Issues in Emerging Market Economies

Alper Sönmez / Dilek Çetin (eds.)

Issues in Emerging Market Economies

PETER LANG

Bibliographic Information published by the Deutsche Nationalbibliothek
The Deutsche Nationalbibliothek lists this publication in the Deutsche Nationalbibliografie; detailed bibliographic data is available online at http://dnb.d-nb.de.

Library of Congress Cataloging-in-Publication Data
A CIP catalog record for this book has been applied for at the Library of Congress.

ISBN 978-3-631-76614-9 (Print)
E-ISBN 978-3-631-76615-6 (E-PDF)
E-ISBN 978-3-631-76616-3 (EPUB)
E-ISBN 978-3-631-76617-0 (MOBI)
DOI 10.3726/b14784

Peter Lang – Berlin · Bern · Bruxelles · New York · Oxford · Warszawa · Wien

This publication has been peer reviewed.

www.peterlang.com

This book is dedicated to *Mine Kalay*, who passed away in the process of publishing this book, for her endless enthusiasm about economics and her devotion to academic life until the last minute of her life. She will always be remembered as a good economist and a great friend.

Contents

List of Contributors

Alper Sönmez
Selçuk University, Department of Economics, Konya, Turkey, alpersonmez80@gmail.com.

Dilek Çetin
Süleyman Demirel University, Isparta, Turkey, dilekchetin@gmail.com.

Ümit K. Seyfettinoğlu
Akdeniz University, Antalya, Turkey, umitk@akdeniz.edu.tr.

Mehmet Zanbak
Akdeniz University, Antalya, Turkey, mehmetzanbak@akdeniz.edu.tr.

Yasemin Asu Çırpıcı
Yıldız Technical University, Istanbul, Turkey, yusanmaz@yahoo.com.

Emre Aksoy
Kırıkkale University, Kırıkkale, Turkey, emreaksoy66@gmail.com.

Gülsüm Akarsu
Ondokuz Mayıs University, Samsun, Turkey, akarsu.gulsum@gmail.com.

Sinem Pınar Gürel
Pamukkale University, Denizli, Turkey, pgurel@pau.edu.tr.

Mine Kalay
Hacettepe University, Ankara, Turkey, minekalay@gmail.com.

Duygu Yolcu Karadam
Pamukkale University, Denizli, Turkey, dyolcu@pau.edu.tr.

Fatih Şahan
Istanbul University, Istanbul, Turkey, fatihsahann@gmail.com.

Selen Işık Maden
Suleyman Demirel University, Isparta, Turkey, selenmaden@sdu.edu.tr.

Aykut Sezgin
Suleyman Demirel University, Isparta, Turkey, aykutsezgin@sdu.edu.tr.

Nazan Şahbaz Kılınç
Kırıkkale University, Kırıkkale, Turkey, nazan_sahbaz@hotmail.com.

Alper Sönmez and Dilek Çetin

1 Introduction: Issues in Emerging Market Economies

The term *emerging market* was first used in 1981 by Antoine van Agtmael who was working in the International Finance Group (IFC) at World Bank. In 1980, IFC analyzed ten local markets[1] in a project which had interesting outcomes than expected. Van Agtmael generated the term "*emerging market*" for this new investment fund, originally named "*Third World Equity Fund*", for these countries (IFC, 2016). IFC constructed the Emerging Markets Data Base (EMDB) where they collected the emerging market data available for investors. This database was later sold to a private company. Emerging markets have always attracted the attention of the investors.

As stated in an IMF working paper by Mody (2004), no unique definition is classified for "emerging markets". The most common definition is that an emerging market economy (EME) is a developing country which has potential to become developed in the future due to the high growth rates. The EME can also be defined by the financial perspective. According to the financial definition, an EME is a financial market with high return rates accompanied with a high risk. IMF (2016a) classified countries as advanced, emerging, and developing according to per capita income, export diversification, and globalization level. According to this definition, Emerging Market Economies (EMEs) are the transition economies which the market economy rules put into effect with the economic regulations. Besides this, the globalization level of countries is important in this definition.

Jean-Claude Trichet (2007) former president of European Central Bank (ECB) summarized the importance of EMEs in his speech at India. He emphasized four main points: Demographic importance, economic importance (micro- and macroevidence), long-term economic outlook, and cultural and scientific importance. China and India have the highest population rates in the world. This population is both the source of production and cheap labor force. The magnificent

1 Argentina, Brazil, Chile, Greece, India, Jordan, Korea, Mexico, Thailand, and Zimbabwe.

amount of GDP they produce and export level make them an important role in the world economy. The projections made by IMF and World Bank indicate that the growth rates of EMEs are higher than the developed ones and expected to increase in the long run. IMF Managing Director Christine Lagarde (2016) made a similar speech about the importance of EMEs.

In this book, the IMF classification (IMF, 2015; 2016b) for EMEs is used in all the chapters. The countries are classified according to their continent to see if there are any similarities in the continent countries or not. The statistical tables in this book are constructed as in Tab. 1.1 by using the country abbreviations instead of their names. Twenty-three EMEs from four continents are under investigation in this book.

This book consists of thirteen chapters including the introduction under three parts. In the first part of the book, EMEs are analyzed through sectorial division: Agriculture, Industry, and Services Sector. In the second part, EMEs are evaluated according to the factors of production, namely labor, capital, and total factor productivity. The effect of the 2008 global financial crisis on EMEs is scrutinized in detail in the ultimate part. The crisis initially started from the United States and influenced the world including EMEs. The economic effects of the crisis are analyzed through the various macroeconomic indicators: economic growth, inflation, unemployment, foreign direct investment (FDI), labor force participation, and monetary policy.

Chapter two highlights the role of agricultural sector. In their study *Structure of the Agricultural Sector in EMEs, Ümit K. Seyfettinoğlu and Mehmet Zanbak* analyze the agricultural developments in EMEs through selected indicators over the period of 2000–2015. The authors explain the agricultural structures of the EMEs by using the index values calculated from the secondary data obtained from the World Bank and ILO. The authors classify indicators under three groups. Firstly, they determine and interpret the indicators which reveal the agricultural efficiency and added value structures in EMEs. Secondly, they evaluate the EMEs by using indicators regarding food production safety and efficiency structure. Finally, they discuss indicators regarding rural life in EMEs. They explore that the efficient use of agricultural land is more important than the amount of land. Also, they conclude that no country has a distinguishing feature when the development of the agricultural sector in all EMEs is evaluated. They suggest that differences in efficiency result from human capital, and they consider that technical know-how levels of the EMEs play a major role in this process.

Industrialization is seen as the main driver for economic development process especially for the developing countries. *Dilek Çetin and Alper Sönmez* in

Tab. 1.1: Emerging Market Economies (EMEs) Abbreviations and Continental Disaggregation

Regions	**Countries**
Latin America	
ARG	Argentina
BRA	Brazil
CHL	Chile
COL	Colombia
MEX	Mexico
PER	Peru
VEN	Venezuela
Asia	
BGD	Bangladesh
CHN	China
IND	India
IDN	Indonesia
MYS	Malaysia
PAK	Pakistan
PHL	Philippines
THA	Thailand
Europe	
BGR	Bulgaria
HUN	Hungary
POL	Poland
ROM	Romania
RUS	Russia
TUR	Turkey
UKR	Ukraine
Africa	
ZAF	South Africa

their study *The Industry Structure in EMEs* analyze the industrialization structure of EMEs. They propose that industry sector plays a major role in the transformation procedure of the country from a developing to developed one. With industrialization process, the share of industry in GDP and employment increases while the share of agriculture decreases. In their study, they investigate the shares of industry in employment and in the value added as percentage of GDP. Moreover, they analyze the growth rate of industry in value added. They also explore the structure of manufacturing industry by using the share of value added of manufacturing industry in GDP. Their findings show that the highest employment levels are from EMEs in the European region, although they create the lowest value added in the industry compared to other EMEs in both Asian and Latin American regions. They conclude that China has a remarkable industry growth with high levels of industrialization. China produces nearly 19 % of the world industry production and half of the EMEs in total. Their findings also reveal that the highest value added in industry also belongs to China.

As industrialization takes place, the share of agricultural sector in the economy decreases, while the share of industrial sector increases. Also, in the advanced stage of the economy, the service sector starts to take an increasing share in the economy. *Yasemin Asu Çırpıcı* in her study *Service Sector in EMEs* discusses general outlook of the service sector of EMEs. The author analyzes the development process of the service sector to get an idea about the development level of the EME. She compares the countries according to certain indicators of the sector. Firstly, she analyzes the share of the sector in GDP. She indicates that some countries display lower shares than others, and she provides the reasons behind this. Also, she reveals that the growth rates of the value added in the service sector are very volatile; they mostly go hand in hand with GDP growth rates. She suggests that the financial crisis of 2008 can be a reason for these growth rates. Secondly, the author analyzes the employment structure in the service sector. In this context, she discusses the handicap of low productivity and high wages in the sector. Finally, she argues the international trade of the service sector, and the role of the service sector for providing exports of intermediates.

Labor Force Markets (LFMs) in EMEs is analyzed by *Emre Aksoy*. He investigates the structural features, similarities, and differences of the LFMs with the aid of the key indicators. The course of LFM indicators in the long run and the correlations among the variables are valuable indicators used to understand the structures of the LFMs. His study provides significant insights about the courses and functions of LFMs, and also gives valuable hints about social dynamics. He also discusses the LFM performances of the economies in question. He provides an overall picture of the labor supply for EMEs via labor and labor force participation indicators and analyzes the unemployment rates. He discovers that EMEs do not utilize their labor force resources similarly. Also, he suggests that EMEs which have low unemployment rates and high labor force participation rates (LFPRs), and more effectively utilize their female labor force have a greater potential in the future. He concludes that LFMs differ remarkably from one another due to their cultural and demographic structures, although there are economic similarities and common features of emerging markets.

Gülsüm Akarsu in her study *Capital Market Developments in EMEs* analyzes the differences and the similarities in the capital markets of EMEs by using time-series data on the indicators of capital markets from 2000 to 2014. She uses the most recent data covering all EMEs, including the period after the 2008 global financial crisis. Her study discovers that some important problems in the EMEs are stock market volatility (SMV), bank dominance, stock market concentration, segmentation, illiquidity, short-termism, low saving rates, lack of financial literacy and investor education, and difficulty in the access of Small and Medium Size Enterprises (SMEs) to financing sources using capital markets. Her findings confirm that (i) the stock markets of South Africa, Malaysia, and Chile are more developed when compared to the other EMEs; (ii) bond market development is higher in Chile, Malaysia, and Thailand for private bonds and in Brazil, Hungary, and Malaysia for public bonds; (iii) among the countries under investigation, South Africa, Hungary, and Argentina seem to benefit more from globalization and internationalization of capital markets on the average, as these countries have experienced higher levels of portfolio equity inflows, foreign direct investment inflows, and international debt issuance. She suggests that EMEs should give importance to macroeconomic stability, building necessary institutional, supervisory, regulatory and legal framework as well as financial infrastructure.

Total factor productivity (TFP) is seen as a key determinant for the analyses of growth process among countries and as a useful instrument to understand how much of the GDP growth comes from growth in labor, how much comes from capital, and how much comes from improvements in TFP. *Total Factor Productivity in EMEs* is analyzed by *Sinem Pınar Gürel.* Her study investigates the TFP growth in EMEs in detail and explores the factors behind the growth process of EMEs. Her study shows that TFP has increased in all regions, but after the Great Recession, global factors played a significant role in the growth process of EMEs and in the TFP growth rates. She suggests that EMEs need policies which promote investments in human capital and innovations to boost TFP growth. Also, she concludes that the countries that want to improve their TFPs should maintain real and financial sector developmental policies.

After 1980, globalization has increased the flow of goods; services and production between countries have also become integrated. This integration of economies also accelerated the spread of the crises which started in developed countries to other countries of the World. *Mine Kalay* in her study *The Global Economic Crisis and Its Effects on the Growth Rate of EMEs* examines the effects of the crises on the growth rates of EMEs. Her study investigates the effects of the

Financial and Real Sector Crisis in the USA (2006–2009), the Global Economic Crisis (2007–2012), and the European Debt Crisis (2009–2012) as part of the Global Economic Crisis.

Duygu Yolcu Karadam in her study *Inflation as a Historical Problem in EMEs* investigates the inflation and the changing factors behind the inflation process from the 1980s to recent years. EMEs have had to deal with high and volatile inflation throughout their histories. Especially Latin American countries have had the worst performance in inflation and inflation volatility and have had to deal with a number of hyperinflation episodes. She argues that many EMEs have managed to reduce their inflation rates considerably during the second half of the 1990s with the contribution of a number of domestic and external factors such as greater fiscal discipline, institutional and structural reforms, and low external inflation environments. She shows that EMEs succeeded in removing the structural domestic factors behind the inflation process and have entered the 2000s in a mild inflation environment with a few exceptions such as Turkey, Romania, and Venezuela. Also, she explores that the changing nature of inflation dynamics has become one of the new challenges for both emerging and industrial countries due to the intensified economic globalization. She reveals that global factors have played a dominant role in inflation in EMEs. She also discusses that global factors have started to replace domestic factors as the primary determinants of inflation. She explores that the increased level of competition in both the product and the labor markets and low demand during the global financial crisis have put downward pressure on prices in EMEs. Moreover, she argues that rising commodity prices emerged as an important driver of the inflation process for both EMEs and industrial countries after the 2000s. Her findings reveal that given their high demand for commodities, Asian countries have faced a much greater increase in inflation relative to Latin American and European EMEs after 2007. She proposes that considerable decline in oil prices after 2012 has led to a downward pressure on inflation for most of the EMEs during this period except for oil exporting countries.

The impacts of the global financial crisis on the labor markets are analyzed by *Fatih Şahan*, in his paper *Global Financial Crisis and Unemployment in EMEs.* He argues that the world economy experienced a serious slowdown with the 2008 global economic crisis, and as a result many countries recorded negative income growths and unemployment rates rose after the crisis. He discusses that advanced economies felt the negative outcomes of the crisis more deeply than the emerging ones on their economies in terms of macroeconomic indicators. He proposes that the harmful effects of the crisis are especially seen on the labor markets and unemployment. He conducts his analyses by using various important labor market indicators such as unemployment rates, labor force participation rates, labor productivity, wages, and prices. He concludes that EMEs had modest negative impacts on their labor markets following the crisis. Furthermore, his findings reveal that Asian countries showed lower unemployment rates and higher growth rates throughout the 2000s. Also, he shows that Latin American countries began the 2000s with high rates of unemployment and low rates of economic growth and throughout 2000s they stabilized these figures. On the other hand, he explores that European countries felt the negative impacts of the crisis more than the other countries and their recovery occurred at a slower pace. His study discovers that European countries experienced a decline in unemployment rates before the crisis; however, after the crisis, the unemployment rates started to increase again, which is parallel to their economic growth trend in the postcrisis period.

With the globalization process, the importance of FDI inflows (especially through MNCs) has increased for the EMEs. Many EMEs see the FDI inflows as a major channel for the economic development and technology diffusion so they compete with each other to attract more FDI inflows from the developed countries. *Alper Sönmez* in his study *Foreign Direct Investment Inflows to EMEs* analyzes the net foreign direct investment (FDI) inflows to EMEs in detail on a country and regional basis between 2000 and 2015 by using the World Bank data. In his study, analysis of the FDI inflows to EMEs is performed in two ways: first, the FDI inflows as current US$ and second, the FDI inflows as percentage of GDP. His study discovers a steady increase in FDI inflows to EMEs over the whole period. Also, his findings explore that Asian region has gained increasing importance in terms of FDI inflows, while the importance of both European and Latin American regions has decreased. In addition, his study reveals that Europe region was more adversely affected by the 2008 global crisis when compared to Asian and Latin American regions. His study also provides evidence that China in Asia, Brazil in Latin America, and Russia in the European region have a dominant role in attracting the FDI inflows. Moreover, his results show that the share of EMEs in World FDI inflows indicates an increasing trend over the whole period. He also explores that Chile in Latin America, Indonesia in Asia, and Turkey in the European region have gained more importance in recent years in terms of attracting the FDI inflows when economic size is taken into consideration.

Monetary Policies in EMEs is analyzed by *Selen Işık Maden* and *Aykut Sezgin*. In their study, they argue that the growth performances are closely related to the monetary policies. They propose that EMEs have high growth potentials, although they have weak institutional structures, low levels of credibility, and shallow financial systems. Moreover, they discuss that some of the EMEs have managed to integrate into developed markets over the last decades and have had high growth performances. They argue that Central Banks of EMEs that apply monetary policies face various operational and technical constraints. Their study provides a short history of Central Banking together with the monetary policy targets. They also discuss the constraints which EMEs face in achieving these targets. They analyze foreign exchange regimes and monetary transmission mechanism of the EMEs before and after the 2008 global financial crisis in order to discuss the applications and their effects on EMEs.

Nazan Şahbaz Kılınç in her study *Labor Force Participation in EMEs* investigates the impact of the global financial crisis on labor force participation. Her study examines the changes occurring in the structure of employment and labor participation rate in EMEs. Also, she evaluates the effects of the 2008 global financial crisis on the employment in the light of various indicators. Her study adopts a comparative analysis of EMEs. Her findings show that LFPRs of EMEs are below the average of both developed countries and world countries for 2003–2014. Also, she concludes that LFPRs remained at 65–67 % in EMEs, while LFPRs in developed countries remained at 70–72 %.

References

IFC (2016). Establishing 'Emerging Markets', https://www.ifc.org/wps/wcm/connect/corp_ext_content/ifc_external_corporate_site/about+ifc_new/ifc+history/establishing-emerging-markets (Last Access Date: 18.07.2016).

International Monetary Fund (IMF) (2015). World Economic Outlook, Adjusting to Lower Commodity Prices, http://www.imf.org/external/pubs/ft/weo/2015/02/pdf/text.pdf (Last Access Date: 15.06.2016).

International Monetary Fund (IMF) (2016a). World Economic Outlook, Frequently Asked Questions, https://www.imf.org/external/pubs/ft/weo/faq.htm#q4b (Last Access Date: 15.06.2016).

International Monetary Fund (IMF) (2016b). World Economic Outlook, Too Slow for Too Long, https://www.imf.org/~/media/Websites/IMF/imported-flagship-issues/external/pubs/ft/weo/2016/01/pdf/_textpdf.ashx (Last Access Date: 15.06.2016).

Lagarde, C. (2016). The Role of Emerging Markets in a New Global Partnership for Growth. By Christine Lagarde, Managing Director, International Monetary Fund, University of Maryland, February 4, 2016, http://www.imf.org/en/News/Articles/2015/09/28/04/53/sp020416 (Last Access Date: 23.08.2016).

Mody, A. (2004). What Is an Emerging Market, IMF Working Paper, WP/04/177, https://www.imf.org/~/media/Websites/IMF/imported-full-text-pdf/external/pubs/ft/wp/2004/_wp04177.ashx (Last Access Date: 15.07.2016).

Trichet J.-C. (2007). The growing importance of emerging economies in the globalized world and its implications for the international financial architecture. Speech by President of the ECB, Tenth L. K. Jha Memorial Lecture, Reserve Bank of India, Mumbai, 26 November 2007, https://www.ecb.europa.eu/press/key/date/2007/html/sp071126 1.en.html (Last Access Date: 23.08.2016).

Part A Sectoral Analysis

Ümit K. Seyfettinoğlu and Mehmet Zanbak

2 Structure of the Agricultural Sector in EMEs

Abstract: Although the concept has a positive notion, EMEs differ within themselves as to extent in which the individual countries use their own resources completely and efficiently. The agricultural sector shows inefficiency in acquiring, using, and most significantly distributing the existing resources. The labor force and the land ownership problems unique to the agricultural sector intensify over time and may result in differences in agricultural efficiencies in various parts of the same country. In addition, the agricultural sector is characterized by a narrow product pattern in many EMEs. This chapter analyzes the agricultural developments in EMEs through selected indicators over the period of 2000–2015. The countries may converge to or diverge from each other according to their levels of development. The data was obtained from the World Bank and ILO. The agricultural structures of the EMEs are explained using the index values which were calculated from the secondary data. The indicators are classified under three groups. Primarily, the indicators revealing the agricultural efficiency, and added value structures in EMEs are determined and interpreted. Next, EMEs are evaluated by using indicators regarding food production safety and efficiency structure. Finally, indicators regarding rural life in these economies are discussed.

Keywords: Agricultural Sector, Agriculture Efficiency

2.1 Introduction

The concept of EMEs was first cited by the International Finance Corporation (IFC) in 1981 (Merchant, 2016). The concept, which has gained recognition in a short time, defines EMEs and refers to those countries with low or medium per capita income. The concept has expanded over time, and the concept has evolved to include all developing countries. According to the definition of Sauvant, EMEs include 28 countries, where China and India are the leading countries (Sauvant, 2006). When the factors discussed in the World Investment Report of the United Nations are considered, Brazil, China, India, Russia, Mexico, Indonesia, and Turkey are also included in the classification (UNCTAD, 1998). Another classification made by the IMF covers 23 countries from different regions in the world[1]. Argentina, Bangladesh, Brazil, Bulgaria, Chile, China, Colombia, Hungary, India, Indonesia, Malaysia, Mexico, Pakistan, Peru, Philippines,

1 In this study, classification of IMF was used.

Poland, Romania, The Russian Federation, The Republic of South Africa, Thailand, Turkey, Ukraine, and Venezuela are on the list (Wikipedia, 2016).

Although the concept of emerging markets sounds positive, it includes negative aspects in regards to economic efficiency (Küçükaksoy, 2009). Therefore, countries in the emerging markets group differ from each other in terms of how completely and efficiently they use their resources and, as a result whether they are considered to be on an advanced level or on an undeveloped level. The greatest gap in obtaining, using, and most importantly distributing existing resources is observed in "the agricultural sector". Sector-specific problems, such as labor and ownership structures, may widen the gap and may result in differences even among different regions of the same country. Moreover, the agricultural sector in most countries listed can be characterized with "limited number of" goods and commodities (Atik, 2005).

In this study, the agricultural sectors of countries which are considered emerging markets and which are expected to converge in terms of development levels were analyzed with selected indicators for the period from 2000 to 2015. With this purpose in mind, an overall evaluation of the agricultural sector in EMEs was followed by detailed statistical analysis of the sector. The final part presents prominent factors in the agriculture industry.

2.2 Overview of Agricultural Sector in EMEs

Data constraint was the determining factor in selecting the indicators in the current study where agricultural analysis of 23 EMEs was conducted for the same period. The determined indicators were evaluated under three titles: "Agricultural Efficiency and Value Added Structure", "Relationship Between Production Indicators and Efficiency", and "Rural Life Indicators".

The share of agricultural value added provides information on the development levels of the countries. A decrease in the share of agricultural value can be interpreted as an indicator of an increase in the development level of the national economy. In this case, production technology used in the value added becomes more important. An analysis of agricultural value added share in EMEs revealed that Pakistan had the highest share of agricultural added value both at the beginning and at the end of the analysis period. In 2000, Bangladesh, India, and Ukraine also had relatively high agricultural value added. EMEs with the lowest agricultural value added were Poland and the Republic of South Africa, which were followed by Mexico and Chile in 2014.

In 2000, The Republic of South Africa, Bangladesh, and Ukraine had the largest amounts of lands used for agriculture. In the Russian Federation, Peru, and Chile, less than 20 % of the total land was being used for agriculture. At the end of the period, The Republic of South Africa, Ukraine, and Bangladesh had the largest shares of agricultural land, and The Russian Federation, Peru, and Venezuela had the smallest shares of agricultural land. Despite its high share in agricultural land, The Republic of South Africa had a relatively lower added value. This indicates that the lands in the country were not used efficiently and there was low efficiency in production.

Bangladesh had the highest female employment rate for the year 2000 while this rate was lowest in Argentina, Colombia, and Venezuela. The greatest change in terms of the female employment rate took place in Turkey. This ratio was 60 % in 2000, whereas it declined to 31.7 % in 2014 with a regression of approximately 29 points. A similar tendency was observed in Romania and Indonesia. For the period analyzed, Colombia experienced the highest increase in the ratio of male employment in agriculture. India, Bangladesh, and Thailand had the highest share in male employment in agriculture at the beginning of the 2000s. In 2010, the situation prevailed with a recession. Examination of the economies with data for 2014 revealed that Pakistan had the highest share. It was followed by Romania and Colombia. When discussing agricultural employment, it should be noted that this type of employment is in the form of an unpaid family labor force in many countries.

In agricultural production, Bulgaria has the greatest increase in its labor force efficiency. Bulgaria was followed by The Republic of South Africa, China, and The Russian Federation as countries which had experienced an increase in labor force efficiency. For the period analyzed, Peru had the lowest increase in agricultural labor force efficiency. Argentina, Brazil, and China had relatively higher efficiency values. Argentina had the highest labor force efficiency in animal production. The Republic of South Africa, which was among the countries with the lowest level of production at the beginning of the period, displayed a significant increase in efficiency in 2013 and ranked at the top of the list of countries having relatively high labor force efficiency in animal production.

Crop production index is important as it indicates the change in the agricultural sector of countries over time. At the beginning of the period analyzed, Romania, Hungary, Ukraine, and Brazil were the leading countries which lagged in production in the mid-2000s. While a decrease of 10–20 points was observed in most other countries, Poland and The Republic of South Africa had higher production levels at the beginning of the 2000s. For the mentioned period, Ukraine had the greatest increase in agricultural production, whereas Poland was the only country whose production decreased when compared to the year 2000.

Analysis of change in crop production in 2013 compared to the 2004–2006 period revealed that greatest change occurred again in Ukraine with an increase of 62.5 % in production. Hungary was the only country where production decreased by 14 %. It can be deduced that Hungary, The Republic of South Africa, and Turkey were the countries with relatively less changes at the end of the period when compared to the beginning of the period.

Product efficiency in arable land is significant as it indicates the change in crop production per unit of land by years. In 2013, the leading countries in product efficiency were primarily Ukraine, which displayed a significant leap, followed by Chile, India, Indonesia, and Bangladesh. In the mentioned period, Bulgaria had the greatest decrease in animal efficiency in arable land, and Turkey was the country with the greatest increase in animal efficiency.

The study also discusses the relationship between food production and efficiency for the period analyzed in EMEs, and the changes in the indicators were emphasized. Hungary was the only country whose food production index value regressed over the period. When the decline in agricultural value added of Hungary is considered, it can be deduced that the negative effect of food production played a major role in this regression. Positive developments, especially in efficiency, had significant results in Peru, where the greatest increase in production index was observed.

Another aspect that should be considered regarding food production efficiency is the fact that efficiency displayed a positive trend over the period 2000–2013 for all the countries except for Pakistan and Hungary. This recession in efficiency for Hungary has primarily reflected on production and then to agricultural value added with a negative trend. Brazil, which had a low level of food production efficiency at the beginning of the period, had a significant increase at the end of the period. Brazil had an improvement in efficiency of crop production and in food production. This finding indicates possible improvements in the technology used.

Analysis of change in the livestock production index for the period of 2000–2013 in EMEs reveals that Turkey was among the leading countries with the fastest growth in animal production, and Turkey was followed by Peru. When the analysis is extended to incorporate the last fourteen years, the greatest decrease in animal production was observed in Bulgaria and Hungary.

The study also discussed some selected rural life indicators. Rural population, improved sanitation facilities, and access to clean water were evaluated for EMEs. The rural population density showed a decreasing trend although remaining close to values seen at the beginning of the period. In 2014, the rural population densities in China and Thailand showed the greatest decrease when compared to the beginning year. India, Bangladesh, Pakistan, and Thailand had a recession, but at the end of the analysis period, had a high rural population density. One out of every two people in these countries was living in rural areas and was occupied with agriculture. Argentina, Venezuela, and Chile were the countries with the lowest rural population density.

In EMEs, the level and the development of sanitation facilities in rural areas are important as they provide information regarding the living conditions. More than 90 % of the rural population in Hungary, Argentina, Poland, Thailand, Malaysia, and Ukraine had access to improved sanitation facilities whereas only one out of four people in India and only one of two people in Pakistan, Brazil, and Peru had access to these facilities.

When access percent of the population to clean water sources is considered, it is apparent that as of 2015, 100 % of the population in rural areas had access to clean water in Argentina, Hungary, Romania, and Turkey. Moreover, the majority of the population in rural areas in Ukraine, Bulgaria, Thailand, and Poland had access to clean water sources. However, Peru led the countries with the least access to clean water sources with only 70 % of rural population having access to clean water. Colombia, Venezuela, and Indonesia can also be listed as having limited access to clean water sources.

2.3 Detailed Statistics on Agricultural Sector in EMEs

In this section, agricultural efficiency and agricultural value added in emerging market economies (EMEs) were evaluated over the period of 2000–2015[2]. This analysis was followed by a discussion of rural life indicators through the relationship between food production indicators and efficiency.

2.3.1 Agricultural Efficiency and Value Added in EMEs

Under this title, agricultural value added and efficiency structures of 23 EMEs were handled comparatively for the period analyzed. With this purpose in mind, agricultural value added was analyzed. This analysis was followed by evaluation of agricultural land, male and female employment in the agricultural sector,

2 Analysis periods of selected indicators end in 2013 for some indicators and in 2014 and 2015 for some others. Despite the effort to use recent data, limitations in obtaining data resulted in this difference. Therefore, the research period was indicated as spanning between 2000 and 2015.

agricultural labor efficiency in the production of crop and livestock, crop production index, and production efficiency in arable land.

2.3.1.1 Share of Agricultural Value Added

In determining the development levels of the economies, it is important to identify the share of agricultural value added to the gross domestic product obtained from the economic activities of the residents. As national economies improve, the share of agriculture in total income decreases while the shares of industry and especially the service sector increase. Analysis of the share of agricultural value added to the domestic income of the EMEs as presented in Tab. 2.1 revealed that Pakistan had the highest agricultural share with 25.9 % as of 2000 which means that out of four units of income created in the economy, one unit was derived from the agricultural sector. In addition to Pakistan, Bangladesh, India, and Ukraine were among the countries with relatively high agricultural added value. EMEs with the lowest agricultural value added were Poland, The Republic of South Africa (3.3 %), and Mexico (3.5 %) (see Tab. 2.1).

Over the period of analysis, the share of the agricultural sector in the total domestic income has declined in all EMEs except for Argentina, Malaysia, Poland, Thailand, and Venezuela. In Bangladesh, the share has regressed 7.7 points in 2014 to 16.1 % from the beginning of the period (see Tab. 2.1).

At the end of the period analyzed (2014), the country with the largest share of agriculture was Pakistan as it was at the beginning of the period analyzed. Indonesia, Ukraine, and Philippines maintained relatively high levels of agricultural share despite the decrease in percentages. However, The Republic of South Africa, Mexico, Chile, and Poland were listed among the countries which had the smallest share of agricultural value added during this period with approximately 3 %.

Analyses of agricultural value added according to continents and five-year average values revealed that there was a regression in all Latin American and European countries, and in Asian and African countries except for Malaysia, Pakistan, and Thailand (Fig. 2.1). There was a remarkable regression in agricultural value added in Bulgaria and Romania. A similar decline was observed in the value added for Bangladesh and China in Asia, and for Peru in Latin America.

In terms of five-year periods, the highest agricultural value added was seen in Argentina and Colombia among the Latin American countries; in Pakistan, India, and Bangladesh among the Asian countries; and Ukraine and Turkey among the European countries.

Tab. 2.1: Agricultural Value Added (%of GDP). World Bank, 2016

	2000	2001	2002	2003	2004	2005	2006	2007	2008	2009	2010	2011	2012	2013	2014
Latin America															
ARG	5.1	4.9	10.8	11.0	9.0	8.4	7.7	8.8	7.2	6.2	8.2	7.5	6.7	7.4	8.3
BRA	5.5	5.6	6.4	7.2	6.7	5.5	5.1	5.2	5.4	5.2	4.8	5.1	4.9	5.3	5.2
CHL	5.9	5.2	5.5	5.3	4.7	4.6	3.9	3.7	3.6	3.6	3.5	3.6	3.2	3.2	3.3
COL	8.9	9.0	9.2	9.0	8.6	8.4	8.1	7.8	7.5	7.5	7.1	6.8	6.3	6.0	6.3
MEX	3.5	3.7	3.6	3.6	3.6	3.4	3.2	3.3	3.3	3.3	3.3	3.2	3.3	3.3	3.3
PER	9.0	8.7	8.3	8.2	7.8	7.8	7.4	7.3	7.7	7.9	7.2	7.5	7.4	-	-
VEN	4.2	4.5	4.1	4.6	4.0	4.0	4.0	4.1	4.4	6.1	5.8	5.4	5.5	-	-
Asia															
BGN	23.8	23.0	21.7	20.9	20.3	19.6	19.0	18.7	18.5	17.9	17.8	17.7	17.1	16.3	16.1
CHN	14.7	14.1	13.4	12.4	13.0	11.7	10.7	10.4	10.3	9.9	9.6	9.5	9.5	9.4	9.2
IND	23.0	22.9	20.7	20.7	19.0	18.8	18.3	18.3	17.8	17.7	18.2	19.0	18.7	18.6	17.8
IDN	15.6	15.3	15.5	15.2	14.3	13.1	13.0	13.7	14.5	15.3	13.9	13.5	13.4	13.4	13.4
MYS	8.6	8.0	9.0	9.3	9.3	8.3	8.6	10.0	10.0	9.2	10.1	11.5	9.8	9.1	8.9
PAK	25.9	24.1	23.4	23.4	22.2	21.5	23.0	23.1	23.1	23.9	24.3	26.0	24.5	24.8	25.0
PHL	14.0	13.2	13.1	12.7	13.3	12.7	12.4	12.5	13.2	13.1	12.3	12.7	11.8	11.2	11.3
THA	8.5	8.6	8.7	9.4	9.3	9.2	9.4	9.4	10.1	9.8	10.5	11.6	11.6	11.3	10.5
Europe															
BGR	12.6	12.1	10.9	10.4	9.8	8.5	7.2	5.4	7.0	4.9	4.9	5.3	5.3	5.3	5.3
HUN	5.7	5.6	4.8	4.5	5.0	4.3	4.1	4.0	4.0	3.5	3.6	4.6	4.6	4.6	4.5
POL	3.3	3.4	3.1	2.9	3.7	3.3	3.1	3.4	2.9	2.9	3.0	3.3	3.2	3.3	3.4
ROM	12.0	14.5	12.6	12.9	14.0	9.5	8.7	5.5	6.6	6.0	6.3	7.3	5.3	6.2	5.4
RUS	6.4	6.6	6.3	6.3	5.6	5.0	4.5	4.4	4.4	4.7	3.9	4.4	3.9	4.0	4.2
TUR	11.3	9.9	11.7	11.4	10.9	10.8	9.4	8.5	8.5	9.1	9.5	9.0	8.8	8.3	8.0
UKR	17.1	16.4	14.6	12.1	11.9	10.4	8.7	7.5	7.9	8.3	8.3	9.5	9.1	10.2	11.8
Africa															
ZAF	3.3	3.5	3.7	3.3	3.1	2.7	2.6	3.0	3.2	3.0	2.6	2.5	2.4	2.3	2.5

2.3.1.2 Agricultural Land

Tab. 2.2 shows the agricultural land as percentage of land area. In 2000, the countries which had the largest share of agricultural land were The Republic of South Africa, Bangladesh, and Ukraine. More than 70 % of the total amount of land in these countries was being used for agricultural facilities. In The Republic of South Africa, this rate was over 80 %. Hungary, Romania, India, and Poland were among the countries having significant amounts of agricultural land. While less

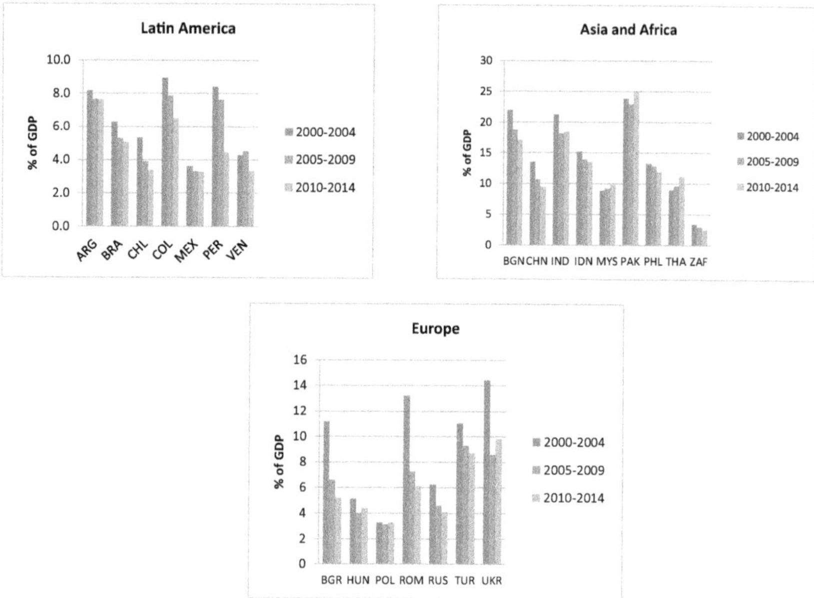

Fig. 2.1: Agricultural Value Added (% of GDP). Calculated by the authors using the data of World Bank (2016)

than 20 % of the total amount of land was used for agricultural purposes in The Russian Federation, Peru, and Chile, half of the land was used for this purpose in Bulgaria, China, and Turkey.

Besides the fluctuations in the period analyzed, agricultural land has diminished in some countries while increasing in others. The Republic of South Africa was the country with the highest share of agricultural land at the end of the period. It was followed by Ukraine and Bangladesh. Countries which had the smallest share of agricultural land in 2013 were The Russian Federation, Peru, and Venezuela. Despite the fluctuations over the period mentioned, Argentina, Indonesia, Thailand, Philippines, and Malaysia have increased their agricultural land shares. Hungary, Bulgaria, Turkey, and Bangladesh were listed among the countries where agricultural land share has diminished.

The point deserving attention is that in the analysis of the data, we observed that The Republic of South Africa created a relatively low added value when compared to its large amount of agricultural land. This situation indicates that The Republic of South Africa had a problem using the available land efficiently and effectively.

Tab. 2.2: Agricultural Land (% of Land Area). World Bank, 2016

	2000	2001	2002	2003	2004	2005	2006	2007	2008	2009	2010	2011	2012	2013
Latin America														
ARG	47.0	47.0	47.0	47.8	49.1	50.4	51.6	52.6	52.7	52.5	53.9	54.2	54.5	54.5
BRA	31.3	31.5	31.8	32.1	32.6	32.6	32.6	32.5	32.7	32.7	32.7	32.9	33.0	33.4
CHL	20.3	20.4	20.9	20.7	21.4	21.4	21.2	21.2	21.2	21.2	21.2	21.2	21.3	21.2
COL	40.4	37.6	37.5	37.9	38.2	38.4	38.0	38.2	38.4	38.3	38.3	37.6	38.4	40.4
MEX	54.7	54.8	54.8	54.8	54.8	54.8	54.8	54.9	54.9	54.9	54.9	54.9	54.9	54.9
PER	18.1	18.1	17.8	17.9	17.9	18.2	18.3	18.4	18.5	18.7	18.8	18.8	19.0	19.0
VEN	24.5	24.5	24.4	24.4	24.5	24.5	24.4	24.4	24.5	24.4	24.5	24.5	24.5	24.5
Asia														
BGN	72.2	72.2	71.9	71.7	71.6	71.5	71.3	71.2	71.1	71.0	71.0	70.1	70.1	70.0
CHN	55.6	55.4	55.2	55.0	55.0	55.1	54.8	54.8	54.8	54.8	54.8	54.8	54.8	54.8
IND	60.9	60.7	60.7	60.6	60.7	60.6	60.5	60.4	60.5	60.6	60.4	60.4	60.4	60.6
IDN	26.0	26.3	26.6	28.2	29.5	28.6	28.4	29.3	29.8	30.7	30.7	31.2	31.2	31.5
MYS	21.4	21.3	21.3	21.6	21.6	21.7	21.6	22.0	21.9	22.2	22.7	23.2	23.5	23.9
PAK	47.6	48.0	47.8	47.8	46.8	46.7	46.9	46.7	45.8	45.8	45.7	46.6	46.8	47.1
PHL	37.7	37.5	37.3	37.7	38.5	38.1	38.8	39.5	40.3	40.6	40.6	41.1	41.7	41.7
THA	38.8	38.8	38.5	38.3	38.3	38.4	38.6	38.8	39.2	40.9	41.2	41.2	42.8	43.3
Europe														
BGR	50.5	49.7	48.9	49.0	49.0	48.5	47.8	47.1	47.0	46.3	46.5	46.9	47.2	46.0
HUN	65.3	65.4	65.3	65.4	65.4	65.4	64.8	64.8	64.6	63.9	59.0	59.0	59.0	59.0
POL	60.1	58.1	55.2	52.8	53.3	51.9	52.1	50.5	50.9	51.0	47.2	48.3	47.4	47.1
ROM	64.7	64.4	64.5	64.4	61.4	61.7	61.0	59.3	59.3	59.2	61.5	60.7	59.7	60.4
RUS	13.3	13.2	13.2	13.2	13.2	13.2	13.2	13.2	13.2	13.2	13.1	13.1	13.1	13.2
TUR	52.6	53.2	53.5	52.8	53.5	53.6	52.6	51.3	50.8	50.6	50.7	49.7	49.9	49.9
UKR	71.5	71.4	71.5	71.4	71.4	71.3	71.3	71.2	71.3	71.2	71.2	71.3	71.3	71.2
Africa														
ZAF	80.9	80.8	80.8	80.7	80.5	80.4	79.9	79.9	80.1	80.0	79.9	79.4	79.8	79.8

Another noticeable finding is that no observable change has occurred in Ukraine and Venezuela during this period.

2.3.1.3 Female Employment in Agricultural Sector

Especially in underdeveloped countries and EMEs, employment mainly centers on the agricultural sector. The share of agricultural employment in some EMEs increases while it is replaced by industry and services in other economies.

Tab. 2.3: Employment in Agriculture, Female (% of Female Employment). World Bank, 2016; ILO, 2016

	2000	2001	2002	2003	2004	2005	2006	2007	2008	2009	2010	2011	2012	2013	2014
Latin America															
ARG	-	-	-	-	-	-	-	-	-	-	-	-	-	-	-
BRA	10.6	16.1	16.5	16.1	16.0	16.0	15.0	13.9	13.1	12.2	-	11.2	10.0	10.1	-
CHL	4.6	4.6	4.7	4.9	-	-	-	-	-	-	5.9	5.3	5.6	4.6	-
COL	0.5	14.2	5.5	7.0	6.4	8.1	6.1	5.8	5.9	6.2	6.6	7.0	7.3	6.8	6.6
MEX	7.2	6.2	6.5	5.7	6.0	4.9	4.7	4.4	4.0	4.4	4.0	3.6	4.1	3.7	-
PER	3.9	6.1	7.5	7.7	7.6	8.0	7.5	5.5	5.5	-	-	-	-	-	-
VEN	1.6	1.7	1.9	2.3	2.1	2.0	1.8	1.8	1.9	1.8	1.8	1.6	-	-	-
Asia															
BGN	76.9		58.6	58.6		68.1	-	-	-	-	64.8	-	-	-	-
CHN	-	-	-	4.2	4.1	3.8	3.7	3.5	-	-	-	-	-	-	-
IND	74.8	-	-	-	-	70.9	-	-	-	-	65.3	-	59.7	-	-
IDN	46.7	44.5	45.4	47.5	44.6	44.3	41.1	41.4	39.9	38.8	37.6	-	-	33.4	-
MYS	14.0	12.0	11.6	11.0	10.5	10.2	10.0	10.0	9.0	9.0	8.5	6.6	8.2	8.3	-
PAK	72.9	72.9	64.6	64.6	67.3	67.3	68.8	72.4	75.0	75.7	76.3	77.0	-	76.9	74.0
PHL	23.9	24.6	24.8	24.3	23.3	23.7	23.6	23.2	23.2	24.0	21.8	21.7	21.0	20.1	-
THA	47.3	43.6	44.0	42.5	40.3	40.7	40.5	40.0	40.3	36.5	36.0	39.2	37.8	39.3	-
Europe															
BGR	9.9	6.5	7.5	7.4	7.6	6.4	5.8	5.4	5.5	5.2	5.1	4.7	4.2	4.3	4.5
HUN	3.3	3.4	3.7	2.7	2.7	2.6	2.6	2.3	2.3	2.6	2.3	2.6	2.8	2.6	2.6
POL	16.9	18.0	17.7	15.9	15.7	15.7	14.3	13.4	13.2	12.6	12.2	11.8	11.3	10.6	10.0
ROM	41.3	40.5	33.9	35.1	28.9	29.0	27.5	26.7	26.0	26.7	28.4	27.2	27.2	26.5	25.6
RUS	11.7	9.3	8.9	8.2	7.9	8.0	7.8	6.9	6.7	6.4	5.7	5.7	5.4	5.4	5.2
TUR	60.5	63.3	60.0	58.5	57.2	51.6	42.2	41.3	40.6	36.7	38.3	38.3	36.1	34.6	31.7
UKR	-	-	-	-	-	-	-	-	-	19.2	-	19.7	19.1	19.3	13.0
Africa															
ZAF	15.7	-	-	7.4	7.4	4.5	5.2	4.5	4.3	3.7	3.8	3.5	3.7	3.6	3.2

Tab. 2.3 presents the rate of women employed in agriculture within the overall female employment. In 2000, Bangladesh had the largest share of women employed in agriculture with 76.9 % of the employed women working in this sector. India is another country which had a large share of women employed in agriculture, and more than 60 % of the women employed in Pakistan and Turkey were working in the agricultural sector. The countries with the smallest share of female employment as of 2000 were Argentina, Colombia, and Venezuela.

In 2014, 74 % of the women who were employed in Pakistan were working in the agricultural sector. Turkey has displayed the greatest change in female employment where the share was 60 % in 2000 but decreased to 31.7 % in 2014. Romania and Indonesia have experienced a similar trend.

The greatest change in female employment value in agriculture was observed in Asia. Female employment share in the sector, which is relatively less in other continents, is greater in Asia.

2.3.1.4 Male Employment in Agricultural Sector

The share of male employment in agriculture in EMEs is presented in Tab. 2.4. Over the period analyzed, Colombia had the most significant increase in terms of male employment share in agriculture, rising from 16.6 % to 23.2 %. In addition to this development, it was noticed that male employment in agriculture mainly regressed in EMEs. India, Bangladesh, and Thailand had the highest male employment share in agriculture at the turn of the 21st century. In 2010, this situation persisted despite a decline in percentages. When the countries with data for 2014 were considered, Pakistan emerged as the country with the highest share, which was followed by Romania and Colombia.

According to the graph below which reflects the share of male employment in the agricultural sector, most men in Asia are involved in agricultural activities, as are the majority of the women. In other words, the majority of the male population living in Asia is employed in the agricultural sector, surpassing the number of men who work in the agriculture sector on other continents. For example, when expressed with the recent data, on the average, one in every three men living in Asia is employed in the agricultural sector, whereas this ratio is one in every five men for some continents and even one in every ten men on other continents.

2.3.1.5 Labor Efficiency in Crop Production

Comparison of the crop production index with the agricultural employment index, which reflects the efficiency of employment in the agricultural sector in EMEs, revealed that Argentina had the highest efficiency at the beginning of the 2000s. Argentina was followed by Brazil and Venezuela, and Peru, The Republic of South Africa, and Romania were the countries with the lowest labor force efficiency in crop production. Bangladesh, Hungary, The Russian Federation, and Ukraine were also among the countries with relatively low labor force efficiency. At the end of the period analyzed, Bulgaria had the greatest increase in its labor force efficiency, and was followed by The Republic of South Africa, China, and

Tab. 2.4: Employment in Agriculture, Male (% of Male Employment). World Bank, 2016; ILO, 2016

	2000	2001	2002	2003	2004	2005	2006	2007	2008	2009	2010	2011	2012	2013	2014
Latin America															
ARG	-	-	-	-	-	-	-	-	-	-	-	-	-	-	-
BRA	23.2	23.6	23.5	23.9	24.5	23.7	22.5	21.5	20.6	20.5	-	19.0	17.9	17.7	
CHL	19.3	18.1	17.9	18.1	-	-	-	-	-	-	14.5	13.8	13.6	12.4	
COL	16,6	26.2	29.2	29.3	28.3	30.4	27.3	25.4	25.0	26.8	26.5	25.8	24.6	24.0	23.2
MEX	23.7	24.0	23.9	22.6	22.1	20.6	19.9	18.9	18.6	18.9	18.6	19.2	19.2	19.4	-
PER	8.9	10.9	12.7	14.3	13.1	13.1	12.6	10.5	10.3	-	-	-	-	-	-
VEN	15.7	14.5	15.0	16.0	15.5	14.4	13.6	13.1	12.7	13.2	13.1	11.9	-	-	-
Asia															
BGN	53.3	-	49.8	49.8	-	41.8	-	-	-	-	40.1	-	-	-	-
CHN	-	-	-	4.5	4.3	4.0	3.7	3.6	-	-	-	-	-	-	-
IND	53.9	-	-	-	-	49.3	-	-	-	-	46.1	-	42.9	-	-
IDN	44.4	43.3	43.7	45.7	42.6	43.8	42.5	41.1	40.6	40.2	38.8	-	-	35.6	-
MYS	20.7	16.8	16.8	16.1	16.8	17.1	17.2	17.5	16.7	16.0	16.0	14.2	15.1	15.4	-
PAK	44.4	44.4	38.2	38.2	38.1	38.1	37.2	36.4	36.9	29.4	28.6	28.1	-	26.8	34.2
PHL	45.0	45.1	44.8	44.3	43.7	43.6	43.5	42.7	42.9	42.3	40.5	40.3	39.4	38.1	-
THA	49.5	48.0	47.8	46.8	43.9	44.2	43.1	43.3	44.3	41.0	40.1	42.5	41.2	44.1	-
Europe															
BGR	14.5	11.4	12.1	12.2	11.8	10.1	9.3	8.8	8.4	8.3	8.1	8.4	8.2	8.5	9.0
HUN	9.0	8.4	8.1	7.7	7.4	6.7	6.5	6.5	6.0	6.3	6.5	6.8	7.0	6.5	6.3
POL	17.8	17.9	19.1	18.3	17.6	17.1	15.7	14.5	13.4	12.8	12.9	13.0	12.9	12.5	12.2
ROM	37.0	35.9	31.0	32.2	29.0	28.7	27.0	25.0	24.1	24.8	27.2	25.1	26.1	25.9	25.2
RUS	17.1	14.6	13.6	13.4	12.4	12.3	12.1	11.0	10.5	10.4	10.0	9.6	9.2	8.5	8.2
TUR	27.0	27.7	24.8	24.4	25.6	21.7	15.8	15.3	15.5	15.8	16.1	16.5	16.4	16.0	14.6
UKR	-	-	-	-	-	-	-	-	-	20.8	-	20.6	20.2	20.7	16.5
Africa															
ZAF	14.3	-	-	12.6	10.4	6.8	7.3	6.2	6.8	6.2	5.7	5.5	5.8	6.2	5.7

Russia in terms of increases in efficiency. In other words, the crop yield for agricultural employment, which was 0.9 in 2000, rose to 5.3 in 2013. When compared to other countries, Argentina, Brazil, and China can be listed among the countries with relatively higher efficiency values. However, Peru was the country with the lowest agricultural labor force efficiency in 2013, as it was also the lowest in 2000. Colombia and Hungary were in a relatively disadvantaged situation with low agricultural labor force efficiency.

2.3.1.6 Labor Force Efficiency in Livestock Production

In EMEs, where the share of agricultural employment is higher than the share in developed countries, livestock production is a significant source of income. In 2000, Argentina was the leading country in labor force efficiency in livestock production as well as leading in crop production. Bulgaria, Brazil, and Venezuela were among the countries with high labor force efficiency in livestock production. Labor force efficiency in livestock production was low especially in Peru, Romania, and The Republic of South Africa.

In 2013, Bulgaria performed an increase of two points in efficiency. Education opportunities and developments in technology have affected this positive development. The Republic of South Africa was among the leading countries with relatively higher labor force efficiency in 2013. However, a regression occurred in this value in Peru and Hungary.

2.3.1.7 Crop Production Index

Crop production index shows the change of production in the agricultural sector over time, and therefore this index is considered an important indicator. When calculating the index value, the average of the years 2004, 2005, and 2006 were taken to be 100. An index value higher than 100 indicates an increase in production whereas index values lower than 100 indicates a decrease. In analyzing the trend of crop production in EMEs, Romania, Hungary, Ukraine, and Brazil emerged as the countries whose productions lagged at the beginning of the period analyzed when compared to the mid-2000s. While most countries had experienced a decline of 10 to 20 points at the beginning of the 2000s, Poland and The Republic of South Africa had higher production values at this time. Ukraine has displayed the greatest increase in crop production over the period with approximately 86 points in index value. It was followed by Peru, India, China, and Bangladesh. Over the period analyzed, the only country which had regressed in production value when compared to the beginning of the period was Poland with a decrease of 2 points.

Comparison of crop production at the end of 2013 with the average values of 2004–2006 revealed that Ukraine had experienced the greatest change with an increase of 62.5 % in production. India and Peru can be included among the countries displaying a rapid increase in production values of 41.9 % and 40.4 %, respectively. Hungary was the only economy where production decreased by 14 %. At the end of the period, Hungary, The Republic of South Africa, and Turkey have displayed limited change in production.

Tab. 2.5: Crop Production Index (2004–2006 = 100). Calculated by the authors using the data of World Bank (2016)

	2000	2001	2002	2003	2004	2005	2006	2007	2008	2009	2010	2011	2012	2013
Latin America														
ARG	81.5	86.2	86.1	93.7	91.7	103.8	104.5	118.9	113.8	84.8	124.0	126.4	108.0	126.0
BRA	77.3	82.8	87.5	95.5	99.0	98.0	103.0	112.4	121.8	118.8	126.6	135.3	130.6	140.3
CHL	82.0	89.0	90.6	94.3	95.8	100.7	103.5	96.6	98.7	101.0	109.8	117.3	112.5	117.2
COL	88.3	89.4	92.3	97.7	100.3	99.3	100.4	104.4	103.1	100.2	96.8	96.0	98.6	108.2
MEX	88.5	95.2	92.7	97.2	99.9	96.9	103.2	105.3	108.0	101.9	106.4	102.3	112.9	117.0
PER	86.3	85.8	91.1	94.5	93.6	99.3	107.2	108.2	117.2	117.9	125.3	128.6	134.7	140.4
VEN	98.8	97.2	89.7	91.2	96.0	102.2	101.8	105.1	109.7	102.5	95.3	104.4	110.5	126.6
Asia														
BGN	90.6	88.3	90.6	92.9	90.3	103.1	106.7	113.0	122.2	123.1	131.4	135.0	135.3	137.8
CHN	84.8	86.9	90.8	90.5	97.4	100.1	102.5	108.0	114.7	116.8	120.5	126.7	131.1	133.6
IND	92.3	95.0	84.7	97.1	94.1	99.9	106.1	116.4	117.5	112.9	125.2	134.4	136.5	141.9
IDN	78.6	80.9	85.4	91.0	94.9	98.5	106.6	109.8	114.8	120.9	123.5	127.1	135.6	136.6
MYS	78.1	82.0	82.5	90.7	95.4	99.6	105.0	103.4	111.4	108.4	107.3	117.5	116.3	117.6
PAK	89.7	83.9	83.7	87.4	99.1	102.4	98.5	102.4	107.0	108.7	99.9	106.8	101.3	107.1
PHL	84.6	87.9	90.6	94.0	98.0	100.5	101.6	108.8	113.0	112.3	110.9	113.4	117.9	117.6
THA	90.7	94.4	95.5	101.6	101.2	97.9	100.9	110.5	110.0	111.4	110.1	119.7	128.2	128.6
Europe														
BGR	87.5	99.2	105.5	92.2	118.4	87.4	94.2	64.4	105.4	98.3	112.7	114.4	103.5	128.6
HUN	76.5	98.2	80.3	72.4	111.1	95.4	93.6	71.3	103.5	89.4	74.3	84.1	71.4	87.4
POL	107.9	112.2	101.6	95.8	111.9	98.3	89.9	98.9	105.7	109.5	98.2	101.5	108.6	105.8
ROM	71.1	93.1	79.9	91.0	116.5	92.3	91.2	58.2	88.3	85.0	89.6	105.1	71.8	102.5
RUS	79.2	90.0	93.2	87.2	96.2	100.6	103.2	102.6	112.8	108.1	74.9	118.6	98.3	115.7
TUR	95.6	88.0	96.3	94.3	95.1	101.7	103.2	95.6	101.1	103.5	105.2	110.2	113.0	114.6
UKR	76.7	86.5	88.5	73.6	100.5	100.7	98.8	88.8	126.9	117.8	111.5	150.1	136.2	162.5
Africa														
ZAF	102.5	94.0	102.6	99.0	100.7	105.5	93.8	93.1	113.3	109.0	107.7	107.5	112.1	114.7

In Fig. 2.2, which was calculated based on the average of period 2004–2006 of the crop production index and by using the five-year average values, an increase was observed in the index values of the last five years. This tendency to increase index values on all continents and in all countries was more noticeable in Argentina, Peru, and Brazil in Latin America; in Bangladesh, Indonesia, and India in Asia; and in Ukraine and Bulgaria in Europe. Especially in Ukraine, the crop production index had increased more than 50 % when compared to the

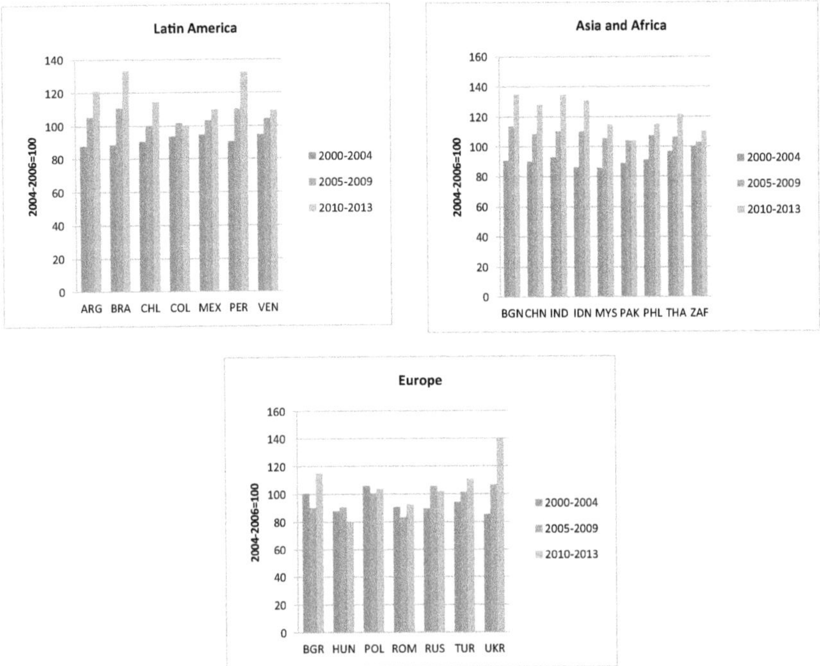

Fig. 2.2: Crop Production Index. Calculated by the authors using the data of World Bank (2016)

average value for the first five years. For the analysis period, a regression was observed in the index values for Hungary and Poland.

2.3.1.8 *Crop Efficiency in Arable Land*

Crop efficiency in arable land is obtained by comparing the crop production index with the arable land index, and crop efficiency is important as it indicates the change by years in crop per unit of land. In 2000, countries with the highest crop efficiency were Brazil, Indonesia, The Republic of South Africa, and Venezuela, whereas countries with the lowest efficiency were Chile, Colombia, Peru, and Romania. Over the thirteen-year period, all countries displayed an increase in efficiency. Ukraine and Chile had the greatest change in efficiency with increases of 0.85 and 0.70 units in efficiency, respectively. Similar developments were observed in other EMEs. In all countries except for Hungary, efficiency value was calculated over one. It is possible to say that those technological advances in agriculture contributed to this improvement.

At the end of the analysis period, in 2013, the prominent countries in regards to crop efficiency were Ukraine, Chile, India, Indonesia, and Bangladesh. EMEs which, despite the improvements observed, stayed in relatively lower positions in crop efficiency when compared with previous years were Hungary, Argentina, Philippines, Romania, and Pakistan.

2.3.1.9 Livestock Efficiency in Arable Land

During the period between the years 2000 and 2013, Bulgaria experienced the greatest decline in livestock efficiency per arable land and it was followed by Hungary and Argentina. The greatest improvement occurred in Turkey with an increase of one point in efficiency. Chile, Colombia, Malaysia, and Peru were countries with relatively higher increases in livestock production. Bulgaria, Hungary, and Argentina were countries with high efficiency in 2000; Chile, Colombia, and Peru were among the low-efficiency countries for the same year. In 2013, Bulgaria experienced a significant decline in livestock efficiency. Improvements were observed in all countries except for Argentina and Hungary. In 2013, Turkey had the highest efficiency with 1.9 points. For the same year, Bulgaria and Pakistan were the countries with the lowest efficiency.

2.3.2 Relationship between Production Indicators and Efficiency

Under this title, food production index, food production safety, and livestock production index were discussed.

The food production index values presented in Tab. 2.6 reflect the trend of food production in EMEs over the period analyzed. Compared to the mid-2000s, countries with the lowest food production in 2000 were Brazil, Malaysia, and Indonesia. Production values in these countries were approximately 20 % less than the base year. The case of Bulgaria was remarkable as its food production index for the same period was 14.8 % higher.

In 2013, the greatest increase in production was observed in Peru with 46.8 %. Countries which experienced the lowest increase in food production index in 2013 when compared to the base year were Mexico, Bulgaria, and Philippines. Primarily Hungary but also Pakistan and Romania experienced a recession in food production when compared to the base year (2004–2006).

When the change in the period 2000–2013 is analyzed, the only country whose food production index regressed was Hungary with a value of 2.5 %. The greatest increase occurred in Peru with a change of 61.4 %. Brazil, India, China,

Tab. 2.6: Food Production Index (2004–2006 = 100). Calculated by the authors using the data of World Bank (2016)

	2000	2001	2002	2003	2004	2005	2006	2007	2008	2009	2010	2011	2012	2013
Latin America														
ARG	85.9	86.5	85.0	91.0	92.7	103.0	104.3	114.5	111.7	96.9	115.7	115.9	106.0	118.4
BRA	76.8	81.4	86.5	94.2	97.4	99.4	103.2	110.9	116.7	116.9	123.9	129.0	127.1	136.7
CHL	83.3	89.9	90.1	91.8	95.1	99.6	105.3	102.0	104.6	104.3	109.8	115.8	114.9	117.4
COL	87.4	88.6	90.5	93.3	97.6	98.9	103.6	106.8	110.7	106.8	104.2	106.2	110.7	116.6
MEX	88.4	92.6	92.5	94.9	98.1	98.5	103.4	104.8	105.3	105.1	107.1	108.0	112.3	115.0
PER	85.4	84.7	90.1	93.7	93.0	99.9	107.2	110.6	120.2	123.3	129.9	133.3	140.8	146.8
VEN	97.0	99.9	99.3	94.0	90.7	102.2	107.1	114.5	108.6	108.3	108.0	120.7	123.3	131.2
Asia														
BGN	89.5	87.6	90.2	92.8	91.0	102.9	106.2	112.1	120.4	121.6	129.7	132.1	132.8	135.4
CHN	83.3	84.8	88.7	90.7	96.5	100.4	103.1	108.1	113.9	116.8	120.0	123.3	127.6	129.5
IND	91.7	94.8	87.4	96.5	94.7	100.0	105.3	114.7	117.2	114.4	123.4	131.1	134.1	138.8
IDN	78.3	80.9	86.1	91.8	95.7	98.1	106.3	108.9	113.8	121.1	123.8	127.4	136.3	137.5
MYS	78.0	82.8	84.4	91.6	94.9	100.3	104.8	105.1	114.6	114.8	115.0	124.5	124.8	128.1
PAK	88.3	86.6	88.2	91.9	96.2	100.5	103.3	108.4	113.2	115.3	113.8	117.9	117.9	93.8
PHL	84.0	87.7	90.9	94.1	97.5	100.3	102.2	109.8	113.0	112.8	112.6	115.5	120.0	121.6
THA	93.2	95.9	97.8	104.0	100.2	97.9	101.9	111.9	110.3	114.4	113.2	121.3	129.6	128.5
Europe														
BGR	114.8	112.9	103.9	94.1	110.2	89.3	100.5	77.0	109.4	101.1	110.5	113.8	108.0	120.4
HUN	91.3	104.7	91.2	83.5	110.6	95.2	94.3	79.4	103.7	92.8	79.3	87.8	79.0	88.8
POL	92.3	95.8	95.2	97.0	100.9	98.7	100.4	100.2	102.1	106.3	102.1	103.0	108.3	107.5
ROM	81.5	91.5	84.5	95.3	109.3	93.9	96.9	80.9	95.4	94.6	94.7	101.3	87.4	98.3
RUS	88.9	94.3	99.5	93.8	98.3	99.3	102.4	108.4	111.3	112.6	102.1	117.5	113.9	122.4
TUR	94.2	87.0	92.5	93.8	94.3	101.7	104.0	100.5	105.4	108.9	113.5	118.9	126.6	129.8
UKR	88.1	93.9	95.2	86.8	96.6	102.3	101.1	94.1	114.1	116.9	106.9	123.7	126.6	138.4
Africa														
ZAF	96.1	89.7	97.7	96.9	98.7	102.1	99.2	102.4	119.6	117.5	118.7	117.3	120.5	122.3

and Bangladesh are among the countries whose food production accelerated in the same period.

According to Fig. 2.3, which reflects intertemporal change in the food production index, the index values for all countries have increased when compared to the beginning of the period. The greatest fluctuation is observed in Europe. Ukraine has been a determining factor in this change on the continent. Similarly, Peru in Latin America and Indonesia in Asia have emerged in terms of increases

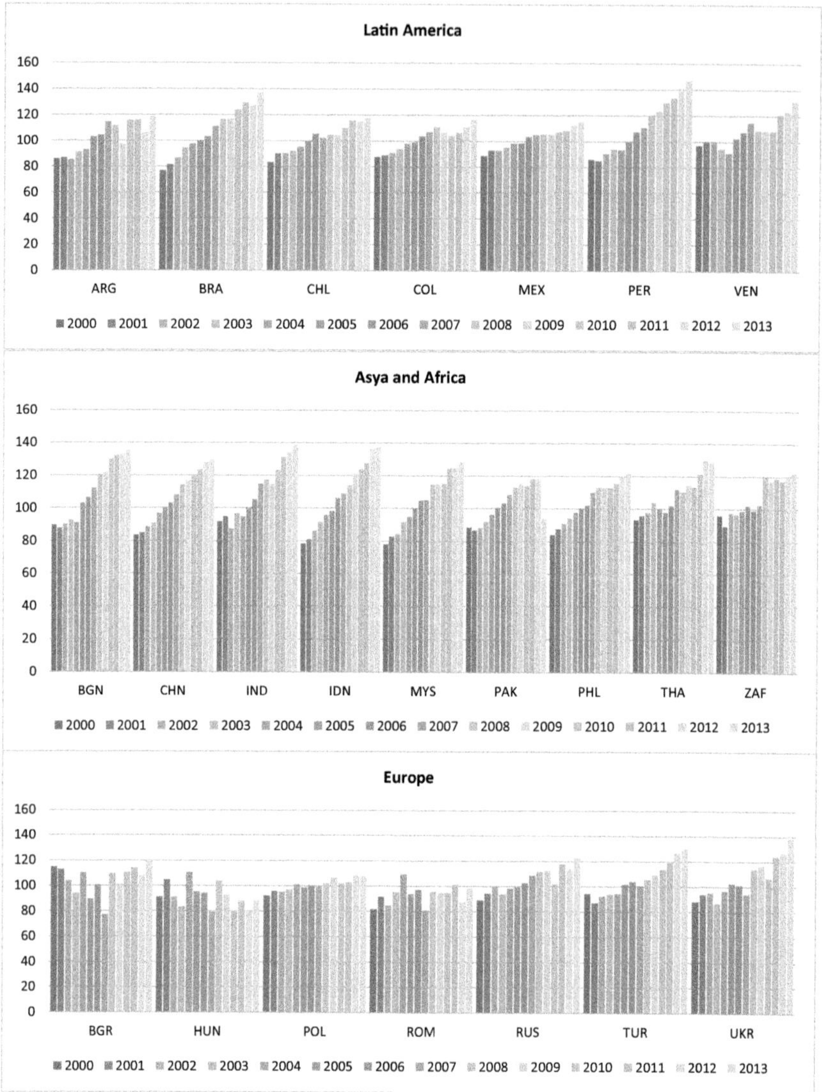

Fig. 2.3: Food Production Index (2004–2006=100). Calculated by the authors using the data of World Bank (2016)

in their index values. Moreover, the striking change in the graph of Asia/Africa is the regression in the index value of Pakistan in 2013.

Food safety is obtained by comparing food production with the population. This value had a positive trend between 2000 and 2013 in all countries except for Pakistan and Hungary and continued generally with an increase in efficiency. Brazil was among the countries with low efficiency in food production in 2000. However, a significant increase in efficiency was observed at the end of the thirteen-year period. Meanwhile, a regression occurred in Pakistan. In 2000, countries with the highest food production efficiency were Bulgaria and Venezuela whereas the lowest efficiency was observed in Brazil, Indonesia, Romania, and Ukraine. In 2013, the ratings of the countries changed and Ukraine became the economy with the highest food production efficiency. In the same year, Brazil, Bulgaria, Peru, and Thailand ranked among the countries with higher food efficiency values than other economies. Pakistan and Hungary had the lowest efficiency values in 2013 when compared with other EMEs.

Livestock production is a major branch of agricultural activities. Tab. 2.7 presents livestock production index values for the 2000–2013 periods. The index values of the countries vary between 74 and 163. Compared to the base year, countries which had the lowest livestock production index value in 2000 were Indonesia, Malaysia, and China. The index values in these countries were about 20 % less than the base year (2004–2006).

Bulgaria and Hungary were among the countries with higher livestock production at the beginning of the 2000s and were providing 50 % and 20 % more production, respectively. However, livestock production decreased notably in 2013 despite the high index values which were especially notable in 2000. A decline of 62 points was observed for Bulgaria while the value for Hungary decreased 33 points.

In 2013, the greatest increase occurred in Turkey with a rise of 63.2 % in livestock production when compared to the base year. Turkey was followed by Peru with an increase of 52.7 %. Venezuela, Indonesia, and Malaysia can be included among the countries experiencing a sharp increase in livestock production when compared to the base year. When the evaluation was extended to incorporate the last fourteen years, the greatest decrease in livestock production was observed in Bulgaria and in Hungary as previously mentioned. Turkey, Peru, and Indonesia witnessed an increase of more than 60 % in production.

As seen in Fig. 2.4, which reflects the change in the index value of livestock production, Venezuela and Argentina in Latin America and Bulgaria, Turkey, and Hungary in Europe differ from the others in terms of the amount of change. Moreover, a great regression was recently observed in Pakistan.

Tab. 2.7: Livestock Production Index (2004–2006 = 100). Calculated by the authors using the data of World Bank (2016)

	2000	2001	2002	2003	2004	2005	2006	2007	2008	2009	2010	2011	2012	2013
Latin America														
ARG	93.9	87.3	83.0	85.4	93.7	102.4	103.9	106.7	107.7	113.8	100.1	100.8	101.5	110.7
BRA	77.6	80.4	85.7	89.6	96.3	100.9	102.8	107.7	111.5	111.4	116.6	118.9	121.4	127.5
CHL	83.1	88.9	87.6	87.9	94.3	98.1	107.6	108.8	112.8	108.1	108.6	112.2	116.7	116.5
COL	86.1	88.0	89.1	89.4	95.0	98.4	106.6	108.7	116.3	106.3	106.2	110.3	116.5	120.0
MEX	86.8	89.3	91.1	93.8	97.5	99.2	103.4	103.8	104.5	106.9	109.4	114.3	113.5	113.2
PER	83.8	83.1	87.8	90.2	92.2	99.2	108.6	113.0	121.7	128.5	133.8	141.0	148.3	152.7
VEN	97.0	103.4	105.4	96.3	88.8	100.4	110.8	123.2	111.2	115.1	118.9	133.9	134.2	139.8
Asia														
BGN	82.4	84.2	88.4	92.3	95.2	101.0	103.8	107.3	111.5	112.5	119.2	123.2	127.6	130.5
CHN	84.0	85.3	88.0	92.9	96.0	100.3	103.8	107.6	111.8	115.7	119.0	119.7	124.7	126.5
IND	84.5	87.8	89.5	91.6	95.8	99.8	104.4	111.1	114.6	118.7	123.8	128.5	132.2	135.2
IDN	74.4	80.5	89.8	94.5	99.4	95.4	105.2	104.7	106.2	110.6	119.1	127.5	134.2	139.9
MYS	78.1	81.3	87.9	90.9	95.0	99.8	105.2	109.0	112.5	115.9	126.0	129.6	132.9	138.8
PAK	85.6	87.9	90.5	93.2	95.7	98.3	106.0	109.6	113.3	117.3	121.6	126.0	130.4	81.2
PHL	84.2	89.2	93.0	95.4	96.8	98.5	104.7	112.3	114.1	115.7	118.3	120.5	122.9	126.5
THA	95.5	95.8	101.1	107.5	92.6	100.8	106.6	112.8	114.8	122.3	124.8	124.9	133.2	130.2
Europe														
BGR	152.8	138.9	106.9	92.4	98.8	99.1	102.0	94.3	94.9	94.7	93.0	91.5	90.9	90.5
HUN	121.5	116.3	117.3	112.6	107.0	97.8	95.2	96.7	97.8	96.0	89.7	92.5	91.1	87.7
POL	93.7	92.8	97.2	99.7	96.8	98.7	104.5	106.2	100.7	102.6	104.9	104.7	107.0	107.8
ROM	89.2	88.5	94.4	103.4	97.6	98.3	104.1	104.3	99.2	99.1	92.3	92.6	90.0	86.4
RUS	97.0	98.0	101.3	103.0	101.2	98.4	100.5	105.1	109.4	112.6	115.0	116.7	121.2	122.4
TUR	91.5	86.7	83.8	94.8	97.2	99.4	103.4	111.1	109.3	112.9	126.4	134.9	153.8	163.2
UKR	97.2	96.4	103.0	103.0	99.5	99.1	101.4	98.8	96.2	96.6	98.6	98.9	100.0	104.8
Africa														
ZAF	89.6	86.0	89.7	92.1	94.9	98.7	106.5	113.5	124.0	125.2	129.6	127.7	130.4	131.4

Furthermore, whereas an increase was noticed in the overall view of Latin America and Asia-Africa, no such change was observed in Europe. In other words, while the livestock production index had regressed for some European countries during the analysis period, no change was observed in others. Turkey, on the other hand, differed from other countries with a significant increase in its index values.

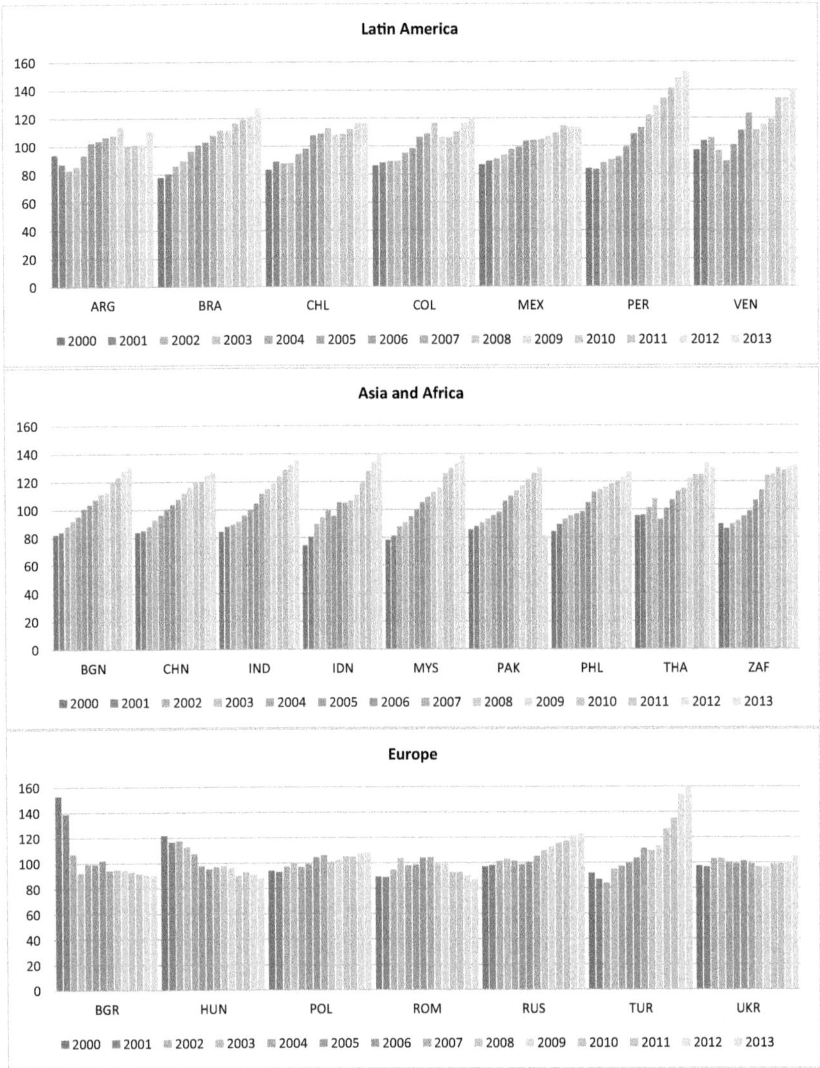

Fig. 2.4: Livestock Production Index (2004–2006 = 100). Calculated by the authors using the data of World Bank (2016)

2.3.3 Rural Life Indicators

Under this title, rural life indicators were explained in emerging market economies (EMEs). The ratio of the rural population within the total population, access of the urban population to improved sanitation facilities, and access to clean water resources were analyzed.

2.3.3.1 Rural Population

An indicator for the development levels of countries is the urban or the rural density of the population. Urban population density means a relatively advanced economic structure, whereas the population density in rural areas denotes the importance of agriculture in the economic structure. As a general rule, the agricultural sector affects value added and development less when compared to other sectors. Tab. 2.8 should be analyzed in order to monitor this trend in EMEs for the analysis period. As it is clear in the table, in 2000, the countries with the highest rural population density were Bangladesh, India, Thailand, Pakistan, and China. The ratio of the rural population to the total population in these countries for the year 2000 was over 60 % where it exceeded 70 % in Bangladesh and India. Countries with the lowest rural population density over the period were Argentina, Venezuela, and Chile.

Rural population density has generally displayed a decreasing trend until 2014 although it was still close to values displayed in 2000. China and Thailand had a regression of 18 % in 2014. India, Bangladesh, Pakistan, and Thailand experienced decreases, yet at the end of the period these countries still had high rural population densities. One out of every two persons in these countries was occupied with agriculture. Moreover, Tab. 2.8 reveals the fact that Argentina, Venezuela, and Chile were the countries with the lowest rural population in 2014 and also in 2000. The rural population of other countries generally varied between 20 % and 50 % and the rural population has increased in Philippines and Poland over the period.

Comparison of rural population density among continents reveals Asia as the leading continent. In Asia, except for Malaysia, nearly half the population lives in rural areas. At the end of the analysis period, Asia is followed by Africa, Europe, and Latin America in regards to rural population density. Moreover, while livestock production index increases over time in Asia, decrease in the rural population together with male and female employment should be emphasized as an expected and positive improvement.

Tab. 2.8: Rural Population (% of Total Population). World Bank, 2016

	2000	2001	2002	2003	2004	2005	2006	2007	2008	2009	2010	2011	2012	2013	2014
Latin America															
ARG	10.9	10.7	10.5	10.3	10.1	9.9	9.7	9.6	9.4	9.2	9.0	8.9	8.7	8.5	8.4
BRA	18.8	18.4	18.1	17.8	17.5	17.2	16.9	16.6	16.3	16.0	15.7	15.4	15.1	14.8	14.6
CHL	13.9	13.6	13.4	13.1	12.8	12.6	12.3	12.1	11.8	11.6	11.4	11.2	11.0	10.8	10.6
COL	27.9	27.6	27.3	27.0	26.7	26.4	26.1	25.8	25.5	25.3	25.0	24.7	24.4	24.1	23.8
MEX	25.3	25.0	24.6	24.3	24.0	23.7	23.4	23.1	22.8	22.5	22.2	21.9	21.6	21.3	21.0
PER	27.0	26.6	26.2	25.8	25.4	25.0	24.6	24.2	23.8	23.4	23.1	22.7	22.4	22.0	21.7
VEN	12.0	11.7	11.6	11.5	11.5	11.4	11.4	11.4	11.3	11.3	11.2	11.2	11.1	11.1	11.1
Asia															
BGN	76.4	75.9	75.2	74.6	73.9	73.2	72.5	71.8	71.0	70.3	69.5	68.8	68.0	67.2	66.5
CHN	64.1	62.9	61.6	60.2	58.9	57.5	56.1	54.8	53.5	52.1	50.8	49.4	48.1	46.8	45.6
IND	72.3	72.1	71.8	71.4	71.1	70.8	70.4	70.1	69.8	69.4	69.1	68.7	68.4	68.0	67.6
IDN	58.0	57.2	56.4	55.6	54.9	54.1	53.3	52.5	51.7	50.9	50.1	49.3	48.5	47.7	47.0
MYS	38.0	37.1	36.1	35.2	34.3	33.4	32.5	31.6	30.8	29.9	29.1	28.3	27.5	26.7	26.0
PAK	66.8	66.6	66.3	65.9	65.6	65.3	64.9	64.6	64.2	63.8	63.4	63.0	62.6	62.1	61.7
PHL	52.0	52.3	52.6	52.9	53.1	53.4	53.7	53.9	54.2	54.5	54.7	55.0	55.2	55.4	55.5
THA	68.6	67.4	66.2	65.0	63.7	62.5	61.2	59.9	58.6	57.3	55.9	54.6	53.3	52.1	50.8
Europe															
BGR	31.1	30.8	30.5	30.1	29.8	29.4	29.1	28.7	28.4	28.0	27.7	27.4	27.0	26.7	26.4
HUN	35.4	35.3	34.9	34.5	34.1	33.6	33.1	32.6	32.1	31.6	31.1	30.7	30.2	29.7	29.2
POL	38.3	38.2	38.2	38.3	38.4	38.5	38.7	38.8	38.9	39.0	39.1	39.2	39.3	39.4	39.4
ROM	47.0	47.1	47.2	47.1	47.0	46.8	46.7	46.6	46.4	46.3	46.2	46.0	45.9	45.8	45.6
RUS	26.7	26.7	26.7	26.6	26.6	26.5	26.5	26.4	26.4	26.4	26.3	26.3	26.2	26.1	26.1
TUR	35.3	34.7	34.0	33.4	32.8	32.2	31.6	31.0	30.4	29.9	29.3	28.7	28.2	27.6	27.1
UKR	32.9	32.8	32.7	32.6	32.4	32.2	32.0	31.9	31.7	31.5	31.3	31.1	30.9	30.7	30.5
Africa															
ZAF	43.1	42.6	42.1	41.6	41.0	40.5	39.9	39.4	38.8	38.3	37.8	37.3	36.7	36.2	35.7

2.3.3.2 Improved Sanitation Facilities

Hygiene conditions and sanitation facilities in a country are among the crucial factors affecting human health. Deficiencies in this aspect can prevent raising healthy generations. The level of sanitation facilities, especially in rural areas in EMEs, and its trend is presented in Tab. 2.9. According to this table, which can also be referred to as the percentage of access to improved sanitation facilities by the rural population, low values in this ratio reflects the deficiencies in the

Tab. 2.9: Improved Sanitation Facilities, Rural (%of Rural Population with Access). World Bank, 2016

	2000	2001	2002	2003	2004	2005	2006	2007	2008	2009	2010	2011	2012	2013	2014	2015
Latin America																
ARG	82	83	84	86	87	88	89.1	90	92	93	94	95	96	98	98	98
BRA	40	40	41	42	43	44	45	46	46	47	48	49	50	51	52	52
CHL	69	71	73	74	76	78	79	81	83	84	86	88	89	91	91	91
COL	52	53	54	56	57	58	59	60	61	62	63	65	66	67	68	68
MEX	52	53	55	56	58	60	61	63	65	66	68	70	71	73	75	75
PER	30	31	33	34	36	37	39	41	42	44	45	47	49	50	52	53
VEN	56	57	58	59	60	61	62	64	65	66	67	68	69	70	70	70
Asia																
BGN	44	45	46	47	49	50	51	52	54	55	56	57	58	60	61	62
CHN	50	51	52	52	53	54	55	56	57	58	59	60	61	62	63	64
IND	15	16	17	18	19	20	21	22	23	24	25	26	27	28	29	29
IDN	34	35	36	37	38	39	40	41	42	43	44	45	46	47	48	48
MYS	89	89	90	90	91	91	92	93	93	94	94	95	95	96	96	96
PAK	20	22	24	26	28	30	32	34	36	39	41	43	45	47	49	51
PHL	56	57	58	59	60	61	62	63	64	65	66	67	68	69	70	71
THA	92	93	94	94	95	95	96	96	96	96	96	96	96	96	96	96
Europe																
BGR	83	83	83	84	84	84	84	84	84	84	84	84	84	84	84	84
HUN	99	99	99	99	99	99	99	99	99	99	99	99	99	99	99	99
POL	76	77	79	80	82	83	85	86	88	89	91	92	94	95	97	97
ROM	56	56	57	57	58	58	59	60	60	61	61	62	62	63	63	63
RUS	59	59	59	59	59	59	59	59	59	59	59	59	59	59	59	59
TUR	72	73	74	75	76	77	77	78	79	80	81	82	83	84	85	86
UKR	90	90	91	90	91	91	91	91	91	92	92	92	92	92	93	93
Africa																
ZAF	46	47	48	49	50	51	52	53	54	55	56	57	58	59	60	61

country. Among all 23 EMEs, India and Pakistan were the countries with the worst conditions at the beginning of 2000s. Less than 20 % of the population in these countries had access to suitable sanitation facilities, especially WC. In the same period, the rates in Peru, Indonesia, Brazil, Bangladesh, and The Republic of South Africa were less than 50 %. However, the value exceeds 90 % in Hungary and Thailand, which was far better than some other countries. Moreover, Ukraine, Malaysia, Bulgaria, and Argentina had relatively better conditions.

It is evident that sanitation facilities in a healthy environment have improved over the period in all countries. In 2015, Hungary, Argentina, Poland, Thailand, Malaysia, and Ukraine were among the leading countries with the best facilities. More than 90 % of the rural population in these countries had access to improved sanitation facilities. However, only one out of four people in India, and one out of two people in Pakistan, Brazil, and Peru had this access.

2.3.3.3 *Improved Water Resources*

Tab. 2.10 presents the access of the rural population in EMEs to clean water resources. It can be stated that Bulgaria was the country which had the best conditions at the beginning of the 2000s. Hungary and Ukraine were also among the countries with high levels of access to clean water resources in 2000. Countries which were the most disadvantaged regarding access to clean water in rural areas were Peru, Chile, and The Republic of South Africa followed by China, Colombia, Venezuela, and Romania. This situation especially poses a threat for irrigation.

In 2015, Argentina, Hungary, Romania, and Turkey succeeded in providing access to clean water resources in all rural areas. This ratio was also high in Ukraine, Bulgaria, Thailand, and Poland. The rural population in Peru had the lowest access to clean water resources with only 70 % of the rural population having such access. Colombia, Venezuela, and Indonesia were also among countries with relatively low levels of access to clean water resources.

2.4 Conclusion

Analysis of EMEs in terms of agricultural facilities reveals that some countries and some continents emerge with positive or negative trends. For example, Pakistan, which is among the leading countries in terms of agricultural value added and male and female employment, has, along with India, the lowest percentage of rural population with access to improved sanitation facilities. South Africa is at the top of the list in terms of rural areas, in addition to a limited

Tab. 2.10: Improved Water Resources, Rural (%of Rural Population with Access). World Bank, 2016

	2000	2001	2002	2003	2004	2005	2006	2007	2008	2009	2010	2011	2012	2013	2014	2015
Latin America																
ARG	81	83	84	85	86	88	89	90	91	93	94	95	96	98	99	100
BRA	76	77	77	78	79	80	81	81	82	83	84	85	85	86	87	87
CHL	68	70	72	74	76	78	80	82	84	85	87	89	91	93	93	93
COL	71	71	71	72	72	72	72	73	73	73	73	73	74	74	74	74
MEX	73	74	76	77	79	80	81	83	84	85	87	88	89	91	92	92
PER	54	55	56	57	58	59	60	61	62	63	64	65	66	67	68	69
VEN	73	73	73	74	74	75	75	75	76	76	77	77	78	78	78	78
Asia																
BGN	74	75	76	76	77	78	79	80	81	82	83	84	84	85	86	87
CHN	71	72	74	75	77	78	80	81	83	84	86	87	89	90	92	93
IND	76	77	78	80	81	82	83	84	86	87	88	89	90	92	93	93
IDN	68	69	70	71	71	72	73	74	74	75	76	77	77	78	79	80
MYS	89	89	89	90	90	90	91	91	91	91	92	92	92	93	93	93
PAK	85	85	86	86	86	87	87	87	88	88	88	89	89	89	90	90
PHL	83	83	84	84	85	85	86	86	87	87	88	88	89	89	90	90
THA	90	90	91	92	92	93	93	94	94	95	96	96	97	97	98	98
Europe																
BGR	99	99	99	99	99	99	99	99	99	99	99	99	99	99	99	99
HUN	96	97	97	98	98	98	99	99	100	100	100	100	100	100	100	100
POL	91	91	928	92	93	93	94	94	94	95	95	96	96	97	97	97
ROM	73	75	77	79	81	83	85	87	90	92	94	96	98	100	100	100
RUS	86	86	86	87	87	88	88	88	89	89	90	90	90	91	91	91
TUR	85	86	87	88	89	90	91	93	94	95	96	97	98	99	100	100
UKR	93	93	94	94	94	95	95	95	96	96	96	97	97	97	98	98
Africa																
ZAF	71	71	72	73	74	74	75	76	76	77	78	79	79	80	81	81

increase over time; yet, interestingly, it has lagged behind in terms of agricultural value added. This finding presents the importance of the efficient use of agricultural land rather than the amount of land. Agricultural land and value added numbers of Bangladesh support this finding.

Another significant finding of the study is the negative situation of Hungary in terms of food, crop, and livestock production index. It is worthy of notice that the country, with access to improved health facilities, has limited efficiency in agricultural production. The said index values are high in Peru and, especially, in India; however, these countries have relatively worse conditions in regards to health facilities and access to clean water, which are indicators of an improved living condition.

Evaluation of the change in agricultural activities in terms of continents reveals that Asia is in a good position in regards to many indicators. For example, whereas the density of agricultural land increases over time, it also emerges in terms of agricultural value added. High levels of female employment ratio and crop production efficiency is noticeable.

Crop and food production indexes have displayed a positive change on all continents. The change in Europe is irregular. This index value fluctuates in European countries, except for Turkey and Russia, where it has regressed recently. An irregular change is also observed in the livestock production index in Europe.

Asia is the leading continent in regards to rural population density. Europe is in a relatively good position in terms of access to clean water and improved health facilities. Africa is at the end of the list in terms of these indicators. Access to healthy living conditions is difficult on this continent.

Finally, when the development of the agricultural sector in all EMEs is evaluated for the last fifteen years, it can be concluded that no country has a distinguishing feature for this period. A country displaying significant improvement in one indicator can experience a regression in another. It is possible to say that this situation is an obstacle for the economies aspiring to reach the levels of developed countries. Another finding of the study is that whereas countries converge in one indicator, they diverge in another. In divergence of the agricultural structures of the countries and the changes observed in these structures, differences in efficiency resulting from human capital and technical know-how levels are considered to play a major role.

References

Atik, A.H, (2005). "Finansal Krizlerin Gölgesinde Yükselen Piyasa Ekonomileri", Türkiye Kalkınma Bankası A.Ş. GA-05-01-02, Ankara.

ILO, (2016). Statistics and Databases, ILOSTAT Databases, http://www.ilo.org/global/statistics-and-databases/lang-en/index.htm, (Last Accessed: 25.07.2016).

Kharas, H. (2010). The Emerging Middle Class in Developing Countries OECD Development Centre, Working Paper No. 285.

Küçükaksoy, İ., (2009). "Yükselen Piyasalarda Gelir Dağılımı Eşitsizliği ve Yoksulluk", e-Journal of New World Sciences Academy SocialSciences, 3C0025, 4(4), 358–378.

Merchant, H., (2016). Handbook of Contemporary Research on Emerging Markets, Edward Elgar Publishing, Cheltenham, UK.

OECD, (2009). Agricultural Policies in Emerging Economies 2009: Monitoring and Evaluation, http://www.oecd.org/chile/agricultura lpoliciesinemergingeconomiesmonitoringandevaluation2009.htm, (Last Accessed: 11.06.2016).

OECD, (2013). Agricultural Policies in Emerging Economies 2013: Monitoring and Evaluation, http://www.oecd-ilibrary.org/agriculture-and-food/agricultural-policy-monitoring-and-evaluation-2013_agr_pol-2013-en, (Last Accessed: 11.06.2016).

Sauvant, P. K., (2006). "Inward and Outward FDI and the BRICs", Emerging Economies and the Transformation of International Business: Brazil, Russia, India and China (BRICs), Edited by: Subhash C. Jain, Edward Elgar Publishing, United Kingdom.

UNCTAD, (1998). "World Investment Report 1998: Trends and Determinants", United Nations, New York and Geneva.Wikipedia, (2016). Emerging Markets (IMF), https://en.wikipedia.org/wiki/Emerging_markets, (Last Accessed: 25.07.2016).

World Bank, (2016). Agriculture and Rural Development/Data, http://data.worldbank.org/, (Last Accessed: 01.05.2016).

Dilek Çetin and Alper Sönmez

3 The Industry Structure in EMEs

Abstract: Industrialization is the main driver for increasing the standards of living and the economic development of a country especially for underdeveloped and developing nations. The industry sector is the sector which influences the transformation from being a developing nation to being a developed one. In the first phase of industrialization, as the countries developed, the share of industry in GDP and employment increases while the share of agriculture decreases. To distinguish the industrialization level of the countries, the structure of the industry can be used. To understand the industry structure, the share of industry in employment and value added in GDP are used. Moreover, the growth rate of industry in value added has been a good indicator for the industrialization rate. Manufacturing industry is the most important part of the industry as all the production process is executed. The share of value added of manufacturing industry in GDP is used to analyze the structure of manufacturing industry. China is a remarkable country with high levels of industrialization. Since the industrial revolution, countries utilize industry sector especially the manufacturing industry as engine for growth and to develop.

Keywords: Industry, Manufacturing, Employment, Value Added, Emerging Markets

3.1 Introduction

Industrial development has a vital role for the countries which pursue prosperity and sustainable growth. "Industrialization" has been the main goal for the underdeveloped and developing countries. Industrialization is a driver for economic growth although it is supposed to shrink after the development process. The importance of industrialization has been in question since Adam Smith's (1776) *The Wealth of Nations*. The standard of living increases as the industry benefits from labor division (Eltis, 1988). In the Encyclopedia of Britannica (2017), "industrialization" is defined as "the process of converting to a socioeconomic order in which industry is dominant". Naudé and Szirmai (2012, 5) defined it as "a single global process in which the industrial mode of production has diffused across the globe". The most basic definition of industry is that it is the sector which deals with the manufacturing and the production of products. It consists of mining and quarrying, manufacturing, construction, and public utilities (electricity, gas, and water)[1] (World Bank, 2016b). Industrialization is a way

1 This is in accordance with divisions 2-5 (ISIC 2) or categories C-F (ISIC 3) or categories B-F (ISIC 4).

to convert a developing nation into a developed one. The main distinguishable factor between a developed country and a developing country is the value added distribution among the sectors.

The economic activities are divided into three main sectors according to the three-sector theory which was developed by Allan Fisher (1939), Colin Clark (1940), and Jean Fourastié (1954). The industry sector is referred to as the secondary while the agriculture (extraction of raw materials) and the service sector are the primary and tertiary sectors, respectively. The share of employment and value added in these three sectors indicate the level of transformation of countries from being a developing country to being a developed one. The main definition of EMEs is that they are considered to be developing, but they must have potential to be a developed country in the future. As the countries are developed, the main driver is the industrialization level of the countries.

Structural transformation of sectorial division from developing to developed country has three phases according to Fourastié (1954). As the countries are becoming advanced, the labor moves from the primary to the secondary sector, and after this process they pass onto the tertiary sector. Industry sectors first expand and then they shrink. In the first phase, which is called the traditional civilizations, the shares of agriculture, industry, and service sector in employment are 65 %, 20 %, and 15 %, respectively. The second phase is referred to as the transitional period, and the shares of primary, secondary, and tertiary sectors are 40 %, 40 %, and 20 %, respectively. These are the expectations for a developing country. Finally, the developed or the industrialized countries are in the third phase which is referred to as the tertiary civilization. In this phase, the shares of agriculture, industry, and service sectors are 10 %, 20 %, and 70 %, respectively.

In developed economies, the share of industry sector is so high, economists add a quandary or a quaternary sector to the three-sector theory. The quandary or quaternary sector is the knowledge-based intellectual services which are based on the creation and distribution of knowledge (Busch, 2008; Selstad, 2008).

3.2 Structure of the Industry

To understand the industry structure of EMEs, primarily the employment share of the industry sector in total employment is analyzed. In the second section, the value added of the industry is studied.

Tab. 3.1: Employment in Industry (% of Total Employment). World Bank, 2016a

	2000	2001	2002	2003	2004	2005	2006	2007	2008	2009	2010	2011	2012	2013	2014
Latin America															
ARG	22.7	21.9	20.2	21.7	23	23.5	23.6	24.2	23.9	23.1	24.1	25.3	23.5	23.7	24
BRA	21.2	20	21.4	20.9	21	21.4	21.4	22	22.6	22.1	24.1	21.7	22.7	22.6	22.9
CHL	22.9	23.5	23.5	22.8	23.2	22.8	23.5	23.4	23.4	23.1	23.5	23.6	23.9	23.7	
COL	25.5	18.2	20.3	19	19.9	19.3	19.8	20.2	19.8	19.8	19.8	20.5	20.5	19.4	19.6
MEX	26.8	25.9	24.8	24.8	24.8	25.5	25.6	25.7	25.5	25.7	25.5	24.1	23.3	23.6	
PER	18.8	17.9	19	17.9	19.2	18.6	19.4	20.4	20.8	22.3	23.9	23.7	23.8	22.9	22.9
VEN	22.8	22.1	20.6	19.8	20	20.8	22.8	23.3	23	22.5	22.1	21.9	21.2	21.3	
Asia															
BGD	10.3		13.7	13.7		14.5					17.7				
CHN	28.1	28.1	28.0	29.4	29.4	29.6	29.9	30.0	30.1	30.1	30.2	30.0	29.5	28.8	28.1
IND	16					19					22.4		24.8	21.5	
IDN	17.4	18.7	18.8	17.7	18	18.7	18.6	18.8	18.8	18.8	19.3	20.9	21.5	20.4	21
MYS	32.2	33.1	32	32	30.1	29.7	30.3	28.5	28.7	27	27.6	28.9	28.4	27.9	27.4
PAK	18	18	20.8	20.8	20.3	20.3	20.7	21	20.1	20.5	20.9	21.2		22.3	22.5
PHL	16.2	16.2	15.6	15.8	15.8	15.6	15.3	15.3	14.8	14.6	15	14.9	15.3	15.6	15.9
THA	17.9	18.8	19.8	19.7	20.5	20.2	20.6	20.7	19.6	20.8	20.6	19.4	20.9	20.3	
Europe															
BGR	33	33	32.9	32.6	33.3	34.5	34.8	35.8	36.8	35.5	33.4	31.6	31.5	30.4	30.3
HUN	33.9	34.5	34.3	33.5	33.1	32.6	32.4	32.7	32.4	31.3	30.8	31	29.9	30	30.5
POL	31.7	31.3	29.1	29	29.5	29.7	30.3	31.1	32.3	31.4	30.6	31	30.7	30.8	30.8
ROM	28.7	28.8	32.2	31.1	32.8	32.1	32.2	33.1	33.3	31.5	29.7	29.9	29.5	29.5	30.1
RUS	28.4	29.4	29.5	30.4	29.7	29.8	29.3	29.2	28.9	27.5	27.7	27.5	27.8	27.7	27.5
TUR	24	22.7	23	22.8	23	24.8	27.4	27.3	27.4	25.9	26.8	27.1	26.6	27	28.4
UKR	20.8	26.3	25.2	24.6	24.6	24.2	24.2	23.9	23.4	25.7		25.7	25.8	24.8	26.1
Africa															
ZAF	23.7	25.7	25.2	24.5	26.1	25.3	25.1	25.7	25.8	25.3	24.5	24.3	23.6	23.6	23.5

3.2.1 Employment in the Industry

The share of the industry sector in the total employment indicates the development level of the country. The shares of industry sector in total employment for EMEs between 2000 and 2015 are presented in Tab. 3.1. Bangladesh and India do not have the complete data set. No country has a sharp increase or decrease trend as stated in the introduction part. After reaching its maximum level, the share of the industry employment is expected to decrease. In China, the share is 28.1 %

in 2000, it reached its maximum for the 2000–2014 period in 2010 with 30.2 % then, it showed a declining trend and finally reached 28.1 %.

In Latin America, all EMEs' average is 22 % between 2000 and 2014 while this ratio is 22.2 % for Asian EMEs. The European EMEs have the highest averages at 29.5 %. The lowest among Latin American EMEs is Colombia at 19.6 % in 2014 while Philippines has the lowest value among all EMEs at 15.9 %. The result is interesting for Europe because Ukraine which has the lowest in Europe has higher averages than rest of the other EMEs except China. When EMEs are compared according to continents, Latin American and European EMEs have similar properties, but for Asia the situation is more complicated. In Latin America, all the EMEs look similar and they all have higher than 20 % averages, but their average is around 20 %. In Europe, all the EMEs have higher rates than other EMEs except for China and Malaysia.

The changes in the industry employment are not easily understood from Tab. 3.1, so to analyze the increasing or decreasing trend in this ratio, the five-year averages are calculated. The five-year averages of employment in the industry can be seen in Tab. 3.2. The direction of the change is easier to analyze from this table. In Latin American EMEs, small increasing trend occurs. The sharp increasing trend is verified for Asian EMEs especially for Bangladesh and India for the 2000–2014 period. The European EMEs have a decreasing trend except for Turkey and Ukraine. These two EMEs are reaching the level of Europe in this period. The averages of the shares of employment in industry in EMEs are 23.6 %, 25 %, and 25.2 % for 2000–2004, 2005–2009, and 2010–2014 period, respectively. A small but constant increase is seen during this fifteen-year period.

China holds a position of importance in the world due to the capacity within. If China fulfills all expectations, it is expected to rule the world economy in the future. China is not only feared because of its potential ruling capacity, but also because of its potential ability to increase competitiveness due to its cheap labor force (Mesquita Moreira, 2007; Jenkins et al., 2008). At the beginning and at the end of the period, industry share of China in employment is 28.1 %. In fifteen years, China increases this share to 30.2 % (maximum level for this period) then it decreased to the initial level.

Fig. 3.1 depicts the five-year averages of employment in industry. Bangladesh and Philippines, which are far behind the all other EMEs, have the lowest share while Bulgaria and Hungary have the highest values. Most of the EMEs fall in the 20–30 % range. Latin American EMEs have a range between 20 and 25 % while European EMEs have a range between 25 and 30 %. Asian EMEs have the lowest share when compared to other EMEs except for China and Malaysia.

Tab. 3.2: The Five-Year Averages of Employment in Industry (% of Total Employment). World Bank, 2016a

	2000–2004	2005–2009	2010–2014
Latin America			
ARG	21.9	23.7	24.1
BRA	20.9	21.9	22.8
CHL	23.2	23.2	23.7
COL	20.6	19.8	20.0
MEX	25.4	25.6	24.1
PER	18.6	20.3	23.4
VEN	21.1	22.5	21.6
Asia			
BGD	12.6	14.5	17.7
CHN	28.6	29.9	29.3
IND	16.0	19.0	22.9
IDN	18.1	18.7	20.6
MYS	31.9	28.8	28.0
PAK	19.6	20.5	21.7
PHL	15.9	15.1	15.3
THA	19.3	20.4	20.3
Europe			
BGR	33.0	35.5	31.4
HUN	33.9	32.3	30.4
POL	30.1	31.0	30.8
ROM	30.7	32.4	29.7
RUS	29.5	28.9	27.6
TUR	23.1	26.6	27.2
UKR	24.3	24.3	25.6
Africa			
ZAF	25.04	25.44	23.9

3.2.2 Value Added of the Industry

The share of industry in GDP is also an indicator as to how far the country has industrialized. Increasing competitiveness of China is due to the structural reforms made after World War II. The industrialization of this country is analyzed according to the share of industry in GDP and employment (Kniivilä, 2006). According to The World Bank (2016b), the average value added of industry as a

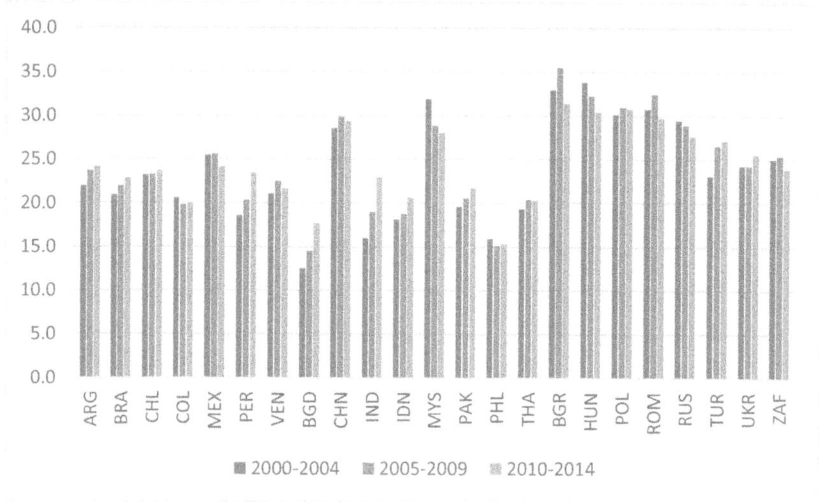

Fig. 3.1: The Five-Year Averages of Employment in Industry (% of Total Employment). World Bank, 2016a

percentage of GDP for all countries in the world is 28 % in 2014 while this value is 31 % for EMEs.

The value added share of industry as a percentage of GDP is given in detail in Tab. 3.3. The highest share of value added of industry from Latin American EMEs is Venezuela where industry forms almost 50 % of its GDP while the lowest share is Brazil with 24 % in 2014. China, Indonesia, and Malaysia draw attention with 40 % among Asian EMEs. Bangladesh has the lowest share in Asia with 27.6 %. Europe has the lowest industry value added in GDP when compared to other EMEs.

The five-year averages of industry value added to GDP are given in Tab. 3.4. The trends (increasing or decreasing) for this variable are easier to detect with this table. In Latin American EMEs, an increasing trend in this ratio is seen for 2005–2009 while for the 2010–2014 period, shares of all EMEs decrease. This generalization cannot be made for other EMEs. The EMEs' averages are 33.6 %, 34.7 %, and 33.5 % for the 2000–2004, 2005–2009, and 2010–2014 periods, respectively. Venezuela has the highest value added in the industry where almost half of the GDP is constructed by the industry. Venezuela is followed by China, Indonesia, and Malaysia which are all Asian EMEs.

Tab. 3.3: Industry, Value Added (% of GDP).World Bank, 2016b

	2000	2001	2002	2003	2004	2005	2006	2007	2008	2009	2010	2011	2012	2013	2014
Latin America															
ARG	28.1	27.0	32.4	34.9	34.7	34.7	35.1	33.6	33.1	31.7	30.9	31.1	29.8	28.8	28.8
BRA	26.7	26.6	26.4	27.0	28.6	28.5	27.7	27.1	27.3	25.6	27.4	27.2	26.1	24.9	24.0
CHL	32.2	32.8	33.1	32.7	35.3	36.9	44.9	43.7	38.5	38.0	39.6	38.7	36.6	35.0	34.6
COL	29.4	29.4	29.8	31.4	32.4	32.8	33.8	33.7	35.5	34.5	35.0	37.6	37.8	37.1	35.6
MEX	34.9	33.0	32.9	33.7	35.4	35.2	36.4	36.1	36.6	34.3	35.1	36.3	36.4	34.4	34.3
PER	31.6	31.2	32.3	33.0	35.2	37.0	39.3	41.1	39.2	36.5	38.8	40.7	38.9	37.3	35.2
VEN	49.7	46.1	49.8	51.6	55.5	57.8	56.5	53.3	54.1	44.2	52.2	52.7	49.3		
Asia															
BGD	23.3	23.8	24.0	23.7	24.0	24.6	25.4	25.7	26.0	26.4	26.1	26.4	26.7	27.6	27.6
CHN	45.4	44.7	44.3	45.5	45.8	46.9	47.4	46.7	46.8	45.7	46.2	46.1	45.0	43.7	42.7
IND	26.0	25.1	26.2	26.0	27.9	28.1	28.8	29.0	28.3	27.8	27.2	32.5	31.7	30.8	30.0
IDN	45.9	46.5	44.5	43.7	44.6	46.5	46.9	46.8	48.1	47.7	42.8	43.9	43.6	42.6	41.9
MYS	48.3	46.2	45.1	46.6	48.5	45.9	46.1	44.2	44.7	40.5	40.5	39.8	40.1	39.9	40.0
PAK	23.3	24.0	23.9	23.9	27.0	27.1	20.9	21.1	22.3	20.2	20.6	21.2	22.1	21.0	20.9
PHL	34.5	34.5	34.6	34.6	33.8	33.8	33.5	33.1	32.9	31.7	32.6	31.3	31.2	31.2	31.4
THA	36.8	36.5	37.0	38.1	38.0	38.6	39.3	39.5	39.6	38.7	40.0	38.1	37.5	37.0	36.9
Europe															
BGR	25.8	26.9	26.7	27.5	26.7	28.2	29.8	30.5	29.5	30.5	27.5	29.6	29.5	27.6	27.2
HUN	31.8	31.5	30.8	30.6	31.2	31.4	31.4	31.2	30.2	29.7	30.2	30.1	30.3	30.1	31.2
POL	32.8	31.1	30.3	31.2	32.4	32.1	32.8	32.8	32.9	33.1	33.3	34.0	33.6	32.3	32.5
ROM	27.7	29.4	30.1	27.9	28.0	28.2	28.0	26.2	25.3	26.3	31.3	32.5	28.6	28.6	28.1
RUS	37.9	35.7	32.8	32.6	36.3	38.1	37.2	36.4	36.1	33.6	34.7	33.8	33.5	32.9	32.1
TUR	31.3	30.2	28.6	28.6	28.4	28.5	28.2	27.7	27.2	25.3	26.4	27.5	26.7	26.6	27.1
UKR	36.3	34.7	34.5	34.6	35.9	32.3	36.1	36.7	33.6	29.6	31.3	29.1	28.4	26.2	25.4
Africa															
ZAF	31.9	32.4	32.5	30.7	30.3	30.3	29.4	29.7	31.4	30.4	30.2	29.9	29.7	29.9	29.5

The five-year averages for the share of industry in GDP are depicted in Fig. 3.2. European EMEs have the highest employment share when compared to other EMEs although the value added share of industry does not differ as expected from data in Fig. 3.2. Venezuela presents an interesting situation, not much higher of employment in the industry nevertheless very high level of value added in the industry.

In India, only 20.6 % of labor works in industry where they make up 30.4 % of the GDP for the 2010–2014 period (see Tab. 3.2 and Tab. 3.4). During this period, in China, only 29.3 % of the employed worked in the industry sector, but

Tab. 3.4: The Five-Year Averages of Industry, Value Added (% of GDP). World Bank, 2016b

	2000–2004	2005–2009	2010–2014
Latin America			
ARG	31.4	33.6	29.9
BRA	27.1	27.2	25.9
CHL	33.2	40.4	36.9
COL	30.5	34.1	36.6
MEX	34.0	35.7	35.3
PER	32.7	38.6	38.2
VEN	50.5	53.2	51.4
Asia			
BGD	23.8	25.6	26.9
CHN	45.1	46.7	44.7
IND	26.2	28.4	30.4
IDN	45.0	47.2	43.0
MYS	46.9	44.3	40.1
PAK	24.4	22.3	21.2
PHL	34.4	33.0	31.5
THA	37.3	39.1	37.9
Europe			
BGR	26.7	29.7	28.3
HUN	31.2	30.8	30.4
POL	31.6	32.7	33.1
ROM	28.6	26.8	29.8
RUS	35.1	36.3	33.4
TUR	29.4	27.4	26.9
UKR	35.2	33.7	28.1
Africa			
ZAF	31.6	30.2	29.8

they produced 44.7 % of the GDP. Nevertheless, this is not the case for Bulgaria where 31.4 % of the employed working in this sector produced only 28.3 % of the GDP. Venezuela has a remarkable situation. In this country, for this period only, 21.6 % of the labor worked in industry where they produced 51.4 % of the GDP. This case is examined in Fig. 3.3.

As can be seen from Fig. 3.3, there is a correlation between the employment in industry and the industry value added. Outlier countries are easier to detect with visualization. China and Chile have higher employment and value added in

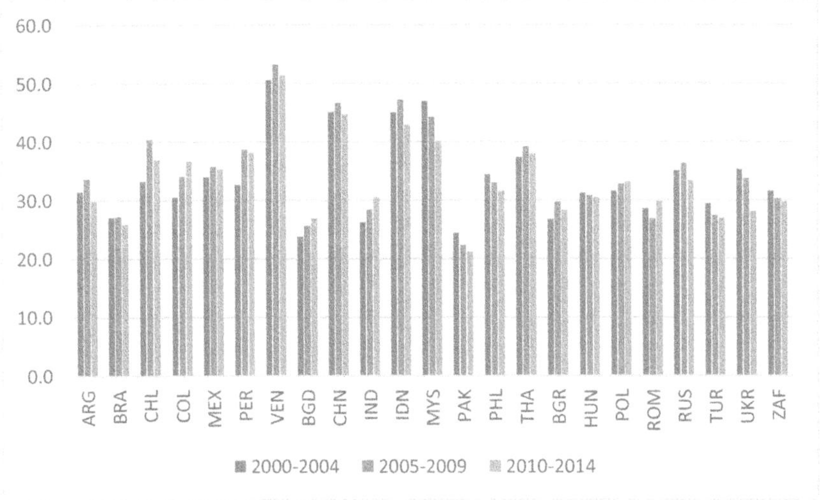

Fig. 3.2: The Five-Year Averages of Industry, Value Added (% of GDP). World Bank, 2016b

Fig. 3.3: The Relationship between Industry's Employment and Value Added. World Bank, 2016a, 2016b

Tab. 3.5: Industry, Value Added (Annual % Growth).World Bank, 2016c

	2000	2001	2002	2003	2004	2005	2006	2007	2008	2009	2010	2011	2012	2013	2014
Latin America															
ARG	-3.4	-6.5	-13.8	16.5	13.4	8.0	10.0	6.3	2.2	-1.1	9.7	9.2	-1.7	0.7	-0.8
BRA	5.3	-1.5	3.8	0.1	8.2	2.0	2.0	6.2	4.1	-4.7	10.2	4.1	-0.7	2.2	-0.9
CHL	-17.6	3.5	-0.4	38.3	5.5	2.0	1.1	0.3	1.3	-1.8	2.5	2.7	4.9	3.9	1.7
COL	-4.4	0.4	2.6	4.7	5.8	4.8	6.6	5.9	3.9	1.6	3.6	7.6	2.9	4.5	2.8
MEX	4.7	-1.5	0.0	1.3	4.1	2.5	4.4	1.5	-0.5	-6.2	4.6	3.4	2.9	-0.5	2.6
PER	1.9	3.3	8.2	3.9	6.5	8.3	6.0	8.7	9.5	-1.5	8.1	4.8	4.6	5.7	-1.2
VEN	3.8	3.2	-11.8	-9.8	17.6	6.8	7.1	4.1	3.7	-5.0	-3.4	3.1	4.7	-0.4	-5.8
Asia															
BGD	6.3	7.5	5.8	6.6	7.0	7.9	9.8	9.0	7.0	6.9	7.0	9.0	9.4	9.6	8.2
CHN	9.4	8.4	9.8	12.7	11.1	12.1	13.4	15.0	9.8	10.1	12.7	10.6	8.2	7.9	7.3
IND	6.0	2.6	7.2	7.3	9.8	9.7	11.6	9.7	4.4	9.2	7.6	5.2	3.6	5.0	5.9
IDN	5.9	2.7	4.3	3.8	3.9	4.7	4.5	4.7	3.7	3.6	4.9	6.3	5.3	4.3	4.3
MYS	10.7	-2.5	4.2	7.4	7.0	3.1	4.3	3.2	0.3	-6.7	8.4	2.5	4.9	3.7	5.9
PAK	1.3	4.1	2.7	4.2	16.3	12.1	4.1	7.7	8.5	-5.2	3.4	4.5	2.5	0.6	4.5
PHL	6.5	1.0	2.9	4.3	5.2	4.2	4.6	5.8	4.8	-1.9	11.6	1.9	7.3	9.2	7.9
THA	2.7	2.3	8.4	9.0	7.2	5.2	5.2	6.6	2.3	-2.0	10.5	-4.1	7.4	1.3	-0.6
Europe															
BGR	11.3	5.3	4.9	7.1	4.1	5.2	8.7	12.8	5.6	-3.5	-7.0	5.6	0.7	0.2	0.9
HUN	3.9	3.9	7.1	3.9	4.6	5.0	4.2	4.8	-5.3	-12.3	4.9	0.6	-2.8	-1.4	7.6
POL	3.9	-0.9	-2.1	5.9	8.6	3.2	10.8	9.1	4.2	2.5	8.0	9.2	0.9	-0.3	4.9
ROM	5.5	8.3	6.0	4.8	7.4	2.7	7.5	0.0	6.1	-1.1	4.6	0.1	-7.0	3.8	3.7
RUS	12.1	5.8	3.8	9.1	9.7	4.1	4.5	4.8	1.9	-10.4	6.6	5.1	3.8	0.6	0.1
TUR	6.2	-9.0	4.7	7.7	11.6	8.8	10.2	5.8	-1.3	-8.6	13.9	10.0	1.6	4.1	3.5
UKR	11.3	14.2	7.0	3.3	11.3	0.3	7.2	10.5	-5.7	-19.5	9.6	15.2	0.2	-3.8	-14.6
Africa															
ZAF	3.8	1.4	2.4	1.4	4.1	4.7	4.1	4.1	0.1	-6.0	4.7	1.3	0.3	1.8	-0.1

industry. Venezuela has a smaller share in employment but not in value added. Bangladesh has both the lowest employment and the lowest value added share in industry.

Annual growth of industry value added is shown in Tab. 3.5. In Latin American EMEs, all the EMEs shrank in 2009 which is after the 2008 crisis, except for Colombia. In the Asian EMEs, half of the EMEs (namely, Bangladesh, China, India, and Indonesia) waned although the other half (namely Malaysia, Pakistan, Philippines, and Thailand) enlarged its share after the crisis. All the European

EMEs derogated in 2009. In 2008, the growth rate decreases in Mexico, Hungary, Turkey, and Ukraine. A shrinkage in the industrial sector is seen in 2000 for Argentina, Chile, and Colombia, after Argentine great depression. In 2012, two Latin American EMEs (Argentina and Brazil) and two European EMEs (Hungary and Romania) have experienced contraction in industry. Bangladesh, China, India, and Indonesia never experienced a slowdown in industry for the 2000–2014 period.

The five- and fifteen-year averages of value added in industry is shown in Tab. 3.6. The growth rate of China, which is 10.6 % on an average for the fifteen-year period, is remarkable. It is followed by India and Peru with 7 % and 5.1 %, respectively. Hungary and Ukraine shrink during the 2005–2009 period while Venezuela contracted for the 2010–2014 period. The minimum growth belongs to Venezuela with 1.2 % for the fifteen-year period. Venezuela is followed by Hungary and South Africa with 1.9 %.

The five-year averages of value added in industry are depicted in Fig. 3.4. The growth rates of China for all the periods are higher than any other EMEs. Even the 2008 crisis did not slow down the growth rate of China. In the first period, Ukraine has a higher growth rate which is followed by a shrinkage in the next period. Bangladesh and India have a remarkable growth rate in the industry for all three periods.

EMEs are different in amplitude by GDP, population, etc. Nominal values of economic variables are actually not a good indicator by which to compare the countries although it still tells us a story. Tab. 3.7 shows the nominal values of the industry value added according to the 2010 constant prices in US dollars. In 2014, the world value added in industry (constant, 2010 US$) is 20.61 trillion (World Bank, 2016c) while the total value for the EMEs is 7.82 trillion which is 38 % of the world value. China produces the 18.7 % of the world and 49.4 % of the EMEs industry value added. The population of China is 1.364 billion and the population of India is 1.294 billion which is 19 % and 18 % of the world population, respectively. These two countries are similar in both population and population density but their industry value added are totally different. India has the industry value added of 3 % of the world and 7 % of the EMEs. During these fifteen years, China has quadrupled (4.1) its industry value added while India has only doubled (2.6) it.

3.3 Structure of the Manufacturing Industry

The manufacturing industry is the backbone of the industrial sector. For all the developed countries, the share of manufacturing in GDP and trade is

Tab. 3.6: The Five- and Fifteen-Year Average of Industry, Value Added (Annual % Growth).World Bank, 2016c

	2000–2004	2005–2009	2010–2014	2000–2015
Latin America				
ARG	1.2	5.1	3.4	3.2
BRA	3.2	1.9	3.0	2.7
CHL	5.9	0.6	3.1	3.2
COL	1.8	4.6	4.3	3.6
MEX	1.7	0.3	2.6	1.6
PER	4.8	6.2	4.4	5.1
VEN	0.6	3.3	-0.4	1.2
Asia				
BGD	6.6	8.1	8.6	7.8
CHN	10.3	12.1	9.3	10.6
IND	6.6	8.9	5.5	7.0
IDN	4.1	4.2	5.0	4.5
MYS	5.4	0.8	5.1	3.8
PAK	5.7	5.4	3.1	4.8
PHL	4.0	3.5	7.6	5.0
THA	5.9	3.5	2.9	4.1
Europe				
BGR	6.5	5.8	0.1	4.1
HUN	4.7	-0.7	1.8	1.9
POL	3.1	6.0	4.5	4.5
ROM	6.4	3.0	1.0	3.5
RUS	8.1	1.0	3.2	4.1
TUR	4.2	3.0	6.6	4.6
UKR	9.4	-1.4	1.3	3.1
Africa				
ZAF	2.6	1.4	1.6	1.9

remarkable. The world leadership path of the countries passes through since the industrial revolution. It is the case for England and the United States of America (Naudé and Szirmai, 2012). All the production process, innovation, and the way to globalization and competitiveness use this path of industrialization through manufacturing industry. In this part, the structure of the manufacturing industry is analyzed with the value added share in GDP.

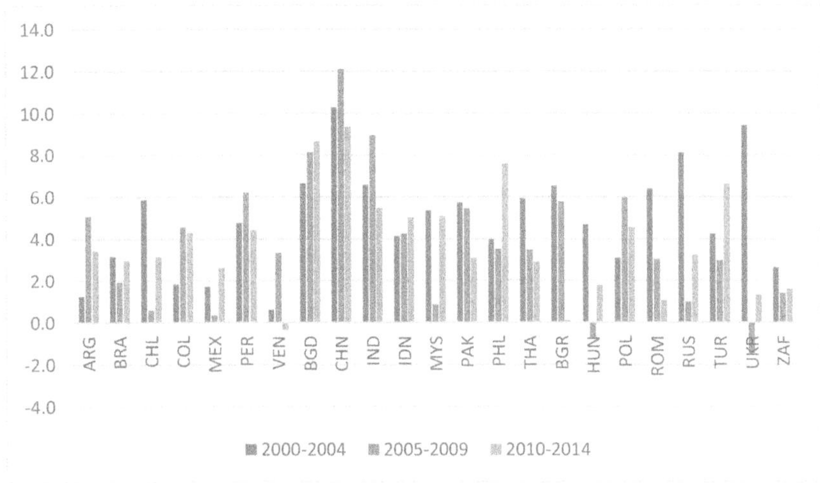

Fig. 3.4: The Five-Year Average of Industry, Value Added (Annual % Growth). World Bank, 2016c

3.3.1 Value Added in the Manufacturing Industry

The value added in the manufacturing industry indicates the production values of light engineering and heavy industry. The world average of value added in the manufacturing industry is 19.2 % and 16.3 % for 2000 and 2014, respectively. This rate is 20 % for Japan and 12 % for the United States (World Bank, 2016d). Tab. 3.8 presents the shares of value added of manufacturing industry in GDP as a percentage for EMEs. In all the EMEs, the share of manufacturing in GDP decreases with the exception of Hungary and Poland for the 2000–2014 period. It is coherent with the situation in the world. The continent averages for 2014 are 13.9 %, 20 %, and 16.6 % for Latin America, Asia, and Europe, respectively. The highest share belongs to China with 30 % while Russia has the lowest value with 6.5 %.

The five-year averages of the manufacturing industry are depicted in Fig. 3.5. The Asian EMEs have the highest share of the manufacturing industry value added of GDP while the lowest belongs to Latin American EMEs. The manufacturing industry of China has an advantage over the other EMEs. According to a consulting firm report for China, the major forces behind China becoming an economic leader are going from the manufacturing industry with the help of the government support for technology and innovation (Deloitte, 2011). Since the

Tab. 3.7: Industry, Value Added (Constant 2010 US$) (1,000,000,000).World Bank, 2016c

	2000	2001	2002	2003	2004	2005	2006	2007	2008	2009	2010	2011	2012	2013	2014
Latin America															
ARG	83	78	67	78	88	95	105	112	114	113	124	135	133	134	133
BRA	384	378	393	393	425	434	443	470	489	466	514	535	531	543	538
CHL	50	52	52	72	75	77	78	78	79	77	79	81	85	89	90
COL	62	63	64	67	71	74	79	84	87	89	92	99	102	106	109
MEX	321	317	317	321	334	342	357	362	361	338	354	366	376	374	384
PER	29	30	33	34	36	39	42	45	50	49	53	55	58	61	60
VEN	174	180	159	143	168	180	192	200	208	197	191	197	206	205	193
Asia															
BGD	14	15	16	17	18	20	22	24	25	27	29	31	34	38	41
CHN	940	1019	1119	1261	1401	1570	1781	2048	2249	2475	2789	3084	3336	3599	3862
IND	203	208	223	239	262	288	321	352	368	402	432	455	471	494	524
IDN	217	222	232	241	250	262	274	287	297	308	323	344	362	377	394
MYS	79	77	80	86	92	95	99	102	102	95	103	106	111	115	122
PAK	20.2	21.0	21.6	22.5	26.2	29.3	30.5	32.9	35.7	33.8	35.0	36.6	37.5	37.7	39.4
PHL	43	44	45	47	49	51	54	57	59	58	65	66	71	78	84
THA	81	82	89	97	104	110	116	123	126	124	137	131	141	142	142
Europe															
BGR	8	8	9	9	10	10	11	13	13	13	12	13	13	13	13
HUN	28	29	31	32	33	35	36	38	36	32	33	33	33	32	34
POL	88	87	85	90	98	101	112	123	127	130	141	154	155	155	162
ROM	30	32	34	36	39	40	43	43	45	45	47	47	44	45	47
RUS	314	332	345	376	413	429	449	470	479	429	458	481	499	502	502
TUR	115	105	110	118	132	144	159	168	166	151	172	190	193	200	207
UKR	27	31	33	34	38	38	41	45	43	34	38	43	44	42	36
Africa															
ZAF	84	85	87	88	92	96	100	104	104	98	103	104	105	106	106

industrial revolution, the manufacturing industry is believed to be the driving force in becoming a "super power" like the United States of America (Naudé and Szirmai, 2012). China uses this historical path to reach its goals.

The relationship between the manufacturing industry and the industrial share of value added is shown in Fig. 3.6. The outliers are easily detected with the help of the figure. The positive relationship between the manufacturing industry and industry is expected as seen from the figure. Venezuela has the highest industry share although the manufacturing share is lower when compared to other EMEs.

Tab. 3.8: Manufacturing, Value Added (% of GDP).World Bank, 2016d

	2000	2001	2002	2003	2004	2005	2006	2007	2008	2009	2010	2011	2012	2013	2014
Latin America															
ARG	17.8	17.2	21.6	24.0	22.7	21.9	21.3	19.9	19.9	18.7	18.2	17.9	16.8	15.9	14.5
BRA	15.3	15.4	14.5	16.9	17.8	17.4	16.6	16.6	16.5	15.3	15.0	13.9	12.6	12.3	11.7
CHL	16.9	17.6	17.6	16.1	15.6	14.7	13.8	13.0	12.2	12.3	11.8	11.9	11.8	11.9	11.7
COL	15.0	15.2	15.2	15.5	15.7	15.4	15.6	15.9	15.2	14.3	13.9	13.5	13.4	12.9	12.4
MEX	20.3	19.4	18.8	18.2	18.2	17.2	18.1	17.4	17.0	16.6	17.3	17.0	17.9	17.5	17.6
PER	16.7	16.9	17.1	16.8	17.4	17.7	17.0	18.0	17.6	16.6	16.9	16.5	16.6	16.2	15.3
VEN	19.8	18.2	17.5	18.1	17.9	16.4	15.1	14.4	14.9	15.4	13.9	13.8	13.8	12.6	13.6
Asia															
BGD	14.7	14.9	15.1	14.9	15.2	15.6	16.1	16.7	16.9	17.2	16.9	16.9	16.8	17.3	17.4
CHN	31.9	31.5	31.2	32.7	32.2	32.3	32.7	32.6	32.4	31.9	31.9	31.6	31.0	30.6	30.4
IND	15.3	14.6	14.9	14.9	15.3	15.4	16.1	16.0	15.4	15.1	14.8	17.4	17.1	16.5	16.1
IDN	27.7	29.1	28.7	28.3	28.1	27.4	27.5	27.0	27.8	26.4	22.0	21.8	21.5	21.0	21.0
MYS	30.9	29.3	29.2	29.9	30.4	27.5	27.6	26.1	24.6	23.8	23.4	23.3	23.1	22.8	22.9
PAK	14.7	15.5	15.5	16.0	17.2	18.6	13.8	14.0	15.2	13.4	13.6	14.3	14.5	14.1	13.9
PHL	24.5	24.7	24.7	24.6	23.9	24.1	23.6	22.7	22.8	21.3	21.4	21.1	20.6	20.4	20.6
THA	28.6	28.0	28.7	29.8	29.6	29.8	30.3	30.7	30.7	29.6	31.1	29.2	28.2	27.7	27.8
Europe															
BGR															
HUN	22.4	22.2	21.4	21.6	22.0	22.0	22.7	22.3	21.4	20.3	21.7	22.1	22.4	22.6	23.5
POL	18.1	16.6	16.3	17.7	19.1	18.4	19.0	18.8	18.6	18.3	17.7	18.1	18.4	17.9	18.6
ROM	22.1	24.3	24.1	22.8	23.4	23.8	23.6	22.1	21.5	21.6	23.9	24.5	22.6	23.0	23.7
RUS			17.1	16.3	17.4	18.3	17.9	20.2	20.3	17.9	20.0	7.7	7.4	7.0	6.5
TUR	22.3	21.3	20.1	20.2	19.8	19.8	19.3	18.6	17.8	16.6	17.4	18.2	17.4	17.3	17.8
UKR	19.2	19.7	20.1	20.7	22.8	19.6	23.1	23.1	20.0	17.8	17.5	13.8	14.3	13.0	13.1
Africa															
ZAF	19.2	19.3	19.4	19.0	18.6	18.1	16.4	16.1	16.0	15.0	14.4	13.3	13.1	13.2	13.3

Russia also has an outlier with a very low level of manufacturing industry share in GDP. On the other hand, China and Malaysia have both shares higher that other EMEs.

3.4 Conclusion

The industrial sector is the engine of the economies. Since the industrial revolution, one of the main aims of the developing countries has been to industrialize like the developed countries. From the definition of EMEs, these countries all

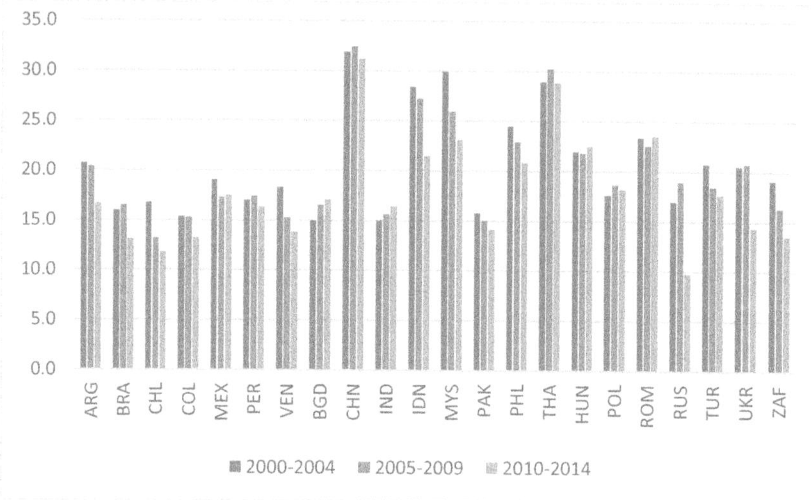

Fig. 3.5: The Five-Year Average of Manufacturing, Value Added (% of GDP). World Bank, 2016d

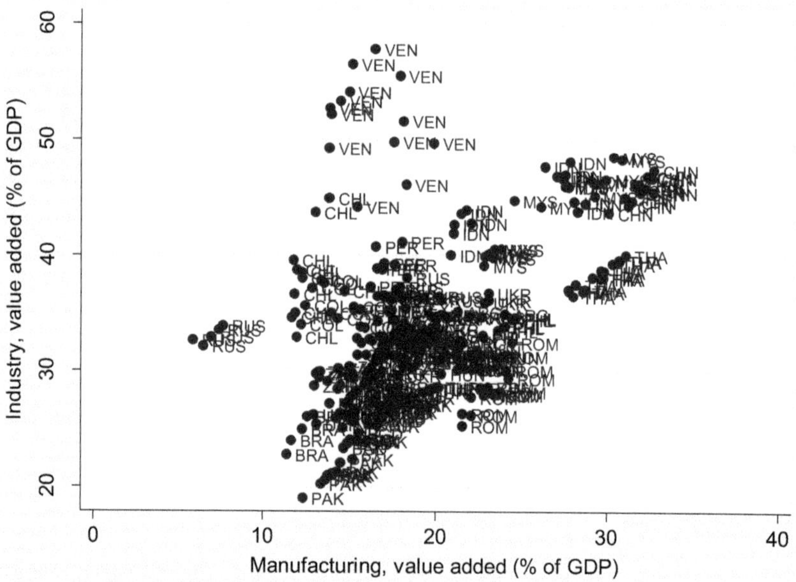

Fig. 3.6: The Relationship between Industry's Value Added and Manufacturing's Value Added (%of GDP). World Bank, 2016b, 2016d

have the potential to be future developed countries although they are still considered developing countries. China as seen by the majority of economists and politicians is the future economic and political leader of world due its potential, although its potential now mostly depends on its population.

The structure of the industry is analyzed with the labor and value added statistics from World Bank. The highest employment levels are from the European EMEs although they create the lowest value added in the industry when compared to other EMEs. Venezuela has the opposite situation. Venezuela has a lower employment level although high industry value added. China's industry growth is remarkable with a 10 % growth on an average every year for fifteen years. It quadrupled its initial level in 2014. China produces 18.7 % of the world industry production and half of the EMEs in total. The highest value added in industry also belongs to China. For further analysis, the relationship between the labor shares and the value added in industry should be analyzed. The European EMEs and Venezuela have a contractor result.

References

Busch, P. (2008). Tacit Knowledge in Organizational Learning, Pennsylvania, PA: IGI-Global Hershey.

Clark, C. (1940). The Morphology of Economic Growth. The Conditions of Economic Progress. London: Macmillan.

Deloitte, (2011), Where Is China's Manufacturing Industry Going? Deloitte China Manufacturing Competitiveness Study 2011, https://www2.deloitte.com/content/dam/Deloitte/global/Documents/Manufacturing/gx_mfg_2011MFGreport_281211.pdf (Last access date: 15.09.2016).

Eltis W. (1988). The Role of Industry in Economic Development: The Contrasting Theories of François Quesnay and Adam Smith. In: Arrow K.J. (eds) The Balance between Industry and Agriculture in Economic Development. International Economic Association Series. London: Palgrave Macmillan.

Encyclopedia of Britannica. (2017). Industrialization, https://www.britannica.com/topic/industrialization (Last access date: 15.06.2016).

Fisher, A.G.B. (1939). Production, Primary, Secondary and Tertiary. The Economic Record, 15 (1939), pp. 22–38.

Fourastié, J. (1954). Die große Hoffnung des 20. Jahrhunderts. ("The Great Hope of the 20th Century"). Köln: Deutz.

Jenkins, R., Dussel Peters, E., Mesquita Moreira M. (2008). The Impact of China on Latin America and the Caribbean, World Development, Volume 36, Issue 2, February Pages 235–253.

Kniivilä, M. (2006). Industrial Development and Economic Growth: Implications for Poverty Reduction and Income Inequality. In: Industrial Development for the 21st Century, 295–332, http://www.un.org/esa/sustdev/publications/industrialdevelopment/3_1.pdf (Last access date: 15.06.2016).

Mesquita Moreira, M. (2007). Fear of China: Is There a Future for Manufacturing in Latin America? World Development, Volume 35, Issue 3, March 2007, Pages 355–376.

Naudé, W., Szirmai, A. (2012). The Importance of Manufacturing in Economic Development: Past, Present and Future Perspectives. MERIT Working Papers 041, United Nations University - Maastricht Economic and Social Research Institute on Innovation and Technology (MERIT).

Selstad, T. (2008). The Rise of the Quaternary Sector. The Regional Dimension of Knowledge-Based Services in Norway, 1970–1985, Norsk Geografisk Tidsskrift - Norwegian Journal of Geography, 44:1, 21–37.

Smith, A. (1776). An Inquiry into the Nature and Causes of the Wealth of Nations, 2 vols. (London); republished Campbell, R. H., Skinner, A. S. and Todd, W. B. (eds) (1976) 2 vols, as vol II of The Glasgow Edition of the Works and Correspondence of Adam Smith (Oxford: Oxford University Press).

World Bank. (2016a). Employment in Industry (% of Total Employment), https://data.worldbank.org/indicator/SL.IND.EMPL.ZS (Access Date: 15.06.2016).

World Bank. (2016b). Industry, value added (%of GDP), https://data.worldbank.org/indicator/NV.IND.TOTL.ZS (Access date: 15.06.2016).

World Bank. (2016c). Industry, value added (constant 2010 US$), https://data.worldbank.org/indicator/NV.IND.TOTL.KD (Access date: 15.06.2016).

World Bank. (2016d). Manufacturing, value added (%of GDP), https://data.worldbank.org/indicator/NV.IND.MANF.ZS (Access date: 15.06.2016).

Yasemin Asu Çırpıcı

4 Service Sector in EMEs

Abstract: In this chapter, a general outlook of the service sector for the twenty-three emerging market economies (EMEs) is discussed. In EMEs, as industrialization takes place, we typically observe a decline in the agricultural sectors share in the economy and an increase in the share of the industrial sector. In the advanced stage of the development, one can observe that the service sector starts to take an increasing share in the economy. It is important to observe the development of this sector in EMEs as it gives an idea as to the level of the development of the country. Here, the countries of concern are compared according to certain indicators of the sector. First, the share of the sector in GDP is analyzed. It is observed that some countries display lower shares than others. The reasons behind this are briefly analyzed. The growth rates of the value added in the service sector are very volatile. They mostly go hand in hand with GDP growth rates. The effect of the financial crisis in 2008 can be easily observed from these growth rates. In fact, almost all countries examined experienced a sharp decline in 2009, followed by a fast recovery in 2010 but suffered a declining trend afterwards due to the general slowdown in the growth rates of EMEs. Here, some of the reasons behind this are addressed briefly. The employment structure in the sector is also analyzed. The handicap of low productivity–high wages in the sector is discussed. Since the productivity analysis requires a country-wise and further subsector analysis, a detailed examination is left to future studies. Finally, the international trade of the sector is examined. The role of the sector for providing exports of intermediates is mentioned.

Keywords: Service Sector, Emerging Markets, Tertiary Sector

4.1 Introduction

Third stage in the development process is agreed to be the increase in the significance of the service sector, referred to as the tertiary sector. In fact, as knowledge and technology improve, the industrialization stage evolves into a post-industrialization phase in which people demand more of the services rather than the material goods (Soubbotina, 2004). Most high- and middle-income countries are at this stage. Even for other countries there is an increasing trend in the share of service sector in the whole economy. In fact, while the service sector was about half of the world GDP in the early 1980s, it became two-thirds of the world GDP at the end of the 1990s (Soubbotina, 2004). World Bank data shows that in 1995, the share of the service sector in GDP worldwide was about 58.5 % where it is 68.3 % in 2014 (World Bank, 2016). When it is compared according with the income levels, one can observe that the shares increase with the income levels of the countries. In 2014 high, upper-middle, lower-middle, and low-income countries have 73.8, 56.7, 51.4, and 47.5 % of service sector shares, respectively.

In the World Bank database, Services are defined to include "*value added in wholesale and retail trade, transport, and government, financial, professional, and personal services such as education, health care, and real estate services. Also included are imputed bank service charges, import duties, and any statistical discrepancies noted by national compilers as well as discrepancies arising from rescaling*". Although there are several branches of the service sector, some common features are mentioned in the literature (Citeman, 2006; Bastos and Perobelli, 2012; Chand, 2016):

- Inseparability: They have to be produced and consumed simultaneously.
- Intangibility: Products are intangible.
- Variety: There is high variety of services since service providers differ, and also where and when they are provided varies.
- Perishability: Cannot be stored.
- Lack of ownership: In the case of tangible products the buyer has full use of the product. However, here the customer may only have access to or use of a facility, such as hiring a hotel room or using a credit card.

4.2 Service Sector Structure

In this part, the general structure of the sector is given in terms of the share of the sector in GDP, sector's growth rates, employment structure, and international trade.

4.2.1 GDP Share

It is particularly important to examine the service sector since it forms more than 50 % of the GDP of the EMEs. The exceptions are China and Malaysia with percentages ranging from 40 % to 51 %, Indonesia with a range of 37 %–43 %, and Venezuela with 38 %–50 %. India and Thailand have a share below 50 % only for the years 2011 and 2010, respectively. The highest share belongs to Brazil with 70 % in 2014. For Venezuela data is between 2000 and 2010 (Tab. 4.1).

Grouping the countries according to the continents may help make the picture clearer. From Fig. 4.1, one can see that in Europe, although the starting values are different for different countries, in the end the shares in GDP converge with each other somewhere between 60 and 70 % range. Even Ukraine, which has the lowest starting point, had values close to the other countries. One

Tab. 4.1: Percentage Share of Service Sector in GDP. World Bank, 2016

	2000	2001	2002	2003	2004	2005	2006	2007	2008	2009	2010	2011	2012	2013	2014
Latin America															
ARG	66.9	68.1	56.8	54.1	56.3	56.9	57.2	57.6	59.7	62.0	60.9	61.4	63.5	63.8	62.9
BRA	67.7	67.8	67.2	65.8	64.7	66.0	67.2	67.7	67.3	69.2	67.8	67.7	69.0	69.8	70.8
CHL	61.9	62.1	61.4	62.0	60.0	58.5	51.2	52.6	57.9	58.4	57.0	57.7	60.1	61.7	61.7
COL	61.6	61.7	61.0	59.6	59.0	58.8	58.1	58.5	57.0	58.0	57.9	55.6	55.9	56.8	58.0
MEX	61.6	63.3	63.5	62.7	61.0	61.5	60.4	60.6	60.2	62.2	61.5	60.3	60.1	62.1	62.2
PER	59.4	60.0	59.4	58.9	57.0	55.2	53.3	51.6	53.1	55.5	53.8	51.5	53.8	55.6	57.6
VEN	46.1	49.4	46.1	43.9	40.5	38.2	39.5	42.6	41.5	49.7	42.1	..	..	..	..
Asia															
BGD	52.9	53.2	54.3	55.3	55.7	55.8	55.6	55.6	55.6	55.7	56.0	55.9	56.2	56.1	56.3
CHN	39.8	41.3	42.3	42.1	41.2	41.4	41.9	42.9	42.9	44.4	44.2	44.3	45.5	46.9	48.1
IND	51.0	52.0	53.1	53.2	53.0	53.1	52.9	52.7	53.9	54.5	54.6	49.0	50.0	50.9	52.6
IDN	38.5	38.3	40.1	41.1	41.0	40.3	40.1	39.5	37.5	37.1	40.7	40.6	40.9	41.5	42.3
MYS	43.1	45.8	45.9	44.1	42.2	45.8	45.3	45.8	45.3	50.2	49.4	48.7	50.1	51.0	51.2
PAK	50.7	51.9	52.8	52.7	50.8	51.4	56.0	55.8	54.6	55.9	55.1	52.7	53.4	54.2	54.1
PHL	51.6	52.3	52.3	52.7	52.9	53.5	54.1	54.5	53.9	55.2	55.1	55.9	56.9	57.6	57.3
THA	54.7	55.0	54.3	52.5	52.7	52.2	51.3	51.1	50.3	51.5	49.4	50.3	51.0	51.8	52.7
Europe															
BGR	61.6	61.0	62.4	62.1	63.5	63.3	63.0	64.0	63.6	64.6	67.6	65.1	65.1	67.1	67.6
HUN	62.5	62.9	64.3	64.9	63.8	64.3	64.6	64.8	65.8	66.7	66.3	65.2	65.1	65.3	64.4
POL	63.9	65.5	66.6	65.8	63.9	64.6	64.2	63.7	64.2	64.0	63.8	62.7	63.4	64.5	64.6
ROM	60.2	56.1	57.4	59.2	58.0	62.3	63.3	68.4	68.2	67.7	62.4	60.2	66.1	65.3	66.5
RUS	55.6	57.7	60.9	61.2	58.1	57.0	58.2	59.1	59.5	61.7	61.4	62.2	62.9	63.3	63.7
TUR	57.4	59.9	59.7	60.0	60.6	60.7	62.4	63.7	64.4	65.6	64.2	63.5	64.5	65.1	64.9
UKR	46.6	48.9	50.8	53.3	52.2	57.3	55.2	55.8	58.5	62.1	60.4	61.4	62.5	63.6	62.8
Africa															
ZAF	64.8	64.1	63.8	65.9	66.7	67.1	68.0	67.4	65.5	66.6	67.2	67.5	67.9	67.8	68.1

can see that Asian countries mostly lie in the range of 50–60 %. Three countries with lower values than the others can be given in descending order as Malaysia, China, and Indonesia. South Africa is above all the Asian countries with a percentage share above 65 % after 2002. Latin American countries show different figures ranging between 50 and 70 %, the only exception being Venezuela with shares below 50 %.

There are various studies concerning the share of the service sector in different countries or country groups. The countries which lag behind the averages in

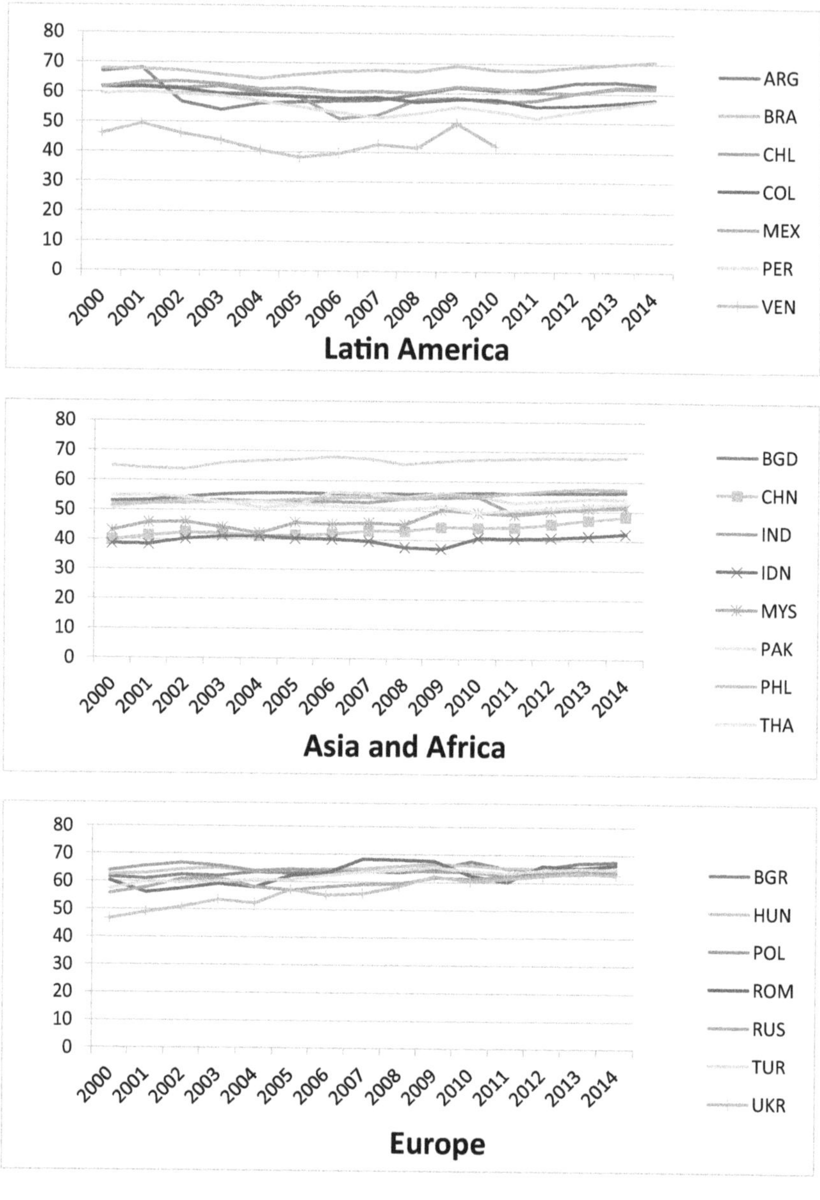

Fig. 4.1: Percentage Share of Service Sector in GDP by Continents

terms of the share of service sector in GDP are of special concern. As mentioned above, some developing countries have lower shares than expected. Especially China has interested many researchers as it undoubtedly has a leading position among the rising economies. Looking at China's development process, the service sector share in GDP is lower than expected. The reason has been analyzed in various studies[1]. Not only the studies on China, but other studies for the other developing countries point out similar facts. Specifically, labor productivity is seen to be the main indicator behind this low performance. In fact, the overall labor productivity in the service sector is lower than for the manufacturing sector. Other factors may be some legal barriers on trade and foreign investment, low R&D expenditures, and low ICT (information and communication technologies) investments[2].

4.2.2 Growth of Value Added in Service Sector

The growth rate in the service sector is more or less constant in developed countries, but in developing and transition economies growth rate does not show a regular pattern (Cuadrado-Roura, 2013). In fact, data for the countries considered in this study also confirms this trend (Tab. 4.2). Very volatile growth rates for almost all countries in the Tab. 4.2 were observed, except for Bangladesh.

Trend of the growth of the service sector value added mostly goes hand in hand with GDP growth. As seen in Fig. 4.2, the average of the service sector growth rates for the twenty-three EMEs that are analyzed shows a very similar trend with the average growth rates of GDPs.

In some countries, however, differences between the two series can be observed. As seen from Fig. 4.3, in India, Pakistan, and Poland there are differences between the two series. Although not shown in the figure, in Romania changes in services growths are sharper than the changes in GDP growth, and in Bulgaria, growth in the service sector is much volatile than the GDP growth.

In 2009, there are dramatic falls in growth rates. One exception is India where there is no change when compared to the previous year. In Philippines, a sharp decline is observed in 2008 and then there is a further but smaller decline in 2009. In China there is no dramatic change in 2009. In fact, the growth rates mostly range between 8 and 10.5 %. In three successive years (2005, 2006, and 2007), the growth rates are highest with 12.3, 14.1, and 16.6 %, respectively.

---

1 See Zheng et al. (2010), Lee and McKibbin (2014), Lee (2016), and ITC (2016).
2 Soubbotina (2004), Alejandro et al. (2010), Noland et al. (2012), Cuadrado-Roura (2013), Sauian et al. (2013), MPC (2016).

Tab. 4.2: Annual Percentage Growth of Value Added in Services Sector. World Bank, 2016

	2000	2001	2002	2003	2004	2005	2006	2007	2008	2009	2010	2011	2012	2013	2014
Latin America															
ARG	0.53	-4.02	-9.16	4.19	6.83	8.95	8.01	8.88	5.54	1.22	8.90	9.23	3.17	3.62	0.57
BRA	1.64	2.82	3.12	1.03	5.04	3.58	4.25	5.88	4.80	1.94	5.87	3.35	2.87	2.69	0.34
CHL	-15.47	3.32	4.14	19.54	5.86	7.83	6.58	7.90	3.73	0.19	7.17	7.68	6.30	4.37	2.37
COL	10.24	2.16	2.46	3.39	5.51	4.91	6.69	7.11	3.73	2.49	4.25	5.91	4.64	5.03	5.22
MEX	5.92	-0.20	0.24	1.39	4.47	3.88	5.31	4.29	2.57	-3.90	5.68	4.74	4.52	2.44	1.86
PER	2.56	-0.68	3.74	4.68	4.00	4.80	8.75	9.22	8.34	3.29	8.48	7.83	6.91	6.15	5.61
VEN	3.39	2.84	-3.81	-3.59	15.22	12.22	11.00	11.40	6.88	-0.79	-0.13	5.13	6.03	3.52	..
Asia															
BGD	5.28	5.37	4.84	4.98	5.21	6.20	6.60	6.49	5.76	5.08	5.53	6.22	6.58	5.51	5.62
CHN	9.73	10.23	10.46	9.53	10.09	12.32	14.12	16.06	10.46	9.47	9.68	9.51	7.96	8.26	7.85
IND	5.07	6.61	6.74	7.89	8.28	10.91	5.23	8.19	11.91	11.76	10.01	9.85	8.14	7.84	10.34
IDN	5.17	4.89	5.20	6.36	7.11	7.87	7.33	9.00	8.66	5.83	8.41	8.41	6.82	6.39	6.01
MYS	7.49	4.39	7.47	3.96	7.15	8.57	6.90	10.75	9.51	2.77	6.86	7.14	6.61	6.04	6.67
PAK	4.15	3.09	4.76	5.22	5.84	8.71	6.28	5.58	4.94	1.33	3.21	3.94	4.40	5.13	4.37
PHL	3.31	4.04	4.22	5.50	8.26	5.79	6.02	7.58	3.99	3.40	7.16	4.94	7.15	6.98	5.94
THA	5.25	4.28	5.60	5.16	6.98	4.14	5.09	5.22	1.05	-0.41	6.94	3.79	8.41	4.52	1.97
Europe															
BGR	5.05	4.71	9.55	3.52	5.64	9.76	7.23	9.45	3.42	-0.40	4.00	0.51	-0.84	1.32	1.90
HUN	5.17	3.40	4.69	4.01	2.64	4.76	4.37	-0.49	1.03	-3.50	0.57	1.81	-0.16	3.64	1.68
POL	4.24	2.13	3.00	2.24	3.83	3.77	4.42	6.44	3.92	2.68	1.35	2.74	2.59	1.99	2.47
ROM	5.52	1.02	6.86	5.73	6.97	8.12	8.96	15.35	8.04	-7.97	-4.81	-1.11	7.61	1.32	2.49
RUS	7.09	3.57	5.54	7.55	5.06	8.03	10.88	11.52	7.64	-4.82	4.00	3.37	3.69	1.56	1.22
TUR	6.61	-0.96	4.68	4.13	9.84	8.57	7.09	6.39	2.31	-1.81	7.64	8.76	2.55	5.54	4.25
UKR	3.96	7.02	6.28	11.07	10.78	-0.35	6.96	10.18	4.67	-14.92	3.15	-4.38	1.58	-1.34	-4.29
Africa															
ZAF	3.65	3.03	3.54	4.07	4.53	5.43	5.98	6.14	4.25	0.73	2.27	3.83	3.09	2.54	2.15

For almost all countries there is a sudden recovery in 2010 after a sharp decline in 2009. But afterwards, growth rates start to decline. For some, this decline starts from 2012. This decline is due to a general slowdown in the EMEs. Compared to 1990s, EMEs showed significant speedups in growth rates during the 2000s. Favorable external conditions accounted for about half of the increase in growth across the EMEs in the 2000s when compared to the 1990s (Cubeddu et al., 2014). These external conditions are: Buoyant global trade, easy financing conditions driven by low interest rates in advanced economies, and high commodity prices. Together with these external factors, some structural reforms

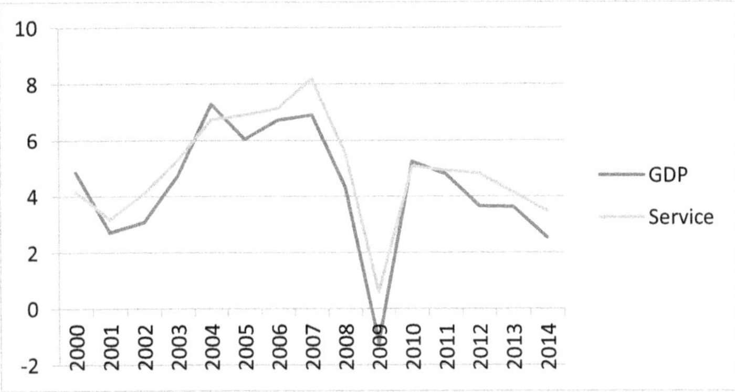

Fig. 4.2: Average Growth of GDP and Services in EMEs

implemented in the EMEs and liberalization in trade and finance contributed to these high growth rates (Cubeddu et al., 2014). However, external factors have disrupted since the global financial crisis. External demand declined, commodity prices increased.

Cubeddu et al. (2014) used a pooled panel ordinary least square (OLS) regression for a sample of twenty-four EMEs for the period 2010–2013 to analyze the external and internal factors affecting the synchronized slowdown in the EMEs. They showed that lower demand in trading countries largely explains the slowdown in growth for 2010–2011 through 2012. In 2013, this has a smaller effect but is still statistically significant. Furthermore, they concluded that the change in external demand for EMEs is explained by advanced economies and China.

The decline in commodity prices, particularly in oil prices since the mid-2014, affected commodity importers and exporters oppositely. While lower prices increased the domestic demand in importers, the terms of trade have deteriorated in exporters resulting in contractions in investment in commodity-related sectors and slowdown in GDP growth (ECB 2016; Buysse and Vincent 2015).

An empirical study, using the data for twelve EMEs from the first quarter of 1998 to the third quarter of 2015, showed that external factors have accounted for around half of all variations in growth dynamics in the last two decades. External factors were especially important in the initial downturn observed in 2010. But, domestic factors have been more effective since 2014 (ECB, 2016).

The World Bank (2014) estimates show that two-thirds of the slowdown in EMEs is a result of a decline in the cyclical component of growth, while the remaining one-third is structural, driven by slowing growth in total factor productivity.

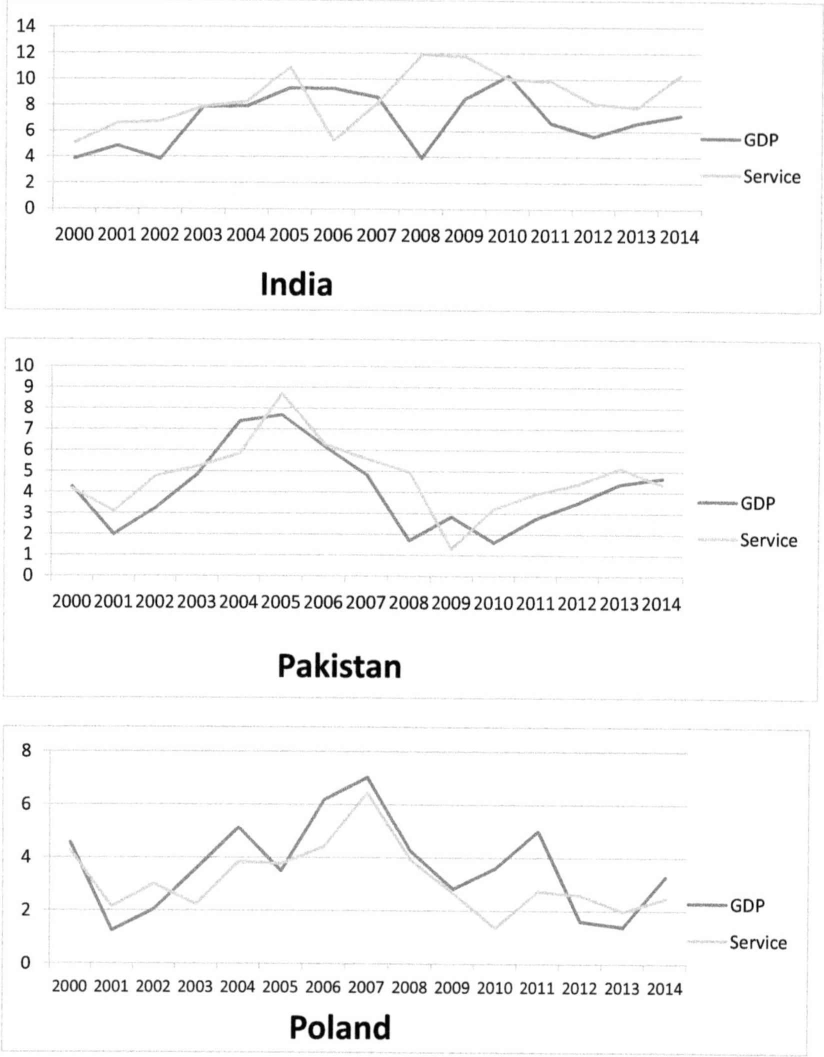

Fig. 4.3: Percentage Growths of GDP and Service Sector of Selected Countries

In both major advanced economies and in EMEs there have been many economic policy uncertainties after the global financial crisis. In fact, political risk in EMEs measured by political risk index of the International Country Risk Guide (ICRG) has increased. This resulted in bouts of stock market and currency volatility (Didier et al., 2015).

As external factors ebbed after the global financial crisis and populations age in parts of the emerging world, it will be important for EMEs to raise potential growth by implementing some structural reforms (Bailliu and Hajzler, 2016). An estimate based on a Cobb-Douglas production function showed that about one-third of the slowdown in the seven largest EMEs since 2010 was due to a fall in potential growth (ECB, 2016).

4.2.3 Employment

In general terms, service sectors are highly labor-intensive. As the sector expands, this leads to a high share of employment in the service sector within the overall employment. In fact, this share goes above 80 % in developed countries. On the other hand, the labor productivity in services is declining. In general, the labor productivity may increase because of increase in capital per worker, improvements in technology, increase in labor skills, better management, and economies of scale (Heilbrun, 2003).

In industries, productivity increase may be achieved by, for example, the use of more machinery and equipment. But when it comes to the service sector, things change. Baumol (1967) points out this by dividing economic activities according to the role played by labor. Labor may be an instrument for producing the final product or labor itself may be the final product. Examples for the latter are teaching or live performances. In fact, performing a symphony requires a certain number of instruments and also certain number of musicians. This will not change over the years. The difficulty comes in terms of productivity. Of course, there may be different technologies used in various live performances such as stage lighting, electronic controls, better sound scheme, and so on but these are not central to the business (Heilbrun, 2003).

Soubbotina (2004) points out that within the service sectors knowledge and information related subsectors grow most rapidly. Some examples for these subsectors are education and business services.[3] Technological innovation

3 *"Include financial intermediation, insurance and pension funding (except compulsory social security), activities auxiliary to financial intermediation, real estate activities,*

became the major factor in economic growth. This requires enhancement of the knowledge base. But most developing countries, in this manner, are far behind the developed countries. It is not easy for developing countries to bear the high cost of innovation. Moreover, they may not have the required number of scientists and engineers. In fact, about 85 % of the global R&D expenditure is made in high-income countries. Also, 80 % of the world's personal computers and about 90 % of its internet users are in these countries (Soubbotina, 2004).

Although the productivity levels are low in the service sector, it is not possible to decrease the wage rates here. High wage rates in progressive sectors force the non-progressive sectors to increase their wages as well. This phenomenon is referred to as "cost disease" by Baumol (1967). This results in cost increase in the service sector.

When the subsectors are analyzed, a different picture may be seen. For example, according to the work by Sauian et al. (2013), in Malaysia, three subsectors, transportation, communication, and financial services, show increasing labor productivity between 2000 and 2010. They attribute this to the increase in the quality of labor due to the increase in the skills of laborers and the use of ICT in the operations of the organizations in these sectors. Oulton (2001) argues that the Baumol's argument is true only if the service sector produces final products. If they produce intermediate products, expansion of these sectors may result in an increase in the productivity, contributing to an aggregate productivity growth. Also, some studies point out the fact that the trade in producer services as a middle input results in increase in productivity in services (see Markusen and Strand, 2007; Markusen, 1989; Francois and Woerz, 2007; Hodge and Nordås, 2001).

When the countries which lag behind the other countries in terms of the contribution of service sector to GDP, namely China, Malaysia, Indonesia, and Venezuela, are analyzed, it can be observed that a productivity analysis must be done on a country level, and more specifically has to be done for the subsectors of the service sector. Lee and McKibbin (2014) constructed a general equilibrium model to examine the impact of increase in productivity on the growth of the service sector in Asian economies. They conclude that productivity growth is beneficiary for all sectors, but the adjustment process differs among countries. In fact, "*adjustment depends on the sectoral composition of each economy, the capital*

---

renting of machinery and equipment, computer and related activities, research and development (R&D), legal, technical, advertising and other business activities", Breitenfellner and Hildebrandt (2006:114).

intensity of each sector and the openness of each sector to international trade". As mentioned before, in Malaysia, while overall labor productivity in the service sector is low, for three subsectors productivity is increasing (Sauian et al., 2013). Alejandro et al. (2010) also analyzed the subsectors of services in Malaysia separately.[4] Here, only the employment structure in the service sector will be examined. Detailed analysis will be left for further studies.

The first indicator used is the employment in services as a percentage of total employment. Data is available for Bangladesh for the years 2000, 2002, 2003, 2005, and 2010 and for India for 2000, 2005, 2010, 2013, and 2014. Also, for Venezuela the data is available up to 2013 and for China up to 2011. The data for all years is given in Tab. A1 in the Appendix. In Tab. 4.3, the data is given as five-year averages together with the overall average in the last column. This enables us to trace the data easily.

The highest employment percentages are observed for Argentina and Peru with values above 70 %. For Argentina, the highest value is 79 % in 2002 while for Peru it is 76 % in 2009. Venezuela follows with a range of 67–71 %. In Brazil, employment in the service sector is about 60 % of the total employment, but for 2010 and 2014 it is above 75 %.

There is an increasing trend in the share of employment in the service sector throughout the period for Hungary, Malaysia, Mexico, Poland, and Russian Federation ranging from 50 to 66 %. For Bulgaria, in 2010 the share is 54 %, in 2001 it is 58 %, and it declines to 56 % in 2008, then it continuously increases to 63 % in 2014.

In Chile, employment is above 60 % in the first and last four years of the period while it decreases to 43–45 % for the years 2004–2009. In China, in 2000 and 2001 employment is about 12.7 % of the total employment, then it sharply increases to 50.5 % in 2003 and stays close to 50 % in the rest of the period. Columbia has a share of 73 % in 2000, 44 % in 2001. Later on it is around 60 %.

The share is 13.3 % in 2000 for Ukraine, 53 % in 2001, then stabilizes at 53–61 %. In South Africa, the share ranges between 53 and 61 % until 2010 then suddenly it rises over 70 % and remains above 70 %. Philippines, Turkey, and Romania experience a continuous increase from 47 to 54 %, from 40 to 52 %, and from 32 to 45 %, respectively.

4 See MPC (2016); Jajri (2011); Alejandro et al. (2010); Zheng et.al. (2010); Koonnathamdee (2013), and Manning and Aswicahyono (2012) for further analysis.

Tab. 4.3: Average Employment in Services (% of Total Employment). World Bank, 2016

	2000–2004	2005–2009	2010–2014	2000–2014
Latin America				
ARG	76.7	74.9	73.6	75.1
BRA	58.5	59.4	68.0	61.9
CHL	58.7	44.5	66.2	55.8
COL	59.6	60.8	62.6	61.0
MEX	57.1	59.8	61.9	59.4
PER	71.8	71.9	75.3	73.0
VEN	68.2	68.2	70.2	68.8
Asia				
BGD	30.9	37.4	35.3	33.1
CHN	28.5	49.1	47.9	40.3
IND	24.0	25.2	27.8	26.5
IDN	37.3	39.7	43.6	40.2
MYS	52.7	56.9	59.5	56.3
PAK	35.6	35.5	34.0	35.1
PHL	47.3	49.4	52.7	49.8
THA	35.0	37.9	39.4	37.3
Europe				
BGR	56.6	57.1	61.9	58.5
HUN	60.2	63.1	64.7	62.7
POL	52.3	54.7	57.1	54.7
ROM	34.9	41.0	43.9	39.9
RUS	58.7	61.8	65.1	61.9
TUR	41.6	49.9	51.1	47.6
UKR	46.2	57.6	55.8	53.0
Africa				
ZAF	55.5	59.6	71.3	62.1

The share of employment is the smallest for India (average of 26.5 %). It is followed by Bangladesh (average of 33 %), Pakistan (average of 35 %), Thailand (average of 37 %), Indonesia (average of 40 %), and China (average of 40 %).

4.2.3.1 *Female Employment*

Another indicator for analyzing the structure of service sector is female employment in that sector as a percentage of total female employment. The complete

Tab. 4.4: Average Employment in Services, Female (% of Female Employment). World Bank, 2016

	2000–2004	2005–2009	2010–2014	2000–2014
Latin America				
ARG	88.4	88.8	89.6	88.9
BRA	72.6	72.6	77.4	73.7
CHL	83.1	…	84.3	83.7
COL	73.2	77.3	77.9	76.1
MEX	72.9	76.8	79.2	76.1
PER	83.1	81.6	…	82.4
VEN	85.9	86.3	87.3	86.3
Asia				
BGD	19.4	19.4	21.9	19.9
CHN	53.2	52.5	…	52.8
IND	13.7	14.7	18.2	16.2
IDN	39	43.7	49.3	42.6
MYS	60.6	67.4	71.5	66.2
PAK	18.7	12.9	5.1	12.8
PHL	63.5	65.4	68.8	65.7
THA	37.9	41.5	44.1	41
Europe				
BGR	63.4	65.8	71.1	66.8
HUN	72.5	76.6	77.7	75.6
POL	64.8	68.5	72.3	68.5
ROM	38.6	47.2	51.8	45.9
RUS	68.5	73	77.4	73
TUR	26.8	41.5	48.2	38.8
UKR	…	64.5	67.5	66.9
Africa				
ZAF	63.9	65.5	82.8	71.8

table is given in the Appendix in Tab. A2, while here in Tab. 4.4 the five-year averages and overall averages are given. It can be observed that in general there is an increasing trend in female share. The only exception is Pakistan where there is a decreasing trend from 18 % to 13 % in 2009 and a very sharp decline in 2009 to 3 %. This value increased to 12 % in 2014. There are limited values for both Bangladesh and India showing low values. For Bangladesh, the latest available data is for 2010 with 22 %, and for India it is 19 % in 2012.

Indonesia, Malaysia, Romania, and Turkey exhibit increasing trends, but stay below 54 %. China also has values below this but between 2003 and 2010 these values are all above 50 %. In Thailand, from 2000 to 2010 there is an increase from 36 % to 46 %, then a decline to 43 % in 2014. For the other countries, at the final stage one can observe values above 70 %. It goes above 80 % for Chile, Peru, South Africa, and Venezuela. The highest percentage is observed in Argentina values above 87 % and grew almost 91 % in 2014.

4.2.3.2 Male Employment

Whole data for male employment is given in the Appendix while in Tab. 4.5 one can observe five-year averages and overall averages. Brazil, Bulgaria, Hungary, Malaysia, Mexico, and Russia have an average of around 50 %. China is slightly below 50 % with data only between 2003 and 2007 showing a decline from 49 % to 46 %. Three other countries have more than 50 % employment rates. Chile has 53 % on average with no data between 2003 and 2010. Argentina has about 65 % on average. Peru has 67 % in 2000 and declines to 61 % in 2004 then increases back to 62 % in 2008. There is no data after 2008.

Venezuela has small swings but, on the average, the employment rate is 57 %. On the other hand, some other countries have rates ranging from 30 % to 40 %: Thailand, India, Indonesia, Pakistan, and Romania. Philippines and Poland show continuous increases from 37 % to 43 % and from 40 % to 45 %, respectively (Tab. 4.5).

Bangladesh has data for 2000, 2002, 2003, 2005, and 2010. First, there is an increase from 30 % to 43 %, and then a decline to 41 %. In Columbia, it starts from 68 % then shows a sharp decline in 2001 to 37 %, then an increase again to 48 % and stabilizing at 50 %. South Africa shows an increasing trend from 52 % to 62 % but has no data for 2001 and 2002. In Turkey, it first increases from 45 % to 54 % in 2009, then declines slightly to 52 % in 2014. Ukraine has data for 2009, 2011, 2012, 2013, and 2014 showing a rate of about 44 % (Tab. A3).

4.2.4 International Trade

Trade in services may be difficult to visualize at first glance. The best way to understand it, perhaps, is to refer to the definition given in GATS (General Agreement on Trade in Services). According to GATS, four different types of service trade, referred to as "the four modes of trade services", are mentioned: cross-border trade, consumption abroad, commercial presence in a foreign country, and movement of natural persons across borders (Jensen, 2011).

Tab. 4.5: Average Employment in Services, Male (% of Male Employment). World Bank, 2016

	2000–2004	2005–2009	2010–2014	2000–2014
Latin America				
ARG	68.4	64.9	62.5	65.3
BRA	48.9	49.7	51.8	49.9
CHL	52.3	...	54	53.2
COL	50.6	50.2	51.9	50.9
MEX	48.9	49.8	51.2	49.9
PER	63	61.9	...	62.5
VEN	57.5	56.8	58.1	57.3
Asia				
BGD	35.4	43	41.1	38
CHN	48.8	46.9	...	47.6
IND	28.2	29.8	30.4	29.7
IDN	36.3	37.5	40.1	37.4
MYS	48.3	51	52.3	50.4
PAK	38.6	38.8	33.4	37.2
PHL	37.3	39.4	41.9	39.3
THA	32.7	34.8	35.4	34.2
Europe				
BGR	50.4	49.2	53.6	51.1
HUN	50	51.6	53.4	51.7
POL	41.9	43.4	44.9	43.4
ROM	31.7	36.1	37.7	35.2
RUS	49.3	50.9	53.2	51.1
TUR	47.3	52.9	52.3	50.8
UKR	...	42.8	44.8	44.4
Africa				
ZAF	51.3	54.9	61.6	56.7

International trade in services may be beneficiary both for developed and developing countries. International trade may increase the competition which may lead to lower costs and prices, also more efficiency and innovation. Reducing the trade barriers for services may favor the industries using services in their production process (OECD, 2005b).

Fall in travel costs, new communication opportunities, increasing use of computers and the internet gave many trading options for services (Jensen, 2011). In fact, growth of trade in services is higher than trade in goods

(Cuadrado-Roura, 2013). Still, the share of service trade in value added remains quite low when compared to other trading activities (OECD, 2005a). World Bank data shows that the share of service trade in GDP worldwide was 13 % in 2015.

In the subsections below exports and imports of the service sector are examined.

4.2.4.1 Service Export

For Bangladesh, Brazil, Bulgaria, Chile, Columbia, Hungary, India, Malaysia, Philippines, Poland, and Thailand there is an increasing trend except in 2010. Bangladesh, Bulgaria, Columbia, and Chile have values of about $3, $9, $9, and $11 billion in 2015, respectively. Higher values are for Philippines with $26 billion, for Hungary with $25 billion, for Brazil with $40 billion, for Malaysia with $42 billion, and for Thailand with $55 billion. India has the highest export value with $156 billion (Tab. 4.6).

We observe swings in export values. China, Indonesia, Mexico, Pakistan, Peru, Romania, South Africa, Turkey, and Venezuela all exhibit swings. But comparing 2000 and 2015, except for Pakistan and Venezuela, there is an increase for all countries. In fact, except for South Africa, the highest values are for 2015. In Mexico, there was an increase from $12 billion in 2000 to $21 billion in 2015; in South Africa, from $5 billion in 2000 to $17 billion in 2015; in Turkey, from $16 billion in 2000 to $52 billion in 2015; in China from $66 million in 2000 to $281 million in 2015; and in Indonesia from about $5 billion in 2000 to $24 billion in 2015. Pakistan has swings with significant jumps, in 2011, 2013, and 2015. While its value is $1 billion in 2010 it increases to about $7 billion in 2011. It drops to $5 billion in 2012, increases to $7 million in 2013 then suddenly drops to $5 million in 2014, and increases again to $6 billion in 2015. Venezuela shows swings especially up to 2009 but afterwards it has small changes stabilizing at $2 billion. In Peru, export values are increasing except for a small decline from 2000 to 2002, and again in 2011. It experienced a sharp increase after 2013, starting at $1 billion in 2000 to approximately $6 billion in 2015. Romania has swings with dramatic increases in 2006 and 2014 ($4 to $10 billion from 2005 to 2006, and $13 to $18 billion from 2013 to 2014), then experiencing a sharp fall in 2010, from $16 in 2009 to $12 billion in 2010 (Tab. 4.7).

China gave special importance to the service trade by implementing its 12th Five Year Plan (2011–2015). The plan focused on the subsectors where China has comparative advantages, namely transport, tourism, and construction sectors (ITC, 2016). In fact, service export values showed a significant increase afterwards (see Tab. 4.7). China on one hand enlarges the scale of its service trade and on the other hand increases technological and knowledge intensity.

Tab. 4.6: Service Exports (BoP, Current US$). World Bank, 2016

(billion $)	2000	2001	2002	2003	2004	2005	2006	2007	2008	2009	2010	2011	2012	2013	2014
Latin America															
ARG	4.7	4.9	4.6	3.4	4.4	5.2	6.5	7.8	10.1	11.8	10.7	13.4	15.3	15.0	14.6
BRA	6.3	8.4	8.3	8.6	9.6	11.7	15.0	18.5	24.0	30.5	27.7	30.8	37.1	39.1	38.2
CHL	3.9	4.1	4.1	4.4	5.1	6.0	7.1	7.8	9.0	10.8	8.5	11.1	13.1	12.4	12.4
COL	1.9	2.1	2.2	1.9	1.9	2.5	3.0	3.8	4.0	4.6	4.6	5.1	5.6	6.4	6.9
MEX	11.5	13.5	12.4	12.5	12.4	13.7	15.7	15.9	17.2	17.7	14.8	15.2	15.6	16.1	20.2
PER	1.4	1.3	1.1	1.2	1.5	1.8	2.0	2.3	2.8	3.3	3.4	3.3	3.6	4.2	5.2
VEN	1.4	1.2	1.4	1.0	0.9	1.1	1.3	1.5	1.9	2.2	2.1	1.8	1.9	2.2	2.2
Asia															
BGD	0.8	0.8	0.8	0.9	1.1	1.1	1.5	1.7	2.0	2.2	2.0	2.4	2.5	2.7	3.0
CHN	66.1	78.7	90.1	102.2	57.7	79.2	78.5	94.1	125.4	145.3	122.6	117.5	201.0	201.6	207.0
IND	14.5	16.7	17.3	19.5	23.9	38.1	52.2	69.4	86.6	106.1	92.9	117.1	138.5	145.5	148.6
IDN	4.6	5.2	5.5	6.7	5.3	12.7	13.0	9.1	11.0	13.8	12.1	16.7	21.9	23.7	22.9
MYS	12.1	14.0	14.6	14.9	13.6	17.3	19.7	21.1	29.1	30.8	28.3	34.7	38.8	40.6	42.1
PAK	1.3	1.3	1.4	2.4	2.9	2.7	3.7	3.5	3.7	4.2	4.0	6.6	5.1	6.6	4.9
PHL	5.2	5.6	4.9	5.6	5.7	6.7	8.6	11.1	13.5	13.1	14.1	17.8	18.9	20.4	23.3
THA	14.6	13.9	13.0	15.4	15.8	19.0	19.9	24.6	30.1	33.1	30.2	34.3	41.6	49.6	58.6
Europe															
BGR	1.8	2.2	2.1	2.2	3.0	4.0	4.4	5.2	6.8	7.9	6.9	8.9	9.1	8.7	9.1
HUN	6.6	7.3	8.5	8.7	10.5	11.5	12.6	13.6	17.1	20.5	18.6	19.4	22.3	20.6	22.6
POL	8.4	10.4	9.8	10.0	11.2	15.2	18.2	22.6	31.8	38.3	31.4	35.4	40.9	41.0	44.6
ROM	1.4	1.8	2.1	2.4	3.1	3.7	9.7	12.3	13.1	16.4	11.8	10.4	12.1	12.7	17.9
RUS	12.7	11.3	12.7	15.1	18.4	23.0	28.8	35.7	43.9	57.1	45.8	49.2	58.0	62.3	70.1
TUR	16.3	19.4	15.2	14.0	18.0	23.1	27.8	26.1	30.0	37.1	35.8	36.5	41.3	43.6	48.2
UKR	4.4	4.7	4.9	5.5	5.9	8.9	10.4	12.2	15.2	19.3	14.9	18.3	21.3	22.1	22.6
Africa															
ZAF	5.2	5.0	4.8	5.1	8.7	10.2	11.8	13.1	14.8	14.0	13.2	16.1	17.3	17.6	16.8

In Argentina, up to 2003, export values are about $5 billion, then declines to about $3 billion in 2003, then reaches $12 billion in 2009 but suffers another decline to about $11 billion in 2010, however, shows an increase in 2011, 2012, and 2013, but experiences a decreasing trend afterwards and stabilizes at about $13 billion. In Russia, starting from $13 billion in 2000, export values increase to $57 billion in 2009, and decreases about 20 % in 2010 and starts to increase up to 2014 then falls in 2015 to $66 billion. In Ukraine, exports continuously increased

Tab. 4.7: Service Exports (%of Total Exports). World Bank, 2016

	2000	2001	2002	2003	2004	2005	2006	2007	2008	2009	2010	2011	2012	2013	2014
Latin America															
ARG	16.8	15.7	14.7	11.8	12.8	13.0	13.8	14.4	15.3	14.4	16.1	16.4	15.6	15.8	16.1
BRA	11.5	13.2	12.5	12.5	11.6	10.9	11.3	11.8	13.0	13.3	15.3	13.3	12.7	13.9	13.6
CHL	18.4	17.5	18.5	19.4	19.0	15.7	14.7	11.8	11.7	14.0	13.3	13.6	13.9	13.7	13.9
COL	13.7	13.0	14.6	13.2	12.3	12.5	12.1	13.0	11.5	10.6	11.9	11.1	8.8	9.5	10.2
MEX	7.8	7.5	7.3	7.2	7.0	6.8	6.8	6.0	6.0	5.7	6.1	4.9	4.3	4.2	5.0
PER	18.4	15.2	13.9	13.4	14.4	12.2	10.4	8.8	9.2	9.6	11.3	8.4	7.1	8.1	10.8
VEN	6.1	3.4	4.9	3.7	3.1	2.7	2.4	2.3	2.6	2.2	3.5	2.7	2.0	2.2	2.4
Asia															
BGD	12.5	11.3	11.0	13.0	14.1	12.5	13.0	12.8	13.9	12.6	11.7	11.3	9.1	9.7	9.5
CHN	44.1	41.4	43.2	41.3	12.9	13.1	10.1	9.5	10.0	9.7	9.8	7.3	10.0	9.3	8.8
IND	28.2	27.8	27.9	27.6	28.2	32.8	33.8	35.9	36.1	34.8	35.6	33.6	31.0	32.8	31.8
IDN	8.2	7.4	8.7	10.1	7.6	16.2	13.7	8.5	9.0	9.5	9.6	10.0	10.3	11.2	11.2
MYS	12.6	12.5	14.2	13.8	11.5	12.0	12.2	11.5	14.1	13.4	15.2	15.6	15.3	16.3	17.2
PAK	14.9	13.4	13.5	19.6	19.9	17.1	19.2	16.9	17.0	16.7	17.7	23.4	16.2	21.0	16.4
PHL	22.0	20.5	20.2	20.6	19.4	20.7	25.5	26.5	29.2	27.3	32.6	32.6	33.0	30.6	34.4
THA	20.5	17.0	17.1	18.9	16.8	16.7	15.4	16.1	16.6	15.9	16.7	15.2	15.9	18.0	20.6
Europe															
BGR	30.9	31.1	29.6	29.0	29.5	28.8	27.0	25.7	25.7	26.1	29.6	26.6	25.5	25.7	24.4
HUN	24.5	23.6	24.6	22.4	21.7	18.4	17.7	16.2	16.0	16.2	19.0	18.1	18.3	18.7	19.1
POL	21.9	22.4	19.0	17.7	15.5	17.3	17.2	17.3	19.1	18.7	19.1	18.4	18.2	18.5	18.4
ROM	14.2	14.8	15.7	15.3	15.5	14.3	40.1	40.5	30.3	29.1	25.9	19.3	17.8	19.8	23.4
RUS	15.4	10.2	11.6	12.9	12.5	11.4	10.7	10.7	11.2	10.9	13.4	11.1	10.1	10.6	11.8
TUR	35.9	38.6	30.3	25.7	25.6	25.1	26.2	21.8	20.6	20.8	24.6	23.2	22.5	21.2	23.0
UKR	27.7	25.5	24.4	25.0	21.5	22.5	24.5	25.2	24.8	23.4	28.7	27.9	25.4	25.5	27.7
Africa															
ZAF	15.4	13.6	13.5	13.9	18.3	17.5	17.4	16.5	15.9	13.6	15.8	14.9	13.7	14.9	14.8

up to 2009. Then there was a sharp decline in 2010 from $19 to $15 billion. There was an upturn in 2011 to $18 billion and continued to increase until 2015 when there was a sudden drop from $22 billion to 15 billion.

When we analyze exports as a percentage of the total exports, we observe that, on the average, for most countries these percentages are below 20 %. In fact, only six countries experience values greater than 20 % (Romania 22.5 %, Ukraine 25.2 %, Turkey 25.5 %, Philippines 26.8 %, Bangladesh 27.5 %, and India 31.9 %). Venezuela and Mexico have very low values of 3 % and 6 %, respectively.

4.2.4.2 *Service Imports*

Data was collected for the years 2005–2014. However, data is not available for Venezuela and China in 2014. In all countries we observe an increase up to 2008. Many have an increasing trend except in 2009 (Bangladesh, Brazil, India, Malaysia, Mexico, Peru, Philippines, Poland, Turkey, Thailand, and Venezuela). The decline in 2009 in Bangladesh, Brazil, Mexico, Turkey, and Venezuela are relatively smaller than the decline in other countries. Argentina and Russia have two declines, one in 2009 and another in 2014, but except for these two years there is an overall increasing trend. In Bulgaria and Romania, there was not only a decline in 2009 but also in 2010, but afterwards exports increase (Tab. 4.8).

In China and Columbia there is an increasing trend. In China, exports increase from $84 billion in 2005 to about $332 billion in 2013, while in Columbia exports increase from $5 billion in 2005 to about $14 billion in 2013.

Chile and Indonesia have a slight decline only in 2014. While in South Africa, after 2011 there is a decreasing trend. In Pakistan, exports increase up to 2008, then decline sharply in 2009 then increase again. In 2011, 2012, 2013, and 2014 figures stabilize at around $8 billion. In Ukraine, there is an increase again up to 2008, then experiences a sharp decline in 2009. Percentages increase again up to 2013, but suddenly drop in 2014. Hungary shows swings where the largest value is observed in 2008 (Tab. 4.9).

The share of service sector imports in total imports indicates higher percentage values than the share of service sector exports in total exports. During this time, Brazil has the largest value with 29 %. Eleven countries have percentage values greater than 20 % while three have 19 %. Only Mexico has a value less than 10 %. India, in the case of exports, has a high value (in fact the second highest value) of 28.7 %. On the other hand, Venezuela which has one of the lowest values for exports has 23.9 % share of imports. Turkey has the second lowest share at 10.3 %.

4.3 Conclusion

In the post-industrialization phase, it is observed that the share of the tertiary sector within GDP increases above 80 % for developed countries. In the EMEs, this share is expected to be about 50–70 %. The countries analyzed in this study support this expectation. The countries which show lower figures are analyzed separately, and it is concluded that the primary reason for the lower figures seems to be caused by the low labor productivity levels in these countries. When employment rates in service sectors are examined one can see that, typically,

Tab. 4.8: Service Imports (BoP, Current US$)[a]. World Bank, 2016

(billion $)										
	2005	**2006**	**2007**	**2008**	**2009**	**2010**	**2011**	**2012**	**2013**	**2014**
Latin America										
ARG	7.5	8.4	10.7	13.3	12.1	14.6	17.6	18.1	18.5	16.8
BRA	23.5	28.1	37.2	47.1	47.0	62.4	76.2	80.9	86.2	88.5
CHL	7.8	8.5	10.0	11.9	10.5	13.0	16.2	15.1	15.9	14.7
COL	5.3	6.0	6.8	7.9	8.0	9.4	10.8	12.2	12.8	13.5
MEX	22.8	23.6	24.9	25.6	25.0	25.8	30.4	30.7	32.1	34.9
PER	3.1	3.4	4.4	5.7	4.8	6.0	6.5	7.3	7.6	
VEN	5.3	6.0	10.5	13.2	12.2	13.1	15.7	18.2	19.9	
Asia										
BGD	2.3	2.6	3.1	3.6	3.5	4.7	5.3	5.6	6.6	7.6
CHN	84.2	101.0	130.3	159.0	159.2	194.0	238.9	282.1	331.5	
IND	47.2	58.5	70.2	87.7	80.3	114.7	125.0	129.7	126.3	147.9
IDN	22.2	21.6	24.6	28.5	23.2	26.5	31.7	34.2	35.0	33.5
MYS	22.0	23.7	28.7	30.3	27.5	32.5	38.2	42.4	44.6	
PAK	7.6	8.5	8.9	9.8	6.6	7.2	8.0	8.5	7.9	8.2
PHL	6.5	6.6	7.5	11.1	9.2	12.0	12.3	14.3	16.3	20.0
THA	26.8	32.6	38.1	46.0	36.5	45.0	52.1	53.0	54.9	53.2
Europe										
BGR	3.4	4.1	5.2	6.0	5.0	4.2	4.2	4.4	4.9	6.1
HUN	11.5	12.1	15.8	18.5	16.9	15.9	17.7	15.8	17.3	17.9
POL	15.5	19.9	24.2	30.5	24.2	31.0	33.6	33.1	34.3	
ROM	5.5	7.0	8.8	11.7	9.8	8.0	9.4	9.2	11.6	12.2
RUS	40.5	46.3	60.6	77.6	63.4	75.3	91.5	108.9	128.4	121.0
TUR	12.0	12.3	16.1	18.3	17.3	19.9	21.1	21.1	24.3	25.4
UKR	7.6	9.2	11.8	16.2	11.6	12.7	13.4	14.6	16.1	12.5
Africa										
ZAF	12.2	14.1	16.2	17.0	15.4	19.6	20.9	18.9	18.1	17.0

[a] Import values for service sector are only available after 2004.

they show an increasing trend. On the other hand, productivity levels are much lower when compared to the other sectors (OECD, 2005b). Service sectors are generally labor-intensive. This stunts the productivity of labor, at least for most service sectors since labor is not easily replaceable by capital equipment or by technology. On the other hand, many studies question this argument. They suggest that when it comes to analyzing service sectors separately, some subsectors,

Tab. 4.9: Service Imports (% of Total Imports). World Bank, 2016

	2005	2006	2007	2008	2009	2010	2011	2012	2013	2014
Latin America										
ARG	26.9	24.1	26.1	24.9	17.8	29.7	25.7	20.5	22.3	18.7
BRA	29.7	29.1	31.1	29.9	21.3	35.7	31.3	26.8	28.4	27.2
CHL	26.3	22.2	22.6	22.0	15.1	25.7	23.6	17.5	17.5	16.2
COL	26.5	23.8	22.1	20.8	17.5	23.7	22.7	19.4	18.6	19.3
MEX	10.5	9.6	8.9	8.3	7.5	9.9	9.3	8.0	8.0	8.5
PER	25.6	22.8	24.4	24.2	14.3	23.6	18.9	17.1	16.0	..
VEN	24.8	20.4	26.7	22.5	18.9	23.8	28.1	26.2	23.3	..
Asia										
BGD	17.7	17.0	18.3	18.6	13.8	20.5	17.9	14.7	17.4	18.2
CHN	15.2	15.6	16.6	16.8	13.9	18.8	17.3	15.4	17.1	..
IND	36.0	32.2	31.2	31.5	21.2	35.0	28.5	23.4	21.8	26.4
IDN	32.9	25.0	28.1	28.1	17.0	25.4	21.8	18.1	16.4	15.9
MYS	18.5	18.1	19.5	18.1	15.4	22.4	21.0	20.4	20.7	..
PAK	34.5	29.0	25.5	26.1	13.8	20.4	20.1	18.0	16.2	16.7
PHL	16.1	15.0	15.5	20.4	14.3	23.0	18.8	20.1	20.5	25.4
THA	25.0	24.6	25.9	28.3	17.9	29.1	25.2	20.8	20.2	19.4
Europe										
BGR	20.2	19.9	19.8	16.9	12.3	15.3	12.7	12.5	13.6	16.2
HUN	17.5	16.7	18.6	17.5	13.5	17.2	17.7	13.9	17.0	16.5
POL	16.4	18.2	17.5	16.8	10.4	18.4	16.6	14.0	15.2	..
ROM	16.5	20.4	19.5	17.3	11.6	14.0	14.6	11.8	16.0	15.8
RUS	31.5	28.2	28.9	27.3	17.3	30.4	28.5	26.6	28.9	25.8
TUR	11.8	9.9	10.9	10.3	8.1	13.1	10.7	8.4	9.8	9.5
UKR	22.0	21.9	22.9	23.3	11.9	23.5	19.2	15.6	16.0	12.8
Africa										
ZAF	20.6	20.6	19.4	17.4	14.3	23.8	20.3	15.4	14.6	14.0

such as transport, communications, and financial services, show high labor productivity levels. Moreover, there are some debates concerning how to measure the productivity in service sectors (Cuadrado-Roura, 2013). For this reason, the productivity analysis is not considered any further and only the employment rates in the whole sector are examined.

Trade in the service sector gained importance in world trade. The shares in the total trade values for the EMEs are analyzed here. Since subsectoral analysis is beyond the scope of this work, details are not analyzed. But, certain subsectors, if are traded as an intermediate good in manufacturing, contribute on the one hand to the overall trade, and on the other hand to the labor productivity in these sectors. The main obstacles for the service trade in the EMEs are legal barriers on trade and on foreign direct investments.

For the EMEs, it can easily be said that it is important to give special concern to the service sector as it is an indicator for the development level of the country. Nevertheless, as this sector has a broad definition and contains many different subsectors, the analysis should be pursued on a country level and also on subsectors. This will be left to further studies.

Appendix

Tab. A1: Employment in Services (% of Total Employment). World Bank, 2016

	2000	2001	2002	2003	2004	2005	2006	2007	2008	2009	2010	2011	2012	2013	2014
Latin America															
ARG	76.2	76.9	78.6	76.3	75.5	75.1	75.1	74.5	74.4	75.6	72.5	70.8	75.2	74.8	74.7
BRA	59.1	59.4	57.8	58.2	57.8	57.9	59.1	59.5	59.7	60.7	75.3	62.4	62.7	62.9	76.6
CHL	62.2	62.5	62.6	63	43	43.5	44.3	44.6	44.7	45.5	65.3	66.6	65.7	67.1	..
COL	73.3	44.3	59.6	60.4	60.3	58.9	59	62	62.6	61.5	61.7	61.3	62	63.7	64.1
MEX	55.2	56.1	57.3	58.4	58.7	59	59.4	60.1	60.6	60.1	60.6	61.9	62.5	62.4	..
PER	74.4	73.3	70.6	70.7	70.1	70.6	70.2	71.3	71.1	76.4	74.7	75	74.9	75.8	75.9
VEN	66.5	68.2	69.2	69.1	68.2	68.7	67.8	67.7	68.3	68.3	68.9	70	70.7	71.1	..
Asia															
BGD	23.5	..	34.6	34.6	..	37.4	..	..	..	..	35.3	..	..	..	..
CHN	12.7	12.7	16.1	50.5	50.3	49.5	48.9	48.6	49.3	49.1	48.8	47	..	..	..
IND	24	..	..	..	..	25.2	..	..	..	..	26.6	..	28.1	28.7	..
IDN	37.3	37.5	36.9	35.9	38.7	37.2	39.3	39.9	40.8	41.5	42.3	43	43.1	44.8	44.8
MYS	49.5	51.8	53.1	53.7	55.3	55.6	55.1	56.7	57.4	59.5	59.2	59.6	59	59.3	60.3
PAK	33.5	33.5	37.1	37.1	36.6	36.6	35.9	35.4	35.2	34.5	34.2	33.7	..	34.1	34
PHL	46.7	46.6	47.4	47.6	48.2	48.5	48.9	49.6	49.9	50.3	51.8	52.1	52.6	53.4	53.6
THA	33.6	35.1	34	35.3	37.1	37.1	37	37.4	37.9	40.2	41	39.5	39.4	37.5	..
Europe															
BGR	54.1	57.8	57	57.3	56.6	57	57.6	57	56.2	57.6	59.9	61.7	62.2	63.1	62.8
HUN	59.6	59.2	59.5	61	61.6	62.5	62.8	62.7	63.3	64.2	64.7	64.1	65	65.3	64.5
POL	50.9	50.7	52.5	53.7	53.8	53.8	54.6	54.9	54.4	55.8	56.7	56.5	57.1	57.5	57.9
ROM	32.3	33.1	35.5	35.4	38.3	39.1	40.5	41.1	41.7	42.8	42.6	44.1	43.9	44.3	44.5
RUS	57.1	58.6	59.1	58.7	60.1	60	60.7	61.8	62.4	64.1	64.4	64.9	64.9	65.3	65.8
TUR	40	39.7	42.1	43.4	43	45.8	50.1	50.7	50.4	52.6	50.8	50.1	51.2	51.5	51.9
UKR	13.3	52.8	54.2	55.1	55.7	56.4	58.2	59.4	60.7	53.5	..	54.2	54.5	55.2	59.1
Africa															
ZAF	60.7	54.5	52.5	54.7	55.3	59.1	58.7	59.5	59.8	60.8	70.6	71.1	71.5	71.3	71.9

Tab. A2: Employment in Services, Female (% of Female Employment). World Bank, 2016

	2000	2001	2002	2003	2004	2005	2006	2007	2008	2009	2010	2011	2012	2013	2014
Latin America															
ARG	89.2	89	89.7	87.1	87.2	88.1	88.5	88.7	88.8	89.7	90	88	89.6	89.9	90.7
BRA	76.1	73.9	70.7	71.1	71	70.6	71.9	72.8	73.3	74.6	..	76.9	77.5	77.9	..
CHL	83.2	82.5	83.3	83.4	..	..	..	..	..	..	83.5	84.7	84.2	84.8	..
COL	79.5	56.2	77.4	76.8	76.3	75.6	75.8	78.2	78.9	77.9	77.7	77.1	76.8	78.6	79.2
MEX	70.6	71.8	72.9	74.7	74.6	75.8	76.4	77.1	77.5	77.1	77.5	79.8	79.8	79.8	..
PER	84.6	83.8	82.1	82.8	82.2	80.9	81.5	82.2	81.9	..	..	..	..	..	..
VEN	85.6	86.1	86.2	86	85.5	86	86.5	86	86.8	86.4	86.9	87.6	..	..	..
Asia															
BGD	12.1	..	23	23	..	19.4	..	..	..	..	21.9	..	..	..	..
CHN	..	..	..	53.3	53.1	52.7	52.2	52.5	..	..	..	..	..	..	..
IND	13.7	..	..	..	..	14.7	..	..	..	..	17	..	19.4	..	..
IDN	38.3	39.4	38.8	37.3	41.2	39.7	43.5	43.5	45.3	46.3	46.9	..	..	51.6	..
MYS	57	58.3	61.1	62.1	64.6	65.4	65.2	67.3	68.3	71	70.5	72	71.5	71.9	..
PAK	18.1	18.1	19.8	19.8	17.6	17.6	16.2	15	12.9	2.9	3	3	..	2.9	11.7
PHL	62.8	62.8	63.4	63.7	64.7	64.3	64.8	65.7	66.3	66	68.3	68.3	68.9	69.72	..
THA	35.5	37.9	37	38.7	40.4	40.5	40.3	40.7	41.4	44.7	45.7	44	43.8	42.8	..
Europe															
BGR	62.1	64.2	63.3	64.1	63.2	64.3	65.7	65.9	65.6	67.7	69.9	71.3	70.6	71.7	72.1
HUN	71.8	70.8	71.5	73.7	74.5	76	76.4	76.4	76.5	77.9	77.7	77.2	77.9	78.2	77.7
POL	63.8	63	64.6	66.3	66.4	66.9	68	68.5	68.6	70.3	71.5	71.5	72.4	73.1	73.2
ROM	35.7	35.8	39.2	39.1	43.4	44.7	45.7	47	48.6	50.1	50.5	51.8	51.7	52.3	52.6
RUS	66.5	67.9	68.4	69.4	70.4	70.7	71.6	72.9	74.2	75.7	76.5	77.1	77.4	77.6	78.2
TUR	26.4	24.6	26.3	28.1	28.7	33.3	41	42.2	43.3	47.7	45.5	46.2	48.6	49.8	50.9
UKR	..	..	..	..	..	..	..	..	..	64.5	..	65.1	65.8	66.5	72.5
Africa															
ZAF	71.5	..	..	59.6	60.5	64.3	63.6	65.5	66.7	67.2	82.8	79	83.8	83.8	84.7

Tab. A3: Employment in Services, Male (% of Male Employment). World Bank, 2016

	2000	2001	2002	2003	2004	2005	2006	2007	2008	2009	2010	2011	2012	2013	2014
Latin America															
ARG	67.5	68.6	70.5	68.3	66.9	65.6	65.4	64.5	64	65.2	60.6	59.3	65	64.1	63.3
BRA	48.8	49.5	48.6	49.1	48.3	48.7	49.6	49.8	49.8	50.4	..	51.8	51.9	51.8	..
CHL	51.8	52.6	52.4	52.6	..	..	..	..	..	..	53.4	54.5	53.3	54.9	..
COL	68.1	36.8	48.3	49.9	50.1	48.3	48.4	51.5	52.1	50.7	50.8	50.5	51.6	53.1	53.3
MEX	47.2	48.1	49.1	49.9	50.1	49.3	49.4	49.9	50.5	49.9	50.5	51.1	51.8	51.5	..
PER	66.7	64.9	61.6	61.1	60.7	62.3	61.2	62.2	62	..	..	..	..	..	..
VEN	55.7	57.1	58.5	58.6	57.4	57.9	56.4	56.3	56.6	56.8	57.5	58.7	..	..	..
Asia															
BGD	30.3	..	37.9	37.9	..	43	..	..	..	..	41.1	..	..	..	..
CHN	..	..	..	48.9	48.6	47.6	46.8	46.2	..	..	..	..	..	..	..
IND	28.2	..	..	..	..	29.8	..	..	..	..	29.9	..	31	..	..
IDN	36.7	36.4	35.8	35.1	37.3	35.9	37.1	37.8	38.1	38.5	39.5	..	..	40.8	..
MYS	45.4	48.2	48.7	49	50.1	50.2	49.5	50.8	51.3	53	52.8	52.7	51.9	51.8	..
PAK	36.1	36.1	40.1	40.1	40.5	40.5	40.6	40.5	40.9	31.6	31.2	30.7	..	31.2	40.4
PHL	37	36.5	37.1	37.6	38.1	38.6	38.8	39.5	39.6	40.4	41.2	41.7	42	42.79	..
THA	32	32.8	31.6	32.6	34.4	34.1	34.2	34.6	34.8	36.5	37.1	35.7	35.7	33.1	..
Europe															
BGR	47	51.8	51.3	51.2	50.6	50.4	50	49.2	47.8	48.7	50.7	53.2	54.5	55.3	54.5
HUN	49.7	49.6	49.6	50.4	50.8	51	51.4	51.2	52.2	52.3	53.1	52.8	53.8	54.1	53.1
POL	40.3	40.5	42.2	43.2	43.4	43.2	43.7	43.7	42.7	43.8	44.8	44.5	44.7	44.9	45.4
ROM	29.2	30.8	32.5	32.3	33.9	34.6	36.2	36.2	36.2	37.1	36.4	38	37.9	38.1	38.2
RUS	48.2	49.7	50.2	48.4	50.1	49.6	50	51	51.1	52.8	52.7	53	52.9	53.5	53.9
TUR	45	45.6	48.4	49.3	48.2	50.2	53.2	53.6	53	54.4	52.9	51.7	52.2	52.2	52.4
UKR	..	..	..	..	..	..	..	..	..	42.8	..	43.9	44	44.6	46.6
Africa															
ZAF	51.5	..	..	50.8	51.6	55	54.7	54.7	54.5	55.8	61.2	61.6	62	61.4	61.9

References

Alejandro, L, J. B. Powell, S. Brady, and I. Wohl (2010). "An Overview and Examination of the Malaysian Service Sector", US International Trade Commission, Office of Industries Working Paper, No: ID-27.

Bailliu J. and C. Hajzler (2016). "Structural Reforms and Economic Growth in Emerging-Market Economies", Bank of Canada Review, 47–60.

Bastos, S. Q. and F.S. Perobelli (2012). "The Search of Homogeneity in The Heterogeneity: An Analysis of the Service Sector in Brazil", Redlas 2012 Conference Papers, 'Offshore services in Global Value Chains: New drivers of structural change in Latin America and the Caribbean?', Santiago, Chile, October 18–19, 2012, http://www.redlas.net/materiali/priloge/slo/service_sector_brazil_quinet.pdf, (Retrieval Date: 18.02.2017)

Baumol, W. J. (1967). "Association Macroeconomics of Unbalanced Growth: The Anatomy of Urban Crisis", The American Economic Review, 57(3): 415–426, URL: http://www.jstor.org/stable/1812111, (Retrieval Date: 09.01.2017)

Breitenfellner, A. and A. Hildebrandt (2006). "High Employment with Low Productivity? The Service Sector as a Determinant of Economic Development", Monetary Policy and the Economy, 1: 110–135.

Buysse, K and E. Vincent, (2015). "Factors explaining emerging economies' growth slowdown", National Bank of Belgium, Economic Review, 2: 61–79. https://www.nbb.be/doc/ts/enterprise/press/2015/cp150922end.pdf, (Retrieval Date: 26.02.2017)

Chand, S. (2016). "Services Characteristics: 6 Key Distinguishing Characteristics of Services" http://www.yourarticlelibrary.com/services/services-characteristics-6-key-distinguishing-characteristics-of-services/34008/ (Retrieval Date: 14.07.2016)

Citeman, (2006). "Characteristics of Services", http://www.citeman.com/274-characteristics-of-services.html (Retrieval Date: 14.07.2016)

Cuadrado-Roura, J.R. (2013). "Service Industries and Regions: Growth, Location and Regional Effects", Springer Heidelberg New York Dordrecht London, Doi 10.1007/978-3-642-35801-2.

Cubeddu L., A. Culiuc, G. Fayad, Y. Gao, K. Kochhar, A. Kyobe, C. Oner, R. Perrelli, S. Sanya, E. Tsounta, and Z. Zhang (2014). "Emerging Markets in Transition: Growth Prospects and Challenges", IMF Staff Discussion Note, SDN 14/06, INTERNATIONAL MONETARY FUND Strategy, Policy, and Review Department. https://www.imf.org/external/pubs/ft/sdn/2014/sdn1406.pdf (Retrieval Date: 23.02.2017).

Didier, T, M. Moretti, and S. L. Schmukler (2015). The Changing Patterns of Financial Integration in Latin America, Policy Research Working Paper, no. 7190, 27 pages, Washington, DC: World Bank Group. http://documents.worldbank.org/curated/en/358291468272087617/The-changing-patterns-of-financial-integration-in-Latin-America, Access Date: 10 June 2016.

ECB (2016). "The Slowdown in Emerging Market Economies and Its Implications for the Global Economy", European Central Bank, ECB

Economic Bulletin, Issue 3/2016 – Article 1. https://www.ecb.europa.eu/pub/pdf/other/eb201603_article01.en.pdf (Retrieval Date: 21.02.2017).

Francois, J. and J. Woerz (2007). "Producer Services, Manufacturing Linkages, and Trade", Tinbergen Institute Discussion Paper, TI 2007-045/2.

Heilbrun, J. (2003). "Baumol's cost disease", A Handbook of Cultural Economics, Ruth Towse (Ed.), Edward Elgar Publishing, United Kingdom, ISBN: 9781840643381, Doi: http://dx.doi.org/10.4337/9781781008003. http://fgimello.free.fr/documents/ECOCULTURE_Baumol_cost_disease.pdf, [10.01.2017].

Hodge, J and H. Nordås (2001). "Liberalization of Trade in Producer Services - the Impact on Developing Countries", South African Journal of Economics, 69(1): 93–93.

ITC (2016). "China Services Sector Analysis", International Trade Centre Publications, http://www.intracen.org/uploadedFiles/intracenorg/Content/Exporters/Sectors/Service_exports/Trade_in_services/China_ServicesBrief.pdf (Retrieval Date: 14.07.2016).

Jajri, I. (2011). "Total Factor Productivity and Output Growth in Malaysian Service Sector", Annals - Economic and Administrative Series, 5(1): 63–76.

Jensen, J. B. (2011). "Global Trade in Services: Fear, Facts, and Offshoring", Peterson Institute of International Economics, Washington DC, ISBN: 978-0-88132-601-7.

Koonnathamdee P. (2013). "A Turning Point for the Service Sector in Thailand", ADB, Asian Development Bank, Economics Working Paper Series, No: 353.

Lee, J. W. (2016). "China's Economic Growth and Convergence", CAMA Working Paper No. 30/2016. http://dx.doi.org/10.2139/ssrn.2785015 (Retrieval Date:30.01.2017).

Lee, J. W. and W. J. McKibbin (2014). "Service Sector Productivity and Economic Growth in Asia", Asian Development Bank Institute Working Paper No. 490.

Manning C. and H. Aswicahyono (2012). "Trade and Employment in Services in Indonesia", ILO Publications, http://www.ilo.org/wcmsp5/groups/public/@asia/@ro-bangkok/@ilo-jakarta/documents/publication/wcms_185237.pdf (Retrieval Date: 30.01.2017).

Markusen, J. R. (1989). "Trade in Producer Services and in Other Specialized Intermediate Inputs", American Economic Review 79: 85–95.

Markusen, J. R., and B. Strand (2007). "Trade in Business Services in General Equilibrium." NBER Working Paper No. 12816.

MPC (2016). "Malaysian Productivity Corporation, 23rd Productivity Report 2015/2016", http://www.mpc.gov.my/wp-content/uploads/2016/06/Productivity-Report-2016.pdf (Retrieval Date: 11.01.2017).

Noland M., D. Park, and G. B. Estrada (2012). "Developing the Service Sector as Engine of Growth for Asia: An Overview", ADB (Asian Development Bank) Economics Working Paper Series No. 320.

OECD, (2005a). "The Service Economy in OECD Countries", OECD Science, Technology and Industry Working Papers, ISSN: 1815-1965 (online), Doi: http://dx.doi.org/10.1787/212257000720 [07.01.2017].

OECD, (2005b). "Growth in Services: Fostering Employment, Productivity and Innovation", OECD Publishing, Paris, ISBN: 9789264064577, Doi: http://dx.doi.org/10.1787/9789264064577-en [07.01.2017].

Oulton, N. (2001). "Must the Growth Rate Decline? Baumol's Unbalanced Growth Revisited.", Oxford Economic Paper 53, no. 4: 605–627.

Sauian, M. S., N. Kamarudin, and R. M. Rani (2013). "Labor Productivity of Services Sector in Malaysia: Analysis Using Input-Output Approach", International Conference on Economics and Business Research 2013 (ICEBR 2013), Procedia Economics and Finance 7: 35– 41. doi: 10.1016/S2212-5671(13)00215-3.

Soubbotina, T. P. (2004). "Beyond Economic Growth: An Introduction to Sustainable Development", Second Edition, WBI Learning Resources Series, 24894, The World Bank Washington, D.C.

World Bank (2014). "Growth in the Post-Crisis Global Economy: Policy Challenges For Developing Countries." Development Committee of the Board of Governors of the World Bank and the IMF, Development Committee Paper, DC2014-0002, March. http://siteresources.worldbank.org/DEVCOMMINT/Documentation/23554308/DC2014-0002(E)PostCrisis.pdf (Retrieval date: 04.03.2017).

World Bank (2016). Development Indicators, www.worldbank.org (Retrieval date: 06.07.2016).

Zheng J., L. Zhang, and Y. Wang (2010). "The Underdevelopment of Service Industry in China: An Empirical Study of Cities in Yangtze River Delta", MPRA, Munich Personal RePEc Achieve, Paper No: 33125.

Part B Factors of Production

Emre Aksoy

5 Labor Force Markets in EMEs

Abstract: This chapter introduces and analyzes the labor force markets (LFMs) of emerging market economies (EMEs), their structural features, and their similarities and differences with the aid of the key indicators of the LFM. The course of LFM indicators in the long run and the correlations among the variables are valuable indicators used to understand the structures of the LFMs. The examination of LFMs provides us with significant insights about the courses and functions of economies. This examination also gives us valuable hints about social dynamics. LFM is not only a factor market, it also embodies multifaceted and intertwined social and political relationships, in addition to its central economic significance. The education systems, and the demographic and economic positions of the EMEs differ from one another. Countries geographically close to each other have similar economic, cultural, and demographical features, which also affect the LFMs of these economies. Therefore, throughout the chapter, countries that are similar to each other in regards to their LFMs will be examined together, and in this way, an analysis of EMEs will be presented. Firstly, the overall picture of the labor supply for emerging markets will be presented via labor and labor force participation indicators. Then, unemployment rates will be analyzed. The aim of this chapter is to present and compare the LFM performances of the economies in question.

Keywords: Labor Force, Unemployment

5.1 Introduction

One of the prerequisites for the economic development of a country is its ability to utilize production factors at a high and productive level. The production factor with the highest potential of providing added value is the labor force, and since it is based on human resources, it has remarkably different structural features from any other production factor. This difference yields a difference in LFMs as well; because labor force means manpower, so it is impossible to evaluate the labor force without considering the human factor. LFM is different from all other markets due to the structural differences the labor force has. In LFMs, employees offer labor and brain power according to their human capital and employers demand labor according to their needs. An individual's behavior, which is shaped by economic and social dynamics, determines the labor supply and an employer's behavior determines the labor force demand. In the same way, as noneconomic social dynamics influence the LFM, labor relations in the LFM influence humans, and therefore, social life. Considering this reciprocal relationship, there is a two-way interaction between social dynamics and LFMs.

The state of LFMs provides important information about the course and the functions of economies, and also gives valuable insights on social dynamics. With the LFM, labor and awareness of human nature, which are the most valuable assets of a country, are included in the production process. In terms of economic management, it is an important policy goal to direct the labor force towards productive areas with high added value through a well-functioning market. Problems in the LFM may have considerable social repercussions and lead to insolvable social problems other than considerable economic losses. Therefore, LFMs in all countries are in the spotlight in terms of not only economic management, but also politics.

Politicians and economic policy makers are more sensitive to changes in the LFM than in any other markets because the changes in the LFM may directly influence social dynamics and have a greater potential to influence politics faster and more vigorously than other markets. When we consider these aspects, it is apparent that the LFM is not only a factor market; this market, in addition to its vital economic significance, includes multifaceted and intertwined social and political relationships.

As a result of demographic changes, labor force supply might increase or decrease. Birth rates and immigration change the demographic structure of a country and they accordingly influence the labor force supply of a country by changing the ratio of working-age population to total population. When working-age population increases and gravitates towards productive work areas, it can be considered an important opportunity for economic growth. However, when labor force demand cannot meet the increase in the labor force supply and when sufficient employment areas are not provided parallel to the increasing labor force supply, the result is unemployment. In some cases, unemployment might occur even though both labor force supply and demand increase. This might be the result of a situation where there is a faster increase in labor force supply than labor force demand or where there is a shortage of a labor force qualified enough for the labor force demand, that is, an inconsistency between supply and demand. What causes such an inconsistency are factors such as an education system which cannot keep up with the requirements of the LFM.

The most important source of labor force demand is economic growth. Increasing investments and a growing economy leads to more labor force demand on the part of employers. The consistency between labor force supply and demand is the main determinant of unemployment levels. Unemployment ratios are one of the greatest indicators of whether or not an economy is well-functioning because unemployment does not merely refer to an idle production factor; it is also closely related to the income levels of the population. In an economy, the source of income for many people is the wages they earn for the work they do in the LFM, and wage income is a significant part of national income.

LFMs are often exposed to non-market interventions due to their idiosyncrasies and their central role. Reaching LFM equilibrium, or in other words, determining wage levels and employment rates, does not depend only on labor force supply and demand. Market equilibrium is influenced by various social, political, demographic, and economic variables such as legislative regulations regarding work life, demographic changes, unions, minimum wage enforcements, economic policies, education system, labor force costs, and social and cultural norms as well as dynamics resulting from labor force supply and demand.

The most variables mentioned above have different influences on LFM equilibrium and therefore on labor market indicators. The variables differ, of course, according to countries. This chapter will not cover the changes regarding the social, cultural, demographic, and economic policies in the LFMs of the EMEs or their repercussions on LFMs since this topic is too comprehensive to be examined in full within the scope of this chapter.

What shapes or steers LFMs do differ from one country to another; however, in today's globalized environment, economic policies all around the world are drawn together around a free market economy and this has influenced LFMs as well. Moreover, it can be seen that, as a result of globalization, the working life standards implemented by countries are also drawn together in parallel with the increasing functions of international organizations such as International Labor Organization (ILO) and the increasing number of member countries. LFMs all around the world, as is the case for many other markets, have come to have similar legislative regulations and institutional features as a result of the integration of their economies, the development of foreign trade, and the growth of multinational corporations operating in different countries.

With the European Union (EU) and similar regional bodies, some parts of the world labor force have, though limited, gained international freedom of movement. Although financial trends and free trade have accelerated and have crossed borders with the help of globalization, the rigid restrictions between LFMs of countries, with a few exceptions, are obstacles to labor force movement. Therefore, the LFMs of countries with similar economic levels seem to have been less influenced by the dynamics of globalization than other markets and have maintained their unique features although they may be similar in some aspects.

This chapter will introduce and analyze the structural features, and similarities and differences of the LFMs of the EMEs with the help of some main LFM indicators. The long-term course of LFM indicators and the correlation between these variables are invaluable indicators for a better understanding of the LFM structure. Despite their multifaceted and complicated structures, LFMs are one of the central constituents of an economy. LFM indicators provide us with highly useful information to evaluate an economy, to see its trend over time, and to predict any potential developments it might face. This chapter will analyze the LFMs of the EMEs within the framework of the labor force, labor force participation, and unemployment rate data.

Labor force, or to put it differently, the population fit to work, and the participation of the population in the labor force are primary indicators to the supply side of LFMs. These two indicators fail to sufficiently reflect the quality aspect of labor force; nevertheless, they provide us with significant information about the quantity aspect and the behavior patterns of the labor force. Although labor force demand is influenced by several factors such as minimum wage enforcements and legislative regulations regarding working conditions, the fundamental determinant of labor force demand is economic growth. The main source of labor force demand is economic growth but growing economies may not always be able to provide the necessary labor force demand; this is due to whether or not the structural features of the economic growth and labor force supply are consistent with each other.

Evaluations of the economic growth performances and the structural features of the EMEs, and the fundamental determinant of labor force demand, are examined in other chapters of the book, and therefore will not be examined in this chapter. After an evaluation and comparison of the LFMs of the EMEs based on the supply side, an analysis of the LFMs of the EMEs within the framework of the results of the unemployment rates occurring as a result of demand dynamics will be provided. Therefore, unemployment rates have been chosen as the third evaluation criterion following labor force and labor force participation. The unemployment rate is a primary indicator used to monitor an analysis of an economy and LFMs. This indicator might, to some extent, be regarded as a reflection of the surplus supply and also its course, in the long run, gives us valuable information as to whether or not the LFM is operationally efficient.

The EMEs are located in very different parts of the world, and they have both similarities and differences in regards to their historical, cultural, and economic structures. The EMEs differ in terms of their education systems, and their demographic and economic structures. Among them, there are economies which are members of the EU, or the European Customs Union, which holds strong economic relations with the EU. Others are countries which were former members of The Soviet Republic. Also, Latin American countries and Asian countries are categorized as EMEs. South America, which has a very different demographic and social structure and a very different history, is also categorized as an emerging market. To put it simply, among the countries which are categorized as EMEs, while there are countries which have similar features, there are also African, Asian, European, and Latin American countries with diverse demographic, cultural, and social structures. Of all these countries, those which are geographically close to each other and have strong economic bonds are culturally and demographically similar to each other as well; this is also reflected in their LFMs. With this in mind, in this chapter, the countries which are similar to each other in terms of LFMs will be examined together to provide an analysis of their EMEs. The aim of the chapter is to identify and compare the LFM performances of the economies in question and to show how much these economies benefit from their labor force.

5.2 LFM Indicators

The LFMs of the 23 EMEs are analyzed based on a revision of the data on the website of the World Bank. The data are annual and cover the period from 1991 to 2014. There are two reasons why this period has been chosen; the first reason is that uninterrupted and reliable data were received within this period. The second reason is that the dynamics after 1990 is a period when the economic climate in the world changed, when globalization accelerated, and when the so-called EMEs had good economic performances.

Three main LFM indicators have been used to examine EMEs: The first indicator is the labor force, which is the main determinant of labor force supply, or, in other words, the portion of the population that is fit to work and at the same time is economically active. The total population of employed and unemployed working-age people, that is, people who are 15 and above, is defined as "labor force". In this regard, those who are employed and those who are unemployed, but expect to be employed, are considered to be the labor force (TÜİK, 2009: 14). Anyone that is healthy and fit to work is included in the labor force. However, in many countries and according to the standards set by ILO, child labor is considered illegal. According to the working standards defined by ILO, the age limit for child labor is 15, and workers below the age of 15 are regarded as child workers. The age ceiling in terms for being fit to work differs from one country to another. Although there seems to be no standard approach to the age ceiling, the retirement age is generally accepted as the age ceiling. Working-age population is considered to be between 15 and 64 in some countries, and 15 to 59 in others. The population under 15 years of age or above the retirement age is defined as population which is unemployable. The working-age population is the first parameter of the labor force. The second is the economically active population.

Economically active population refers to individuals who are 15 and above, that is, who are of working age and who are not in school, army, prison, hospital, or nursing home, and who have the necessary work capacity to produce goods and services. Labor force, on the other hand, refers to the population aged 15 and above, and the economically active population (World Bank, 2016).

The second LFM indicator to consider is the labor force participation rates (LFPRs). As explained above, the labor force is the part of labor force supply that is fit to participate in the process of producing goods and services. LFPR is the proportional statement of those who participate in the production process in order to produce goods and services and those who offer their work force in proportion to the total labor force (World Bank, 2016). Regarding this, LFPR is defined as the rate of the labor force in 15-and-above age population (TÜİK, 2011: 175).

Firstly, this chapter will present the overall picture of the labor force supply in EMEs with the help of labor force and labor force participation indicators and then the unemployment rates will be analyzed. The concept of unemployment rates refers to the part of the labor force that is fit to work, but unemployed and looking for work (World Bank, 2016).

The LFMs of the EMEs will be analyzed using the three aforementioned indicators. The 23 EMEs will be analyzed after being grouped according to their geographical positions, economical features, and LFMs. Latin American EMEs are Argentina (ARG), Brazil (BRA), Chile (CHL), Colombia (COL), Mexico (MEX), Peru (PER), and Venezuela (VEN). Asian EMEs are divided into two groups: Small and Large Asian EMEs. Large Asian EMEs consists of Bangladesh (BGD), Pakistan (PAK), India (IND), and China (CHN). European EMEs that are members of the EU and the European Customs Union, and are geographically close to these countries with strong economic relationships as well. These countries are Bulgaria (BGR), Poland (POL), Romania (ROU), Hungary (HUN), Russia (RUS), Turkey (TUR), and Ukraine (UKR). The small Asian countries and South Africa form the last group, namely, Indonesia (IDN), Malaysia (MYS), Philippines (PHL), and Thailand (THA), and South Africa (ZAF), which differs drastically from the other 22 countries in terms of the structural features of its LFM.

5.2.1 Labor Force

Labor force refers to the working-age population, and the main determinant for it is the demographic structure. It has already been mentioned above that the working-age population is defined by the ILO as the population of economically active, fit-to-work individuals who are aged 15 and above. This definition includes all people who are employed, looking for work, or unemployed. An increasing rate of fit-to-work individuals in the total population refers to a proportional increase of the economically active population when compared to the dependent population, comprising of children, babies, and the elderly. This increase indicates a significant potential in terms of economic growth because it suggests a great potential in terms of labor force supply.

When there is an increase in the labor force and when accordingly, there is an increase in job opportunities and new productive work areas for the labor force, there are great opportunities for the economic growth of a country. That is why the path that the labor force, the main source of a country's labor force supply, follows is an important indicator in order to understand the dynamics of the labor force supply. The change that the labor force, the main determinant of the labor force supply, undergoes over the years provides valuable insights into the future position of LFMs. Increases in the labor force not only indicate a demographically dynamic society, but also a remarkable economic potential because an increase in the labor force means that a vital production factor has increased.

As is mentioned above, the countries have been grouped according to their common features. However, the demographic structures and population sizes of the countries differ. Latin American EMEs are Argentina (ARG), Brazil (BRA), Chile (CHL), Colombia (COL), Peru (PER), Venezuela (VEN), and Mexico (MEX). Fig. 5.1 shows the developments in the labor force of these countries between 1991 and 2014. When we consider the size of the working-age population, notably Brazil and Mexico, which have larger populations when compared to the other countries in the group, working-age populations are significantly larger than those of the remaining five countries.

Considering the data, it is clear that there are huge gaps between the countries in regards to labor force size and that the labor forces for all countries in the Latin American continent shows an increasing trend. So, we can say that the LFMs of the countries in the Latin America show a tendency to grow. Of the countries in the Latin American continent, Brazil has the largest LFM and also has a greater rate of growth than the other countries. The country with the second largest labor force is Mexico and has second place after Brazil regarding labor force growth rate. The labor force in Colombia surpassed that of Argentina through to the end

Fig. 5.1: Labor Force in the Latin American EMEs. World Development Indicators (World Bank, 2016)

Vertical axis represents the number of people and the horizontal axis the years.

of the 1990s. The labor forces in Peru and Venezuela are close to each other in size. The country with the smallest labor force in this group is Chile. The labor force growth rates in countries other than Mexico and Brazil seem to be close to each other.

The Large Asian EMEs include Bangladesh (BGD), Pakistan (PAK), India (IND), and China (CHN). These four countries are the most populated countries in the world. China, without a doubt, has the most notable labor force and LFM, since China is the most populated country. India, besides its large population, has a notable labor force supply potential regarding the size of its working-age population. Fig. 5.2 shows developments in the labor forces of these four countries.

Fig. 5.2 shows that Bangladesh and Pakistan had similar trends for labor force increase between 1991 and 2014 and also that, for both countries, this trend did not change within that period. India's fit-to-work population in the same period seemed to have a stronger increasing trend when compared to Pakistan and Bangladesh; this increase trend slowed down in 2006 and rose again in 2012. China's labor force increase rate, similar to that of India, was greater when compared to that of Pakistan and Bangladesh. In 2010 there was a slowdown in the labor force increase, but afterwards continued a course close to its previous trend. We can observe an increase trend in the labor forces of all four countries when we consider the changes in their fit-to-work populations. We can also see that the labor force increase rates in China and India were the greatest.

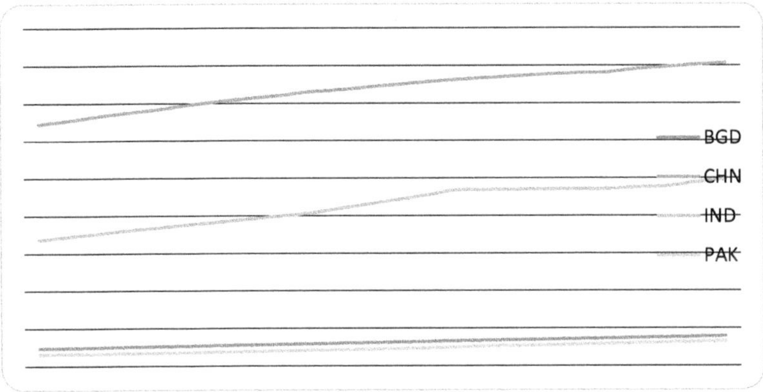

Fig. 5.2: Labor Force in the Large Asian EMEs. World Development Indicators (World Bank, 2016)

Vertical axis represents the number of people and the horizontal axis the years.

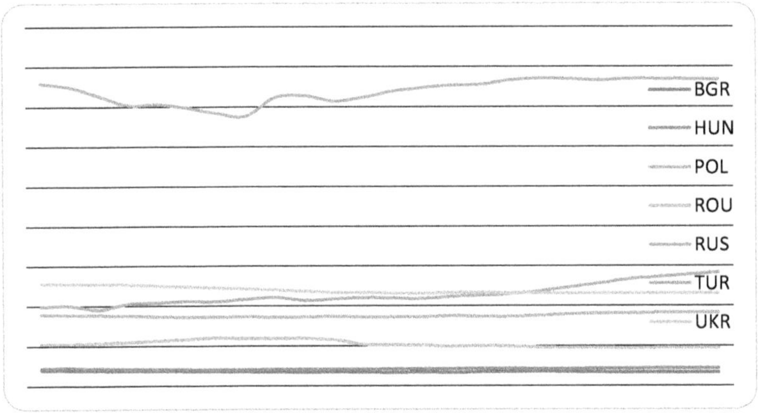

Fig. 5.3: Labor Force in the European EMEs. World Development Indicators (World Bank, 2016)

Vertical axis represents the number of people and the horizontal axis the years.

The European EMEs include Bulgaria (BGR), Poland (POL), Romania (ROU), Hungary (HUN), Russia (RUS), Turkey (TUR), and Ukraine (UKR). Of the countries in Europe, Russia has the largest labor force. As seen in Fig. 5.3, Russia's fit-to-work population showed a decreasing trend between 1991 and

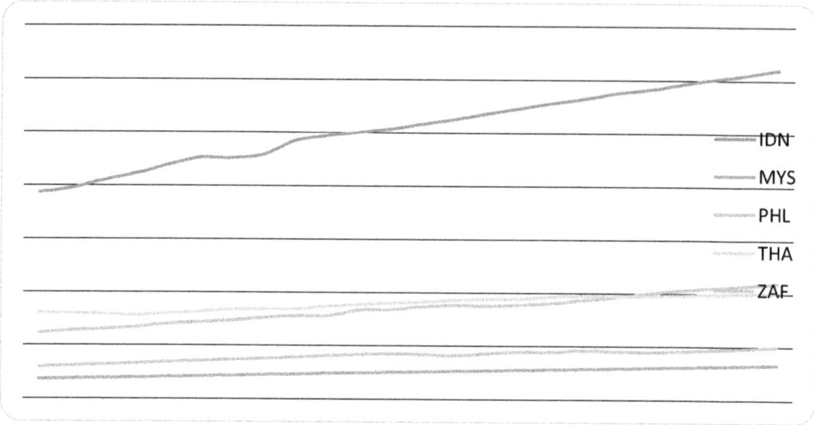

Fig. 5.4: Labor Force in the Small Asian EMEs and South Africa. World Development Indicators (World Bank, 2016)

Vertical axis represents the number of people and the horizontal axis the years.

1998 and then increased again between 1998 and 2008 becoming closer to its level in 1991. Russia's labor force does not seem to have changed in terms of quantity after 2008.

Ukraine and Romania are countries which showed a slight decreasing trend in their labor forces between 1991 and 2014. The labor forces of Hungary and Bulgaria during the same period showed almost no change. Poland, on the other hand, showed a weak increasing trend in the same years. Of all the European EMEs, the most remarkable labor force developments took place in Turkey. The labor force in Turkey showed an increasing trend between 1991 and 2014, and this trend accelerated as of 2008. This acceleration raised the level of Turkey's labor force to that of Ukraine in 2008, and in 2014 Turkey's labor force was larger than Ukraine's labor force. As of 2009, Turkey had the second largest labor force among the European EMEs. All in all, the total labor forces of countries in European EMEs, except for Turkey, were stable and did not show a significant increase.

The last group, Small Asian EMEs and South Africa, includes Asian countries, Indonesia (IDN), Malaysia (MYS), Philippines (PHL), and Thailand (THA) and, in addition to these Asian countries, South Africa (ZAF). The developments in the labor forces of these countries are shown in Fig. 5.4 below.

Indonesia had a strong labor force increase performance between 1991 and 2014 and had a much larger labor force than any other countries in the group. We can see that between 1991 and 2014, the labor forces of all the countries in the Small Asian EMEs and South Africa experienced growth. Indonesia experienced the greatest rate increase, and it was followed by Philippines. Malaysia and South Africa had consistent increase rates, although not as high as those of Indonesia and Philippines. Thailand had the slowest labor force growth rate in the group. Philippines passed Thailand's labor force increase rate in 2011 in regards to labor force size.

When we consider all four groups of countries, Brazil, Indonesia, Bangladesh, Pakistan, and Mexico have notable increases in labor force rates as do China, India, and Philippines. Turkey's labor force increase rate gained momentum in 2008, and as of 2008 it became one of the countries experiencing a sharp increase in the labor force. Of the 23 countries, Chile, Colombia, Peru, Venezuela, Argentina, South Africa, Thailand, and Malaysia have slowly progressing labor force increase rates. Also, there is not a significant change in the labor force increase rates of Hungary, Bulgaria, and Poland where rates are progressing slowly. In Ukraine and Romania, the labor force shows a decreasing trend.

Emerging markets, when considered in terms of their labor force size, differ significantly from each other due to the fact that these economies are of different sizes and have different population dynamics.

Fig.5.5 displays a proportional comparison of labor force positions for emerging markets in 1991. Of the 23 countries, China had the largest labor force with a rate of 42 %. The labor force share of India was 22 %, Indonesia 5 %, Russia 5 %, and Brazil 4 %. Following them, Bangladesh had a rate of 3 %, Mexico and Philippines 2 %, Ukraine 2 %, Thailand 2 %, and Pakistan 2 %. The share of the remaining countries in the EMEs regarding labor force size was 1 % or less.

Fig. 5.6 shows the proportional comparison of the position of labor force sizes in 2014. The figure shows that the distribution of the labor force among countries changed in 2014 due to the demographic dynamics which occurred in the emerging markets between 1991 and 2014. The population growth which took place in the emerging markets prior to and during the given period resulted in an increase in the labor force. The demographic processes that the countries have gone through differ; as shown in the figures given above, labor force increase rates were high in some countries and low in others. It is also apparent that in some countries, labor force increases rates came to a halt and did not have a tendency to increase. Finally, in two of the EMEs, labor forces decreased. These dynamics led to a change in the proportional comparison of the EMEs to the total labor force by 2014. In general, the labor force in the 23 countries increased

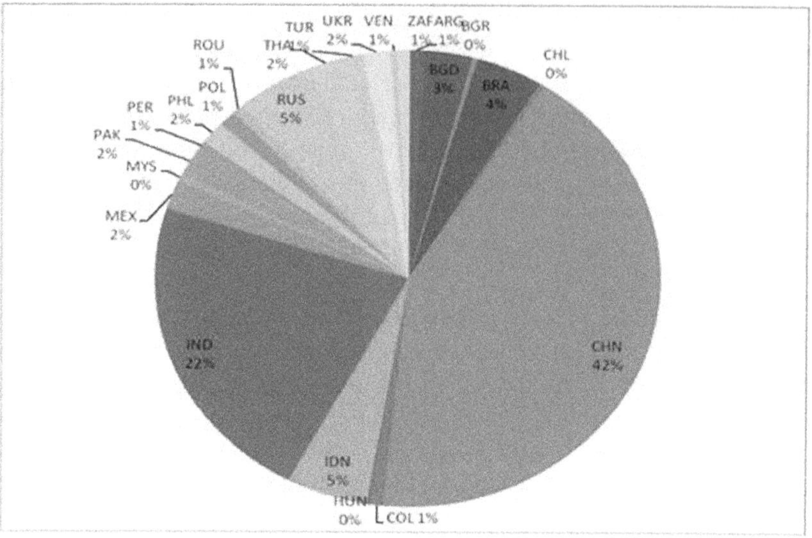

Fig. 5.5: Labor Force Sizes of Emerging Markets in 1991. World Development Indicators (World Bank, 2016)

The share of countries in total labor force in 1991.

in total between 1991 and 2014. However, the proportional weight of the EMEs to the total labor force changed.

When we examine Fig. 5.6, our attention is drawn to the fact that in 2014 China's share in the total labor force of emerging markets decreased. Similarly, there was a decrease in the labor force shares of Russia, Ukraine, and India. However, Brazil, Indonesia, Bangladesh, Pakistan, and Mexico significantly raised their shares in the total labor force of emerging markets. There are also other countries among these 23 countries which had a proportional weight change in their labor force size. The countries mentioned above are those which had the most notable changes.

The total labor force in the world is approximately 3.383 billion and the 23 EMEs have approximately 2.100 billion of the total labor force in the world. In summary, the 23 countries have approximately 2/3 of the world's total labor force.

5.2.2 Labor Force Participation

When we consider the behavior of men and women in the LFM, we see that men and women in every country in the world behave differently. In this regard, it is

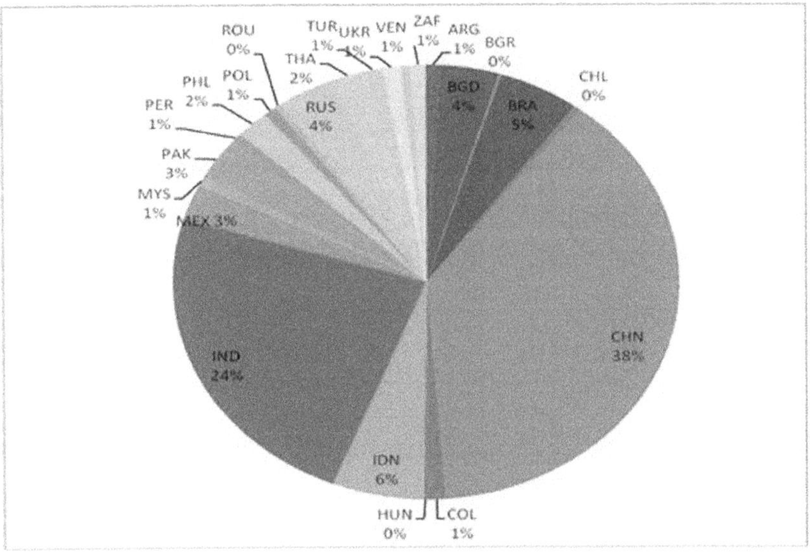

Fig. 5.6: Labor Force Sizes of Emerging Markets in 2014. World Development Indicators (World Bank, 2016)

The share of countries in the total labor force in 2014.

possible to say that gender is one of the determinants for preference and behavior in the LFM. The behavior of men and women in the LFM changes according to the cultural and the social structures of the countries. As far as labor force participation is concerned, clearly, behavior of men and women differ. A review of literature calls to our attention two important facts: Firstly, the LFPRs for women throughout the world are on the rise. Secondly, LFPRs for men either remained stable or did not increase as much as the LFPRs for women (Olsen, 1994; Lewis, Peterson, 1997; Ehrenberg, Smith, 2000; Genre et al., 2010; Bergemann, Van Den Berg, 2008). LFPRs in emerging markets have been separately analyzed for men and women.

Male LFPR is the proportion of the male labor force which offers labor force in order to produce goods and services to the total male labor force. Similarly, LFPR for women is the proportional statement of the female labor force that offers labor force in order to produce goods and services (World Bank, 2016).

For this analysis, as explained in the previous sections of chapter 23, EMEs were analyzed under four groups. The foremost result that the analysis reveals is that male labor force participation is higher than female labor force participation

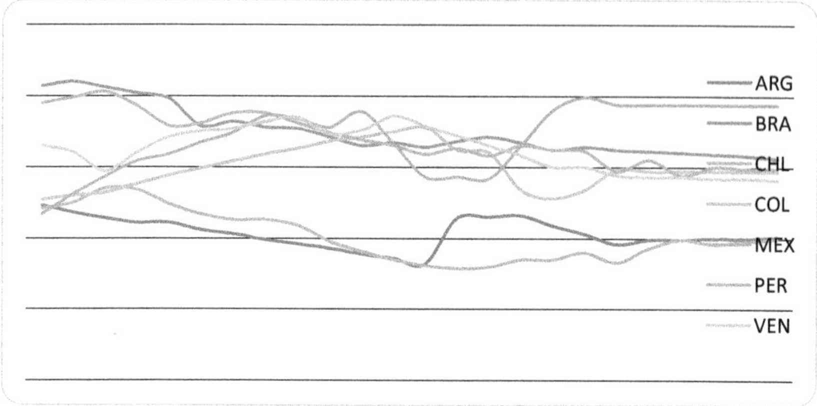

Fig. 5.7: Male LFPRs for Latin American EMEs. World Development Indicators (World Bank, 2016)

Vertical axis represents the percentage and the horizontal axis the years.

in the all EMEs. Also, the differences between the rates of male and female labor force participation changes from one country to another.

5.2.2.1 Male Labor Force Participation

As far as male labor force participation is concerned, there seems to be no consistent pattern in Latin American EMEs. As seen in Fig. 5.7, although participation rates between 1991 and 2014 showed a tendency to decline, the male labor participation rate in Peru rose dramatically especially after 2006. Regarding the countries in the Latin American continent, Peru had the highest male LFP which occurred in 2014. Again, for the same year, the second highest rate was in Brazil. However, following the dynamics from 1991 to 2014, Brazil had an overall decreasing trend in this rate. The male labor participation rates in Venezuela displayed a decreasing trend after 2000. Although the data shows some fluctuations for the period between 1991 and 2014, male LFPRs decreased in Brazil, Chile, Argentina, Venezuela, and Mexico.

Male LFPRs in Peru has increased notably over the last 10 years. In Colombia, male LFPRs increased during the same period, although not as high as in Peru. There are no notable increases in the male LFPRs for the remaining countries in the Latin American continent between 1991 and 2014. In the Latin American EMEs, Chile and Argentina have the lowest rates of male labor force participation with a percentage of 75 %. Still, a percentage of 75 % is not necessarily a very

Fig. 5.8: Male LFPRs for the Asian Countries. World Development Indicators (World Bank, 2016)

Vertical axis represents the percentage and the horizontal axis the years.

low rate considering the percentages of the other continent EMEs and especially the percentages of those countries which fall into Europe.

Fig. 5.8 shows male LFPRs for Large Asian EMEs. The figure shows that in the early 1990s, male LFPRs in Bangladesh, China, India, and Pakistan were high, with a percentage above 84 %. However, in the following years, the rates fell for all countries. The greatest decrease took place in China; Bangladesh and India had similar rates of decline. The decline in Pakistan was relatively smaller than in the other three countries.

For Large Asian EMEs, there was a decline in male LFPRs between 1991 and 2014. Bangladesh stood out as the country with the highest male LFPR during the same period. In 2014, Pakistan had the second highest participation rate after Bangladesh; following Pakistan were India and China. Of the four countries, China stands out as the country with the highest change in male LFPRs. While the rates in China were higher than in Bangladesh and very close to the rates in India in 1991, with a sharp decrease between 1991 and 2014, China became the country with the lowest rate of male labor force participation among all four countries. There was a decrease in male LFPRs for all four countries; nevertheless, male LFPRs as of 2014 were not dramatically low, when compared to the other countries.

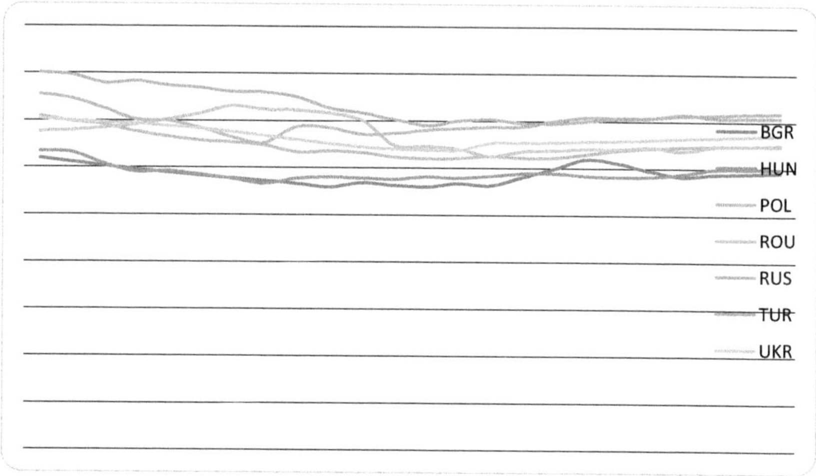

Fig. 5.9: Male LFPRs for the Countries in the European EMEs. World Development Indicators (World Bank, 2016)

Vertical axis represents the percentage and the horizontal axis the years.

Male LFPRs recorded between 1991 and 2014 for the seven countries in the European continent are given in Fig. 5.9. A decrease in male LFPRs is observed for these countries, but the decrease rate is not as great as the decrease rate experienced in the Large Asian EMEs. Another noteworthy fact about the male LFPRs of the European EMEs is that these rates, in total, are lower than the rates in the first two groups of countries. Also, there does not seem to be much volatility or fluctuation in the male LFPRs of the European EMEs.

The figure shows that among the countries in Europe, Russia, and Turkey are the countries with the highest rates of male LFPRs, and Bulgaria and Hungary have the lowest participation rates.

As seen in Fig. 5.9, for the emerging markets in Europe, the rates for male labor force participation were between 60 % and 80 % in 1991, and these rates were 60 % and 70 % in 2014 for almost all countries. Between 1991 and 2014, male LFPRs percentages for the countries in Europe became closer to each other.

Fig. 5.10 shows male LFPRs for the fourth and last group of countries. The most notable observation is that male LFPRs in Indonesia showed an increase between 1991 and 2014, and in 2014 Indonesia had the highest rate of all five countries. In 1991, Thailand had the highest rate, but in the dynamics following 1991, the rates showed a decreasing trend for Thailand, Philippines, and

Fig. 5.10: Male LFPRs for the Countries in Small Asian EMEs and South Africa. World Development Indicators (World Bank, 2016)

Vertical axis represents the percentage and the horizontal axis the years.

Malaysia. South Africa had the lowest participation rate, and it also showed a decreasing trend during the same period.

When we take a look at male LFPRs for all groups of EMEs between 1991 and 2014, the total rate for all countries showed a decreasing tendency. But Peru stands out as the most distinctive country, because unlike other countries, male LFPRs in Peru significantly increased. Except for Peru, and except for the slight increases in Colombia and Indonesia, the rates for the countries either did not show a significant change or show a tendency to decrease. This tendency to decrease in male LFPRs seems to be especially notable in China and India when considering their large LFMs. In addition to these two countries with large LFMs, Brazil and Bangladesh also experienced notable decreases in their rates.

As for Argentina, Brazil, Chile, Colombia, Peru, Venezuela, and Mexico, the rates for male LFP between 1991 and 2014 did not have a consistent course and fluctuated. There was a considerable decline in male LFPRs of the countries in the Large Asian EMEs, but these countries initially had quite high participation rates.

The European EMEs, namely, Bulgaria, Poland, Hungary, Russia, Turkey, and Ukraine, did not experience notable changes in terms of male LFPRs. However, the initial rates for these countries in 1991 were not very high. In the Small Asian EMEs and South Africa countries other than South Africa maintained their high

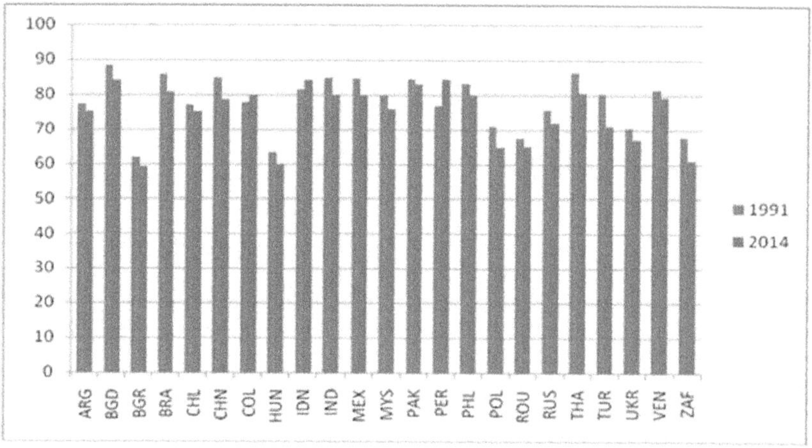

Fig. 5.11: Male LFPRs in Emerging Markets. World Development Indicators (World Bank, 2016)

Vertical axis represents the percentage and the horizontal axis the years.

rates of male labor force participation throughout 2014, despite some slight fluctuations and decreases.

Fig. 5.11 shows male LFPRs of the emerging markets between 1991 and 2014. In the figure, the country with the highest male LFPR was Bangladesh, and Bulgaria had the lowest rate. Overall, male LFPRs showed a tendency to decline in the countries except for Colombia, Indonesia, and Peru.

5.2.2.2 Female Labor Force Participation

Female labor force participation in LFMs is less than male labor force participation throughout the world, but today the rates for female labor force participation have reached a level of 70 % in developed countries and have come closer to the rates for male labor force participation in those countries. In today's developing world, occupations have become gender neutral, allowing women to work in various fields.

Historically speaking, the increases in female LFPRs were the result of sectors requiring an unqualified labor force for low wages and no job insurance benefits (Standing, 1999: 585). This influenced, but did not limit, a woman's place in society due to the fact that they have to take a leave of absence from their jobs to fulfill their maternal duties; cultural differences are also one of the most important

Fig. 5.12: Female LFPRs for Latin American EMEs. World Development Indicators (World Bank, 2016)

Vertical axis represents the percentage and the horizontal axis the years.

determinants of female labor force participation. Therefore, the positions of men and women in LFMs change from one country to another. This difference may apply also to LFPRs. The rates for female LFPRs in developing countries are behind the rates for developed countries (Standing, 1999: 586–599). This difference also yields economic consequences. As far as the literature is concerned, the findings suggest a significant correlation between female labor force participation and economic growth. Another interesting finding is that high levels of discrimination against women bring about negative economic consequences (Goldin, 1994; Balleer et al., 2009; Klasen, Lamanna, 2009; Löfström, 2009).

Female LFPRs in emerging markets will be similarly analyzed in four groups. Fig. 5.12 shows female LFPRs in the Latin America EMEs; the figure shows that for most countries in this group, female LFPRs were low in 1991; however, the rates increased until 2014. The lowest rates of female labor force participation in 2014 were in Mexico and Argentina, respectively.

We have already mentioned in the previous sections of the chapter that Peru and Brazil had the highest male LFPRs in 2014, and we can see that the same applies to the rates of female labor force participation. Although female LFPRs were on the increase for all the countries in the Latin American continent, it should be noted that female LFPRs had increased from very low rates and were behind the male LFPRs for the same countries.

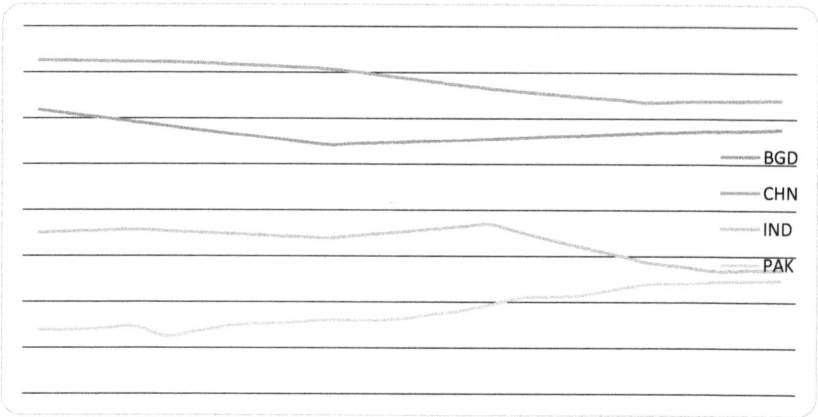

Fig. 5.13: Female LFPRs for the Countries in the Large Asian EMEs. World Development Indicators (World Bank, 2016)

Vertical axis represents the percentage and the horizontal axis the years.

The course of female LFPRs between 1991 and 2014 in China, India, Pakistan, and Bangladesh is given in Fig. 5.12. The most remarkable development as seen in the figure is the fact that the very low female LFPRs in Pakistan increased to a level of more than 20 % in the given period. Still, this rate is considerably low when compared to the rates of other countries.

India's female LFPRs decreased and came close to the rates in Pakistan. Bangladesh had relatively higher rates of female labor force participation than did India and Pakistan, but the rates in Bangladesh showed a decline between 1991 and 2014 from a level of above 60 % to a level of below 60 %. Of the Large Asian EMEs, China has the highest female LFPRs. However, in China there was also a decrease in the rates of female labor force participation, similar to the decrease in male LFPRs. When we consider all Large Asian EMEs, we see that Pakistan was the only country with an increase in its female LFPRs between 1991 and 2014; female LFPRs in the other countries showed a decline.

Female LFPRs for the European EMEs are given in Fig. 5.14. In this group, the country with the lowest rates of female labor force participation is Turkey.

Female LFPRs for Poland and Romania decreased between 1991 and 2014. The other countries in this group such as Bulgaria, Hungary, Russia, and Ukraine did not experience a drastic change despite some fluctuations from time to time. Of the countries in this group, Russia had the highest female LFPRs in 2014.

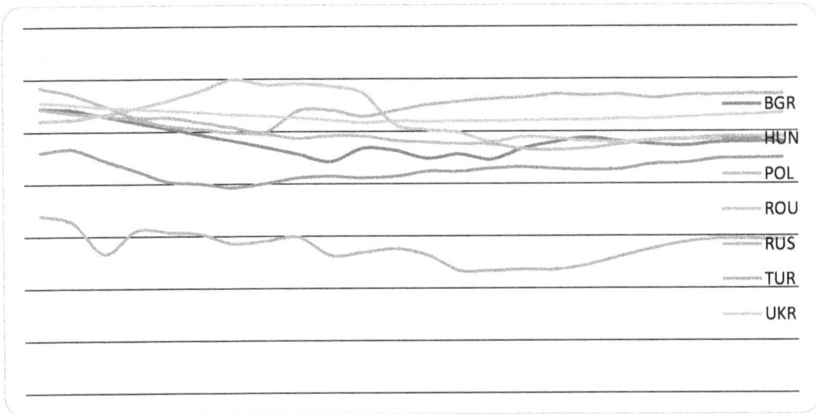

Fig. 5.14: Female LFPRs for the European EMEs. World Development Indicators (World Bank, 2016)

Vertical axis represents the percentage and the horizontal axis the years.

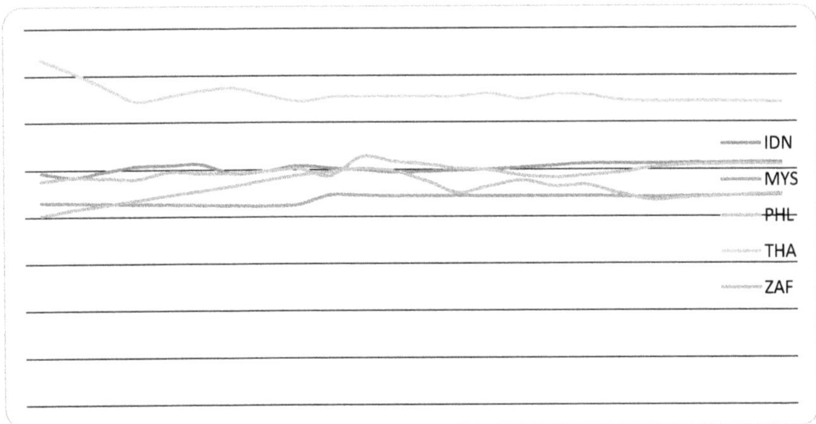

Fig. 5.15: Female LFPRs for the Countries in the Small Asian EMEs and South Africa. World Development Indicators (World Bank, 2016)

Vertical axis represents the percentage and the horizontal axis the years.

As seen in Fig. 5.15, among the countries in the Small Asian EMEs and South Africa, Indonesia had the highest female LFPRs, but these rates in Indonesia declined between 1991 and 2014. In the other four countries, Malaysia,

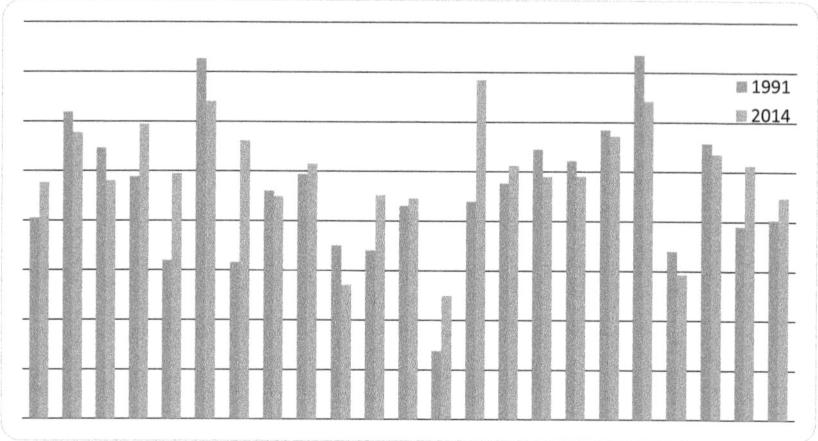

Fig. 5.16: Female LFPRs in Emerging Markets. World Development Indicators (World Bank, 2016)

Vertical axis represents the percentage and the horizontal axis the years.

Philippines, Thailand, and South Africa, female LFPRs did not decrease and showed slight increases.

As far as emerging markets are concerned, in all Latin American countries, female LFPRs have increased. Moreover, of all the emerging markets, Pakistan had the lowest female LFPRs. Yet, there seems to be an increasing trend in the rates in Pakistan. The country with the second lowest rates of female labor force participation after Pakistan is India and the rates in India showed a tendency to decrease. Turkey has the third lowest rates of female labor force participation. The rates in Turkey showed a decline between 1991 and 2014 and were approximately at 30 % in 2014.

In summary, female LFPRs for emerging markets are lower than male LFPRs, and there are considerable differences between the countries. The tendencies and fluctuations also differed from one country to another within the given period. Fig. 5.16 shows female LFPRs in all EMEs for the years between 1991 and 2014.

Female LFPRs were the lowest in Pakistan. The country with the second lowest rates of female labor force participation after Pakistan was India and the rates in India showed a tendency to decline. Turkey had the third lowest rates for female labor force participation at a level of 30 %. Female LFPRs in Chile and Colombia were low but showed a tendency to increase. In Thailand and China, women participated in the labor force at considerably high levels, but there was a decreasing trend in female LFPRs in these two countries.

Bangladesh had high rates of female labor force participation, but the country with the highest rates of female labor force participation was Peru, which was followed by Thailand with the second highest rates. When we compare Fig. 5.16 to Fig. 5.11, clearly, female LFPRs are lagging behind male LFPRs.

5.2.2 Unemployment

Labor force and labor force participation, which have significant impacts on the labor force supply and on the kind of processes these two variables go through in emerging markets, have been explained. The information provided above reflects the supply side of the labor force in emerging markets in terms of quantity. At this point, we should keep in mind that this chapter does not cover information about economic growth, which is one of the determinants of the demand side of LFMs, and that this topic is discussed in the related chapter.

A highly significant indicator resulting from the supply and demand dynamics of LFMs is unemployment. The concept of unemployment and its economic significance have already been explained in previous sections. This section will include analyses of the unemployment rates in emerging markets. Unemployment rates will be covered both as a whole and separately for men and women.

5.2.2.1 Total Unemployment Rates

As in the previous sections, EMEs will be considered in four groups and compared in terms of their unemployment rates. The data for unemployment rates are examined by using annual data for the years between 1991 and 2014 in order to see the process of the countries. Below is the course for the unemployment rates in the Latin American EMEs. Peru had the lowest unemployment rate. When we take a closer look at the LFPRs in Peru, we see that LFPRs for both men and women were on the rise. It can be suggested that within the given period, the low course of unemployment rates in Peru had a triggering effect on the LFP. Similar to Peru, Mexico did not have high rates of unemployment. It should be noted that male LFPRs in Mexico did not show drastic declines and female LFPRs significantly increased.

The economic crises in countries such as Colombia, Argentina, and Venezuela have had impacts on their LFMs. Brazil and Mexico, whose labor force and labor force participation were on a strong rise and had good performances since their unemployment rates, showed only a modest rise. Another noteworthy fact about

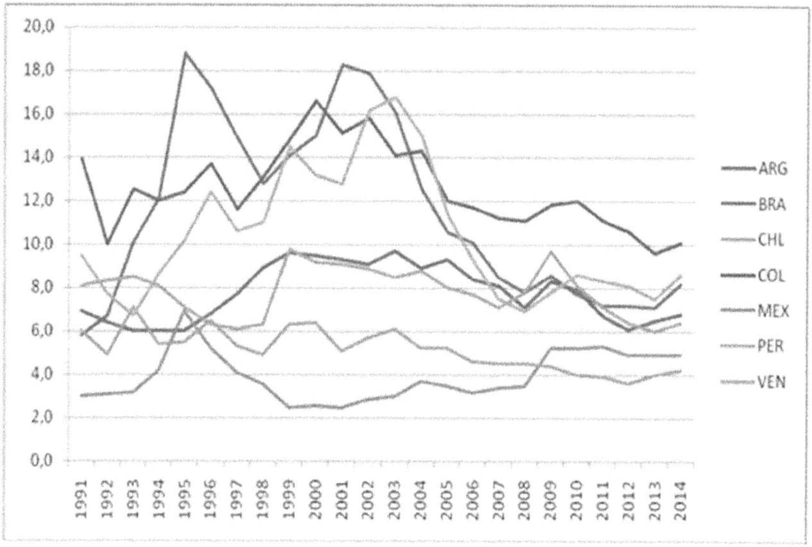

Fig. 5.17: Unemployment in the Latin American EMEs. World Development Indicators (World Bank, 2016)

Vertical axis represents the percentage and the horizontal axis the years.

the Latin American countries is that they were not greatly affected by the global crisis in 2009 in regards to their unemployment rates and that the volatility and fluctuations in their unemployment rates decreased after the crisis.

The data for the unemployment rates of the Large Asian EMEs is given in Fig. 5.18; Pakistan had the highest unemployment rates, and after 1994, unemployment rates fluctuated and then stabilized again between 2003 and 2007. Within the period between 1991 and 2004, the same trend applied to Bangladesh, although it had lower unemployment rates.

China and India are the two countries which have had a more consistent course regarding unemployment rates. Considering the labor force supply dynamics of these two countries, we can say that the LFMs of both countries function well.

Fig. 5.19 shows the unemployment rates for the countries in the European EMEs. The data shows that Bulgaria, which performs poorly in terms of LFP, has the highest unemployment rates. Similar to the countries in the first two groups, the countries in this group still had volatile rates of unemployment after 2009, yet the rates relatively decreased. Russia, Ukraine, and Romania showed good

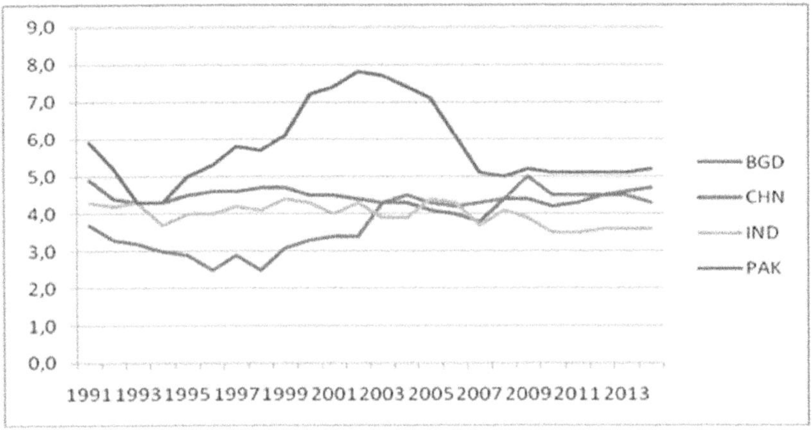

Fig. 5.18: Unemployment in the Large Asian EMEs. World Development Indicators (World Bank, 2016)

Vertical axis represents the percentage and the horizontal axis the years.

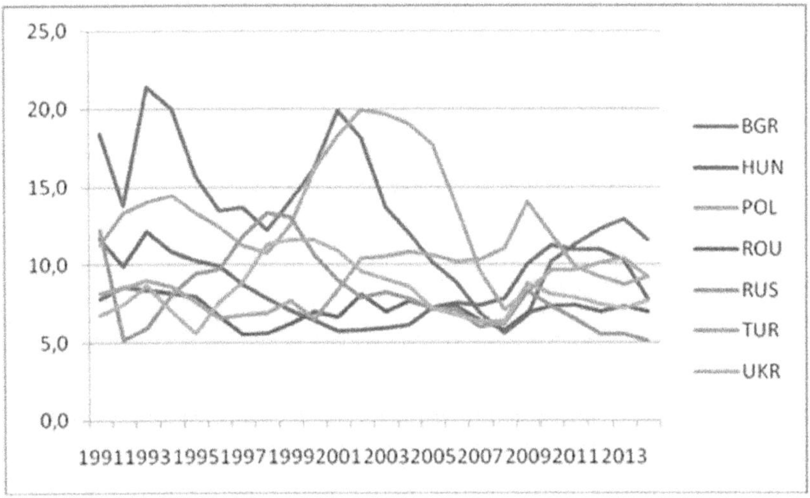

Fig. 5.19: Unemployment in the European EMEs. World Development Indicators (World Bank, 2016)

Vertical axis represents the percentage and the horizontal axis the years.

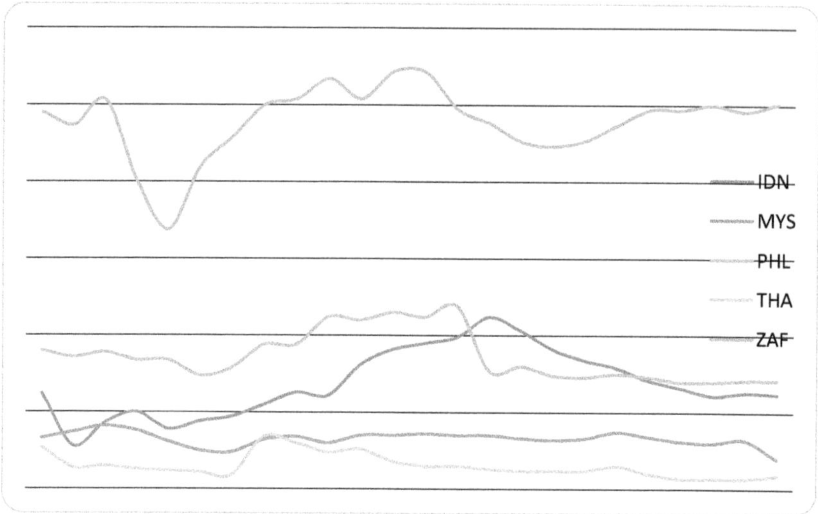

Fig. 5.20: Unemployment in the Small Asian EMEs and South Africa. World Development Indicators (World Bank, 2016)

Vertical axis represents the percentage and the horizontal axis the years.

performances in terms of unemployment rates, and it should be noted that these countries also had high rates of male and female LFPRs.

It is interesting that Ukraine's unemployment rates did not drastically change, and even modestly rose despite its decreasing labor force. It should also be noted that the labor force in Romania also decreased during the same period.

The unemployment rates for the Small Asian EMEs and South Africa are given in Fig. 5.20. Among the countries in the group, South Africa stands out as the country with the highest rates of unemployment, and these rates are also the highest of all the EMEs. South Africa does not have a good LFP performance either, and it seems to be the least efficient country among all EMEs in terms of utilizing labor force. Thailand has the lowest rates of unemployment of all the EMEs and its LFPRs are high for both men and women.

Although the labor force in Indonesia showed a sharp increase, this increase did not seem to have a significant impact on unemployment. Also, unemployment in Malaysia and Philippines had a tendency to decrease.

Fig. 5.21 gives the proportional unemployment rates in emerging markets for the period from 1991 to 2014. The former Soviet economies suffered serious economic problems in the early 1990s, the years which marked their period of transition to a

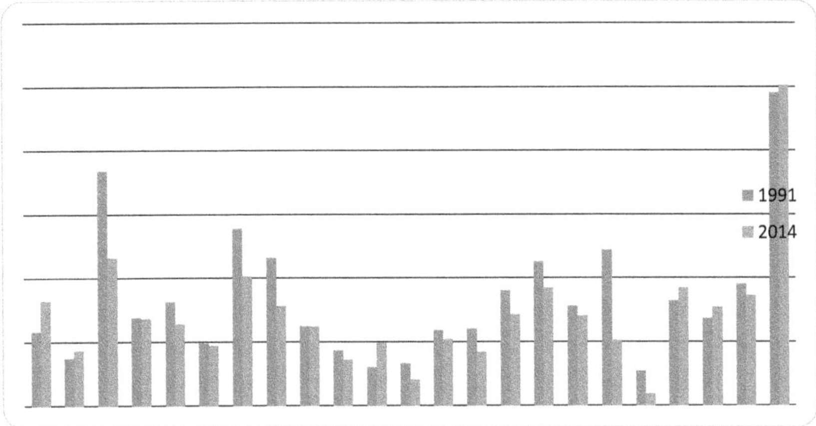

Fig. 5.21: Unemployment Rates in Emerging Markets. World Development Indicators (World Bank, 2016)

Vertical axis represents the percentage and the horizontal axis the years.

market-based economy. As a result, in 1991 Bulgaria, Hungary, Poland, Romania, Russia, and Ukraine had high rates of unemployment. These rates of unemployment decreased in 2014 for all countries except for Ukraine. Among these countries, Russia managed to show a good performance and its rates of unemployment fell by half. The unemployment rates in Bulgaria, Hungary, and Poland were still high. In Ukraine, although there was a decrease in the labor force between 1991 and 2014, unemployment rates in 2014 were higher than in 1991. This is also related to the political and social turmoil that Ukraine had been through. The unemployment rates in Ukraine are lower than in Bulgaria. Regarding the period between 1991 and 2014, Bulgaria and Ukraine had the worst LFM performances in terms of total unemployment. Although the labor force in Ukraine decreased, there was an increase in unemployment in the given period, not a decrease.

When we consider the other countries in terms of total unemployment, in Brazil unemployment decreased, although slightly, regardless of the fast-increasing labor force rates. Also, in Peru, Colombia, Chile, and Venezuela there was a decrease in unemployment, but the rates of unemployment in Colombia were still considerably high. Peru, on the other hand, managed to lower its already-low unemployment rates. In Mexico, unemployment increased, but it did not have very high unemployment rates to begin with. In Argentina, unemployment increased considerably.

Of all the EMEs, Thailand has the best performance regarding unemployment rates. Thailand managed to lower the already low unemployment rates and also had the lowest unemployment rates of all the emerging markets in terms of total unemployment. Malaysia, with the second lowest unemployment rates after Thailand, had a decrease in its already low unemployment rates in 1991. India has a large economy and labor force, with an unemployment rate below 5 %, and it managed to lower its unemployment rates in the period between 1991 and 2014. China has the largest economy and labor force among all emerging markets and managed to lower its already low unemployment rates with the help of its growing economy despite its expanding labor force. In Indonesia, however, the total unemployment rates did not show a notable change. In Bangladesh, unemployment rates remained low despite some moderate increases. In Philippines, unemployment rates declined, but were still above 7 %. In Pakistan, unemployment rates decreased to 5 %. In Turkey, unemployment rates rose. Within the time period which is subject to analysis, the country with the worst rate of unemployment was South Africa. Unemployment in South Africa continued to rise and reached 25 %.

5.2.2.2 Male Unemployment Rates

In the analysis of total unemployment rates, the trends throughout the years and the changes are presented in detail. However, the rates for male and female unemployment will be provided in less detail. The male unemployment rates for emerging markets for the years 1991 and 2014 are given in Fig. 5.22.

As far as male unemployment rates are concerned, there is a similar tendency to the total rates of unemployment for many countries. In countries with rising total unemployment rates, there is also a rise in male unemployment rates. Likewise, in all countries with declining total unemployment rates, there is a decline in male unemployment rates. Although these increases and decreases are not the same in terms of percentages, they represent a similar tendency. There are only two exceptions to this situation: These are Turkey and Indonesia. The total unemployment rates in Turkey showed a rise in the period between 1991 and 2014, but male unemployment rates showed a decline. In Indonesia, although there was not a significant change in the total unemployment rates, male unemployment rates showed a tendency to decline. The LFMs of Turkey and Indonesia notably differ from those of other countries. In both countries being a male lowers the possibility of being unemployed.

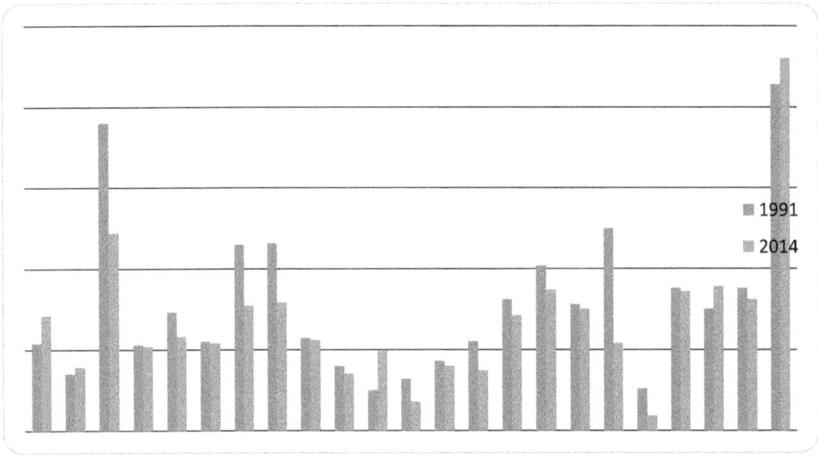

Fig. 5.22: Male Unemployment Rates in Emerging Markets. World Development Indicators (World Bank, 2016)

Vertical axis represents the percentage and the horizontal axis the countries.

5.2.2.3 Female Unemployment Rates

When considering female unemployment rates, we observe a case similar to male unemployment rates, in that countries with an increasing total unemployment rate also have a high female unemployment rate. Fig. 5.23 shows female unemployment rates. Before discussing female unemployment rates, it would be useful to highlight the fact that female LFPRs are lower in almost all the countries.

An analysis of female unemployment rates reveals that Turkey has the highest increase in female unemployment rates. It is necessary here to note that the female unemployment rates in Turkey were considerably low and showed a tendency to decrease within the related period of time. Female unemployment rates in Argentina showed an increase, but male and female and total unemployment rates are very close to each other. Bangladesh also had an increase in female unemployment rates and, similar to the case in Argentina, the rates seemed to be consistent with the other unemployment increase rates. In Pakistan, although female LFPRs were very low and although they considerably increased in the years between 1991 and 2014, female unemployment rates showed a significant decline. In this regard, we can say that the course of Pakistan's LFMs was in favor of women. While in Indonesia the total unemployment rates did not change significantly and male unemployment rates showed a tendency to decline, there

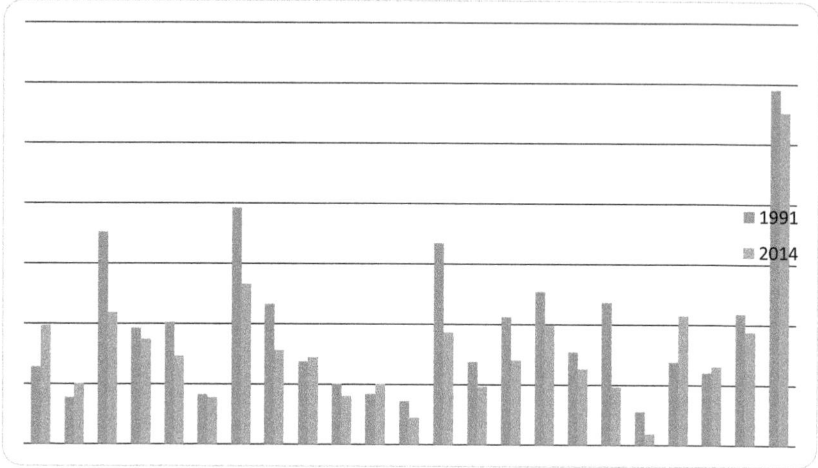

Fig. 5.23: Female Unemployment Rates in Emerging Markets. World Development Indicators (World Bank, 2016)

Vertical axis represents the percentage and the horizontal axis the countries.

was a rise in female unemployment rates. In Romania, female unemployment rates showed a greater decline when compared to the corresponding rates for male unemployment. For Russia, the rates also dropped significantly. In Mexico, female unemployment rates rose, but this rise was still below male unemployment rates. In Philippines, the decline in female unemployment rates was higher than for male unemployment rates.

5.3 Conclusion

The labor forces of the EMEs comprise 2/3 of the total labor force in the world. The most notable fact about these markets is that there are considerable differences between their labor force sizes and labor force increase rates. This is a significant indicator of the differences between the demographic structures of these countries. In countries where unemployment rates are low and chances of getting a job are high, LFPRs are high as well. High levels of unemployment deter the labor force from LFM. LFM indicators in such countries as Turkey, Pakistan, India, and Indonesia give out negative signals regarding women. This implies that cultural differences influence LFMs. In summary, the demographic and cultural differences in emerging markets have perceivable impacts on LFMs.

Labor force increase rates are high in Brazil, Indonesia, Bangladesh, Pakistan, and Mexico. Also, in China, India, and Philippines labor force increase rates are high. Turkey's labor force increases rates accelerated as of 2008. In the other countries, labor force increase rates are either slow or stable, or the labor force shows a tendency to decrease. In this regard, the abovementioned nine countries have potential in terms of labor force sizes in the long run.

Male LFPRs are the highest in Bangladesh. The lowest rates for male LFPRs are in Bulgaria. In all the countries except for Colombia, Indonesia, and Peru, male LFPRs experienced a decline. Yet, in all the countries, male LFPRs are higher than the corresponding rates for female LFP. Pakistan has the lowest female LFPRs, but the rates show a tendency to rise. India has the second lowest female LFPRs. The third lowest rates are in Turkey, and the rates show a tendency to decline.

In regards to total unemployment, the country with the highest unemployment rates is South Africa. Unemployment rates in Ukraine are high and show an increase tendency despite the decrease in its labor force. In Bulgaria, Poland, and Colombia unemployment decreased but still remains at high levels. In Argentina, unemployment increased considerably. Turkey has high levels of unemployment and the rates are on the rise. It can be assumed that these countries are very likely to face serious problems in their LFMs.

The total unemployment rates in Indonesia did not show a notable change. In Brazil, unemployment rates decreased, although slightly, despite a fast-increasing labor force. China, India, and Peru managed to lower unemployment rates, and in Bangladesh unemployment rates remained low despite some increases. When considering the total unemployment rates among emerging markets, Thailand had the best performance of all, managing to lower the already low unemployment rates. Similarly, in Malaysia, the already low rates of unemployment decreased even more. Malaysia, after Thailand, has the second lowest unemployment rates among emerging markets. Russia, also, managed to lower unemployment rates.

In regards to male unemployment rates, we see that they show a similar trend as the total unemployment rates for the countries except for Turkey and Indonesia. In Turkey, male unemployment rates declined although there was a rise in the total unemployment rates in the period between 1991 and 2014. In Indonesia, on the other hand, total unemployment rates did not change significantly, but male unemployment rates declined. The LFM notably of Turkey and Indonesia differ from those of other countries.

As for female unemployment rates, Turkey showed the greatest increase in female unemployment rates. It is necessary to emphasize that the female labor participation rates in Turkey are very low and show a tendency to decline; Turkey cannot utilize its female labor force. In Pakistan, female unemployment rates showed a considerable decline even though female LFPRs are very low, and these rates rose significantly between 1991 and 2014. Considering this fact, the conclusion is that LFMs in Pakistan have taken a positive course; yet, Pakistan cannot efficiently utilize its female labor force, either. In Indonesia, there seems to be an increasing trend in female unemployment rates while the total unemployment rates do not change greatly, and male unemployment rates have a tendency to decrease. In this sense, Indonesia is one of the poorly performing countries.

Thailand benefits most efficiently from its labor force although its rates of labor force increase are not very high. Thailand has high rates of male and female labor force participation and low rates of unemployment. Also, there is not a significant difference between male and female unemployment rates.

The worst LFM performance belongs to South Africa. It not only has very high unemployment rates but also very low LFPRs. Still, there does not seem to be a significant difference between men and women.

In conclusion, although there are economic similarities and common features of emerging markets, their LFMs differ remarkably from one another due to their cultural and demographic structures. Moreover, these countries do not utilize their labor force resources similarly. It can be suggested that countries which have low unemployment rates and high LFPRs, and more effectively utilize their female labor force have a greater potential as EMEs in the future.

References

Balleer, Almut; Gomez, Salvador, Ramon; Turunen, Jarkko (2009). "Labour Force Participation in the Euro Area: A Cohort Based Analysis", European Central Bank Working Paper Series, No: 1049.

Bergemann, Anette; Van Den Berg, Gerard J. (2008). "Active Labor Market Policy Effects for Women in Europe- A Survey", Annals of Economics and Statistics, No: 91–92, July– December, 385–408.

Ehrenberg, Ronald G.; Smith, Robert S. (2000). Modern Labor Economics: Theory and Public Policy, Addison-Wesley Longman Inc., Massachusetts.

Genre, Veronique; Gomez, Salvador, Ramon; Lamo, Ana (2010). "European Women: Why Do(n't) They Work", Applied Economics, Vol. 42, No: 12, December.

Goldin, Claudia (1994). "The U-Shaped Female Labor Force Function in Economic Development and History", NBER Working Paper Series, No: 4707

ILO, (2016). Employment Statistics, www.ilo.org, last date of access 03.09.2016.

Klasen, Stephan; Lamanna, Francesca (2009). "The Impact of Gender Inequality in Education and Employment on Economic Growth: New Evidence for a Panel of Countries", Feminist Economics, Vol. 15, No: 3, July, 91–132.

Lewis, Margaret; Peterson, Janice (1997). "The Labour Supply Decision Differences Between Genders and Races", Bartlett, Robin J. (Ed.), Introducing Race and Gender into Economics, Routledge, London.

Löfström, Asa (2009). Gender Equality, Economic Growth and Employment, Swedish Ministry of Integration and Gender Equality, Sweden.

Olsen, Randall J. (1994). "Fertility and the Size of the U. S. Labor Force", Journal of Economic Literature, Vol. 32, No: 1, 60–100.

Standing, Guy, (1999). "Global Feminization through Flexible Labor: A Theme Revisited", World Development, Vol. 27, No: 3, 583–602.

TÜİK, (2009). İşgücü, İstihdam ve İşsizlik İstatistikleri Sorularla Resmi İstatistikler Dizisi-1, T.C.Başbakanlık Türkiye İstatistik Kurumu, Ankara.

TÜİK, (2011). Türkiye İstatistik Yıllığı 2010, Türkiye İstatistik Kurumu, Ankara, Nisan.

World Bank, (2016). Development Indicators, http://data.worldbank.org/indicator, last date of access 03.09.2016.

Gülsüm Akarsu

6 Capital Market Developments in EMEs

Abstract: Since the 1970s, financial globalization, financial and technological innovations, restructuring in the financial sector, and expansion of the investor base have led to significant changes in the global financial system. These changes have also influenced EMEs, but on various levels in each country. The aim of this chapter is to analyze the differences and the similarities in the capital markets of EMEs by using the data on the indicators of capital markets from 2000 to 2014. The study uses the most recent data covering all EMEs, including the period after the 2008 global financial crisis. The analysis shows that some important problems in the EMEs are stock market volatility (SMV), bank dominance, stock market concentration, segmentation, illiquidity, short-termism, low saving rates, lack of financial literacy and investor education, and difficulty in the access of Small and Medium Size Enterprises (SMEs) to financing sources using capital markets. However, the stock markets of South Africa, Malaysia, and Chile are more developed when compared to the other EMEs. Bond market development is higher in Chile, Malaysia, and Thailand for private bonds and in Brazil, Hungary, and Malaysia for public bonds. Among the countries under investigation, South Africa, Hungary, and Argentina seem to benefit more from globalization and internationalization of capital markets on the average, as these countries have experienced higher levels of portfolio equity inflows, foreign direct investment inflows, and international debt issuance. As policy suggestions, countries should give importance to macroeconomic stability, building necessary institutional, supervisory, regulatory, and legal framework as well as financial infrastructure.

Keywords: Capital Markets, Equities Markets, Bond Markets, Globalization

6.1 Introduction

Because of financial globalization, financial and technological innovations, restructuring in the financial sector, and expansion of the investor base, there have been major changes in the global financial system which grew rapidly starting from the beginning of the 1970s and reaching an elevated level of development throughout the 1990s (de la Torre and Schmukler, 2007: 25). According to de la Torre and Schmukler (2007), EMEs were also affected by these developments in the global markets; however, one can see differences in the domestic capital market developments among these countries and regions, although similar reforms were undertaken to attract international capital flows.

The aim of the chapter is to understand the differences and the similarities in the capital markets of EMEs by using the data on the performance measures of capital markets from 2000 to 2014. Although EMEs have grown rapidly over the past twenty-five years, their capital markets did not develop as much when compared to their growth as these countries had only 22 % of the total global equity market capitalization and 14 % of the bond market value even though EMEs had a 51 % share of global output (Langridge and Valle, 2015). However, there has been transformation in their capital markets. Many reforms have been implemented to develop their capital markets and to ensure their financial integration into the global markets. These reforms aim to increase competition and efficiency in the financial markets and develop domestic capital markets to provide long-term local currency financing, reduce the cost of capital, increase savings and investment, allocate and diversify risks, and create liquidity (de la Torre and Schmukler, 2007). Therefore, because of reforms and capital market liberalization, as well as demand growth expectations, capital markets are expected to become deeper in these countries (Langridge and Valle, 2015).

To understand how capital markets work, some definitions are given as follows. Capital is one of the production factors, i.e., input used in the production process. In other words, "capital includes goods produced by the economic system that are used as inputs to produce other goods and services in the future" (Case and Fair, 1999: 254). Firms need funds to finance their capital purchases which are supplied by private investors and financial institutions through their savings which earn interest on bank deposits, corporation bonds and government bonds, or claims to future profits such as dividends. Some of these transactions take place through capital markets. More specifically, the financial market is a combination of two systems: one is market-based and other is bank-based (ICSA Emerging Markets Committee, 2015). In the bank-based system, banks are the major actors which give financing through the savings of investors to the firms and provide risk management tools, but in the market-based system, securities market in relation to banks provide financing and risk management services. However, there is a shift from a bank-based to a market-based system in both developed and developing countries (ICSA Emerging Markets Committee, 2015). Therefore, in this chapter, the focus is on market-based financing. In this context, capital markets can be defined as "markets for trading long term financial securities, government bonds and other public-sector securities" (Murinde, 2006: 1). Murinde (2006) discussed the structure of the capital market in detail and mentioned the three main functions of capital markets for raising long-term funds for companies through a primary capital market, i.e., the new issues of equity and debt, trading existing shares and bonds through secondary markets, trading the future and contingent claims through derivatives markets. As capital stock has a key role in the economic growth of countries, i.e., it is a principal factor of production, the development of capital markets is very crucial for economic growth and poverty alleviation through many channels which are discussed in detail by de la Torre and Schmukler (2007). Local capital markets also play important roles in risk sharing, efficient allocation of capital, and financial integration (The World Bank, 2015).

For the evaluation of capital market development, different indicators were used such as stock market capitalization, the number of listed companies and the value traded in stock exchanges (SEs), bonds outstanding, and credit from financial institutions. In the next sections, these indicators are analyzed for each country, and each country's indicator was compared by classifying the countries into geographical regions.

This chapter is organized as follows. Following the introduction, section two discusses the capital market development in EMEs emphasizing on equities and bond markets and the effects of globalization on domestic capital markets. The focus of section three is on some issues and problems related to the capital markets of EMEs. Lastly, conclusions are presented.

6.2 Capital Markets in EMEs

To attract international capital to their markets, EMEs have begun reform processes in their domestic markets by starting financial liberalization and deregulation, introducing privatization and implementing policies to ensure macroeconomic stability, strong institutional and economic fundamentals and to create better business environment mentioned by de la Torre and Schmukler (2007). Financial liberalization and reforms include abolishing controls on direct credit, foreign exchange and capital transactions, abandoning foreign investment restrictions, privatization programs, interest rate deregulations, introducing banking regulations and supervision, pension system reforms, introducing laws and regulations related to protecting investors' rights[1], introducing reforms to establish institutions and infrastructure[2], and introducing international standards and codes (de la Torre and Schmukler, 2007; The World Bank, 2015). However, financial integration, reforms, and privatization cause these

1 Such as enforcement of property rights, protection of minority shareholders and creditors, prevention of insider trading.

2 For example, establishment of domestic securities and exchange commissions and centralized exchanges, introduction of regulatory and supervisory framework, custody arrangements and developments in securities clearance and settlements systems and accounting and disclosure standards.

countries to be more prone to financial crisis because of the substantial amounts of capital flows into their countries. This situation is aggravated by the underdeveloped capital markets, the absence of a local currency bond market, and high dependence on bank-based intermediation (de la Torre and Schmukler, 2007; The World Bank, 2015).

Although similar reforms have been implemented, different levels of capital market development are attained due to structural factors, such as levels of savings rates and macroeconomic volatility. Tab. 6.1 shows the average value of some indicators for capital market development for each country from 2000 to 2014. On a regional basis, comparison shows that overall South Africa has reached the highest level of capital market development followed by Asia, Latin America, and Europe on the average, based on the four criteria: depth, access, efficiency, and stability. Among Latin American countries, Asian countries, and European countries, based on most indicators, Chile; China and Malaysia; and Hungary and Turkey have shown better performance in terms of their capital market development. Comparison for all countries shows that Chile, China, Malaysia, and South Africa have higher levels of capital market development than any other EME.

In addition, there seems to be a shift from bank-based to market-based system in both developed and developing countries (ICSA Emerging Markets Committee, 2015). But, the dominance of a bank-based system continues in the majority of EMEs.

Tab. 6.2 presents the percentage of investments financed by bank loans and equities. According to this table, the percentages of investments financed by bank loans are higher than the percentage of investments financed by issuing new equity shares. Therefore, bank loans continue to be an important source of investment financing in EMEs. China and Malaysia give a higher average ratio of bank credits to the private sector when compared to other EMEs. This section discusses the important issues in the capital markets of EMEs. The focus is on equities and bonds markets as the markets for derivatives have shown a strong growth only since 2010 as mentioned by Ehlers and Packer (2013). After explaining the developments in the equities markets of these countries, bonds markets are analyzed. Lastly, the effects of globalization on the domestic markets are discussed.

6.2.1 Equities Markets

For comparison of stock markets' performance, different indicators are considered. One of these indicators is the number of domestic companies listed on

Tab. 6.1: Mean Values of Indicators over the Period from 2000 to 2014*. Based on author's own calculation employing the data obtained from World Bank Global Financial Development Database, 2016

	DEPTH							ACCESS	EFFICIENCY	STABILITY
Regions/ Countries	**Market Cap.[1]**	**Total value traded[2]**	**Private credit[3]**	**Domestic private debt securities[4]**	**Domestic public debt securities[5]**	**International private debt securities[6]**	**International public debt securities[7]**	**Market capitalization excluding top 10 companies[8]**	**Turnover ratio of stock market (%)**	**Volatility of stock price**
Latin America	**39**	**16**	**33**	**15**	**21**	**4**	**9**	**39**	**19**	**24**
ARG	14	1	13	6	18	3	25	26	9	33
BRA	48	25	46	21	55	7	5	48	53	30
CHL	103	68	83	37	10	7	2	55	14	16
COL	37	5	32	0	23	2	8	30	12	21
MEX	29	8	20	14	19	5	5	36	28	22
PER	38	3	23	10	4	3	8	38	8	21
VEN	4	0	16			4	11		8	24
Asia	**52**	**33**	**60**	**19**	**24**	**5**	**3**	**60**	**85**	**21**
BGD	11	1	32						25	17
CHN	45	68	113	24	15	1	0	75	154	25
IND	61	44	39	2	10			67	110	25
IDN	31	10	24	4	15	3	2	50	37	24
MYS	133	41	109	51	38	15	2	63	31	14
PAK	23	44	22		34	0	1		222	21
PHL	50	9	32	1	32	8	14	48	17	22

(continued on next page)

Tab. 6.1: (continued)

	DEPTH							ACCESS	EFFICIENCY	STABILITY
Regions/ Countries	**Market Cap.[1]**	**Total value traded[2]**	**Private credit[3]**	**Domestic private debt securities[4]**	**Domestic public debt securities[5]**	**International private debt securities[6]**	**International public debt securities[7]**	**Market capitalization excluding top 10 companies[8]**	**Turnover ratio of stock market (%)**	**Volatility of stock price**
THA	61	48	112	33	23	4	1	55	84	23
Europe	**24**	**14**	**38**	**4**	**27**	**4**	**8**	**34**	**51**	**30**
BGR	14	2	46			2	12		20	23
HUN	22	17	48	11	42	9	14	6	71	25
POL	28	10	38	1	32	2	9	40	38	25
ROM	9	1	27			1	4		12	27
RUS	48	28	32	5	4	6	5	37	48	36
TUR	27	39	32	1	30	2	7	52	162	36
UKR	19	1	46			4	7		6	39
Africa										
ZAF	199	53	137	17	31	8	3	67	28	19

* Time period differs for some countries based on data availability. The values are rounded to the nearest integers.
[1] Stock market capitalization as a ratio to GDP (%).
[2] Stock market total value traded as a ratio to GDP (%).
[3] Private credit provided by financial institutions as a ratio to GDP (%).
[4] Domestic private debt securities outstanding as a ratio to GDP (%).
[5] Domestic public debt securities outstanding as a ratio to GDP (%).
[6] International private debt securities outstanding as a ratio to GDP (%).
[7] International public debt securities outstanding as a ratio to GDP (%).
[8] Market capitalization excluding top ten companies as a ratio to total market capitalization (%).

Tab. 6.2: Domestic Bank Credit to the Private Sector as a Share of GDP (%), Percentages of Investments Financed by Bank Loans and Equity or Stock Sales over the Period from 2000 to 2014* on Average. Based on author's own calculation employing the data obtained from World Bank Global Financial Development Database, 2016

Regions/Countries	Investments financed by banks (%)	Investments financed by equity or stock sales (%)	Domestic bank credit to private sector (% of GDP)
Latin America	**25**	**3**	**30**
ARG	10	2	13
BRA	32	2	44
CHL	34	1	67
COL	32	2	29
MEX	8	4	17
PER	37	3	24
VEN	22	6	18
Asia	**19**	**4**	**61**
BGD	15	4	33
CHN	5	3	120
IND	23	4	42
IDN	6	3	25
MYS	33	3	113
PAK	5	5	23
PHL	12	4	33
THA	53	10	97
Europe	**16**	**6**	**39**
BGR	20	1	47
HUN	20	10	47
POL	17	3	39
ROM	16	5	26
RUS	8	2	35
TUR	20	10	34
UKR	11	7	44
Africa			
ZAF	26	0	69

*The time period differs for some countries based on data availability. The values are rounded to the nearest integers.

Tab. 6.3: Listed Domestic Companies, Total Between 2000 and 2014* on average. Based on author's own calculation employing the data obtained from World Bank World Development Indicators Database, 2016

Regions/Countries	Listed domestic companies, total
Latin America	**172**
ARG	104
BRA	376
CHL	238
COL	91
MEX	143
PER	200
VEN	53
Asia	**1234**
BGD	274
CHN	1717
IND	5211
IDN	384
MYS	922
PAK	626
PHL	242
THA	499
Europe	**245**
BGR	345
HUN	48
POL	447
ROM	68
RUS	374
TUR	261
UKR	172
Africa	
ZAF	386

*The time period differs for some countries based on data availability. The values are rounded to the nearest integers.

domestic SEs. India has the highest average number of listed domestic companies from 2000 to 2014, as can be seen from Tab. 6.3. Hungary's listing is the lowest for the same period. Fig. 6.1 illustrates this indicator over the period 2000–2014 for different countries grouped by their geographical regions: Latin America, Asia-1 and South Africa, Asia-2, and Europe. While one can see a declining trend in the

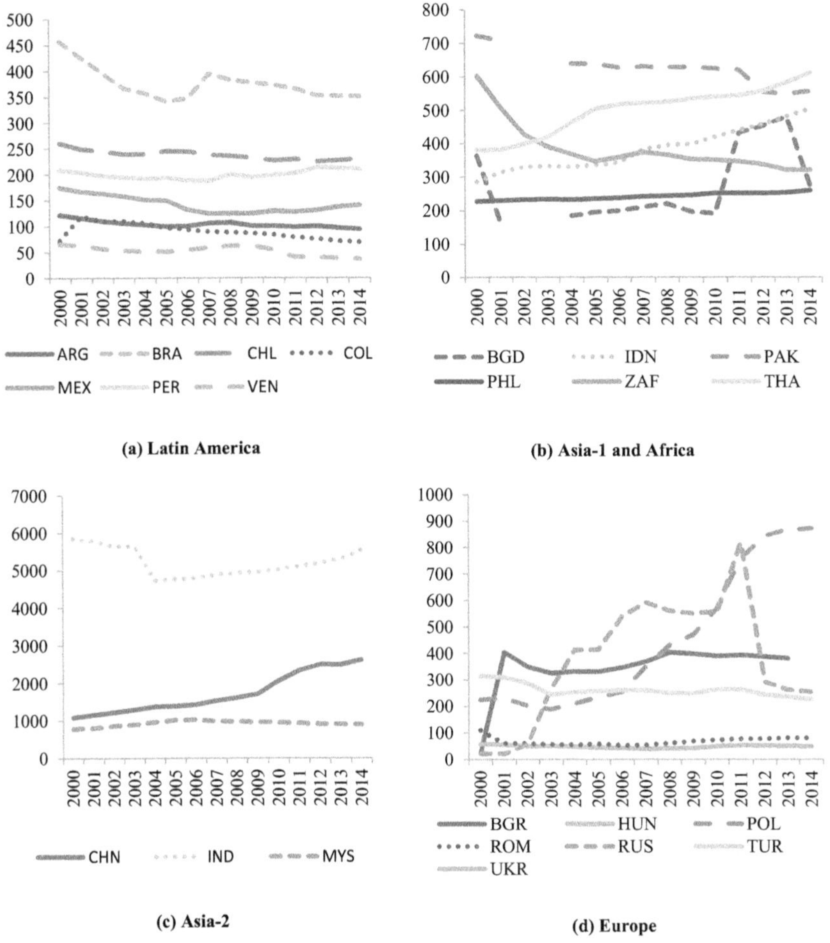

Fig. 6.1: Listed Domestic Companies, Total. Based on author's own elaboration employing data obtained from World Bank World Development Indicators, 2016

listed domestic companies for Latin America and South Africa, listings increased in the majority of countries in Europe and Asia except for Pakistan and Russia; however, there was not any significant effect of the 2008 global financial crisis on this indicator. Among the many reasons for delisting (for example, inability to meet the listing requirements), the most noticeable one was the migration of firms from these countries to international capital markets through depositary receipts, after mergers and acquisitions and privatization processes.

Evaluation of another measure, *market capitalization*, shows that on an average, South Africa and countries in Asia are characterized by higher levels of market capitalization which indicates deeper markets when compared to other countries (see Tab. 6.1). Among Latin American, Asian, and European countries, the stock markets of Chile, Malaysia, and Russia are deeper when compared to their regional counterparts (see Tab. 6.1), recording higher levels of market capitalization. Fig. 6.2 shows a sharp decline in market capitalization for all countries in 2008, showing the adverse effects of the 2008 global financial crisis. Similar decrease in total value of stocks traded (as a share of GDP) can also be seen in 2008 (Fig. 6.3). Although this is a temporary decrease for most of the countries, this adverse effect of Global Financial crisis last more than one period for some countries, for example, Pakistan, Argentina, India, Russia, Romania and Bulgaria.

In Fig. 6.4, evolution of the countries' stock market returns in different regions is given for 2000–2014 for comparison purposes. The sharp declines in the returns are seen for all regions from 2008 to 2009 as a result of the global economic crisis in 2008. After 2011, the stock market of Venezuela outperforms the other countries with a notable difference in stock market returns.

From the examination of the overall averages and five-year averages of the stock market returns given in Tab. 6.4, one can see that although during the period from 2000 to 2004, stock market returns, on the average, were higher in European countries, Latin American countries recorded the highest average stock market returns throughout the whole period as well as for 2005–2010 and 2010–2014, respectively.

6.2.2 Bond Markets

Shifting from monetary financing to debt financing of the public deficit and the aim of decreasing dependency on external funding stimulates the countries to develop their domestic bond markets (de la Torre and Schmukler, 2007; Kawai and Prasad, 2013). This section extends the analysis to bond markets.

Tab. 6.5 shows the average of bond market capitalization (as a ratio to GDP) for both private and public bond markets from 2000 to 2014. Public bond market is deeper than private bond market in all countries except for Chile, Peru, China, Malaysia, Thailand, and Russia. Therefore, one can see a high dominance of public sector debt issuance and trading in EMEs.

Although there is a high dominance of public bond markets, as demonstrated in Fig. 6.5, private bond markets in some countries such as Brazil, Mexico, Malaysia, Thailand, India, South Africa, Poland, Turkey, and Russia experienced a higher level of improvement with an upward growing trend from 2000 to 2014. On the other hand, as shown in Fig. 6.6, public bond markets showed

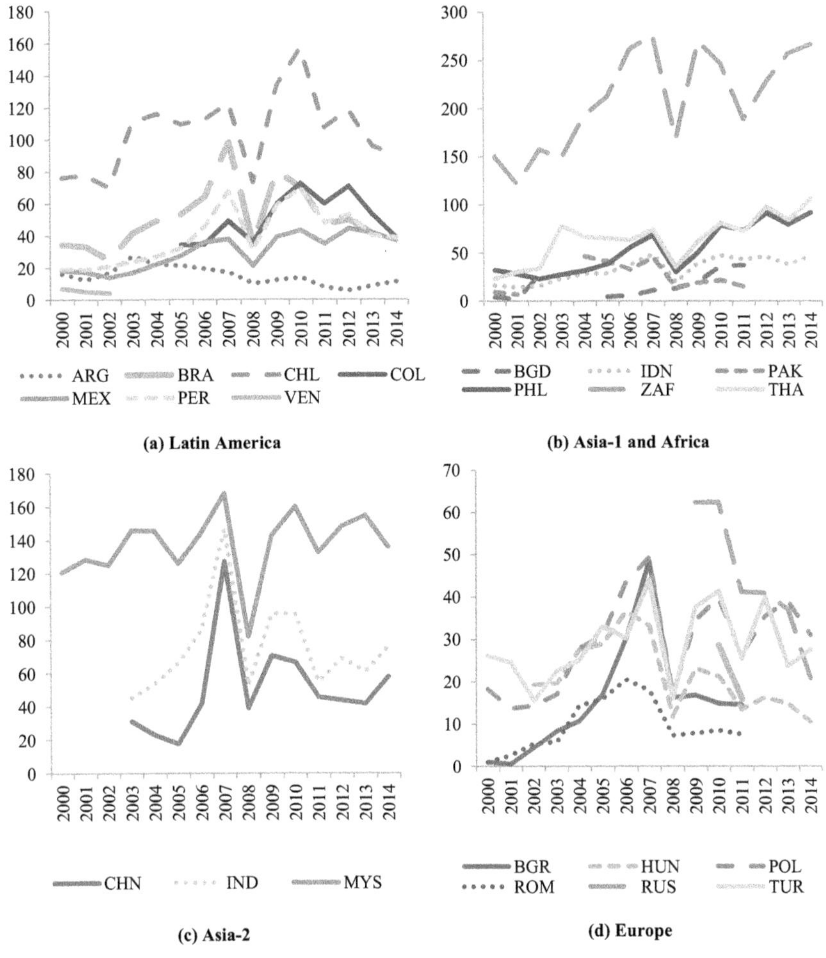

Fig. 6.2: Market Capitalization of Listed Domestic Companies (% of GDP). Based on author's own elaboration employing data obtained from World Bank World Development Indicators, 2016

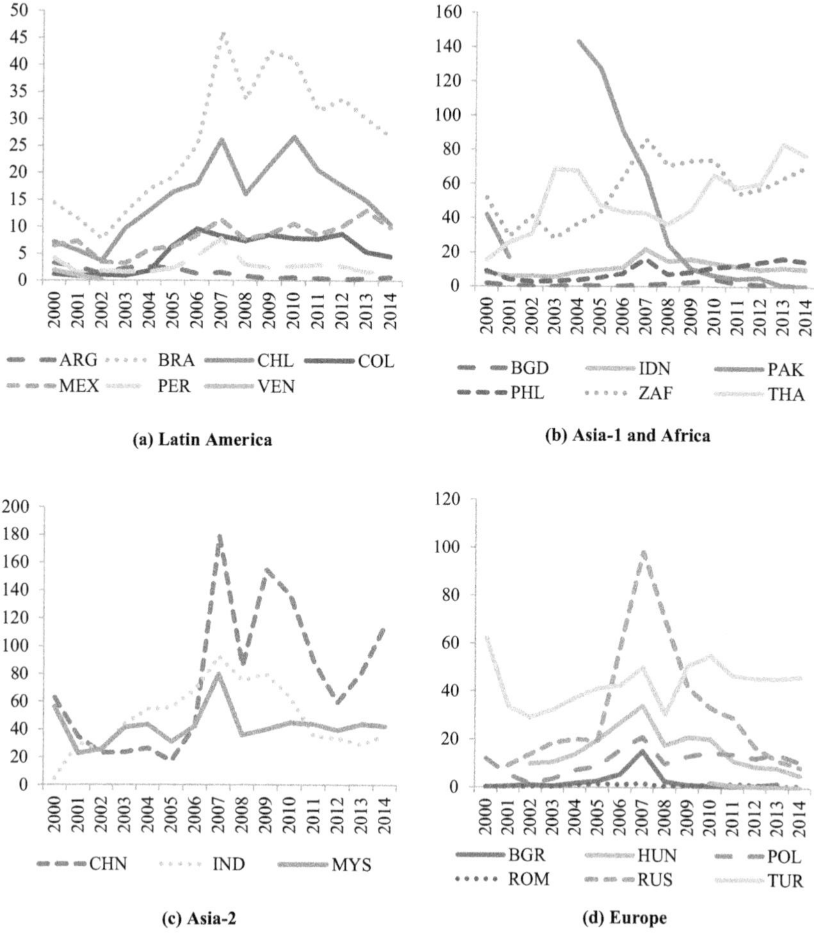

Fig. 6.3: Total Value of Stocks Traded (% of GDP). Based on author's own elaboration employing data obtained from World Bank World Development Indicators, 2016

some improvements in growing patterns, especially in Malaysia, Pakistan, India, South Africa, Hungary, and Poland.

6.2.3 Effect of Globalization on Domestic Markets

Financial globalization can be defined as follows, "the integration of a country's local financial system with international financial markets and institutions"

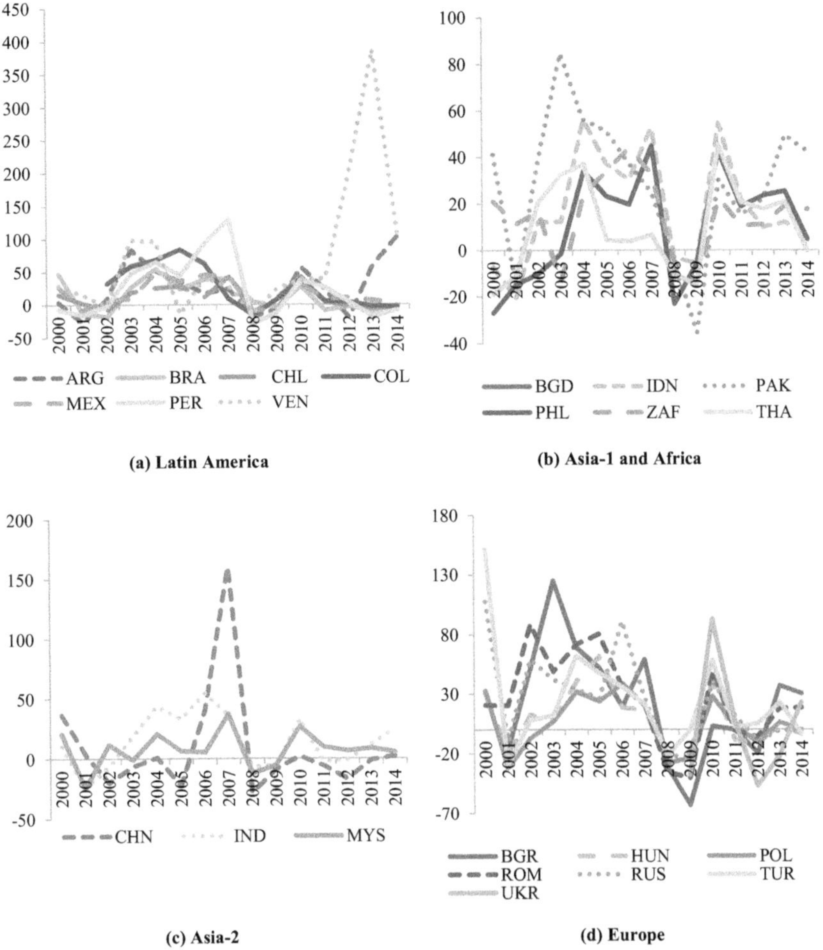

Fig. 6.4: Stock Market Return (%, Year-on-Year). Based on author's own elaboration employing data obtained from World Bank Global Financial Development Database, 2016

(Schmukler, 2004: 1). Financial globalization has led to the increase in capital flows across borders, interrelation among financial markets, emergence of foreign financial firms, SE activities taking place abroad, as well as a cross listing of firms on international exchanges through depositary receipts, increase in use of financial services provided by international intermediaries by local market

Tab. 6.4: 5-Year Averages and Average of Stock Market Return Rate (%) over the Period from 2000 to 2014*. Based on author's own calculation employing data obtained from World Bank Global Financial Development Database, 2016

Regions/Countries	2000–2004	2005–2009	2010–2014	2000–2014
Latin America	**24**	**22**	**33**	**26**
ARG	24	10	44	26
BRA	19	20	1	13
CHL	11	16	6	11
COL	53	29	8	26
MEX	16	22	11	17
PER	17	45	8	23
VEN	47	13	154	71
Asia	**11**	**15**	**17**	**14**
BGD			17	17
CHN	3	28	-4	9
IND	8	22	13	15
IDN	11	22	21	18
MYS	6	6	11	8
PAK	41	15	32	29
PHL	-4	12	23	10
THA	12	-2	21	10
Europe	**36**	**12**	**10**	**19**
BGR	57	7	10	22
HUN	14	11	4	9
POL	7	6	5	6
ROM	50	12	15	26
RUS	47	19	8	25
TUR	41	16	17	25
UKR		-38	11	3
Africa				
ZAF	12	19	16	16

*The time period differs for some countries based on data availability. The values are rounded to the nearest integers.

participants and concentration of capital market activities (measured by liquidity and market capitalization) in only some financial centers which are located in Frankfurt, New York, London, and Tokyo (Sassen, 1999; Schmukler, 2004; de la Torre and Schmukler, 2007). Therefore, in addition to globalization, market

Tab. 6.5: Bond Market Capitalization as a Ratio to GDP (%) Between 2000 and 2014* on Average. Based on author's own calculation employing the data obtained from World Bank Financial Structure and Development Dataset, 2016

Regions/Countries	Private Bond Market Capitalization ratio to GDP (%)	Public Bond Market Capitalization ratio to GDP (%)
Latin America	**15**	**21**
ARG	6	18
BRA	21	55
CHL	37	10
COL	0	23
MEX	14	19
PER	10	4
VEN		
Asia	**19**	**24**
BGD		
CHN	24	15
IND	2	10
IDN	4	15
MYS	51	38
PAK		34
PHL	1	32
THA	33	23
Europe	**4**	**27**
BGR		
HUN	11	42
POL	1	32
ROM		
RUS	5	4
TUR	1	30
UKR		
Africa		
ZAF	17	31

*The time period differs for some countries based on data availability. The values are rounded to the nearest integers.

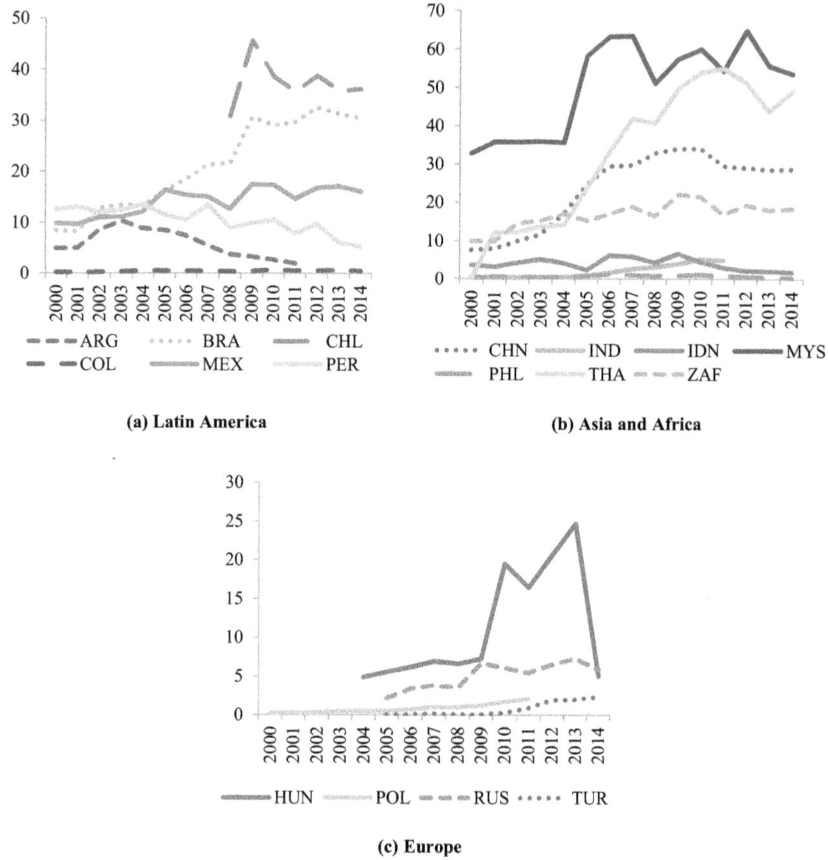

Fig. 6.5: Private Bond Market Capitalization/GDP (%). Based on author's own elaboration employing the data obtained from World Bank Financial Structure and Development Dataset, 2016

integration allows firms to gain access to local and international markets by offering different funding options at different maturities and amounts denominated in different currencies (The World Bank, 2015). But, capital flows make countries to be more vulnerable to external shocks. Sudden capital outflows affect not only the countries' markets, but also the global capital markets by contagion. As consequences of financial globalization, Schmukler (2004) and de la Torre and Schmukler (2007) discuss four main issues. Firstly, migration of equity and

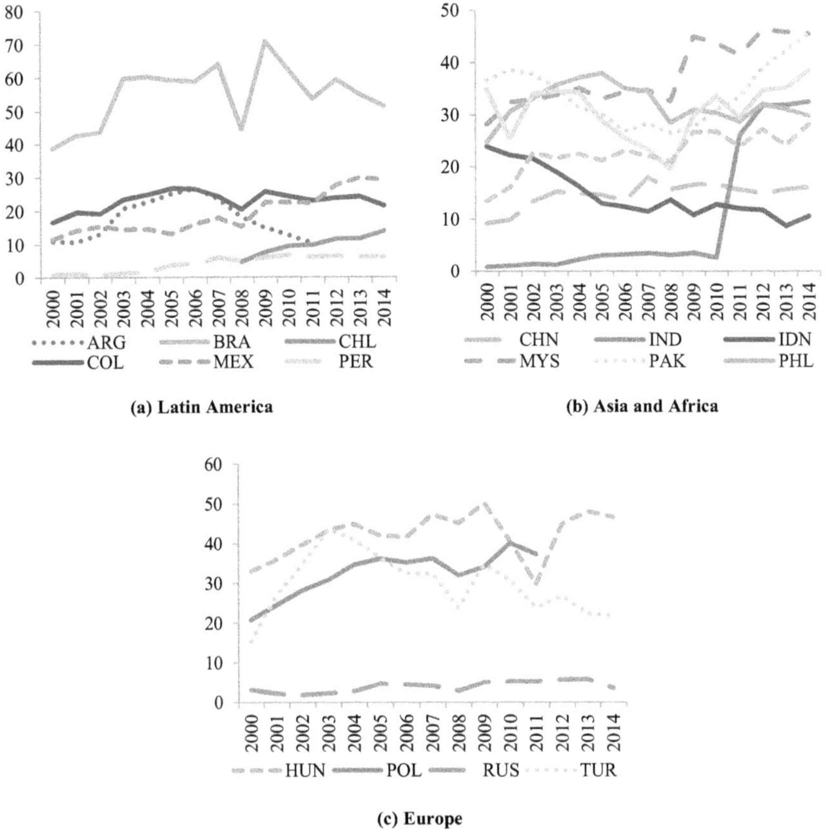

Fig. 6.6: Public Bond Market Capitalization/GDP (%). Based on author's own elaboration employing the data obtained from World Bank Financial Structure and Development Dataset, 2016

bond issuance and trading activities of firms and governments to international markets results in a liquidity decrease on local markets and affects the ability of the firms on the local markets to raise new equity capital, adversely. Secondly, the appeal of internationalized firms causes trade diversion on the domestic market. Thirdly, in contrast, cross listings allow domestic markets to be more integrated by sending positive signals to investors, thus increasing liquidity and trading. Lastly, because of internationalization, firms can access funds with longer maturities at lower costs, also, transparency and monitoring are improved on the local capital markets while information costs decrease. The shares of foreign

Tab. 6.6: Averages of Net Portfolio Equity (PE) Inflows (As a Share of GDP, Basis Point), Net Foreign Direct Investment (FDI) Inflows (% of GDP) and International Debt Issues to GDP (%) over 2000–2014*. Based on author's own calculation using the data obtained from World Bank World Development Indicators, 2016 and World Bank Financial Structure and Development Dataset, 2016

Regions/Countries	Net PE Inflows	Net FDI Inflows	International Debt Issues
Latin America	**25**	**3**	**14**
ARG	-4	2	28
BRA	69	3	12
CHL	65	7	9
COL	27	4	10
MEX	7	3	10
PER	11	4	11
VEN	-3	1	15
Asia	**37**	**2**	**9**
BGD	5	1	
CHN	49	4	2
IND	94	2	
IDN	23	1	5
MYS	2	3	18
PAK	18	1	1
PHL	37	1	23
THA	70	3	5
Europe	**16**	**5**	**12**
BGR	10	10	14
HUN	-8	10	23
POL	28	3	11
ROM	16	4	4
RUS	6	2	11
TUR	35	2	8
UKR	22	4	10
Africa			
ZAF	130	2	12

*The time period differs for some countries based on data availability. The values are rounded to the nearest integers.

investors in the total market capitalization in EMEs are high for 2012 (ICSA Emerging Markets Committee, 2015).

The following measures are analyzed to understand the effects of globalization on EMEs: portfolio equity net inflows, FDI inflows, and international debt issuance.

Sudden capital outflows affect the countries adversely, especially in times of crises. Therefore, the analysis of portfolio equity net inflows is important. Portfolio equity net inflows are negative on the average for Argentina, Venezuela, and Hungary (see Tab. 6.6). Except for China, other countries have also experienced periods associated with portfolio equity net outflows. (See Fig. 6.7). During the 2008 crisis, net portfolio equity inflows to Malaysia and Thailand declined sharply to negative values (Fig. 6.7). Similar situations were also experienced by Latin American countries (Argentina, Brazil, Colombia and Mexico), other Asian countries (Pakistan and Philippines), European countries (Bulgaria, Hungary and Russia), and South Africa. However, the decline in net portfolio equity inflows for these countries was lower than for Malaysia and Thailand.

The analysis of FDI inflows shows that Hungary recorded the highest levels of net FDI on the average from 2000 to 2014 as shown in Tab. 6.6. Fig. 6.8 shows the evolution of FDI net inflows as a ratio of GDP from 2000 to 2014. One can see that the FDI inflows were not stable and fluctuated over the period. Especially after the 2008 global financial crisis, there was a significant drop in the level of FDI inflows with a one-year period lag in many of the countries. Over the period, except for 2001, the greatest FDI inflow was to Europe and Latin America, and therefore there was an uneven inflow of foreign capital into the regions, i.e., segmentation across regions. The country level comparisons show that Hungary and Bulgaria, on the average, attracted FDI inflows more than any other EMEs from 2000 to 2014.

Another measure showing financial integration is international bond issuance. The highest values for international debt issues to GDP are recorded by Argentina in Latin America, Philippines in Asia, and Hungary in Europe, on the average over the period given in Tab. 6.6. Fig. 6.9 shows that a decreasing trend for international debt issues was affected adversely by the crisis in 2008 in Brazil, Colombia, Mexico, Venezuela, China, Poland, Romania, Russia, and Ukraine. For other countries, there is not clear evidence of the impact of the 2008 global financial crisis on international debt issues.

The comparison of outstanding international private and public debt securities relative to GDP between the countries show that Malaysia has the highest international private debt securities while Argentina has the highest level of international public debt securities (Tab. 6.1). The outstanding international debt

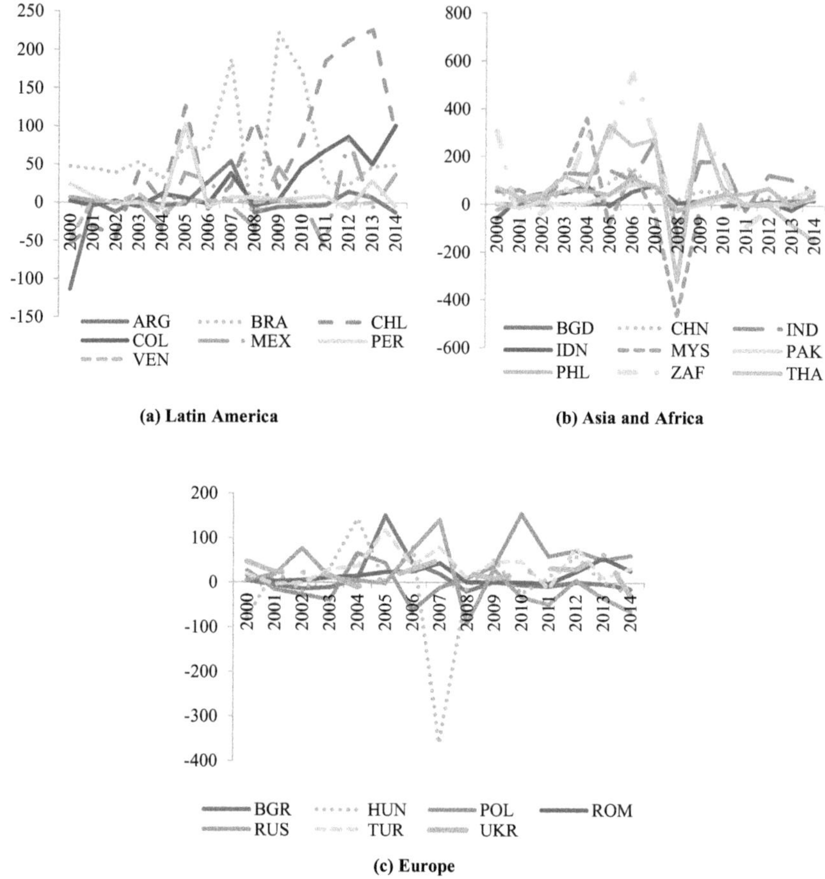

Fig. 6.7: Portfolio Equity Net Inflows (as a Share of GDP, Basis Point) in EMEs. Based on author's own elaboration employing data obtained from World Bank World Development Indicators, 2016

exceeds the outstanding domestic debt for private debt securities in Colombia, Philippines, Russia, Poland, and Turkey and for public debt securities in Russia, Peru, and Argentina.

In conclusion, by globalization, the capital markets of the countries have become more vulnerable to external shocks. The analysis for the period under investigation shows the consequences of the 2008 crisis on international capital

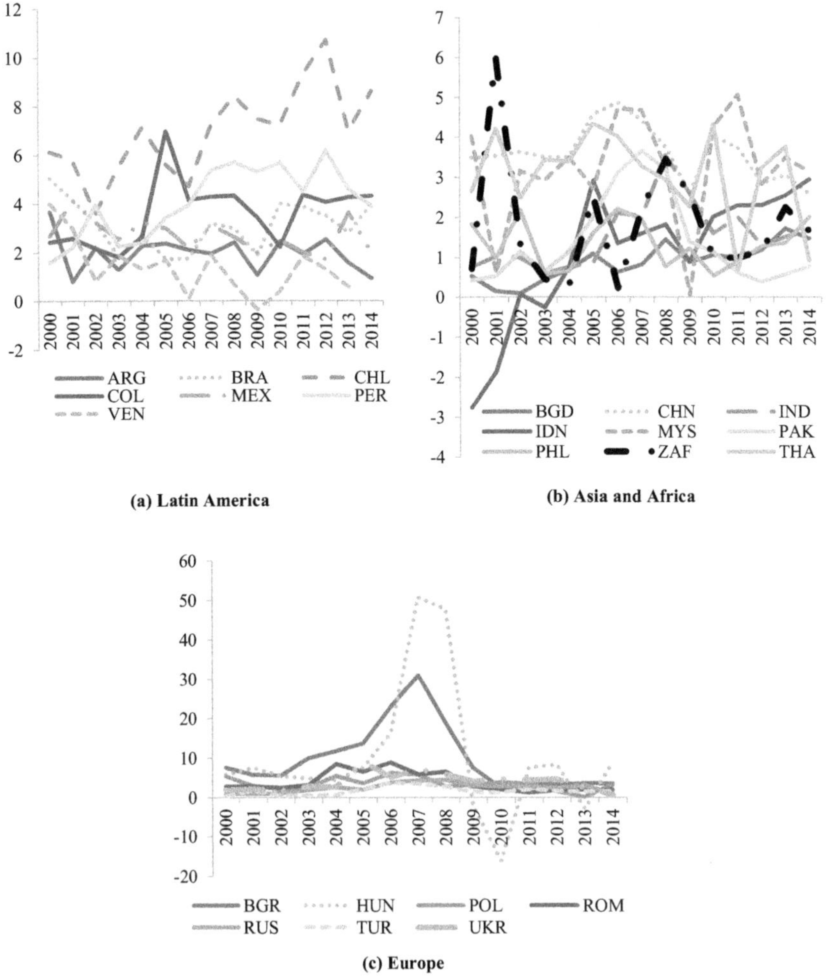

Fig. 6.8: Foreign Direct Investment Net Inflows (% of GDP) in EMEs. Based on author's own elaboration employing the data obtained from World Bank World Development Indicators, 2016

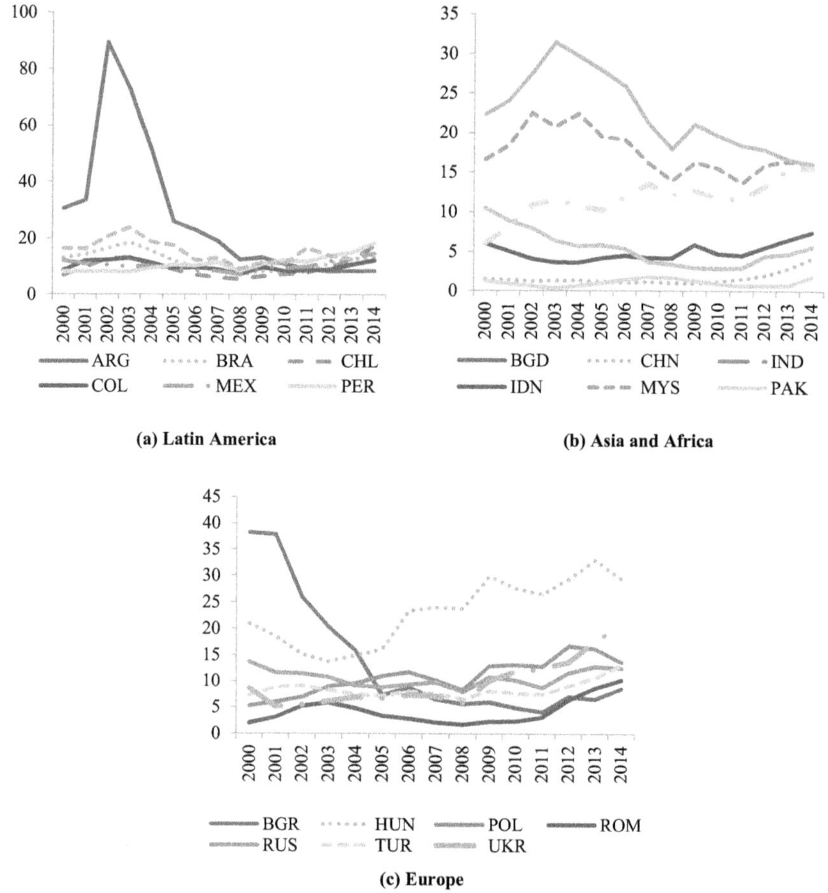

Fig. 6.9: International Debt Issues to GDP (%) in EMEs. Based on author's own elaboration based on the data obtained from World Bank Financial Structure and Development Dataset, 2016

flows, such as sudden portfolio equity outflows, decline in FDI inflows and international debt issuance. Therefore, the development of domestic capital markets and broadening investor bases are important for the mitigation of the adverse effects of international capital flows.

6.3 General Issues and Problems

As the countries and capital markets develop, bank-based financing shifts to market-based financing. Fig. 6.10 illustrates the progression of domestic credit to the private sector by banks in EMEs. Domestic credits by banks to the private sector seem to be decreasing in Venezuela, Pakistan, Bulgaria, Ukraine, Hungary, and Romania. This may signal a shift from financing based on banks to financing based on markets or may be the result of the severe effects of the 2008 global financial crisis on EMEs. In some countries, such as, Malaysia, China, and Thailand, although there was a decline, after 2008, bank credits to the private sector began to increase which was a sign that the financial markets recovered after the global financial crisis.

Some important problems encountered in the majority of EMEs are SMV, bank dominance (as shown in Tab. 6.2), stock market concentration, segmentation, illiquidity, and short-termism. Except for Chile, Bangladesh, Malaysia, and South Africa, EMEs had higher SMVs than the average for high-income countries[3] (with a SMV value calculated as 21[4] from 2000 to 2014) and the average of the world (with a SMV value calculated as 20 (see Footnote 4) from 2000 to 2014). In EMEs, there is speculation in stock markets which increases the SMV and thus decreases market integrity (ICSA Emerging Markets Committee, 2015). Banks are the main actors offering long-term financing. Only a small number of firms can access long-term financing through issuances of equities and bonds (see Tab. 6.2). However, a developed banking system is also important as during crises, banks and capital markets can complement each other. The top ten companies which dominate the stock market account for on the average 53 % and 54 %[5] of the value traded and market capitalization for the period 2000–2014. Some EMEs, especially in Latin America and Europe, such as Venezuela, Ukraine, and Romania, suffered from low stock market liquidity (see stock market total value traded, % of GDP, in Tab. 6.1). Moreover, when compared to high-income countries, the liquidity was very low in all EMEs. The highest average stock market total value traded (% of GDP), calculated as 68 (see Footnote 5), was still very low when compared to the high-income countries'

3 Author employs High income definition of World Bank.

4 This average value is calculated by the author employing the data on SMV obtained from World Bank Global Financial Development Database, 2016. SMV is defined to be the median value of one-year daily stock market index volatility of each country.

5 This average value is calculated by the author employing the data obtained from World Bank Global Financial Development Database, 2016.

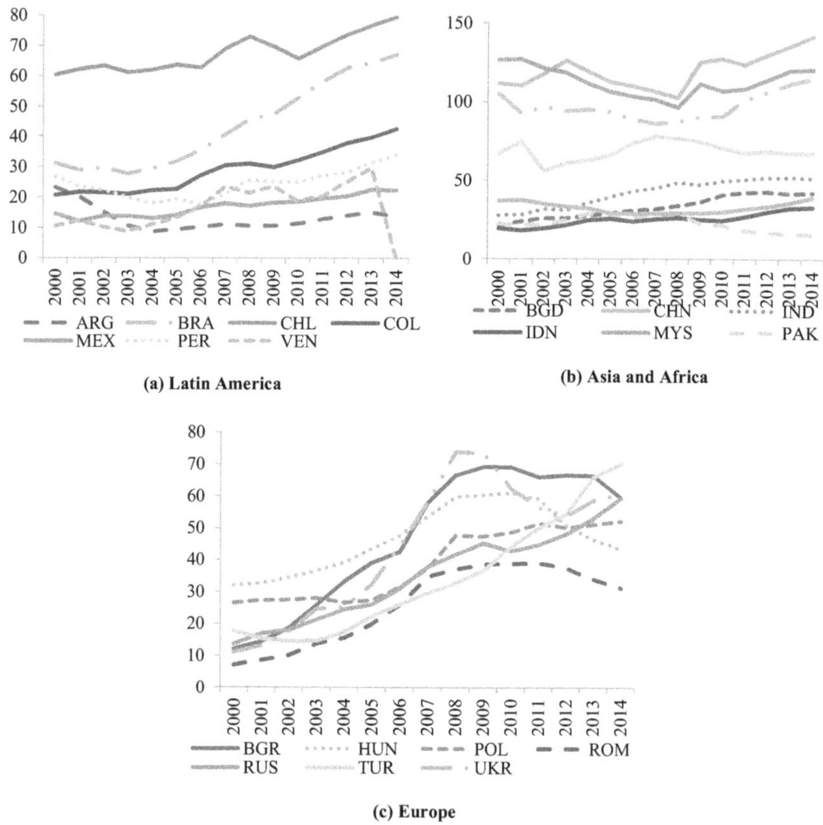

Fig. 6.10: Domestic Bank Credit to Private Sector (% of GDP). Based on author's own elaboration employing the data obtained from World Bank World Development Indicators, 2016

average value of 129 (see Footnote 5) for the same period. Among other factors, as mentioned by de la Torre and Schmukler (2007), and according to a report prepared by OICU-IOSCO (2007), the low level of liquidity may result from the migration of trading and issuance of securities abroad and can signal a tendency for the concentration in the supply and demand side of the stock markets. For example, in Latin American countries, only a few companies can satisfy the

Tab. 6.7: Outstanding Debt Securities to GDP Between 2000 and 2014* on Average. Based on author's own calculation employing the data obtained from World Bank Global Financial Development Database, 2016

	Outstanding domestic debt securities/GDP (%)		Outstanding international debt securities/GDP (%)	
	Private	**Public**	**Private**	**Public**
EMEs	14	-26	-6	6
High-Income Countries	-28	-31	-18	6

*The values are rounded to the nearest integers.

minimum size thresholds and issue sufficient amounts of securities to achieve significant liquidity, and the few institutional investors invest in government securities following buy and hold investment strategies.

In most EMEs, public sector debt issuance and trading dominates the debt market. In fact, deeper public bond markets are a prerequisite for the development of corporate bond markets; however, the crowding out effect of the public bond market should be considered (The World Bank, 2015). Private bond markets in Brazil, Mexico, Malaysia, Thailand, India, South Africa, Poland, Turkey, and Russia showed fast growth (See Fig. 6.5). When compared to high-income countries, emerging countries' debt securities markets are still underdeveloped (See Tab. 6.7). The development of domestic bond markets is essential because they can play a "spare tire" role during the crises (Chan et al., 2012).

Another important issue is the extending maturity structure of finance, i.e., offering long-term financing which is important for faster growth, wealth and prosperity, as well as stability since long-term financing is essential for infrastructure investments, firms' capital investments and households' investments for their life cycle challenges and reduce rollover and interest rate risks (The World Bank, 2015). Moreover, in the bond market, by short-term borrowing, countries became more open to capital outflows and liquidity crises (de la Torre and Schmukler, 2007; The World Bank, 2000). However, short-termism is an important problem in most EMEs.

Firms gain access to long-term finance by issuing equities, bonds and through syndicated loans on both domestic and international markets. Bonds and syndicated loans are used for different purposes. Whereas bonds are suitable for more advanced stages in a project's financing, syndicated loans are more suitable to finance the initial phases of projects and are used mainly for infrastructure projects (The World Bank, 2015). Comparison of the average corporate bond maturity between EMEs and high-income countries shows that in Argentina, European and Asian countries, except for India and Malaysia, the average corporate bond maturity is shorter, on the average, for the period under consideration (See Tab. 6.8). Macroeconomic instability, institutional weaknesses, and market failures may prevent extending the maturity structure of finance.

The average corporate bond maturity decreased in 2008 in high-income countries, Europe, Asia, and Latin America due to the financial crisis indicating an increase in shorter-term bonds, but South Africa experienced a decrease in shorter-term bonds for the same year (Fig. 6.11).

The 2008 crisis affected the average maturity of syndicated loans in high-income countries and some EMEs in Europe and Asia (for example, Bulgaria, Hungary, Ukraine, and Pakistan) after one year following the crisis (Fig. 6.12). South Africa and Malaysia experienced this adverse effect one period earlier. On the other hand, in Russia, there was no significant negative impact of the 2008 crisis on the maturity of syndicated loans.

In Malaysia, Thailand, and Chile, corporate bond issuance was higher than high-income countries. The corporate bond issuance showed an increasing trend after 2008 in Asia, Europe, and Latin America (see Fig. 6.13).

Most syndicated loans come from international markets. Chile was the only country which had a higher syndicated loan issuance volume when compared to high-income countries. However, in all the regions, syndicated loan issuance fell sharply after 2008 (Fig. 6.14).

Argentina, Russia, Ukraine, and South Africa issued syndicated loans with shorter average maturity when compared to high-income countries. Since international markets may offer longer-term financing to domestic firms and governments, most EMEs show a high dependency on the international market for their long-term financing which makes EMEs more open to external shocks as a result of exchange rate risk caused by the foreign currency denominated debt issuance. Therefore, the 2008 global financial crisis affected the firms in the EMEs which received financing through the international financial markets when compared to firms in the high-income countries (The World Bank, 2015). For some countries, because of a weak currency problem, dollarization and short-termism become inevitable on their debt markets. Governments and firms were faced with a domestic and international "original sin" phenomenon which means the inability of governments and firms to obtain longer-term financing in local currency on the domestic market and international financing in local currency abroad. To mitigate the vulnerability to external shocks, and to cope with currency and maturity mismatches, some countries issued local currency-denominated bonds on the international markets with long maturities (Burger

Tab. 6.8: Average Maturity (Years) and Issuance Volume to GDP (%) for Corporate Bond and Syndicated Loans over 2000–2014*. Based on author's own calculation employing the data obtained from World Bank Global Financial Development Database, 2016

Regions/ Countries	Corporate bond average maturity	Corporate bond issuance volume to GDP (%)	International private debt securities outstanding/ GDP (%)	Syndicated loan average maturity	Syndicated loan issuance volume to GDP (%)
Latin America	**10**	**1**	**4**	**6**	**1**
ARG	6	0	3	4	1
BRA	8	1	7	6	1
CHL	13	2	7	7	4
COL	9	1	2	5	1
MEX	11	2	5	5	2
PER	11	1	3	6	1
VEN	11	1	4	7	1
Asia	**7**	**1**	**5**	**7**	**1**
BGD	5	0		7	0
CHN	8	2	1	7	1
IND	8	1		8	2
IDN	7	1	3	6	1
MYS	8	4	15	6	3
PAK	5	0	0	6	0
PHL	7	1	8	6	2
THA	6	2	4	8	2
Europe	**5**	**1**	**4**	**6**	**2**
BGR	5	1	2	7	2
HUN	6	0	9	7	2
POL	6	0	2	6	2
ROM	3	0	1	5	1
RUS	6	2	6	5	2
TUR	6	0	2	7	1
UKR	4	1	4	3	1
Africa					
ZAF	9	1	8	5	2
High income	**8**	**2**	**18**	**5**	**4**

* The time period differs for some countries based on data availability. The values are rounded to the nearest integers.

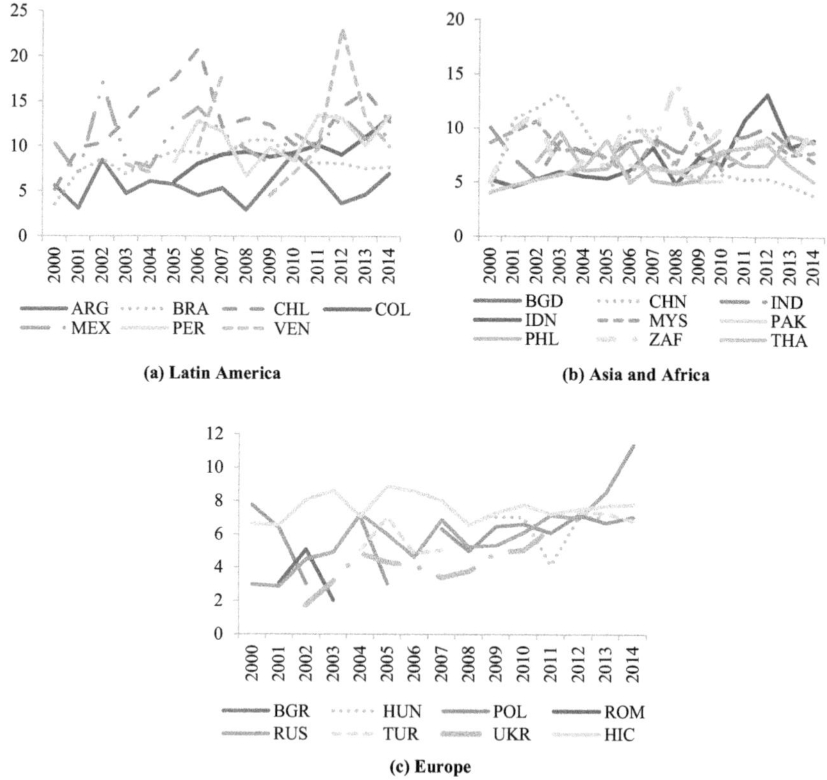

Fig. 6.11: Corporate Bond Average Maturity (Years). Based on author's own elaboration employing the data obtained from World Bank Global Financial Development Database, 2016

and Warnock, 2006). Dollarization could be reversed by implementing macroeconomic tools (for example, imposing flexible exchange rate regimes and targeting inflation), prudential (such as dollar loans imposing higher capital requirements) and financial policies (CPI-indexed contracts), simultaneously (de la Torre and Schmukler, 2004; de la Torre and Schmukler, 2007).

In addition, the development of a local currency bond market was important for the alleviation of banking stress on the real economy during the economic and financial crisis (The World Bank, 2015). Low inflation and implementing flexible exchange rate regimes and inflation targeting policies were suggested for the development of debt markets in local currency (de la Torre and Schmukler,

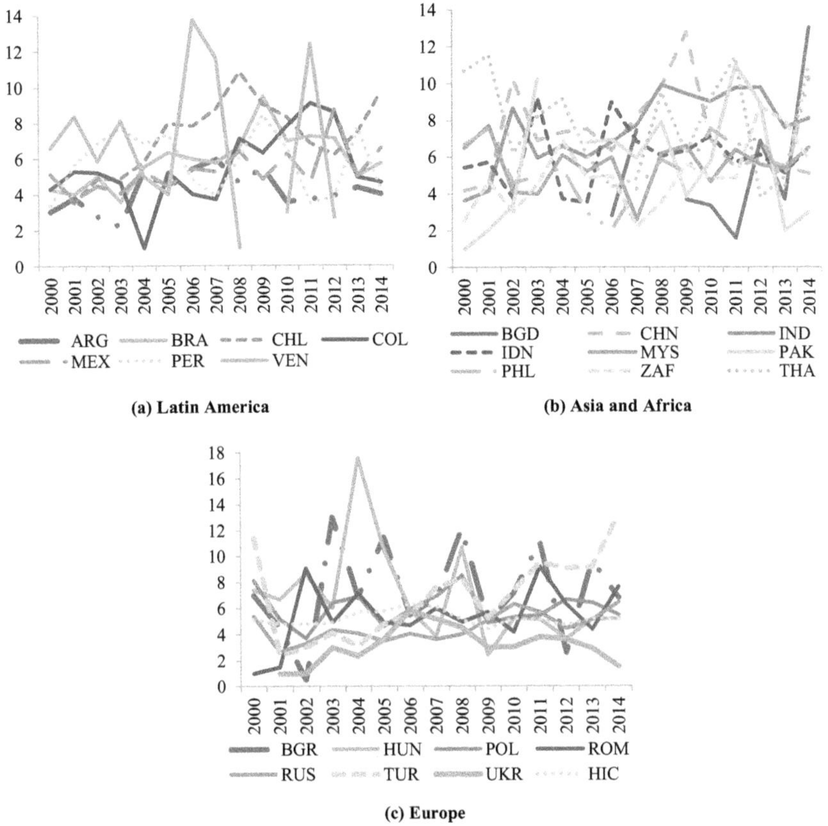

Fig. 6.12: Syndicated Loan Average Maturity (Years). Based on author's own elaboration employing the data obtained from World Bank Global Financial Development Database, 2016

2007). Moreover, public investment companies, state-owned investment funds, private equity funds, and funds given by multinational development banks were other ways to increase long-term financing. Also, Public and Private Partnership was an effective way to increase private investments for infrastructure projects while decreasing the regulatory and political risks (The World Bank, 2015).

In Colombia, Philippines, Russia, Poland, and Turkey, outstanding international private debt securities exceeds domestic private debt securities and a similar situation was seen for public debt securities in Russia, Peru, and Argentina showing the evidence of debt issuers migration to international markets (see Tab. 6.1).

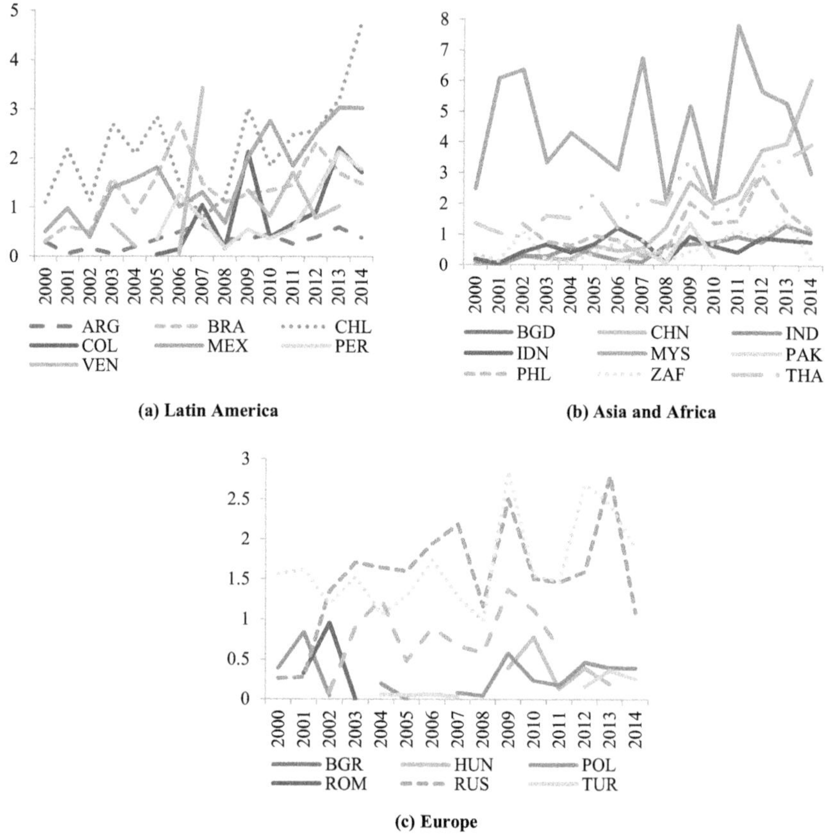

Fig. 6.13: Corporate Bond Issuance Volume to GDP (%). Based on author's own elaboration employing the data obtained from World Bank Global Financial Development Database, 2016

This result may be due to the fact that international markets allow firms to issue bonds at longer maturities (The World Bank, 2015).

On the demand side, the role of institutional investors is important, especially for the promotion of long-term finance, in the capital markets (The World Bank, 2015) and broadening the investor base. The investors in Latin America create a stable demand for fixed income securities (de la Torre and Schmukler, 2007; Heng et al., 2016). Figs. 6.15, 6.16, and 6.17 show the increasing participation of

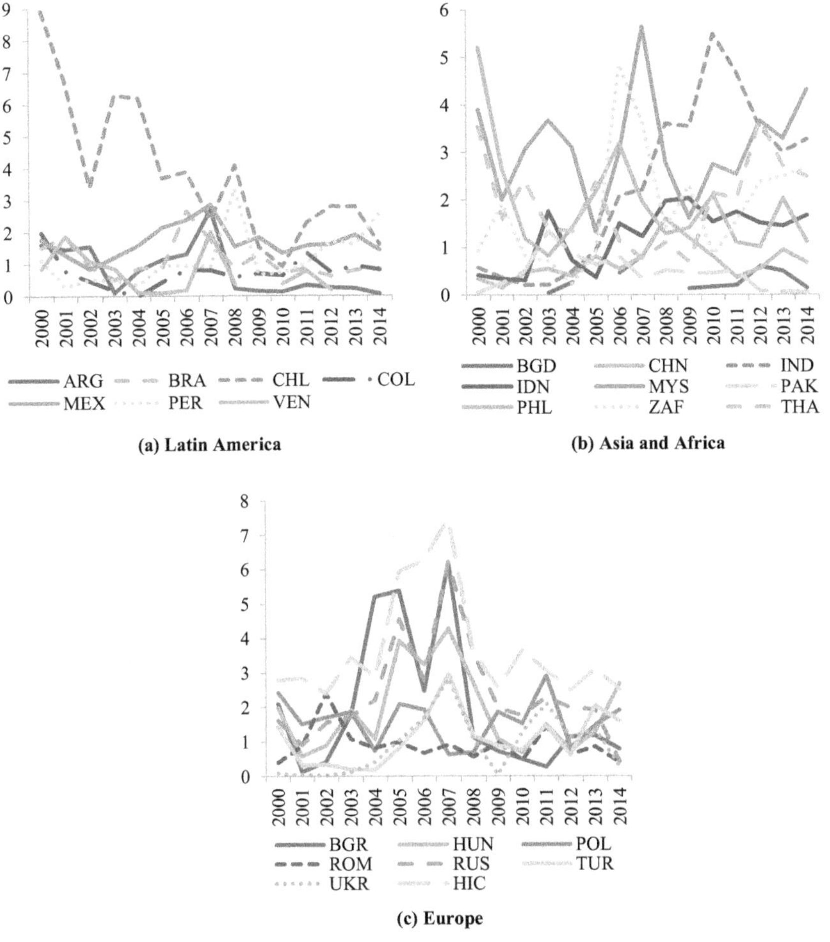

Fig. 6.14: Syndicated Loan Issuance Volume to GDP (%). Based on author's own elaboration employing the data obtained from World Bank Global Financial Development Database, 2016

institutional investors in EMEs. As seen from Tab. 6.9, institutional investors in South Africa participate most actively in capital markets.

Among Latin American, Asian, and European countries, Chile, Malaysia, Hungary, and Poland have a higher ratio of institutional investors' assets to GDP. However, as pointed out by de la Torre and Schmukler (2007) and Heng et al.

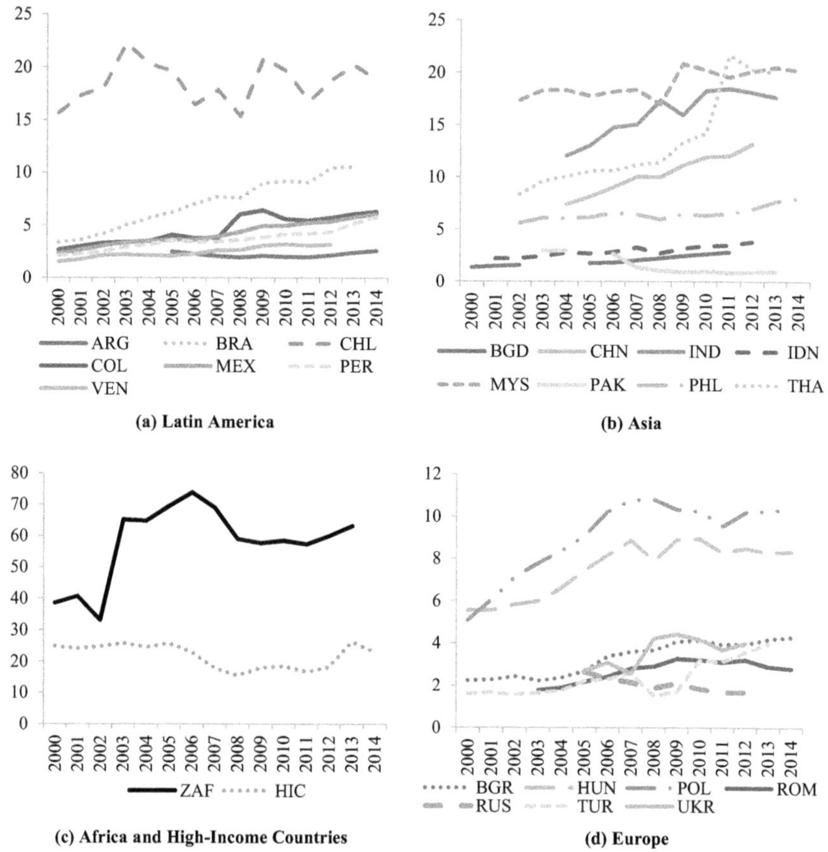

Fig. 6.15: Insurance Fund Assets as a Percentage of GDP. Based on author's own elaboration employing the data obtained from World Bank Global Financial Development Database, 2016

(2016), regulations in some countries forced these investors to concentrate their investments in the highest rated securities and government papers; on the other hand, pension reforms led to the growth of total investments in pension funds and therefore, improve the capital market performance of EMEs by extending the institutional investor base.

Another important issue is the difficulty for SMEs to access financing sources in these markets, so, SMEs heavily rely on bank loans to finance their investments. This creates segmentation on the local and the international capital

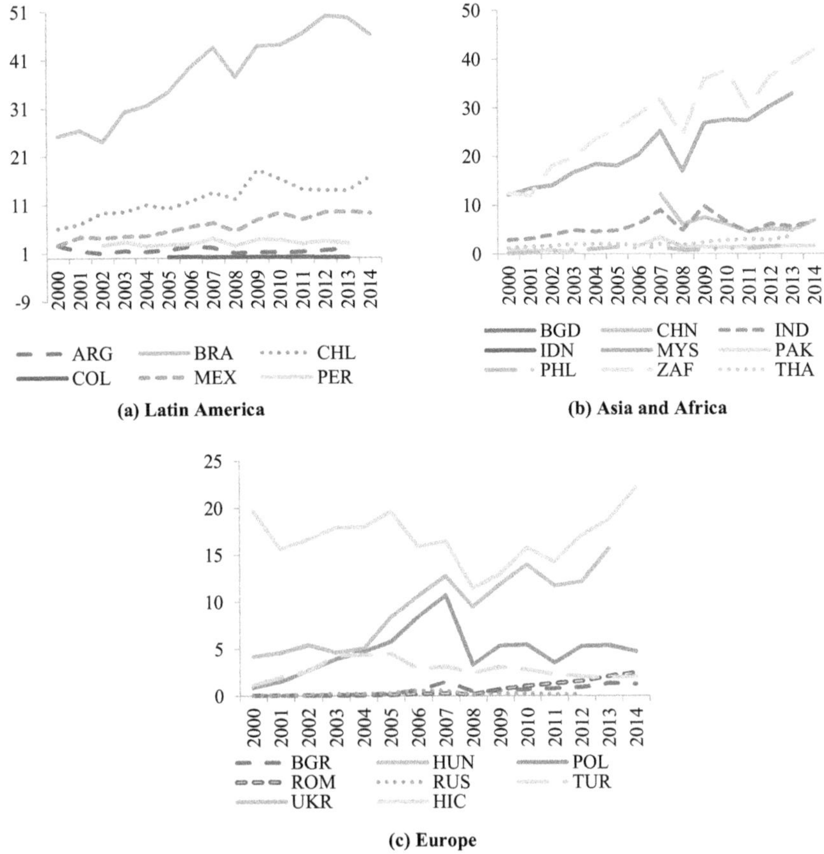

Fig. 6.16: Mutual Fund Assets as a Percentage of GDP. Based on author's own elaboration employing the data obtained from World Bank Global Financial Development Database, 2016

markets. Illiquidity and regulations along with structural factors restricting the institutional investors in their portfolio allocations and risk diversification causes segmentation (de la Torre and Schmukler, 2007; Eiteman, Stonehill and Moffett, 2016). The 2008 global crisis first affected SMEs through deleveraging in developed countries, but, by 2011, larger firms and smaller firms in developing countries which used long-term debts also experienced the adverse impact of the crisis (The World Bank, 2015). After the global financial crisis, most EMEs made some regulations for their capital market development, to increase the

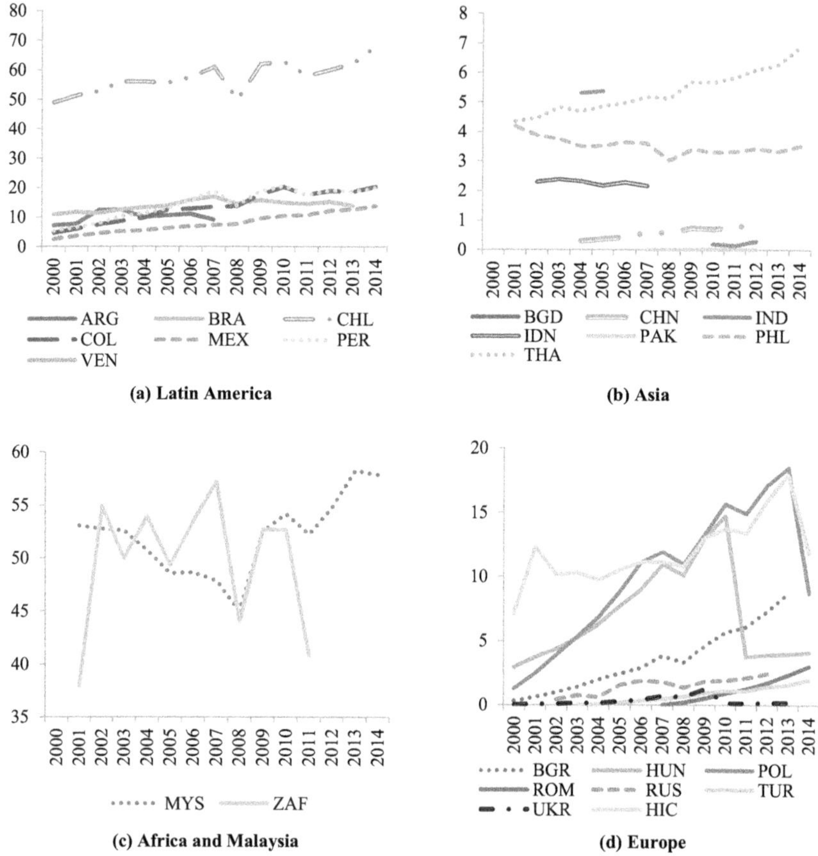

Fig. 6.17: Pension Fund Assets as a Percentage of GDP. Based on author's own elaboration employing the data obtained from World Bank Global Financial Development Database, 2016

capital availability for SMEs, start-ups, and ventures by ensuring their listing on SEs. For example, in Turkey, an emerging companies market was set up in 2010 to fulfill the financing requirements of those SMEs which could not satisfy the stock market listing criteria. Another example was the opening of the SME platform by the Bombay SE Market in India (ICSA Emerging Markets Committee, 2015). Also, government-backed credit guarantee mechanism increased lending to SMEs.

Tab. 6.9: Insurance Company, Mutual Fund and Pension Fund Assets to GDP (%) over 2000–2014*. Based on author's own calculation employing the data obtained from World Bank Global Financial Development Database, 2016

Regions/Countries	Insurance company assets/GDP (%)	Mutual fund assets/GDP (%)	Pension fund assets/GDP (%)
Latin America	**6**	**10**	**20**
ARG	2	2	10
BRA	7	38	14
CHL	19	12	57
COL	5	0	14
MEX	4	7	8
PER	4	3	14
VEN	2		
Asia	**9**	**5**	**9**
BGD	2	0	
CHN	10	7	1
IND	16	6	2
IDN	3	5	2
MYS	19	21	52
PAK	2	1	0
PHL	7	1	4
THA	13	2	5
Europe	**4**	**3**	**3**
BGR	3	1	4
HUN	8	9	7
POL	9	5	10
ROM	3	1	1
RUS	2	0	2
TUR	2	3	1
UKR	4		0
Africa			
ZAF	58	28	50
High income	**22**	**17**	**12**

* The time period differs for some countries based on data availability. The values are rounded to the nearest integers.

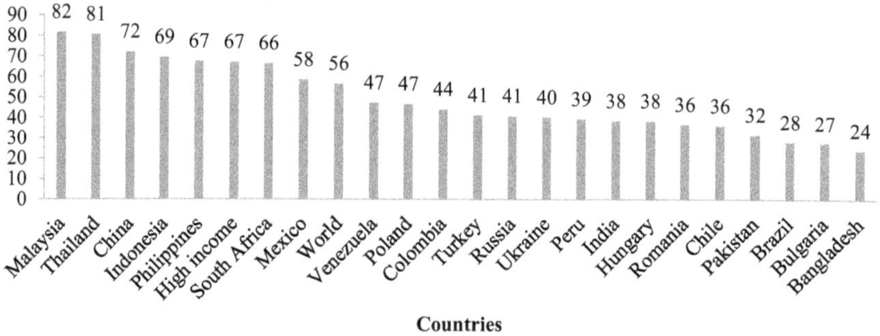

Fig. 6.18: Any Saved Money in the Past Year (% Above Age 15), 2014. Based on author's own elaboration employing the data obtained from World Bank Global Financial Inclusion Database, 2016

A low saving rate can be an obstacle for the development of capital markets. For example, Turkey suffered a low level of development on financial markets due to the low level of the saving rate (ICSA Emerging Markets Committee, 2015). Malaysia has the highest saving rate at 82 %, followed by Thailand, China, Indonesia, and Philippines (Fig. 6.18). These countries' saving rates are above the average of high-income countries.

Other obstacles include lack of financial literacy and investor education in EMEs (ICSA Emerging Markets Committee, 2015).

Lastly, as countries become more developed, one expects that their capital markets also deepen and that their financial markets become more market-based. For high-income countries,[6] earlier analyses show that their capital markets on average are more developed when compared to the EMEs under analysis due to macroeconomic stability (low inflation, low fiscal deficits) and well-developed legal and institutional structures and financial infrastructures. However, among EMEs, although Hungary has the highest level of average GDP per capita from 2000 to 2014, there are other countries with more developed capital markets but lower GDP per capita (Fig. 6.19). Therefore, based on the analyses performed, one cannot see a strong relationship between economic and capital market development. However, this needs further and advanced analysis.

6 See footnote 2.

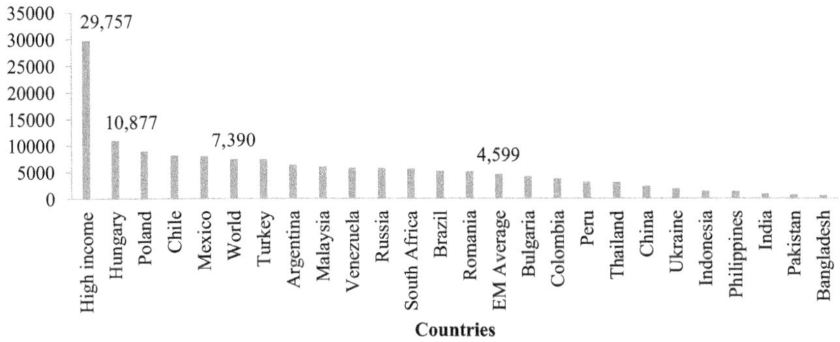

Fig. 6.19: Average GDP per Capita (Constant 2005 USD) over the Period Between 2000 and 2014. Based on author's own elaboration employing the data obtained from World Bank World Development Indicators, 2016

6.4 Conclusion

In this chapter, the capital markets of EMEs were analyzed using time series data on different measures from 2000 to 2014. Overall, the analysis in Section 2 shows that the stock markets in South Africa, Malaysia, and Chile are more developed than other countries. Bond market development is higher in Chile, Malaysia, and Thailand for private bonds and in Brazil, Hungary, and Malaysia for public bonds. Among the countries under investigation, South Africa, Hungary, and Argentina, on the average, seem to have benefited more from globalization and internationalization of capital markets since these countries have experienced higher levels of portfolio equity inflows, FDI inflows, and international debt issuance.

Development of domestic capital markets, i.e., deep and liquid capital markets, depends on macroeconomic stability, institutional, supervisory, a regulatory, and legal framework including collateral, improvement in the disclosure and accounting standards and corporate governance, regulations for insider trading, protection for creditors and minority investors, contract enforcement and promoting local institutional investors (for example, pension funds), and financial infrastructures. To overcome market failures, governments should support information sharing mechanisms, such as credit bureaus. Financial integration also helps to develop capital markets, but with caution, as the markets can become more volatile and vulnerable to international shocks. Other ways of providing financing for domestic firms can be through engaging into regional exchanges and foreign listings.

As policy suggestions, new financial products should be developed, and countries should continue the liberalization of their financial markets with an appropriate level of regulation differing for each country's individual needs and find ways to enhance the efficiency and development of their markets. Therefore, reforms should focus on improving the development of markets and institutional investors, financial literacy, contract enforcement, consumer protection, corporate governance, and information and risk sharing (The World Bank, 2015). Also, the banking system and capital market developments should complement each other.

The limitations of the study are as follows. The analyses did not cover the issues related to the derivatives markets. Because these markets have shown some evidence of strong growth only since 2010, but well development of these markets are important for hedging, i.e., providing insurance for currency and maturity mismatches and for liquidity increase. Other issues which were not discussed are structured finance transactions and repo markets used for liquidity management because the main aim of this chapter was to gain an overall insight into the development of capital markets. As a future study, all these markets and transactions can be analyzed separately.

References

Bekaert, G., Harvey, C. R., & Lundblad, C. T. (2003). Equity Market Liberalization In Emerging Markets. *The Journal of Financial Research*, XXVI (3), 275–299.

Burger, J. D., & Warnock, F. E. (2006). Local Currency Bond Markets. *IMF Staff Papers*, 53 (Special Issue), 133–146. Retrieved from http://www.imf.org/external/ pubs/ft/staffp/2006/03/pdf/burger.pdf, Last Accessed: 28/02/2017.

Case, K. E., & Fair, R. C. (1999). *Principles of Economics*. Upper Saddle River, NJ: Prentice Hall.

Chan, E., Chui, M., Packer, F., & Remolona, E. (2012). Local Currency Bond Markets and the Asian Bond Fund 2 Initiative. *BIS Papers* 63, Bank of International Settlements, Basel.

de la Torre, A., & Schmukler, S. L. (2004). Coping with Risks Through Mismatches: Domestic and International Financial Contracts for Emerging Economies. *International Finance*, 7 (3), 349–90.

de la Torre, A., & Schmukler, S. L. (2007). *Emerging Capital Markets and Globalization the Latin American Experience*. Palo Alto, Calif.: Stanford University Press.

Ehlers, T., & Packer, F. (2013). FX and Derivatives Markets in Emerging Economies and the Internationalization of Their Currencies. *BIS*

Quarterly Review, December 2013. Retrieved from www.bis.org, Last Accessed: 20/02/2017.

Eiteman, D. K., Stonehill, A. I., & Moffett, M. H. (2016). *Multinational Business Finance*. Upper Saddle River, NJ: Prentice Hall Pearson Education, Inc.Heng, D., Ivanova, A., Mariscal, R., Ramakrishnan, U., & Wong, J. C. (2016). Advancing Financial Development in Latin America and the Caribbean. *IMF Working Paper*, WP/16/81, April 2016. Retrieved from https://www.imf.org/external/pubs/ft/wp/2016/wp1681.pdf, Last Accessed: 28/02/2017.

ICSA Emerging Markets Committee. (2015). *Market-Based Financing in Emerging Market Countries*. April 2015, retrieved from http://www.amib.com.mx/images/Study%20on%20EMC%20Market%20Based%20Finance.pdf, Last Accessed: 20/02/2017.

Kawai, M., & Prasad, E. (Eds.). (2013). *New Paradigms for Financial Regulation: Emerging Market Perspectives*. Brookings Institution Press. Retrieved from http://www.jstor.org/stable/10.7864/j.ctt1261n4, Last Accessed: 27/02/2017.

Langridge, K., & Valle, P. (2015). *The Changing Shape of Capital Markets in Emerging Economies*. Retrieved from website of Manulife Asset Management, http://www.manulifeam.com/hk/Research-and-Insights/Market-Views-And-Insights/The-changing-shape-of-capital-markets-in-emerging-economies/, Last Accessed: 20/02/2017.

Murinde, V. (2006). *Capital Markets: Roles And Challenges*. Paper presented at the International Conference on Accelerating Africa's Development Five Years into the Twenty-First Century, Tunis, November 22–24, 2006. Retrieved from http://www.afdb.org/fileadmin/uploads/afdb/Documents/Knowledge/09484315-EN-CAPITAL-MARKETS-ROLES-CHALLENGES-DRAFT1.PDF, Last Accessed: 20/02/2017.

OICU-IOSCO (2007). *Factors Influencing Liquidity in Emerging Markets*. Report of the IOSCO Emerging Markets Committee, December 2007. Retrieved from https://www.iosco.org/library/pubdocs/pdf/IOSCOPD258.pdf, Last Accessed: 28/02/2017.

Sassen, S. (1999). Global Financial Centers. *Foreign Affairs*, 78 (1), 75–87.

Schmukler, S. L. (2004). Benefits and Risks of Financial Globalization: Challenges for Developing Countries. *Federal Reserve Bank of Atlanta Economic Review*, (Second Quarter 2004), 2004–06. Retrieved from http://documents.worldbank.org/curated/en/710321468322735111/Benefits-and-risks-of-financial-globalization-challenges-for-developing-countries, Last Accessed: 22/02/2017.

The World Bank. (2000). *Global Development Finance Analysis and Summary Tables*. Washington, DC: World Bank. Retrieved from http://

siteresources.worldbank.org/INTGDF2000/Resources/CH4--76-95.pdf, Last Accessed: 28/02/2017.

The World Bank. (2015). *Global Financial Development Report 2015/2016: Long-Term Finance*. Washington, DC: World Bank. doi:10.1596/978-1-4648-0472-4.

Sinem Pınar Gürel

7 Total Factor Productivity in EMEs

Abstract: Total factor productivity (TFP) is a key determinant for growth process analyses among countries and a useful instrument to understand how much of the GDP growth comes from growth in labor, how much comes from capital and how much comes from improvements in TFP. This chapter aims to investigate TFP growth in emerging market economies (EMEs) in detail and to make a better understanding for the factors behind the growth process of EMEs. In the past decade, EMEs began to close the income gap with developed economies. Over the last decade, EMEs have benefited from high terms of trade, easy financial conditions, institutional reforms and macroeconomic policies. However, EMEs have recently entered a slowing growth period. Although there are variations among countries, the overall growth rates in the past few years have fallen. While factor accumulation has been the main driver of growth in EMEs in the 1990s, the 2000-2014 period is mainly explained by higher TFP (Tsounta, 2014). The TFP has increased in all regions, but after the Great Recession, global factors played a significant role in the EMEs growth process and the TFP growth rates.

Keywords: Total Factor Productivity, Economic Growth

7.1 Introduction

The TFP in EMEs has shown a decline in the recent years. In 2014, the average TFP growth rate for EMEs showed the lowest performance since the Great Recession. However, EMEs had experienced a remarkable growth over the past decade until the Great Recession. The global financial crisis disrupted the availability of credit, which was important for innovation, slowed down international trade and then effected the productivity via transmission mechanisms (Eichengreen and Shin, 2015). The TFP is a key determinant for sustainable economic growth. Productivity affects the competitive position of an economy, determines a country's ability to compete in the world market, and is a primary source for a high standard of living (Puente et al., 2009). The decline in TFP growth can be explained by several factors. Firstly, the global financial and economic crisis unsettled the world economy. According to Summers (2014), the deceleration in productivity growth predates the financial crises. Some researchers invoked the hypothesis of secular stagnation, suggesting that productivity growth has slowed because of a decline in innovation. Another reason is due to the middle-income trap, where TFP growth slowed down as former low-income countries achieved middle-income status and were no longer able to boost productivity simply by shifting labor from agriculture to manufacturing (Eichengreen and Shin, 2015).

Conceptually, TFP is defined as the portion of growth which cannot be explained by the factors of production, namely capital and labor. It is the growth in 'residual term'. Many factors cause TFP growth, such as institutional changes, trade balances, innovations, spillovers among sectors, political issues, organizational changes and macroeconomic stability. To understand the productivity differences among EMEs, this chapter provides TFP growth rates in EMEs from 2000 to 2014 and compares the dynamics behind the TFP growth rates among countries. In the analysis, Total Economy Database (TED)[1] was used. TED was developed by the Groningen Growth and Development Centre and published every year.

The organization of this chapter is as follows. Section two gives the TFP growth performance in EMEs by emphasizing the sources of TFP growth. This section is followed by a comparison of the countries' TFP growth performance on a regional base, from 2000 to 2014. Section three concludes and discusses policy implications.

7.2 TFP Growth in EMEs

The EMEs experienced high growth rates during the 2000-2014 period (Fig. 7.1). The growth increased by an average of 4.75 %. The underlying drivers of the significant growth rates during this period are the financial and trade integrations which come with the globalization process, favorable external environments (such as increasing liquidity, easy financing conditions and strong external demands) and developments in institutional quality, structural reforms and economic liberalization.

Despite the high overall growth rates in the EMEs, there was a significant growth performance gap among the countries. On regional basis, comparisons showed that Asian and European EMEs have performed high growth rates until the global financial and economic crisis (Fig. 7.2). Among the Asian countries, China, India, and Bangladesh have shown better performances than other Asian EMEs. After the global financial and economic crisis, European countries suffered very low growth rates, especially Bulgaria, Hungary and Romania. On the other hand, Asian EMEs, notably India and Indonesia, showed remarkable growth rates after the global financial and economic crisis. The growth rates for

---

1 https://www.conference-board.org/data/economydatabase/

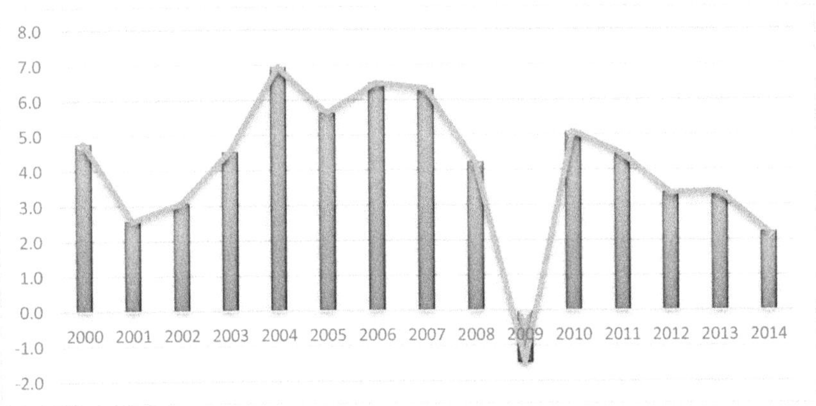

Fig. 7.1: Average GDP Growth Rates in EMEs, 2000–2014. Total Economy Database, 2016

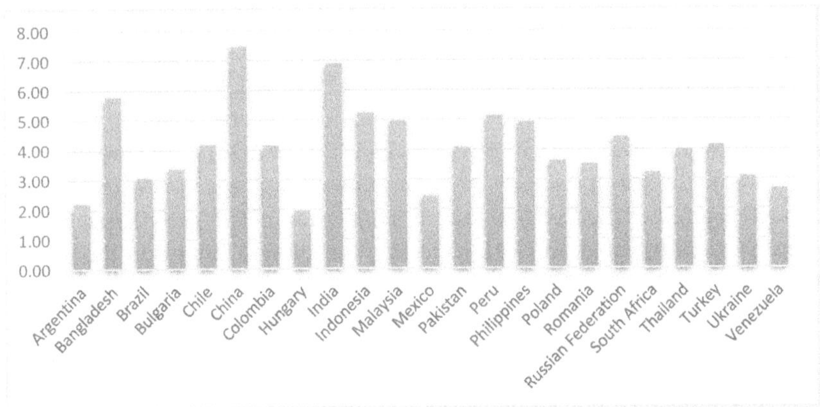

Fig. 7.2: Average GDP Growth Rates Among EMEs, 2000–2014. Total Economy Database, 2016

Latin American EMEs were the lowest. This heterogeneity among the countries and regions is due to the differences in the economic balances among the EMEs.

To understand the dynamics behind the robust growth performances of EMEs, the literature analyses the process in two different perspectives: the supply side perspective (Sosa et al., 2013; Tsounto, 2014) and the demand side perspective

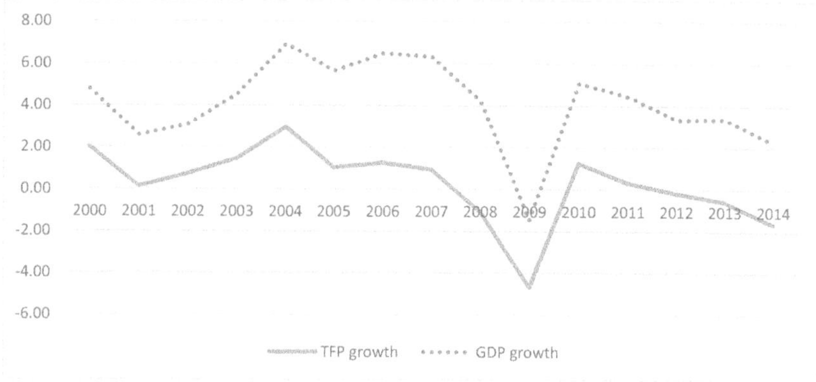

Fig. 7.3: TFP and Real Output Growth of EMEs, 2000–2014. Total Economy Database, 2016

(Cubeddu et al., 2014; Culiuc, 2014). To study from the supply side perspective, researchers used a growth accounting framework that decomposes growth into capital, labor and changes in TFP. High growth rates in 2000–2014 (except during the Great Recession period) are mainly explained by higher TFPs (Fig. 7.3). According to Tsounto (2014), TFP alone explains the 1 percentage point increase in the average growth rate in EMEs between 2000 and 2012. The average TFP growth was stronger in the early 2000s but slowed and began to decrease in the pre-crisis period of the Great Recession. High rates of TFP growth had a spill-over effect among the countries by affecting the living standards of the trading partners and reallocating the resources into more productive areas or industries.

TFP growth is not solely dependent on developments in technology or the quality of factors in production. TFP is also affected by factors such as, investments in education, human capital development, openness of the economy, inflation rates, financial developments, easy access to finance, taxes, research and development, institutional settings and innovations (Berument et al., 2011). Because all these dynamics vary across regions and there are important regional patterns, investigating all EMEs separately on a regional basis, will give a clearer understanding of the TFP dynamics in EMEs. Tab. 7.1 presents the annual TFP growth rates for each country by regional groups between 2000 and 2014.

Comparison of the TFP growth rates confirms that the highest TFP growth rates were in Emerging Asian countries. The average of TFP growth rates in Emerging Asian countries were higher than in other EMEs. Until the global financial and economic crisis, TFP growth was higher in European EMEs than in

Tab. 7.1: Total Factor Productivity Growth in EMEs, 2000–2014. Total Economy Database, July 2016 (https://www.conference-board.org/data/economydatabase)

	2000	**2001**	**2002**	**2003**	**2004**	**2005**	**2006**	**2007**	**2008**	**2009**	**2010**	**2011**	**2012**	**2013**	**2014**
Asia	***1,9***	***-0,7***	***1,2***	***1,6***	***1,8***	***1,6***	***1,5***	***1,4***	***-0,5***	***-1,7***	***1,9***	***-0,1***	***0,9***	***0,4***	***0,3***
Bangladesh	-1	-2.	-1.7	-1.4	-0.8	-1.2	-0.9	-1.1	-0.6	-0.1	0.3	0.4	0.0	-0.3	0.2
China	1.3	0.5	3.8	1.1	1.7	0.7	3.8	3.6	-2.7	-0.5	3.1	-1.6	-3.3	-2.1	-2.7
India	0.1	-1.2	-0.6	1.6	0.6	3.4	4.1	3.3	2.2	1.2	3.7	2.0	-0.6	0.5	0.8
Indonesia	1.6	0.2	1.9	1.9	0.5	2.4	1.1	-0.5	1.0	-0.6	0.9	2.3	1.5	-0.1	2.1
Malaysia	4.0	-2.6	1.9	2.0	3.8	2.5	2.0	2.5	1.6	-4.9	1.3	1.2	1.3	0.0	0.6
Pakistan	1.8	-0.1	0.6	2.8	2.7	3.3	-1.7	-1.5	-3.2	-2.4	-1.9	-0.8	0.5	1.4	0.6
Philippines	4.0	-1.5	1.0	0.7	3.8	0.7	2.4	3.3	-0.3	-2.2	3.2	-1.8	3.7	3.2	1.4
Thailand	2.9	1.2	2.8	4.3	2.3	1.0	1.1	1.5	-2.1	-4.0	4.5	-2.1	4.0	0.4	-0.3
Eastern Europe	***3,3***	***1,9***	***3,5***	***3,3***	***3,7***	***0,2***	***1,2***	***0,8***	***-1***	***-8,3***	***1,6***	***1,4***	***-0,2***	***-0,4***	***-1,4***
Bulgaria	3.9	-0.9	-0.8	-1.4	-1.7	-2.3	-2.6	-2.2	-4.1	-9.2	-1.5	-0.2	-1.7	-1.9	-1.3
Hungary	0.9	1.7	1.0	0.7	0.9	1.0	0.7	-2.3	-0.9	-7.0	-0.4	-0.4	-1.5	-1.0	-0.9
Poland	3.3	0.3	2.3	2.4	2.7	0.5	2.3	2.2	-0.8	0.1	2.7	2.0	-1.0	-0.5	-0.7
Romania	3.1	6.2	11.0	5.1	6.3	0.4	3.5	4.9	6.4	-7.4	-1.4	-0.2	4.1	2.3	0.6
Russia	5.6	6.5	4.5	7.6	6.2	4.4	4.4	2.9	-0.2	-8.3	4.0	3.5	2.8	1.1	-0.3
Ukraine	2.7	7.9	2.7	6.6	7.8	-3.0	1.8	2.0	-3.1	-.	4.0	2.9	-0.4	-1.5	-4.5
Turkey	3.8	-8.7	3.9	2.4	3.9	0.6	-1.5	-1.8	-4.3	-8.0	3.6	2.1	-3.6	-1.3	-2.5
Latin America	***1,0***	***-1,0***	***-2,4***	***-0,6***	***3,9***	***1,6***	***1,2***	***0,5***	***-1,5***	***-4,6***	***0,2***	***0,0***	***-1,1***	***-1,5***	***-4,0***
Argentina	-1.4	-3.4	-6.5	4.9	3.6	3.7	1.9	2.1	-1.3	-4.6	5.0	0.6	-5.3	-1.9	-6.5
Brazil	1.9	-0.2	0.3	-1.4	2.0	-0.7	-0.7	1.0	-0.9	-3.7	1.7	-1.0	-2.1	-0.4	-2.8
Chile	1.0	-0.6	-1.9	-1.2	2.0	1.1	-0.5	-0.7	-2.9	-5.3	-1.1	-0.7	-0.2	-1.2	-2.2
Colombia	0.4	0.1	0.2	0.6	1.2	0.0	1.6	1.0	-1.7	-2.6	-1.1	0.6	-1.4	-0.4	-1.2
Mexico	3.4	-2.7	-3.5	-0.3	1.0	-0.9	1.4	-0.5	-3.5	-6.2	-0.6	0.7	-0.2	-2.3	-1.2
Peru	-0.4	-1.1	3.8	1.4	2.4	3.0	3.1	3.7	2.8	-4.0	2.2	-0.7	-1.2	-2.0	-4.7
Venezuela	1.9	1.0	-9.2	-8.0	15.2	4.7	1.4	-2.8	-3.2	-5.6	-4.6	0.8	3.0	-2.0	-9.2
Africa															
South Africa	***1.4***	***2.5***	***-0.8***	***1.4***	***0.3***	***-1.8***	***0.2***	***1.1***	***-2.6***	***-4.4***	***0.5***	***-2.3***	***-2.2***	***-3.5***	***-3.1***

other countries, but during the crisis period and post-crisis period TFP growth declined considerably in European EMEs. Zero and negative TFP growth suggests that labor and capital efficiency decelerated. The slowdown in TFP growth can also be indicative of weak demand and regulatory challenges which prevented businesses from maximizing their potential through investments in technology and innovation (The Conference Board Productivity Brief, 2015). Among all the countries, TFP growth in Asian EMEs was the less volatile.

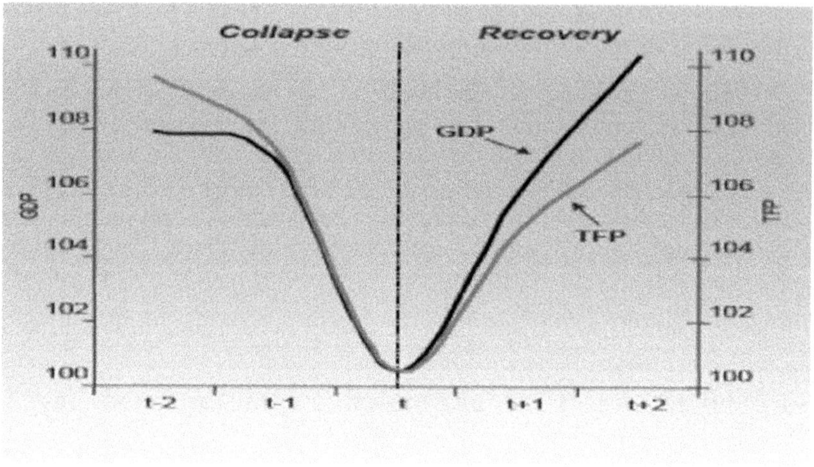

Fig. 7.4: Behavior of (Average) TFP and Real GDP During Emerging Market Crises. Calvo, Izquierdo, and Talvi (2006: 5)

The domestic crisis observed in all emerging economies and the Great Recession had decreased TFP growth significantly during these periods, with the exception of India. According to Calvo et al. (2006), TFP follows a sharp V-shaped trajectory as shown in Fig. 7.4; with a sudden fall, followed by a swift recovery and reaching its pre-crisis level in less than three years following the output trough (Zarazaga, 2006).

The slowdown in TFP growth after the Great Recession has been widespread across EMEs, but there have also been some significant differences among different regions. The average TFP declined to 1 percentage points during the global financial and economic crises, however, Bulgaria's TFP growth (-4.1 and -9.2) and Turkey's (-4.3 and -8.0) experienced substantial declines. India, Indonesia and Malaysia were exceptions because they experienced high positive TFP growth rates during the crisis period. In fact, during the overall period, the average TFP growth was mostly positive except in the crisis periods. The country-based comparisons showed that the countries which had the highest average TFP growth rate over the whole period were Russia, Romania and India. High terms of trade growth, high investments, capital accumulation, and macroeconomic reforms which leads to improvements in resource allocations in EMEs maintained positive TFP growth.

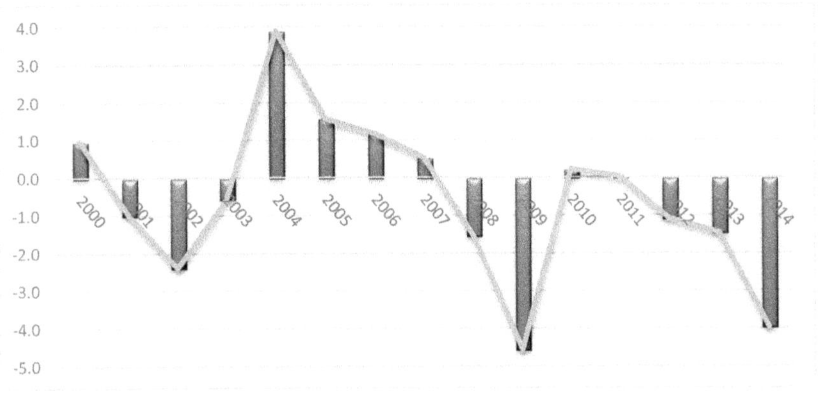

Fig. 7.5: Average TFP Growth of Latin American EMEs, 2000–2014. Total Economy Database, 2016

7.3 Region Based Comparisons

7.3.1 Latin American EMEs

TFP growth rate averages ranged from -4.6 percent to 3.9 percent between 2000 and 2014 in Latin American EMEs (Fig. 7.5). Among the country-based average TFP growth rates, the least productive country was Venezuela (-1.1) (Fig. 7.6).

Latin American EMEs have maintained high TFP growth rates during the 2003–2008 period. The economies have benefited from high terms of trade during the last decade. The high terms of trade level have an impact on short term growth rates via the output channel. In particular, it indirectly affected the TFP. High terms of trade tend to increase profits in trading sectors, it also helps boost investments and through this channel has an indirect positive effect on the TFP. The spillover effect from tradeable to non-tradeable sectors also helps the TFP (Bardalez and Zea, 2014). During the Great Recession period, the Latin American EMEs experienced foreign shocks with the cause of high negative terms of trade shocks and they had substantial effects on TFP. As a consequence, TFP growth began to decline.

Turning to the individual country-based comparisons (Fig. 7.6), TFP growth varies among the countries. Argentina's TFP growth decreased -6.5 percentage points during Argentina's domestic crisis period (2002) and sharply increased 4.9 percentage points after the crisis and continued in high ratios because of the substantial devaluation of the domestic currency. The devaluation effected the

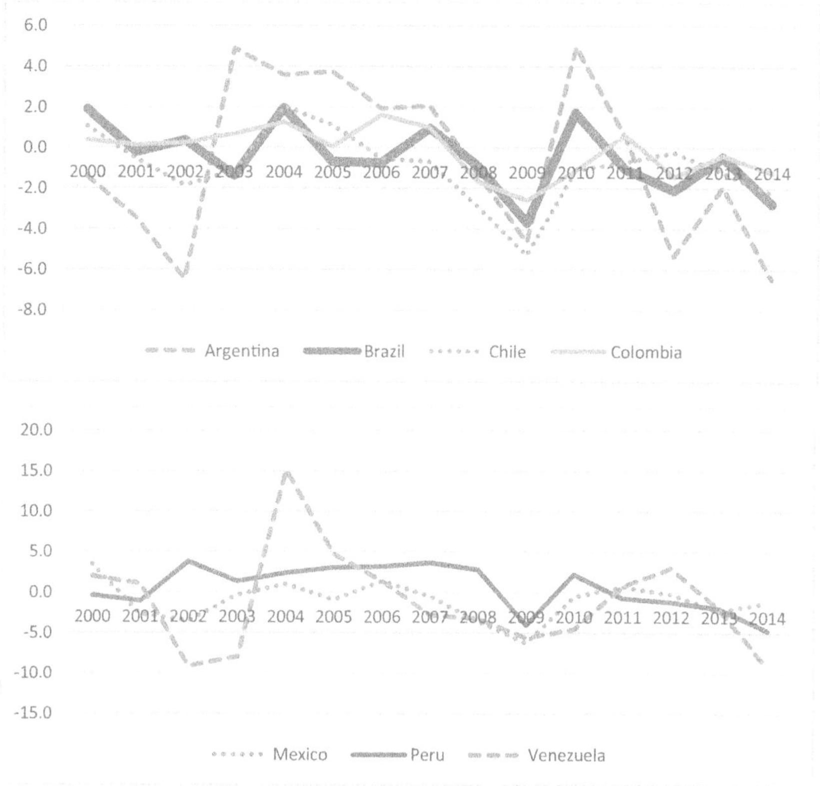

Fig. 7.6: TFP Growth in Latin American EMEs, 2000–2014. Total Economy Database, 2016

tradable goods producing sectors, they had increased their share of GDP and their contribution to GDP growth (Coremberg; 2008).

It should be noted that Venezuela had volatile TFP growth rates over the whole period (the extreme points were in 2002 (- 9.2) and 2004 (15.2)). This volatility of productivity is consistent with macroeconomic instability, and the balance of payments crisis in 2002 (Puent et al., 2009). Devaluation followed after the crisis caused real exchange rate appreciations and an increase in TFP growth rates. Also, the volatility of the oil income influences the TFP growth rates in Venezuela.

Peru and Argentina have the highest TFP growth rates because they were undergoing deep and rapid institution changes.

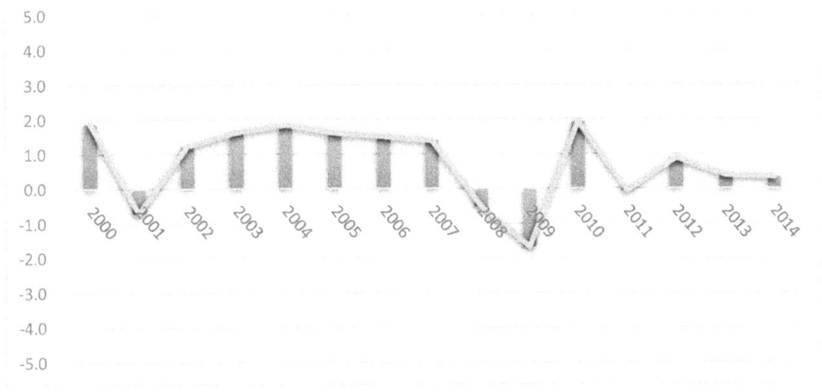

Fig. 7.7: Average TFP Growth Rates of Asian EMEs, 2000–2014. Total Economy Database, 2016

7.3.2 Asian EMEs

The average TFP growth for Asian EMEs appears to be stable, with the exception of the global financial and economic crisis period. The region's average ranged from -1.7 percent to 1.9 in the 2000–2014 period (Fig. 7.7). Among the country-based TFP growths, Bangladesh showed the worst performance, with an -0.7 TFP average. China and Philippines were the best performers (1.4 percentage) when compared to other countries in the region.

Comparisons of individual countries show that Bangladesh had the lowest TFP growth rate, possibly because of low R&D investments, poor infrastructure and difficulties in doing business (see Fig. 7.8). Indonesia had a modest TFP growth rate with strong credit growth and supportive monetary policy which boosted demand and high investment and capital accumulation (Anand et al., 2014). Improved macro management and governance in the Philippines built investor confidence and led to improve its TFP. Malaysia's Economic Transformation Programme (ETP) increased investments and capital accumulations. These favorable developments allowed Asian EMEs to be more successful in maintaining higher TFP ratios than their counterparts.

China's strong TFP growth is due to increased globalization with its entry into the World Trade Organization (WTO), and rapid investments in information technology. China's TFP growth has slowed down since 2011 from -1.6 percent to -2.7 percent (see Fig. 7.9). The average growth decreased to 0.5 percent. The reason

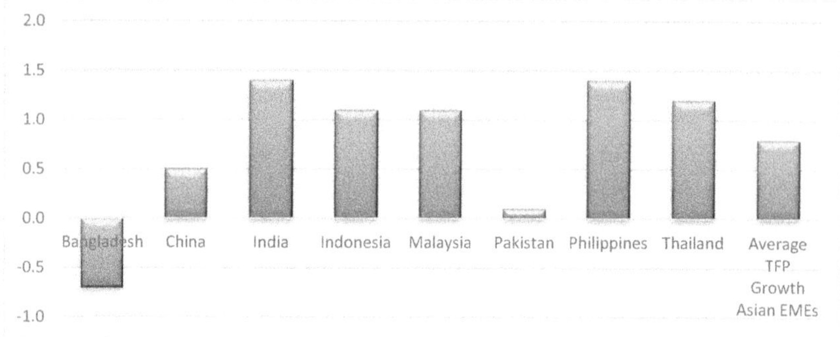

Fig. 7.8: Average TFP Growth for Individual Asian Emerging Countries, 2000–2014. Total Economy Database, 2016

Fig. 7.9: TFP Growth in Asian EMEs, 2000–2014. Total Economy Database, 2016

behind this slowdown resulted from slower GDP growth. Nevertheless, China continues to show one of the highest TFP growth rates among the overall EMEs.

India performed a significant TFP improvement even during the global financial and economic crisis period up until the past few years (see Fig. 7.9). Therefore, India has the highest TFP growth (1.4) in the region. Philippines, which experienced a high growth rate in the same period, shared the spotlight with India. India's economy has shown some improvement in tackling many of its most troublesome macroeconomic challenges including high inflation, slowing exports and current account deficits (The Conference Board Productivity Brief, 2015).

7.3.3 European EMEs

TFP growth developed quite smoothly between 2000 and 2005. However, this positive development was interrupted by the Great Recession. The global financial and economic crisis affected the European EMEs much more than the other EMEs. It disrupted the availability of credit, which is important for innovation, and decreased the growth of international trade due to demand shocks (Eichengreen and Shen, 2015). The average TFP growth sharply decreased in almost all the countries during the crisis period. After the crisis, TFP growth recovered, but remained below the average TFP growth rates seen prior to the 2008 recession. Interestingly, TFP growth has slowed and there is a continuous downward trend even after the recovery process. The average TFP growth rate has sharply slumped from 0.8 to -8.3 during the global financial and economic crisis. The region's averages ranged from -8.3 percent to 3.7 percent between 2000 and 2014 (Fig. 7.10). When compared with their regional counterparts, Bulgaria showed the worst performance with an -1.9 TFP average and Romania showed the best performance with a 3.0 TFP growth rate (see Fig. 7.11).

Poland has shown remarkable economic progress and was the only European EME that survived the global financial and economic crisis without going through a recession (see Fig. 7.12). Poland was the only European country which recorded a positive GDP growth in 2009 (see Fig. 7.12). Moreover, Poland benefited from the catching up process after the end of the central planning and has also benefited by joining the EU in 2004. While in the transformation process, high capital accumulation, the increase in capital deepening and the improvement in workforce composition (developments in education) maintained the TFP growth rate. Thus, Poland has increased its TFP growth significantly. However, after the catching up process, the economy faced a slowdown in TFP growth (Gradzewicz et al., 2014).

Romania is another country which performed well except during the crisis period and made significant progress in the past years by reducing

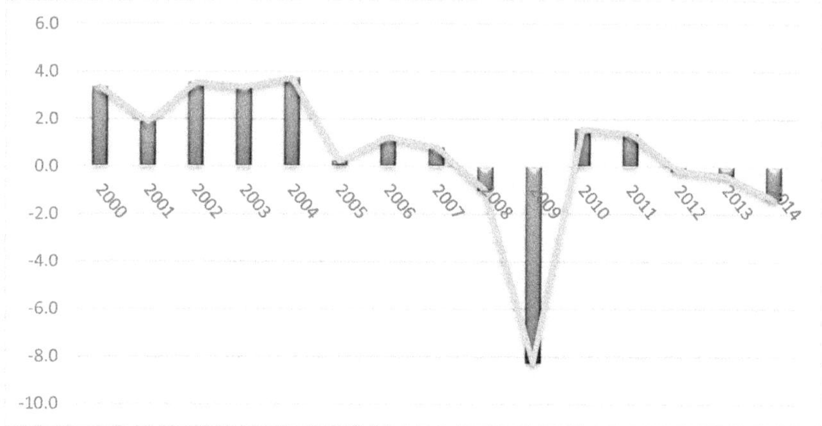

Fig. 7.10: Average TFP Growth Rates of European EMEs. Total Economy Database, 2016

macroeconomic imbalances (see Fig. 7.12). Before the crisis, Romania recorded high GDP growth rates, and capital and labor contributions were positive as a result of increasing investments. Romania's growth acceleration since 2000 was fueled mainly by improvements in TFP, increasingly by a foreign financed credit and investment boom. The sudden decrease in TFP growth in 2008 had a V-shape and TFP immediately recovered in 2011 with the recovery of domestic investments and inflows of EU funds (Government of Romania, 2016).

When comparing Russia with other counterparts in the region, the data shows that there is a high TFP growth except during the global financial and economic crisis period (see Fig. 7.12). This high TFP growth rate is due to Russia's strong efforts for modernization, a prudential macro fiscal policy and the creation and operation of oil funds. The price of energy commodities significantly increased on the international market and this led to a significant capital flow into the country. With the economic transition to a market economy, Russia experienced a shift of resources into the services sector and this transition spurred higher productivity. Labor moved away from low-productive sectors toward high productive sectors (World Bank, 2007). The firms operating in ICT-related industries displayed higher productivity performances with technological spillovers. Although, the global financial and economic crisis had negative effects on the Russian economy, the country recovered within two years. In 2014, TFP growth declined sharply from 1.1 % to -0.3 %. The ongoing geopolitical tensions and the

Fig. 7.11: Average TFP Growth for Individual European Emerging Countries, 2000–2014. Total Economy Database, 2016

decline in oil prices since the middle of 2014 have played important roles in this decline.

Interestingly, Bulgaria's TFP growth remained significantly below the regional average (see Fig. 7.12). Although Bulgaria's real GDP growth was strong, its TFP fell short of other countries in the region and improvements in prosperity achieved before 2008 were not sustainable. The sectors with skilled labor experienced rapid productivity growth. After the global financial and economic crisis, the recovery of the Bulgarian economy has been slow and weak. Misallocation of resources played an important role in this slow and weak productivity growth (World Bank, 2015).

7.3.4 South Africa

South Africa's TFP growth rate has a high volatility and has been on a downward trend due to its unusual sectoral structure (see Fig. 7.13). More than 60 % of the GDP is contributed by the service sectors and employment in service sectors is higher than in industry or in agriculture where there are low-skilled workers (Fedderke, 2014). Although the TFP has a declining trend short productivity growth cycles have been reported. Small recoveries in productivity growth can only be seen during these short periods (2002–2003; 2006–2007).

The integration of South Africa into the world economy has had important outcomes and due to this integration process, growth has improved but its TFP unfortunately be linked to a lack of employment growth (McCarthy, 2005).

Fig. 7.12: TFP Growth in European EMEs, 2000–2014. Total Economy Database, 2016

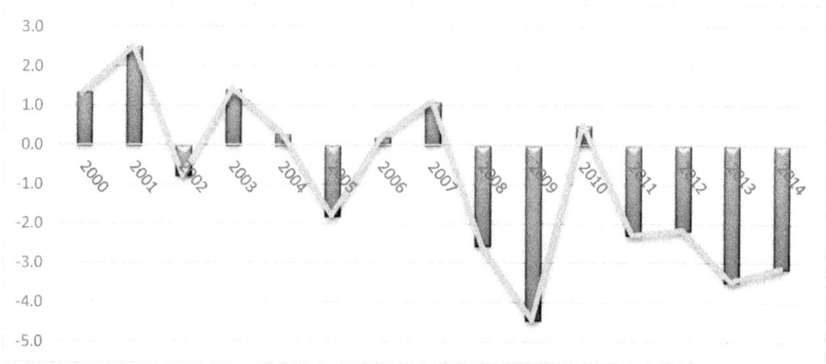

Fig. 7.13: TFP Growth Rate, South Africa, 2000–2014. Total Economy Database, 2016

7.4 Conclusion

Over the past years, EMEs have experienced a slowdown in their productivity performances relative to the last decade and there are negligible TFP differences between the countries. The purpose of this chapter was to shed light on the causes of the TFP slowdowns and the TFP differences among EMEs.

Among the countries investigated in multiple regions (European, Asian, Latin American and South Africa), during the 2000–2014 period Asian EMEs exhibited the highest average TFP growth and their TFP growths were less volatile.

The domestic crisis episodes observed in all EMEs and the Great Recession decreased TFP growth significantly during these periods, with the exception of India. Until the global financial and economic crisis, TFP growth in European EMEs was higher than in other EMEs, but during the crisis period and post-crisis period TFP growth decreased considerably. Possible causes for this decline were that labor and capital efficiency decelerated. Bulgaria's TFP growth (-4.1) and Turkey's (-4.3) had a substantial decline while India was an exception, having a high positive TFP growth rate throughout the crisis period.

The country-based comparisons showed that Russia, Romania and India had the highest average TFP growth rates throughout the whole period. High terms of trade growth, high investments, capital accumulation, and macroeconomic reforms which led to improvements in resource allocation maintained the positive TFP.

According to Ferriera et al. (2010), the slumps in TFP growth in advanced economies are associated with external factors, while in emerging economies the TFP growth slowdowns are attributed to country-specific sources. Therefore, the challenges facing policy makers in order to maintain high TFP growth rates must be well understood on country-specific basis. EMEs need policies which promote investments in human capital and innovations to boost TFP growth. Also, the countries that want to improve their TFPs should maintain real and financial sector developmental policies. Policies that lower trade barriers which help the spillover of technology and efficient factor reallocation can lead to productivity gains. Also, institutional quality and a strong financial system play an important role in improving productivity. Institutional quality helps the country to attract foreign direct investments and strong financial systems enhance investments and boost innovations. Macroeconomic stability along with well-designed tax systems increase TFP growth via investment channels.

References

Anand, R., Cheng, C. K., Rehman, S., Zhang, L. (2014). Potential Growth in Emerging Asia. *IMF Working Paper*, 14/2, Washington, International Monetary Fund.

Ark, B., Erumban, A. (2015). *Global Productivity Growth Stuck in the Slow Lane with No Signs of Recovery in Sight*, New York, The Conference Board Productivity Brief 2015.

Bardalez, C, P., Zea, R, Y. (2014). Terms of Trade and Total Factor Productivity: Empirical evidence from Latin American Emerging Markets. Banco Central De Reserva Del Peru, Working Paper Series, No. 2014-012.

Berument, H., Dinçer, N. N., Mustafaoğlu, Z. (2011). Total Factor Productivity and Macroeconomic Instability. *The Journal of International Trade and Economic Development*, *20* (5), 605–629.

Calvo, A. G., Alejandro, I., Talvi, E. (2006). Phoenix Miracles in Emerging Markets: Recovering without Credit from Systemic Financial Crises. *NBER Working Paper*, 12101, Cambridge, MA.

Cardale, C. P., Zea, R. Y. (2014). Terms of Trade and Total Factor Productivity: Empirical evidence from Latin American emerging markets. *Banco Central De Reserva Del Peru, Working Paper Series,* No.2014-012.

Coremberg, A. (2008). The Measurement of TFP in Argentina, 1990-2004: A Case of The Tyranny of Numbers Economic Cycles and Methodology, *International Productivity Monitor*, No: 17, 52–74.

Cubeddu, L., Culiuc, A., Fayad, G., Gao, Y., Kocchar, K. Kyobe, A., Oner, C., Perrelli, R., Snaya, S., Tsounta, E., Zhang, Z. (2014). Emerging Markets in Transition: Growth Prospects and Challenges. *IMF Staff Discussion Note*, 14/06, Washington, International Monetary Fund.

Culiuc, A. (2014). External Factors and Medium–term Economic Growth. *IMF Working Paper* (forthcoming)

Eichengreen, B., Shin, K. (2015). The Global Productivity Slump: Common and Country-Specific Factors. *NBER Working Paper*, No: 21556.

Fedderke, J. W. (2014). Exploring Unbalanced Growth in South Africa: Understanding the Sectoral Structure of the South African Economy, *ERSA Working Paper*. 468.

Ferreira, P., Galvao, A., Gomez, F. R., Pesoa, S. (2010). *The effects of External and Internal Shocks on Total Factor Productivity*, Unpublished manuscript, Gerulio Vargas Foundation.

Government of Romania. (2016). *Convergence Programme 2016-2019*, 51 pages, Report of European Commission, https://ec.europa.eu/info/sites/info/files/

european-semester-convergence-programme_romania_2016_en.pdf, Access Date: 20 June 2016.

Gradzewicz, M., Growiec, J., Kolasa, M., Postek, L., Strzelecki, P. (2014). Poland's exceptional performance during the world economic crisis: New growth accounting evidence, *Narodowy Bank Polski Working Paper*, No. 186. Warsaw.

McCarthy, C. (2005). *Productivity Performance in Developing Countries, Country Case Studies: South Africa*. United Nations Industrial Development Organization.

Puente, M. J., Gomez, P., Vera, L. (2009). The Political Economy of Productivity: The Case of Venezuela, *Instituto de Estudios Superiores de Administracion*, IESA.

Sosa, S., Tsounta, E., Kim, H. S. (2013). Is the Growth Momentum in Latin America Sustainable? *IMF Working Paper*. No: 13/109, Washington, International Monetary Fund.

Summers, L. (2014). U.S. Economic Prospects: Secular Stagnation, Hysteresis, and the Zero Lower Bound. *Business Economics* No. 49, 65–73.

Total Economy Database, 2016 (https://www.conference-board.org/data/economydatabase), Access Date: 20 June 2016.

Tsounta, E. (2014). Slowdown in Emerging Markets: Sign of a Bumpy Road Ahead? *IMF working Paper*, No. 14/205, Washington, International Monetary Fund.

World Bank. (2007). Russian Economic Report, World Bank Economic Management and Policy Unit, Washington.

World Bank. (2015). Productivity in Bulgaria: Trends and Options, Washington DC, May 2015. http://www.worldbank.org/content/dam/Worldbank/document/eca/Bulgaria/Bulgaria-Productivity-6-26-15-eng-web.pdf, Access Date: 20 June 2016

Zarazaga, E. J. M. (2006). The Role of Total Factor Productivity In "Phoenix Miracles" Insights from An Emerging Market Crisis. *Federal Reserve Bank of Dallas Working Paper*, 0605.

Part C The Effect of 2008 Crisis

Mine Kalay

8 The Global Economic Crisis and its Effects on the Growth Rate of EMEs

Abstract: Within the scope of this study, after briefly mentioning the Financial and Real Sector Crisis in the USA (2006–2009), the Global Economic Crisis (2007–2012), and the European Debt Crisis (2009–2012) as part of the Global Economic Crisis, the effects these crises have had on the growth rate of emerging market economies (EMEs) will be examined. In particular, the main purpose of this study is to see how the Global Economic Crisis has affected the EMEs in terms of growth rates.

Keywords: Global Economic Crisis, Growth Rate, Emerging Markets

8.1 Introduction

Globalization rapidly increased the flow of goods, services and production from the mid-1980s onwards and in particular, the crisis in developed countries accelerated its transition to other countries through these channels. The Financial and Real Sector Crisis of 2006–2009 in the United States spread to other countries by means of the mentioned flows and resulted in a complex financial, debt and trade crisis not previously seen globally: The Global Economic Crisis of 2007 - 2012. The global recession created by the Global Economic Crisis can be compared to the Great Depression in the United States which lasted from 1929 to 1939 and caused a large negative economic impact. This Global Economic Crisis led to crises in other countries and regions under different names. In this sense, the Loan Crisis of the European Union between 2009 and 2011 was an important component of the Global Economic Crisis of 2007–2012.

Even though the Global Economic Crisis first effected the developed countries, the growth rate of many EMEs slowed and, in fact, certain EMEs suffered negative growth rates during the crisis years.

In the second section of this study, the Financial and Real Sector Crisis in the United States and the Global Economic Crisis followed by the European Loan Crisis considered a part of the Global Economic Crisis will be examined. In the third section, what growth is and how it is calculated will be looked at. In the fourth section, an explanation will be given on how the Global Economic Crisis and the European Loan Crisis affected the growth rates of EMEs and in the fifth and final section, concluding remarks (or policy implications) will be presented.

8.2 The Financial and Real Sector Crisis in the United States and the Global Economic Crisis

The event that triggered the Financial and Real Sector Crisis in the United States was the rapid fall in real estate prices as a result of the balloon that burst in real estate prices. Obviously, there were other reasons for the crisis: According to the debate in the literature, the factors that led to the Crisis in the United States and subsequently to the Global Crisis were:

i. The inadequate supervision and regulation of financial markets by governments in many countries, in particular in the United States in the 1970s.
ii. In particular, the "new invention" that "carried excessive risk" of certain financial instruments that began to be rapidly bought and sold by American financial sector firms in the 1990s.
iii. The "bad" economic policies applied by governments of the United States and other countries during the first decade of 2000 (Kibritçioğlu, 2011a:5). These reasons will be reviewed below.

The FED or the Federal Reserve Bank, starting from the beginning of 2001 to 30 June 2004 embarked on an expansionary monetary and a low interest rate policy. The expansionary monetary policy and the low interest rate, created a revival in the US economy and led to a higher growth rate in the country. During these periods when it was thought that this economic boom would continue for a long time, there was an increase in the demand for financial assets by citizens and by financial institutions where risks were high but the returns were high as well. The same event happened in the USA. In order to meet this demand, new, high-risk financial instruments, but which also had high return expectations, were introduced into the financial markets by financial institutions. At the time, it was considered a financial engineering marvel. However, when these new, high- risk and high-return assets began to be issued based on the mortgage-backed housing market, the seeds of the crisis began to be sown. While the economy retained its buoyancy, the financial institutions began to operate with high leverage ratios; in other words, they began to provide loans (provide loans or purchase bonds) above their equity.

The demand for housing and real estate prices began to rise rapidly between January 2001 and 30 June 2004 when the FED kept interest rates low. During this period, when the volume of transactions was very high in the mortgage-backed housing loan market, financial institutions began to buy these mortgage-backed housing loans provided by the financial institutions and converted them to new higher risk, higher return financial assets which were a financial engineering marvel and sold them to savings account owners or to other financial institutions. As previously stated, a crucial reason for the crisis in the USA was the inadequate supervision and regulation of the financial markets by the American Government. If adequate supervision and regulation had taken place, these new high-risk, toxic assets would not have been bought and sold on the markets to this extent and financial companies would not have been able to operate at such high leverage ratios. Thus, the development of a long-term crisis in the financial markets would not have occurred. It was also mentioned that financial institutions operated with high leverage ratios. Under these conditions, financial institutions were providing large amount of loans to individuals where the risk premium was high and, thereby, the possibility of defaulting on the loan was high as well in order to receive higher returns. The loans provided to these high risk premium individuals were called "subprime" loans. Subprime loans mean: Individuals who applied for a housing loan were listed from those who would be able to repay easily to those who would have the most difficulty in repaying the loan. If this list is divided into three categories, the individuals with the highest credit rating would be listed at the top while the individuals listed at the bottom (third category) would be considered subprime. In other words, the section where the bad loan ratio is the highest is the category which is at the bottom of the list and is referred to as the "subprime category".

After June 2004, the FED adapted a tighter monetary policy and a rise in interest rates took place. As a result of an increase in interest rates, the balloon in housing prices burst at the beginning of 2006 and house prices began to decline. This situation put a squeeze on borrowers who received mortgage-backed housing loans by giving the houses they had purchased up as collateral since the borrowers who purchased mortgage-backed housing loans avoided bankruptcy only as long as house prices increased. When borrowers realized that they would have difficulty in repaying these loans, they sold their houses and were able to repay their loans since the sale price was higher than the purchase price.

When the balloon burst in the housing market and house prices began to decline, the damage which incurred was mostly to the financial institutions that gave housing loans to subprime borrowers and to the subprime borrowers who took out these loans. The financial institutions which issued these high-risk, toxic assets to subprime borrowers were left in a predicament. As house prices began to decline, the subprime borrowers began to default on their loans and, as a result, financial institutions began foreclosing. When these financial institutions needed to covert these foreclosed houses into cash, they entered the housing market as sellers which further accelerated the fall in housing prices. This rapid fall in housing prices increased the repayment difficulties of borrowers as well as increasing the number of foreclosed houses which in turn accelerated even further the fall in housing prices.

The financial crisis that appeared on the housing finance market in the USA between 2006 and 2007, rapidly spread first to the domestic financial sector and later to the domestic real sector between 2007 and 2009 and, as a result, an increase in unemployment and a recession began in the United States from December 2007 to June 2009. This financial and real sector crisis, according to some researchers, spread in particular to the financial and real sectors of European Union member nations and the economies of other developed countries particularly due to strong financial relations during the last months of 2007. However, certain other researchers give a later date and indicate the autumn of 2008 as the date the crisis spread to other countries, namely, when it "globalized" (Kibritçioğlu, 2011a:6).

8.2.1 The European Union Loan Crisis under the Effects of the Global Economic Crisis

This section will review the countries which entered a period of crisis and the reasons why, what is termed as the European Loan Crisis, was triggered by the globalization of the economic crisis outside of the USA as of 2008.

When 2009 arrived, the world began to wait for the flames from the Global Economic Crisis to die out. Certain issues began to appear in certain EU countries at the end of 2009. In this period, serious problems emerged beginning with Greece, Portugal, Ireland, Spain and Italy in that order. In fact, the crisis in these EU members (Later to be coined the European Loan Crisis) can be seen as the foundation blocks of the Global Economic Crisis.

Troubles first appeared in Greece towards the end of 2009, with its high public debt problem. Greece was accepted into the EU by fulfilling the Maastricht Criteria. However, this acceptance resulted because Greece downsized its public debt and when the reality of the situation was revealed, The EU saw that Greece's public debt was far above the Maastricht Criteria. Greece's public debt led to a serious debt crisis in 2010. The already very high public debt increased due to the Global Crisis. In 2010, after a long debate, the EU created an 80M Euro fund and the IMF extended another 30M Euro to save Greece. In this way the risk premium of Greece was lowered. The EU was forced to continue to extend loans to Greece during 2011 and 2012 (Özatay, 2014: 168–169).

Portugal's main problem is that its core lies with the banking sector. Additionally, Portugal's debt to GNP was high due to its low growth rate, one of the smallest growth rates among EU member nations. This low growth rate increased the debt to the GNP ratio and the question of debt repayment became an issue. These are the basic reasons for the economic crisis in Portugal.

In Ireland, the low interest rate and lax banking regulations in the 1990s resulted in a ballooning of real estate prices. When this balloon began to deflate, serious problems appeared in the banking sector and on the housing market. The spread of the Global Economic Crisis from the USA to other countries deepened the debt crisis in Ireland. With the bailout, its public debt increased and due to the Global Economic Crisis, the country's debt became unmanageable when interest rates rose.

The debt crisis in Spain, as with Portugal and Ireland, lies in the banking sector. This crisis appeared because of the increase in loans and the ballooning of real estate prices from the end of the 1990s to 2008. In the November of 2010, Spain came under the scrutiny of the EU. In August 2011, the interest rate of Spain's state bonds skyrocketed, in other words, the risk premium of Spain increased. In this situation, in order to decrease the risk premium of Spain, the European Central Bank was forced to buy its state bonds.

Italy did not have any problems in its banking sector or its housing market nor was the public deficit of Italy as high as the countries mentioned above. However, due to low growth expectations and a high level of debt, Italy has always been a country which has received a low rating from credit rating agencies. In particular, after May 2011, Italy's rating continuously declined. When the interest rate of state bonds accelerated in August 2011, the European Central Bank was again forced to buy the country's state bonds in order to reduce its risk premium (Kibritçioğlu, 2011b: 6–8).

The fact that countries which joined the EU could not pursue independent monetary or exchange rate policies outside of other EU members, in other words, since "only a single monetary policy" existed and although this constituted the cause of the crisis in these countries, it was not possible for them to overcome these problems singly without help. During this period, these countries had a single currency and a single monetary policy but each had a separate fiscal policy. Although there are certain limits on budget deficit and public debt in the EU, these limits are quite loose and when exceeded, no sanctions are applied. Whereas, looking from an economic perspective, it is necessary that each country's monetary policy be in harmony with its fiscal policy. This matter, that is, "a single fiscal policy" of EU member nations or, to put it another way, an overdue "fiscal union" among the member nations, makes up another important reason for the crisis in these countries.

If we summarize the European Loan Crisis: The crisis that appeared at the end of 2009 in EU member nations (respectively, Greece, Portugal, Ireland, Spain and Italy) has two causes, domestic and foreign. The internal reason for the crisis is the high level of public debt due to the imprudent policies applied by national governments. The high private debt in the countries listed above led to difficulties for some financial institutions. With the bailout provided by governments to these financial institutions, the loans of the private sector became the debt of the public sector. Another reason for the crisis in these countries, was the lack of regulations and agencies which would regulate, supervise and control the banking and financial sectors in EU member nations, as was the case in the American crisis and for this reason the rise in the private sector and public sector debt is observed. Among the leading reasons for the external causes of the Loan Crisis among the EU member countries is the Global Economic Crisis emanating from the USA. The triggering of the Global Economic Crisis led to a worsening in the financial state of many countries. Another external reason is the application of the "single currency and monetary policy" without the necessary complete infrastructure and not having a "fiscal union" in place. Additionally, the relatively distant approach of EU member nations to each other in "jointly assisting" and the "spirit of solidarity," is not only a reason for the crisis, but also a factor that complicated the exit from the crisis.

Due to the increasing public deficit and debt, the growth rates of these countries tumbled and the low growth rate led to payment difficulties for these countries starting from the end of 2009 to 2011. Thus, the question of a "Debt Crisis" within the EU and the means to exit these countries from this Crisis became an issue for debate.

8.3 The Effects of the Global Economic Crisis and the European Debt Crisis on the Growth of EMEs

In this section, data on the growth rates of EMEs between 2000 and 2014 and how these economies were affected by the European debt crisis as a result of the global economic crisis are provided.

In previous sections, it was shown that the financial crisis which started in the USA spread to the developed European countries as well as the economies of other countries due to the integration of world economies and also showed that the crisis which commenced in the financial sector had a negative impact on the real sector. A world-wide economic crisis causes the most damage to EMEs. In general, these economies have to foot the bill for the crises originating in the USA and the developed countries of Europe (Yıldırım, 2010: 1).

Prior to the global economic crisis, all countries world-wide, that is, "the global economy", grew relatively less in 2005 with an average growth rate of 4.4 % (this rate was 5.1 % in 2006) due to the increase in petroleum prices. Beginning in 2007, the world economy began to shrink because of the financial and real sector crisis in the USA. Because the US economy has the power to give direction to all global economies, within a short period, this crisis had a negative impact first on developed countries and later on developing countries. The growth rate in developed countries remained below the world average.

While the growth rate in developed economies grew 2.6 % in 2005, it has continuously contracted since 2007. The 7.1 % growth rate of developing countries in 2005, after reaching 8 % in 2007, began to fall from 2007 onwards similar to the developed countries. China, India followed by Russia were the economies which showed the greatest growth in 2005.

In this section, the EMEs are examined within the framework of the global economic crisis and the European debt crisis which were triggered by the global economic crisis in Europe, the reasons why the EMEs were affected by the crisis and the effects of the crises on the growth rates of the EMEs will be outlined.

8.3.1 Latin America

The Argentinean economy is accustomed to economic crises. The country entered into its biggest debt crisis in its history in 2001 and the crisis drove the economy to a deep recession. This crisis in 2001 protected the Argentinean economy from the devastating effects of the 2008 global crisis. Because the public confidence in the banking system wavered after the 2001 crisis, the limited use of Argentine bank credits also limited the need for local banks to use credit from the US and European Banks. This protected the Argentinean economy from the devastating effects of the global economic crisis and the country has not entered a recession as was the case in 2001 (Rogers, 2008). Looking at the growth rate of the Argentinean economy during the global economic crisis we note that:

The growth rate of the economy, which was 7.96 % in 2007, declined to 3.07 % in 2008 due to the impact of the global economic crisis. This decline continued in 2009 and the Argentinean economy only grew by 0.05 %. Tab. 8.1 shows that the rate of growth in the economy rose again as of 2010 to 9.45 %. As seen from Tab. 8.1, the Argentinean economy has been affected by the global economic crisis, however, although the country's growth rate has slowed down having been influenced by the global crisis, there was no recession in the economy.

Brazil is an economy that makes notable use of global credit flows. The Brazilian economy experienced a sudden negative shock with the introduction

Tab. 8.1: The Growth Rates of EMEs between 2000 and 2014. World Bank, Development Indicators, 2016

	2000	2001	2002	2003	2004	2005	2006	2007	2008	2009	2010	2011	2012	2013	2014
Latin America															
Argentina	-0,8	-4,4	-10,9	8,8	9,0	9,2	8,4	8,0	3,1	0,1	9,5	8,4	0,8	2,9	0,5
Brazil	4,1	1,7	3,1	1,1	5,8	3,2	4,0	6,1	5,1	-0,1	7,5	3,9	1,9	3,0	0,1
Chile	4,5	3,3	2,2	4,0	6,0	5,6	4,4	5,2	3,3	-1,0	5,8	5,8	5,5	4,2	1,9
Colombia	4,4	1,7	2,5	3,9	5,3	4,7	6,7	6,9	3,5	1,7	4,0	6,6	4,0	4,9	4,6
Mexico	5,3	-0,6	0,1	1,4	4,3	3,0	4,9	3,2	1,4	-4,7	5,2	3,9	4,0	1,4	2,2
Peru	2,7	0,6	5,5	4,2	5,0	6,3	7,5	8,5	9,1	1,0	8,5	6,5	6,0	5,8	2,4
Venezuela	3,7	3,4	-8,9	-7,8	18,3	10,3	9,9	8,8	5,3	-3,2	-1,5	4,2	5,6	1,3	-4,0
Europe															
Bulgaria	5,0	4,2	6,0	5,1	6,6	7,2	6,8	7,7	5,6	-4,2	0,1	1,6	0,2	1,3	1,6
Hungary	4,2	3,8	4,5	3,8	4,9	4,4	3,8	0,4	0,8	-6,6	0,7	1,8	-1,7	1,9	3,7
Poland	4,3	1,2	1,4	3,6	5,1	3,5	6,2	7,2	3,9	2,6	3,7	5,0	1,6	1,3	3,3
Romania	2,4	5,6	5,2	5,5	8,4	4,2	8,1	6,9	8,5	-7,1	-0,8	1,1	0,6	3,5	2,8
Russian Federation	10,0	5,1	4,7	7,3	7,2	6,4	8,2	8,5	5,2	-7,8	4,5	4,3	3,4	1,3	0,6
Turkey	6,8	-5,7	6,2	5,3	9,4	8,4	6,9	4,7	0,7	-4,8	9,2	8,8	2,1	4,2	2,9
Ukraine	5,9	9,2	5,2	9,4	12,1	2,7	7,3	7,9	2,3	-14,8	4,2	5,2	0,2	0,0	-6,8
Asia															
Bangladesh	5,3	5,1	3,8	4,7	5,2	6,5	6,7	7,1	6,0	5,0	5,6	6,5	6,5	6,0	6,1
China	8,4	8,3	9,1	10,0	10,1	11,4	12,7	14,2	9,6	9,2	10,6	9,5	7,8	7,7	7,3
Indonesia	4,9	3,6	4,5	4,8	5,0	5,7	5,5	6,3	6,0	4,6	6,2	6,2	6,0	5,6	5,0
India	3,8	4,8	3,8	7,9	7,9	9,3	9,3	9,8	3,9	8,5	10,3	6,6	5,1	6,9	7,3
Malaysia	8,9	0,5	5,4	5,8	6,8	5,3	5,6	6,3	4,8	-1,5	7,4	5,3	5,5	4,7	6,0
Pakistan	4,3	2,0	3,2	4,8	7,4	7,7	6,2	4,8	1,7	2,8	1,6	2,7	3,5	4,4	4,7
Philippines	4,4	2,9	3,6	5,0	6,7	4,8	5,2	6,6	4,2	1,1	7,6	3,7	6,7	7,1	6,1
Thailand	4,5	3,4	6,1	7,2	6,3	4,2	5,0	5,4	1,7	-0,7	7,5	0,8	7,3	2,8	0,9
Africa															
South Africa	4,2	2,7	3,7	2,9	4,6	5,3	5,6	5,4	3,2	-1,5	3,0	3,2	2,2	2,2	1,5

of foreign capital during the period when the global economic crisis had entered an acute phase. During this period, not only did the stock market in the country collapse but the currency also drastically depreciated. In other words, the financial channel made the Brazilian economy vulnerable to the global economic crisis (Canuto, 2008).

Looking at the growth rate of the Brazilian economy during this period, the rate of 6.07 % in 2007 dropped to 5.09 % in 2008 and to 0.12 % in 2009 due to the impact of the global economic crisis. In 2010, this negative growth rate turned upwards with the growth rate reaching 7.52 %. These growth rates tell us that the Brazilian economy began to shrink after 2007 with the impact of the global economic crisis but that the effect of this recession quickly and unprecedentedly turned into a positive growth rate.

The economy of Chile grew at an average rate of 4.8 % between 2003 and 2008 due to an increase in domestic demand. Although the Chilean economy is a small economy, it was adversely affected by the global economic crisis because of its open economy. The deterioration in the terms of trade and the contraction in global financial conditions, particularly caused by the global economic crisis, led Chile, which has a small but open economy, to be affected by the global economic crisis. The growth rate of the Chilean economy declined to 3.29 % in 2008 from 5.16 % in the previous year due to the global economic crisis. Nevertheless, the Chilean economy was one of Latin America's highest-income countries in 2008 with per capita GDP of $ 10,087. By 2009, the economy contracted to 1.03 %, reaching its lowest growth rate between 2004 and 2012. However, this negative growth, which was the result of the global economic crisis, did not continue for very long. In 2010, the country emerged from this recession and managed to grow at a rate of 5.75 %. Although the growth rates fell due to the crisis, the recession in the country lasted only one year.

Economists generally agree that the Chilean economy has a high debt-financing strength and that the country's financial structure is active and well-regulated so that the country's economy succeeded in surviving the global economic crisis.

The economy of Colombia did not remain isolated from the global crisis environment and the position of the country's economy resembled that of other countries in South America during the crisis: The growth rate of the Colombian economy fell from 6.90 % in 2007 to 3.54 % in 2008 and to 1.65 % in 2009 due to the global economic crisis. The country saw a resurgence in its economy in 2010 with a 3.97 % growth rate and continued at a growth rate of 6.58 % the following year. The Colombian economy was affected by the global economic crisis in 2008 and 2009 but did not see a recession. The rapid drop in the growth rate due to the crisis saw a rapid recovery at the same rate.

Mexico's economy has been one of the EMEs most affected by the global economic crisis. The main reason for this is the export dependency of the Mexican economy on the USA and the combination of these exports. Mexico realizes almost 80 % of its total exports with the USA, and a significant portion of these exports are durable consumer goods. The economic stagnation experienced by the USA during the global economic crisis caused Mexico's exports to decline and the terms of trade to deteriorate. In other words, the first reason why Mexico was affected by the global economic crisis was due its trade channel. Another reason for the shock created by the global economic crisis on the Mexican economy was the anti-risk behavior of international investors during this period and, as a result of the decline in their loans to global financial markets, led to a restriction of access to international finance markets by the Mexican economy. Thus, it can be stated that another reason is the finance channel (Sidaoui et al., 2010). In view of the growth rate, the position of the Mexican economy during the global economic crisis is as follows:

Mexico's growth rate of 4.94 % in 2006 dropped to 3.22 % in 2007 and to 1.37 % in 2008 due to the global economic crisis. In 2009, the Mexican economy entered into a recession and shrunk by 4.74 %. In 2010, the growth rate again returned to a positive figure (growth rate in 2010 was 5.19 %) and did not reach a negative figure in the following years. The global economic crisis led the Mexican economy to enter a recession in 2009, but this recession did not last long.

Peru was also affected by the global economic crisis through the financial channel. Foreign capital entering the country and short-term foreign exchange debts and credits caused the country to be affected by the crisis. Looking at the growth rate of the Peruvian economy during the global economic crisis we saw that:

Peru's growth rate, which was 9.14 % in 2008, dropped to 1.04 % in 2009 due to the global economic crisis (a decline of 8.1 % after one year of growth). The growth rate of 1.04 % in 2009 raised to 8.45 % in 2010 (a year-on-year growth rate of 7.41 %) and the global economic crisis has not hindered the growth of the Peruvian economy after 2010.

At the core of the Venezuelan economy is the production and exports of oil and heavy industrial products such as steel, aluminum and cement. The Venezuelan economy grew at a rate of 8.75 % in 2007 with rising oil prices together with rising government spending. During the global economic crisis, the economic growth of the country slowed down from 8.75 % to 5.27 % in 2008 due to the drop-in oil prices and a reduction in demand for industrial products and hence exports. In 2009, the Venezuelan economy entered into a recession with the growth rate falling to -3.20 %. Entering 2010, the contraction in the economy continued and the growth rate was -1.48 %. In other words, the Venezuelan economy shrank in 2009 and 2010 due to the global economic crisis. In 2011, the economy started to grow again in positive proportions and the growth rate rose to 4.17 %. To

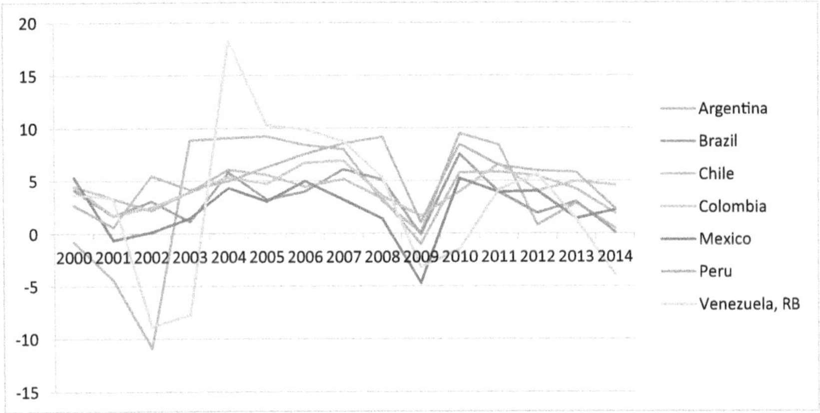

Fig. 8.1: The GDP Growth Rates of EMEs of South America between 2000 and 2014. Authors on calculation based on World Bank Data (2016)

summarize, it can be said that Venezuela's economy had suffered the effects of the global economic crisis and experienced a recession between 2007 and 2010.

As seen in Fig. 8.1, except for Peru, the growth rates of all EMEs of South America experienced a decline in 2008. The countries that had the greatest declines in their growth rates were Argentina, Venezuela and Columbia, respectively. In 2009, however, Peru's growth rate showed a sharp downfall (The 9.14 % growth rate in 2008 dropped by 8.1 % to 1.04 %). Among these South American economies, the countries with the greatest or the sharpest declines were Venezuela, (a drop of 8.47 % in its growth rate) followed by Peru (a decline of 8.1 %) and Mexico (a 6.11 % decline). All the countries experienced their greatest declines in 2009 for 2000 to 2014 period. Some of these countries had negative growth rates or a contraction in their economy. The economies with negative growth rates were: Mexico with -4.74 %, Venezuela with -3.20 % and Chile with -1.03 %. After the greatest decline in their growth rates in 2009, these economies began to recover after 2009 and the countries with the highest growth rates in 2010 were Mexico, Argentina and Peru, respectively. While many South American EMEs saw an upward shift in their economies after 2009, others saw this recovery in 2010 and 2011. In this sense, the country which had the latest revival was Venezuela and the country which had the most rapid revival was Argentina followed by Mexico. Except for Venezuela, all other countries again saw a decline in their growth rates after 2010 with Argentina having the greatest decrease in its growth rate in 2011. Similarly, Brazil and Peru also saw a decline in their growth rates in 2011, while Chile and Columbia saw a decline in their growth rates after 2012.

8.3.2 Europe

In Bulgaria, the period prior to the global economic crisis (2001–2008) was a period in which the income of the country and foreign capital increased rapidly due to the tax revenue from goods and services with production and also employment expanding due to the increased income. However, in 2009, the income level of Bulgaria's tax revenues and non-tax revenues declined rapidly. The country's export volume fell, because its trading partners were affected by the global economic crisis, but more so by the recession created by the European debt crisis. (In particular, at the end of 2008 and during the first quarter of 2009). In the last quarter of 2008, the credit flow in the world resulted in a decline in the GDP of Bulgaria for the first time since the 1996–1997 crises. As a result, unemployment increased rapidly (Center for the Study of Democracy, 2011). Thus, the Bulgarian economy was adversely affected by the crisis environment due to its trade and finance channels. As shown by the growth rates in Tab. 8.1, the growth rates of Bulgaria were 7.67 % in 2007, 5.64 % in 2008 and as a result of the global economic crisis, Bulgaria entered into a recession in 2009 with the growth rate decreasing to 4.12 %. In other words, the economy contracted by – 4.21 % in 2009. Although the Bulgarian economy, affected by the global economic crisis and the European debt crisis, showed a positive growth again in 2010, it was able to grow only between 0.05 % and 1.58 % between 2010 and 2012 because of the impact of the European debt crisis, with rates of (0.05 % in 2010, and 1.58 % in 2011 and 0.24 % in 2012).

Hungary became the first country among former socialist countries to achieve market reforms and gradually liberalized its economy in the 1980s. In the 1990s, Hungary was very close to the EU member states in terms of income level and institutional development. However, this progress in its economy came to an end in 2005. The Hungarian economy's weakness during the global economic crisis and the European debt crisis was its outstanding foreign exchange debt and the budget deficits. Before the global crisis, Hungarian banks borrowed at a high international level in foreign currency and gave loans to households and firms. In other words, it was the finance channel which put the Hungarian economy into difficulty during the crisis. Looking at the Hungarian economy's post-2007 situation in terms of its growth rate we note that:

The growth rate of Hungary, which was 3.80 % in 2006, fell sharply to 0.42 % in 2007 with the global economic crisis. The growth rate of the country was

0.83 % in 2008 and fell to -6.55 % in 2009 and the country entered into a recession. In 2012, the economy also experienced a contraction due to the European debt crisis (-1.68 %) however, this recession lasted only one year.

As the EU nations entered the global recession and the economies of the neighboring countries diminished, a single country in the region continued to grow: Poland. The durability of Poland against the global economic crisis was the prevention of a decline in both demand and supply. In order to prevent a drop-in demand, a tax cut from labor income was implemented and an expanding monetary policy applied. In addition to this, support was provided for the supply side. With the effects of the global economic crisis at its peak in 2009, as a result of the normal activities of the capital markets in the country and the existence of a strong and positive labor force, Poland was relatively less affected by the global economic crisis and the European debt crisis than other European countries. (Gradzewicz, Growiec, Kolasa, Postek, Strzelecki, 2014). When we look at the Polish economy during the global economic crisis and European debt crisis in terms of growth rate it is noted that the growth rate of the Polish economy declined from 7.20 % in 2007 to 3.92 % in 2008 and to 2.63 % in 2009 due to the global economic crisis. The growth rate, which rose to 3.69 % and 5 % in 2010 and 2011, fell to 1.56 % in 2012 under the effects of the European debt crisis. The Polish economy has been one of the countries affected by both the global economic crisis and the European debt crisis.

The economy of Romania was also one of the economies affected by both the global economic crisis and the European debt crisis. The global crisis affected the Romanian economy through its trade and financial channels: From the point of commerce, Romania's export volume declined and from the point of finance, investors' confidence in the financial sector turned negative as a result of many investors withdrawing their investments in the Eastern European region. Access to foreign capital became restricted and the value of the local currency fell considerably (depreciated) (Simona, Marinescu, Toma, 2012). The Romanian economy was affected by the global economic crisis as well as the European debt crisis. When looking at the country's growth rate during the global economic crisis and the European debt crisis period we see that:

While Romania grew at a rate of 8.05 % in 2006, this rate decreased to 6.86 % in 2007 due to the global economic crisis but rose to 8.45 % in 2008. In 2009, the Romanian economy entered a serious recession, this time due to the European debt crisis and its growth rate dropped to a low of 7.06 %. The Romanian economy also grew at a negative rate in 2010 (i.e., shrunk) and the growth rate was realized at 0.79 %. In other words, the European debt crisis caused a recession in Romania for two consecutive years.

In 2011 and 2012, the economy began a positive growth. In other words, the Romanian economy was overcoming the effects of the European debt crisis. However, even though this EME in Eastern Europe started to grow at a positive rate after 2011, this growth rate has been fluctuating as a result of the European debt crisis.

The economy of Russia is the fastest growing EME after China and India. The global economic crisis, having spread to all parts of the globe in 2008, also reached Russia and Russia's export volume, which is mostly based on raw material exports, contracted. In other words, the Russian economy was most affected by the trade channel during the global economic crisis. The drop-in oil prices from $145 to $37 in 2008–2009 caused the unemployment rate in Russia to fall below the natural rate of unemployment. During this period, the domestic currency experienced considerable depreciation against foreign currencies and the amount of loans in foreign currency increased. Despite this unfavorable picture, the significant amount of gold stocks in Russia eased the severity of the foreign exchange and budgetary income crisis (at the end of 2009). When we look at the effects of these facts on the growth rate of the Russian economy we note that:

While the Russian economy grew by 8.53 % in 2007 this rate fell to 5.24 % in 2008 due to the global economic crisis. In 2009, there was a serious recession in the economy and the growth rate of the Russian economy fell drastically to 7.82 %. However, this situation lasted only one year and the country's economy began to grow again in positive numbers in 2010 (the rate of growth in 2010 was 4.50 %). Despite this growth in 2010, with the impact of the European debt crisis, Russia entered a low growth trend after 2010 (4.50 % in 2010, 4.26 % in 2011 and 3.40 % in 2012). These figures show that Russia entered into a serious recession in 2009, which was affected by both the global economic crisis and by the European debt crisis. The economic growth rate of the country continued to lose its tempo until 2013, and nearly suffered a recession in 2014 and a serious economic crisis in late 2014.

The Turkish economy underwent its greatest economic crises since the Second World War with the onset of the global economic crisis. Turkey's growth performance during the crisis was one of the worst performances among the EMEs. As in many EMEs, the global economic crisis hit Turkey mainly with a contraction in exports, namely the trade channel. In addition, the financial difficulties experienced by other EMEs, namely the shortage of foreign capital and foreign exchange market fluctuations (exchange rate shocks), as well as the negative expectations of investors and consumers, caused Turkey to be deeply affected by the crisis. Nevertheless, when compared to the economic crisis in 2001, Turkey's lessons learned from the 2001 crisis and the strengthening of its financial infrastructure has shown that the amount of foreign capital which left the country was less than the amount of foreign capital leaving in the previous crises. When looked at from this perspective, Turkey survived the financial shocks caused by the global economic crisis more successfully in terms of losses and time than it did from the economic shocks from previous crises (Cömert and Çolak, 2014). In summary, due to the global economic crisis, the financial system in Turkey did not collapse as was the case for many EMEs. Given Turkey's growth performance during the global economic crisis it is seen that:

The growth rate of the Turkish economy in 2006 was 6.89 %, fell to 4.66 % in 2007 and fell to 0.65 % in 2008 due to the global crisis. In 2009, the economy entered into a recession and the growth rate dropped to -4.82 %. In 2010, there was a significant revival in the economy and the growth rate rose to 9.15 %. Although Turkey is not a member of the EU, it has been one of the countries affected by the European debt crisis. The growth rate of 9.15 % achieved in 2010 declined in 2011 and 2012 (The growth rate was 8.77 % in 2011 and 2.12 % in 2012) due to the impact of the European debt crisis.

In summary, the Turkish Economy shrunk with the impact of the global economic crisis, entered a recession in 2009, and suffered the effects of the European Debt Crisis in 2011 and 2012.

The economy of the Ukraine was also affected by the global economic crisis as well as the European debt crisis. As a result, the price of the steel exported by the country fell, the dollar's debt burden increased, the banking problems in the country and Russia's natural gas supply cutoff in January 2009 are given as reasons for the crisis. This led to a contraction in the production volume in the metallurgical and machine-building sectors, the main industries in the country, and layoff of workers. The implications of the above on the growth rate of Ukrainian Economy are as follows:

The growth rate of the Ukrainian Economy, which was 7.90 % in 2007, dropped to 2.30 % in 2008 during the global economic crisis for the above-mentioned reasons. In 2009, the economy entered into serious recession and its growth dropped to -14.8 %. Entering 2010, there was a significant recovery in the economy and the growth rate rose to 4.2 %. In 2011, the economy grew by 1 % and the growth rate rose to 5.2 %. However, due to the debt crisis in Europe, the Ukrainian economy started to shrink again from 2012 onwards.

In summary, it can be said that the Ukrainian economy was affected by the global economic crisis combined with the European debt crisis and entered into a recession in 2009.

In Fig. 8.2, the growth rates of the EMEs of the European Union are given for 2000–2014 and a comparison is made between these countries.

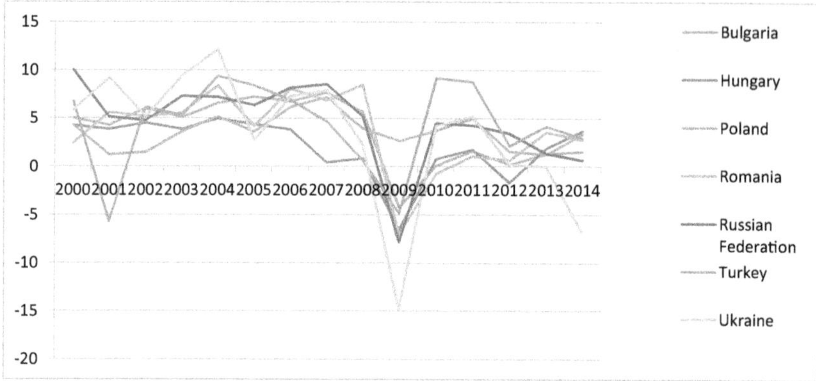

Fig. 8.2: The Growth Rates of the EMEs of the EU between 2000 and 2014. Authors on calculation based on World Bank Data (2016)

With the spread of the global economic crisis there are three EMEs that had a reduction in their growth rate in 2007 when compared to the previous year. Compared to 2006, the economy of Hungary declined by 3.40 %, the economy of Turkey by 2.2 %, and Romania's economy by 1.19 %. In 2008, when we list the countries which suffered the lowest decline in their growth rates to those which suffered the greatest decline, Ukraine was -5.6 %, Turkey -4 %, Poland -3.28 % and Bulgaria -2.03 %.

In 2009, growth rates of these countries again declined due to the European debt crisis. Ukraine had the greatest drop (-16 %) followed by Romania, Bulgaria, Hungary, Turkey and Poland respectively. In 2010, again the economies revived and from the highest growth rate to the lowest, the order was Ukraine, Turkey, Hungary, Bulgaria and Poland. Because of the debt crisis in Europe, Romania experienced a negative growth rate for two consecutive years and entered into a deep recession.

8.3.3 Asia

The economy of Bangladesh has become increasingly integrated into the global economy in recent years, particularly through commodity and financial channels (with portfolio investments and foreign direct investments). The Bangladesh economy's trade gap in 2007 was 43.4 %, and its net exports for the same year corresponded to 10 % of its GDP. About 85 % of its exports and 60 % of its imports is to developed economies (Rahman, Battacharya, Iqbal, Khan, Paul,

2009). The country's economy has not escaped the adverse effects of the global economic crisis because of its commercial and financial links. Due to the global economic crisis, the growth rate of the country started to decrease in 2008 with a growth rate of 7.05 % in 2007 dropping to 6.01 % in 2008 and to 5.04 % in 2009. From 2010 to 2012, the growth rate increased from around 5 % to around 6 %. It appears that the global economic crisis affected the Bangladesh economy with a growth rate of a 2 % decline.

The Chinese economy is neither a fully centralized economy nor a full market economy. However, China has abandoned strict socialism practices since 1978 and has significantly increased production and foreign trade through liberal practices. The economy of China has become one of the most important forces in the world economy with the reforms it has undergone during the last thirty years. The country has experienced a very rapid growth during this period and behind this success lies the fact that the country attracts large amounts of foreign direct investments. Moreover, China is now among the world's largest exporters, with foreign exchange reserves and budget surpluses at record levels. After the country's membership to the World Trade Organization (WTO), exports and growth gained momentum and the export success of this country began to threaten other countries (Morrison, 2009).

Given the country's growth rate prior to the global economic crisis, it is clear how strong the Chinese economy is. In 2004, while the world economy grew at a rate of 5.1 %, China grew at a rate of 9.5 %. In 2005, the world economy grew at around 5 %, while China's growth rate was 9.3 % (World Bank, 2007). China's GDP (according to the purchasing power parity) in 2005 was nearly $ 98,859B and this success made China the world's second largest economy after the USA. In 2007, China passed the USA to become the next largest exporter after the EU. As mentioned above, foreign direct investment (FDI) in China is the most important factor behind the country's productivity and rapid economic growth. In 2007, the amount of FDI in China reached $ 75B and the Chinese economy was the first among EMEs drawing the most foreign capital and third after the EU and the USA.

China has very high reserves in terms of foreign currencies and it is an important force which can create significant effects on the global economy with the policies that it implements. While the conditions for China seemed so positive, the global economic crisis and the global economic slowdown also threatened the Chinese economy despite its having attracted large amounts of FDI with a very high volume of exports. China has, of course, implemented various policies to ease the negative effects of the global economic crisis, but the measures and policies implemented by the developing countries during the crisis will not be considered under this heading in order to make it more self-evident (Morrison, 2009).

Looking at China's growth rate during the global economic crisis, the growth rate of the country was 14.19 % in 2007 and decreased to 9.62 % in 2008 during the crisis which affected the world economy (Tab. 8.1). The drop in the average growth of 4.5 % in 2008 did not last very long and the growth rate of only 9 % for two years rose to 10.63 % in 2010. Although the growth rates in 2008 and 2009 remained below the 2007 growth rate, the Chinese economy did not experience any recession during the global economic crisis. The growth rate of the country has only declined for two consecutive years. The growth rate of the country after 2011 was still below the growth rate in 2007. China's economy lagged behind its previous growth performance as the global crisis and the debt crisis in Europe continued. However, China is one of the few countries that has survived the global economic crisis with minimum damage.

India is the fastest growing emerging market economy after China. The Indian economy slowed down in 2008 due to the global economic crisis but did not undergo a recession. (The growth rate of 9.8 % in 2007 and 3.9 % in 2008). There are several reasons for this positive result. First, while the global crisis entered an acute stage, India's financial markets and banks were able to continue their normal functioning. Secondly, the foreign exchange reserves of the country, despite the decline in the volume of exports and decreasing capital inflows, were sufficient to keep the balance of payments in check. Thirdly, inflation showed a decline during this period and finally, compulsory agricultural credits and social security programs did not result in a decline in demand in the rural areas of the country (Viswanathan, 2010). The Indian economy, which grew at a rate of 9 % during the last four years before the global crisis, entered a slowdown from the last quarter of 2008. Due to the global economic crisis, the economy of India grew by an average of 6 % less in 2008 when compared to the previous year (the 9.80 % growth in 2007 was 3.89 % in 2008). The economy was most negatively affected by the global economic crisis in 2008: still, the economy grew by 3.89 % in 2008 and by 8.47 % the following year. Although the Indian economy did not reach the high growth rates it enjoyed prior to 2007 due to the global decline of financial transactions and the level of demand (as a result of its trading and financial channels), like many EMEs, the Indian economy did not experience a recession (stagnation) due to the global economic crisis.

In Fig. 8.3 the growth rates of the three EMEs (China, India and Russia), which have the highest growth rates since 2005, are shown and compared to each other. Bearing in mind the growth rates of the EMEs, a review was conducted to see whether or not these countries suffered the effects of the global economic

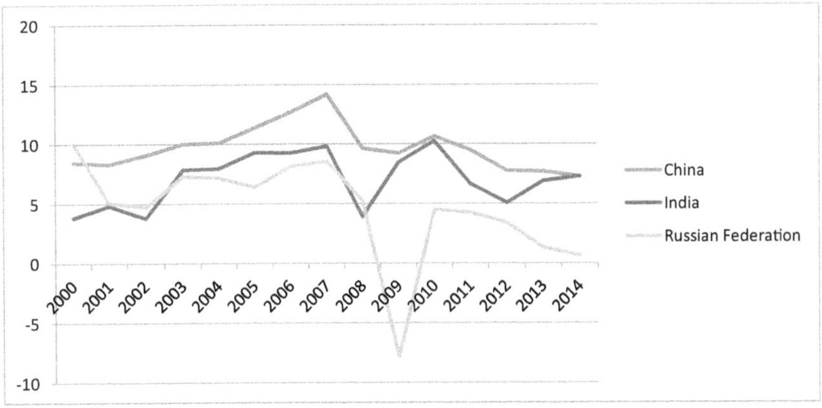

Fig. 8.3: The Growth Rates of China, India and Russia between 2000 and 2014. Authors on calculation based on World Bank Data (2016)

crisis and the European debt crisis and if so, to what extent they were affected and whether or not they entered into a recession.

During 2007, the growth rate of the three countries declined. India's growth dropped by 5.90 % in 2008 when compared to the previous year, China's growth declined by 4.57 % while Russia's declined by 3.29 %. In 2009, the growth rate of China's economy had not changed significantly when compared to the previous year, while the growth rates of India and Russia changed by 4.58 % and -13.06 %, respectively. Among these three EMEs, the country which was affected the least by the crisis and which quickly returned to its growth rate prior to the crisis was India, the country that was most affected by the global crisis was Russia.

Like many other EMEs, the reason for the effect of the global economic crisis on the Indonesian economy has been the trade channel. The declining world demand and the shrinking export market, a result of the global economic crisis, forced sectors in Indonesia which produced for exports to produce less and employ less labor. Less production, fewer exports and unemployment lowered income levels and, as a result, slowed the growth rate (Tambunan, 2010:156). Given the growth momentum of Indonesia's economy, when examined during the global economic crisis and its aftermath it is seen that:

The growth rate of the Indonesian economy in 2008 was almost the same as its growth rate in 2007 (6.34 % in 2007, 6.01 % in 2008). However, with the global economic crisis affecting the country's economy, growth decreased by 1.39 % when compared to the growth rate in 2008 (growth rate was 6.01 % in 2008,

4.62 % in 2009). The 2009 growth rate of 4.62 % increased by 1.6 % to 6.22 % the following year. Although the Indonesian economy grew only by 1.39 % in 2009 when compared to 2008, the country did not experience any recession due to the global economic crisis.

Malaysia has an open economy and the global economic crisis had a negative impact on the country's economy because it caused the contraction of the export volume of the country. The growth rate of the Malaysian economy dropped from 6.29 % in 2007 to 4.83 % in 2008. In other words, the growth rate from 2007 to 2008 declined by 1.46 %. This decrease in the growth rate was not limited to 2008, and in 2009 the Malaysian economy contracted by 1.51 %, that is, the economy entered into a recession. Entering 2010, the economy began to grow again with an increase on an average of 8 % to 7.42 % after declining by 1.51 % in 2009.

The global economic crisis affected the Malaysian economy in 2008 and 2009. In 2009, the economy of the country entered into a recession, but during the same year it was able to exit this recession.

The economy of Pakistan, together with the global economic crisis, was most affected by the shrinking global demand, i.e. the trade channel. Financial channels are given as a secondary reason. In other words, the decrease in the amount of foreign capital entering the country and the decrease in the capital account are other reasons for the effects of the global economic crisis on the Pakistani economy. Looking at the pace of growth of the economy of Pakistan during the global economic crisis we can state that:

The growth rate of Pakistan, which was 4.83 % in 2007, dropped to 1.70 % in 2008 (The growth rate declined by 3.13 % from 2007 to 2008). Rising to 2.83 % in 2009, it again decreased to 1.60 % in 2010. After 2011, the growth rate of Pakistan's economy started to increase. In summary, the Pakistani economy was affected by the global economic crisis, but that the global crisis did not lead the country into a recession.

Behind the impact of the global economic crisis on the Philippine economy, were diminishing exports caused by the crisis, namely trade channels and unresolved structural issues in the country. In terms of the growth momentum of the Philippine economy during the global economic crisis we observe that:

The growth rate of the country, which was 6.61 % in 2007, dropped to 4.15 % in 2008 due to the global crisis. In other words, the growth rate declined by 2.46 % from 2007 to 2008. The growth rate of 4.15 % in 2008 was 1.14 % in 2009, meaning a contraction of 3.01 % from 2008 to 2009. However, the adverse effect of the global economic crisis on the country's economy lost its affect in 2009 and the growth rate increased to 7.63 % in 2010. Although the global economic crisis caused fluctuations in the growth rate of the Philippines, the country did not experience a recession.

The Thailand economy has become an economy that has grown up as an engine of exports and foreign investments. In 2006, 70 % of the country's GDP consisted of export revenues. In the same year, Thailand's GDP was $ 2.5T, while total FDI amounted to $ 1.4T. With the global economic crisis, the export volume of the country and the amount of foreign investments coming to the country decreased. In other words, the crisis affected the country's economy through both trade and finance channels. When we look at the growth rate of the economy during the global economic crisis we note that:

While Thailand's growth rate was 5.43 % in 2007, this rate dropped to 1.72 % in 2008 due to the impact of the global economic crisis. In 2009, the Thailand economy entered into a recession and the growth rate dropped to -0.73 %. In 2010, the country came out of the recession, the economy revived and its growth rate rose to 7.50 %.

To summarize, the Thai economy entered a recession in 2009 with the impact of the global economic crisis, but this recession lasted only one year and the economy revived again the following year.

8.3.4 Africa

When the global economic crisis reached the Republic of South Africa, the country had recently emerged from a long period of growth. South African was also affected by the decline in global demand, that is, the trade channel was the most affected with the export volume of the country declining considerably. However, the strong financial structure of the country helped South Africa to have a smaller decline in its growth rate than was expected.

Fig. 8.4 shows the GDP growth rates of EMEs of Asia and Africa between 2000 and 2014. When looking at South Africa's growth rate during the global economic crisis, we can see that the Republic of South Africa grew at a rate of 5.36 % in 2007, but this rate decreased to 3.19 % in 2008 due to the global economic crisis. In 2009, the South African economy entered into a recession and the economy contracted by -1.53 %. In 2010, there was a recovery in the economy and the growth rate rose to 3.03 %. In summary, the South African economy was affected by the global economic crisis and under its effects went into a recession in 2009.

The first EME of Asia affected by the global economic crisis was Pakistan in 2007 (see Fig. 8.4). Pakistan's growth rate in 2007 decreased by 1.34 % to 4.83 %. In 2008, Malaysia, the Philippines, Thailand and the Republic of South Africa were affected by the global economic crisis: Malaysia's GDP growth rate decreased by 1.46 %, the Philippines by 2.46 %, Thailand by 3.71 % and South Africa by

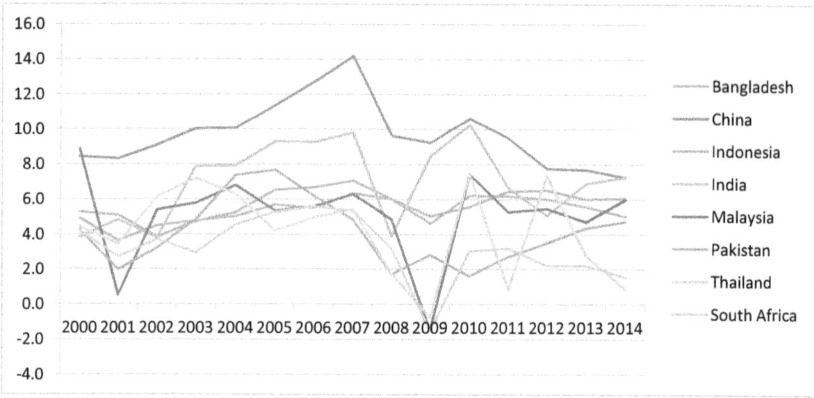

Fig. 8.4: The GDP Growth Rates of EMEs of Asia and Africa between 2000 and 2014. Authors on calculation based on World Bank Data (2016)

2.17 %. In 2009, Indonesia also was affected by the global economic crisis as well. Among these countries, the three economies which had the sharpest decline in 2009 was Malaysia (growth rate dropped by 6.34 % when compared to the previous year), South Africa (the decline in 2009 was 4.72 % when compared to the previous year) and Pakistan (a decline of 3.13 % too place in 2008 when compared to the previous year).

Within the period 2004–2012, these countries reached their lowest growth rates in 2008 and 2009. Some of these countries dropped into the negative area as shown in the figure; that is to say, their GDP growth rates were negative. These countries were South Africa (The growth rate in 2009 was -1.53 %), Malaysia (In 2009 the growth rate was -1.51 %) and Thailand (The GDP growth rate was -0.73 %). The other countries did not undergo a negative growth rate. Having reached their lowest growth rates or negative growth rates in 2008 and 2009, their economies revived in 2009 and 2010. The three countries with the highest growth rates in 2010 were Malaysia, Thailand and the Philippines respectively. The first country to be affected by the crisis was Pakistan (in 2007) and the first country to exit the crisis was again Pakistan (in 2009). In 2011, some countries again had a decline in their GDP growth rates. These countries, from the largest declines to the smallest declines are as follows: Thailand, with an approximately 6.5 % fall in its growth rate, the Philippines with a 4 % decrease and South Africa with a 1 % decrease. None of the other countries saw a fall in their growth rates again.

8.4 Conclusion

The acceleration of globalization from the mid-1980s increased the flow of goods, services and production between countries and the economies of nations have become integrated. This integration of economies accelerated the spread of the crises that started in developed countries to other countries of the world.

In the financial and real sector crisis that started in the USA, in particular by means of the strong financial relations, led to the contagion of first, the financial and real sectors of the developed countries of the EU and later to the same sectors of other developed countries in the world which in turn had a negative impact on these economies or was the cause of these economies entering into an economic crisis.

The crisis began in the USA and became globalized, even though, at first, the crisis affected the developed countries, later many of the EMEs had declines in their growth rates and, in fact, some of these economies exhibited negative economic growth.

All of the Latin American, EU, Asian EMEs and South Africa were affected by the global economic crisis as well as the European debt crisis and experienced decreases in their growth rates. Even though the EMEs were not affected by the crises to the same extent as the developed countries, certain EMEs saw their growth rates in negative figures. However, the recessions which took place in these EMEs did not become a full blown economic crisis and their economies revived within a short period.

Appendix: What is Growth and How is it Measured?

The continuous increase of goods and services produced by a country within a given time period is said to be "economic growth." As can be understood from this definition, in order for the amount of goods and services to be considered as growth or in other words, for an increase in real Gross Domestic Product (GDP) to be considered as growth, this increase has to be continuous (not temporary). Economic growth is the only path to follow in order to increase the living standards of individuals living in a country and for this reason one of the basic economic targets of nations is to able to attain a rapid growth rate (Ünsal, 2003: 15).

Economic growth is measured as "average growth rate (g)". The average growth rate or real GDP shows the annual growth rate. The average growth rate can also be referred to as the "long-term growth rate" and is calculated as follows:

$$g = \left[\frac{Real\ GDP\ at\ the\ End\ of\ the\ Period}{Real\ GDP\ at\ the\ Beginning\ of\ the\ Period}\right]^{1/n} - 1 \quad (1.1)$$

where “n” is the number of years.

Economic growth is sometimes measured as “the annual growth rate.” The annual growth rate is the difference between the change in real GDP during t and t-1 years with the rate of real GDP in t-1 year multiplied by 100.

$$\text{Growth Rate in } t \text{ year} = \frac{GDP_t - GDP_{t-1}}{GDP_{t-1}} \cdot 100 \quad (1.2)$$

While a decline in a country’s current growth rate indicates a contraction in the economy, an increase in the growth rate signals growth in the economy (Ünsal, 2003: 16).

References

Canuto, O. (2008). The Impact of The Global Financial Crisis on Developing Countries. Impacts of The Financial Crisis on Brazil. Sussex: Institute of Development Studies. Retrieved from https://www.ids.ac.uk/files/dmfile/BRAZILOtavianoCanuto.pdf. Access Date: 14 July 2016

Cömert, H., Çolak, M. S. (2014). *The Impacts of the Global Crisis on the Turkish Economy and Policy Responses.* (No.1417). Ankara: ERC-Economic Research Center, Middle East Technical University (METU), Retrieved from http://www.erc.metu.edu.tr/menu/series14/1417.pdf. Access Date: 24 June 2016

Gradzewicz, M., Growiec, J. Kolasa, M., Postek, T., Strzelecki, P. (2014). *Poland’s Exceptional Performance During the World Economic Crisis: New Growth Accounting Evidence.* (Working Paper No: 186). Warsaw: Naradowy Bank Polski (NBP) Retrieved from https://www.nbp.pl/publikacje/materialy_i_studia/186_en.pdf. Access Date: 10 July 2016

Kibritçioğlu, A. (2011a, 20 September). The Components and Complexity of the Global Economic Crisis of 2006–2011. *Munich Personal Repec Archieve.* Retrieved from http://mpra.ub.uni-muenchen.de/33515. Access Date: 4 May 2017

Kibritçioğlu, A., (2011b, 25 September). Current Sovereign Debt Crisis in Eurozone Countries. *Munich Personal Repec Archieve.* Retrieved from http://mpra.ub.uni-muenchen.de/33528. Access Date: 4 May 2017

Morrison, M. W. (2009). *China and the Global Financial Crisis: Implications for the United States.* Congressional Research Service: CRS Report for Congress (Prepared for Members and Committees of Congress). Retrieved from https://fas.org/sgp/crs/row/RS22984.pdf. Access Date: 17 July 2016

Özatay, F., (2014) Finansal Krizler ve Türkiye, (5th Edition) İstanbul: Doğan Press.

Rahman, M., Bhattacharya, D., Iqbal, M. A., Khan, T. I. and Paul, T.K. (2009). *Global Financial Crisis Discussion Series: Bangladesh.* (Series. 1). London: Overseas Development Institute (ODI). Retrieved from https://www.odi.org/sites/odi.org.uk/files/odi-assets/publications-opinion-files/4319.pdf. Access Date: 17 April 2017

Rogers., M. (2008, 10 October). Argentina and the Global Financial Crisis. The Argentina Independent, Argentina, p. 12. Retrieved from http://www.argentinaindependent.com/currentaffairs/latest-news/newsfromargentina/argentina-and-the-global-financial-crisis/. Access Date: 14 April 2017

Sidaoui, J., Ramos-Francia, M., Cuadra, G. (2010). *The Global Financial Crisis and Policy Response in Mexico* (BIS Papers No:54). Mexico: Bank for International Settlements (BIS). Retrieved from http://www.bis.org/publ/bppdf/bispap54q.pdf. Access Date: 14 July 2016

Simona, O., Marinescu, P., Toma, S. G. (2012). *World Economic Crisis and Its Effects on Romanian Economy.* (No.93). Siedlice: Institute of Management and Marketing, Siedlice University of Natural Sciences and Humanities. Retrieved from http://www.tstefaniuk.uph.edu.pl/zeszyty/archiwalne/93-2012_4.pdf. Access Date: 8 July 2016

Tambunan, T.H. (2010). The Indonesian Experience with Two Big Economic Crises. Modern Economy, 1, 156–167 Retrieved from: http://www.SciRP.org/journal/me. Access Date: 20 July 2016

The Hidden Economy in Bulgaria After the Economics Crisis. (2011, April). Brief No: 28). Sofia: Center for The Study of Democracy Retrieved from http://library.fes.de/pdf-files/bueros/sofia/08099.pdf. Access Date: 14 July 2016

Ünsal, E. (2003). *Makro İktisat.* Ankara: Turhan Kitapevi

Viswanathan, K. G. (2010). The Global Financial Crisis and its Impact on India. *Journal of International Business and Law*, 9 (1), 40–62. Retrieved from http://scholarlycommons.law.hofstra.edu/cgi/viewcontent.cgi?article=1112&context=jibl World Bank Data (2016), Development Indicators, http://databank.worldbank.org/data/home.aspx. Access Date: 26 April 2017

World Bank (2007). Development and the Next Generation, world development report 2007, 317 pages, The World Bank, Washington DC.

Yıldırım, S., (2010). 2008 Yılı Küresel Ekonomi Krizinin Dünya ve Türkiye Ekonomisine Etkileri. KMÜ Social and Economic Research Magazine *12*(18), 47–55. Retrieved from http://hdl.handle.net/11492/333. Access Date: 22 March 2017

Duygu Yolcu Karadam

9 Inflation as a Historical Problem in EMEs

Abstract: This chapter presents an analysis of inflation in emerging market economies (EMEs) and the changing factors behind their inflation process from the 1980s to recent years. Due to the structural problems in their economies, many EMEs have had to deal with high and volatile inflation throughout their histories. Among these countries Latin American countries have had the worst performance in inflation and inflation volatility and have had to deal with a number of hyperinflation episodes. However, the majority of EMEs have managed to reduce their inflation rates considerably during the second half of the 1990s with the contribution of a number of domestic and external factors such as greater fiscal discipline, institutional and structural reforms, and low external inflation environments. They have, to a large extent, succeeded in removing the structural domestic factors behind the inflation process and have entered the 2000s in a mild inflation environment with a few exceptions such as Turkey, Romania and Venezuela. However, associated with intensified economic globalization, the changing nature of inflation dynamics has become one of the new challenges for both emerging and industrial countries. During this process, global factors have played a dominant role in inflation in EMEs. Consistent with the globalization of inflation hypothesis, global factors have, to a large extent, started to replace domestic factors as the primary determinants of inflation. On one side, the increased levels of competition in both the product and the labor markets and low demand during the global financial crisis have put downward pressure on prices in EMEs. On the other side, rising commodity prices emerged as an important driver of the inflation process for both EMEs and industrial countries after the 2000s. Given their high demand for commodities, Asian countries have faced a much greater increase in inflation relative to Latin American and European EMEs after 2007. However, considerable decline in oil prices after 2012 has led to a downward pressure on inflation for most of the EMEs during this period except for oil exporting countries.

Keywords: Inflation, Commodity Prices, Globalization of Inflation

9.1 Introduction

Accruing at two or triple-digit levels, inflation has been one of the leading problems of EMEs, particularly until the end of the 1990s. However, as a result of some global and domestic factors, the majority of the EMEs have experienced dramatic declines in the level and the volatility of inflation since the second-half of the 1990s. The fall in global inflation and the adoption of sounder macroeconomic policies have played important roles during this disinflation process. Even though inflation performance has been widely varied across regions, a major part of those economies has eradicated the structural factors behind high and persistent inflation in the first half of the past decade.

However, as EMEs grow and become more integrated into world trade and finance, the set of policy challenges they face becomes increasingly more complex. Associated with the rise in economic globalization, the dynamics of inflation has been changing for both industrial and emerging countries. In this respect, global factors have started to play a more important role in causing inflation. Consistently, changes in commodity prices have become the most important factor behind the changes in price levels in EMEs after 2000. Despite the repressive impact of the global financial crisis by slowing down the growth of demand, inflation in EMEs has continued to be affected by global food and energy prices according to their extent of global market integration.

This chapter basically analyzes the inflation performance of EMEs since the 1980s.[1] Section two presents a historical analysis of the inflation experience of EMEs in order to understand the main factors behind their high and volatile inflation. Section three focuses on the performance of inflation in the 1990s and examines how EMEs have achieved to lower inflation. Section four reviews the developments in inflation performances in the 2000s and analyzes how globalization has affected the dynamics of inflation in EMEs. Section five represents the inflation process during and after global financial crisis. Finally, section six concludes.

9.2 Historical Inflation Process in EMEs

High and persistent inflation has been one of the main macroeconomic challenges of EMEs. The majority of EMEs have had a history of moderate to high inflation in the 1970s and the 1980s. Even though it has never reached very high levels in emerging markets, accommodative monetary policy responses to the 1970s' supply shocks have also led to inflation in industrial countries. However, governments in advanced countries succeeded in bringing inflation under control during the second half of the 1980s by setting fiscal and monetary discipline with the aid of institutional and operational changes (IMF, 2001). While the average inflation in industrial countries has been around 9 % and has had a wide

1 The analyses in the book cover mainly the period 2000–2014. Since inflation experiences of EMEs during 1980s and 1990s are important for the changing dynamics of inflation in those economies in recent years, this chapter's analysis also covers some period before 2000s.

Tab. 9.1: Inflation in Industrial Countries and EMEs in 1980–2004 Period[1]. World Economic Outlook Database, April 2016

	1980–1984	1985–1989	1990–1994	1995–1999	2000–2004
World	14.8	16.5	31.2	8.8	4.1
Industrial Countries	9.1	4.0	3.8	2.0	2.0
EMEs	38.6	126.0	269.6	35.5	8.7
EMEs Excluding Argentina, Brazil, Bulgaria, Peru, Russia and Ukraine[2]	18.9	21.7	35.9	21.1	8.6

[1] Average of annual percentage change of the consumer price index.
[2] Those are the countries which experienced episodes of hyperinflation in the late 1980s and early 1990s.

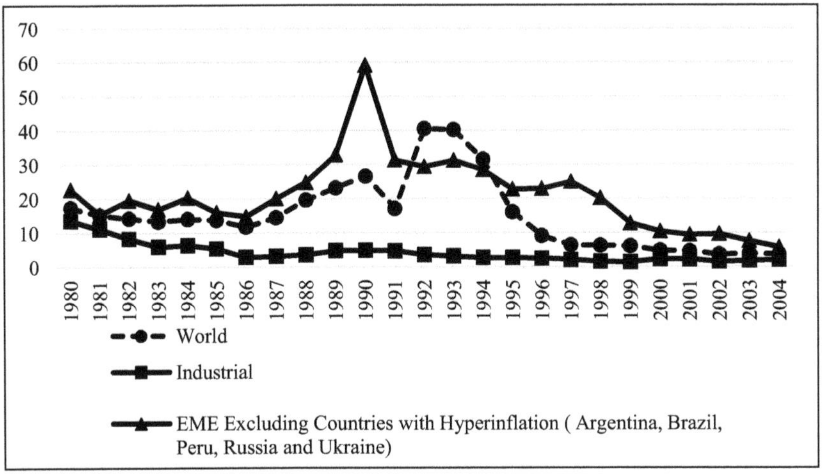

Fig. 9.1: Inflation in Industrial Countries and EMEs in 1980–2004 Period. World Economic Outlook Database, April 2016

dispersion across countries in the early 1980s, industrial countries have lowered their inflation levels to around 3–4 % and dispersion has been lower since the second half of the1980s (Tab. 9.1 and Fig. 9.1).

Contrary to the industrial countries, inflation has accrued at two- digit and triple-digit levels in the majority of EMEs in the 1970s and the 1980s. Accelerating in the second half of the 1980s, inflation has reached its maximum levels in the first half of the 1990s for the majority of EMEs. As shown in Tab. 9.1, inflation has risen to 126 % in the 1985–1989 period and to around 38 % in the 1980–1984 period and rose to 269.6 % in the 1990–1994 period. The reason behind this high increase in the average inflation was mainly the hyperinflation episodes of countries such as Argentina, Brazil, Bulgaria, Peru and Ukraine in the late 1980s and the early 1990s[2].

For the majority of the EMEs, inflation has been one of the foremost issues which they have had to cope with until the end of the 1990s. However, it is clearly evident from Tab. 9.2 that different regions have displayed different inflation performances. Emerging Asian countries have had the lowest inflation among the other EMEs which can be attributed to their stronger fiscal stance and sounder macroeconomic policies. Except for a few countries such as Bangladesh, Indonesia and Philippines, inflation rates were generally lower than 10 % even in the early 1980s. Contrary to the performance of Asian economies, Latin American countries have had the highest levels of inflation among EMEs which has been realized in two-digit or triple-digit for almost all of the countries in the region until the second-half of the 1990s. Among them, Argentina, Brazil and Peru have exhibited several episodes of hyperinflation in the late 1980s and early 1990s. Inflation levels of emerging Eastern European and African countries have been between the levels for those of Asian and Latin American countries. Except for Russia and Ukraine, whose data were not available before 1993, inflation has been persistently high (over 50 %) in Poland and Turkey while Bulgaria and Romania had low levels in inflation in the 1980s.

9.2.1 Why has Inflation been Historically High in Emerging Markets?

High inflation in developing and emerging countries can be attributed to various factors. There are two mainstream views on the dynamics of the inflation process. The first view states that inflation is determined by real factors, mostly by supply shocks and these real shocks cause price levels to be barely controllable by complicating the monetary transmission mechanism. According to the other view, inflation is a monetary phenomenon in the long run and non-monetary factors affect inflation only in the short-run. IMF (1996) states that on this basis, while inflation in industrial countries is generally explained by real factors such

2 For example, Brazil's inflation rate realized as 1430 % and 2947 % in 1989 and 1990. Similarly, the rate of inflation in Peru was 3398 % and 7481 % in 1989 and 1990, respectively.

Tab. 9.2: Regional Inflation in EMEs. World Economic Outlook Database, April 2016

	1980–1984	1985–1989	1990–1994	1995–1999	2000–2004
Asia	***9.7***	***7.1***	***8.2***	***8.3***	***3.5***
Bangladesh	11.8	10.0	6.3	6.5	3.9
China	2.3	12.0	10.3	5.2	1.1
India	10.2	7.2	10.4	8.6	4.0
Indonesia	12.4	6.9	8.6	20.6	8.0
Malaysia	6.0	1.3	3.9	3.5	1.5
Pakistan	8.4	6.1	9.5	9.8	3.8
Philippines	18.4	9.9	11.6	7.3	4.4
Thailand	8.5	3.2	4.8	5.1	1.7
Europe	***22.3***	***28.0***	***565.2***	***87.4***	***15.6***
Bulgaria	2.1	3.4	121.6	253.5	6.4
Hungary	7.2	10.7	25.5	18.9	7.1
Poland	45.8	73.9	153.3	16.4	4.4
Romania	5.0	1.0	178.5	66.1	25.9
Russia	-	-	591.1	74.7	16.5
Ukraine	-	-	2813.1	101.2	11.0
Turkey	51.6	51.0	73.4	81.0	37.7
Latin America	***84.4***	***347.6***	***554.4***	***18.7***	***8.0***
Argentina	268.1	863.3	505.1	0.8	8.3
Brazil	123.9	532.3	1667.1	19.3	8.7
Chile	22.4	20.4	17.5	6.0	2.8
Colombia	22.8	24.0	26.4	17.9	7.3
Mexico	56.2	81.9	16.3	24.5	6.0
Peru	84.1	878.5	1607.4	8.4	2.4
Venezuela	13.1	33.0	41.0	53.8	20.8
Africa	***13.6***	***15.7***	***12.4***	***7.4***	***5.5***
South Africa	13.6	15.7	12.4	7.4	5.5

as output gap and oil shocks, nominal factors provide the main mechanisms behind the sustained high inflation in EMEs.

Among the research on the mechanisms behind the high and persistent inflation in emerging and developing countries, the nexus between fiscal deficits, monetary growth and inflation emerges as the most important factor (Montiel, 1989; Dornbusch, 1992). Inflation problems tend to be generally associated with the monetization of excessive fiscal deficits and it generally gained persistence with a high degree of indexation of wages. Seigniorage has been widely used as an easy and costless way of financing fiscal deficits by many governments in EMEs. One reason for this is the limited access of developing and emerging countries to international markets which forces these countries to rely on domestic financing of fiscal deficits. Government revenue from seigniorage has been the lowest in Asian economies while it has been the highest in Latin American countries (IMF, 2001).

Exchange rate movement is another factor that has led to inflation in emerging and developing countries. Changes in exchange rates have affected inflation by raising import prices and reshaping inflation expectations (Bailliu et al., 2003). Due to the high dependence of their consumption and production on imports, pass-through of depreciations to domestic prices can be much greater in EMEs.

Besides these factors, shocks in food and energy prices play an important role on these countries' inflation processes since they account for a larger share in the CPI of EMEs than for industrial countries (Mohanty and Klau, 2001). Supply shocks can also create demand-driven inflationary pressure when they are accommodated by monetary policy.

9.3 The Trends in 1990s and Global Disinflation

High inflation process in the 1980s has continued for the majority of the EMEs peaking in the first-half of the 1990s especially in Latin America and Eastern Europe. The average inflation rate for EMEs has increased from 89 % in the 1980s to 257.4 % in the early 1990s (Tab. 9.1). Excluding hyperinflation countries, average inflation rate has risen from around 20 % to 36 %. Countries such as Argentina, Brazil, Peru, Russia and Ukraine suffered hyperinflations in the 1990–1995s which was mainly caused by monetary expansion due to central bank financing of fiscal deficits.[3] For instance, Brazil's inflation rate exceeded 1000 % in almost all the years between 1989 and 1993. On the other hand, countries such as Chile, Colombia, and Mexico, witnessed relatively moderate inflation rates, averaging around 20 % in this period. However, on the average, emerging Asian countries have had the best performance among other regions pursuing 8–10 % inflation during this period. Associated with boom in investments, only China has experienced a remarkable rapid rise in inflation in the 1992–1995 period reaching 25 % levels.

During the second half of the 1990s, emerging economies have exhibited dramatic declines in inflation. In fact, inflation has been reduced all around the

---

3 See Dijkstra (1997), Fraga (2004), and Singh et al. (2005) for the analysis of the reasons of severe inflation in Latin America in early-1990s.

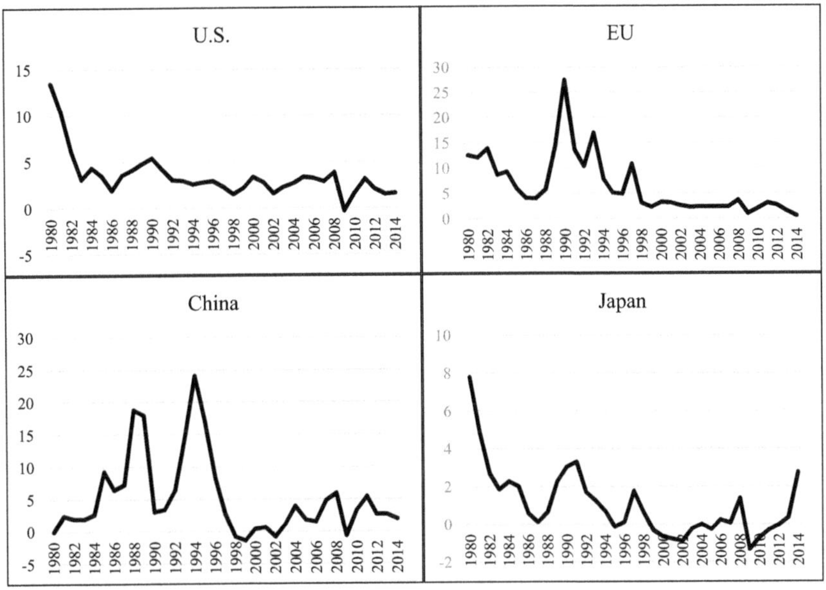

Fig. 9.2: Inflation in Large Industrial Countries and China. World Economic Outlook Database, April 2016

world – not just in emerging markets, but also in the United States, Japan and Europe (Fig. 9.2). All around the world, greater inflation focuses, awareness and central bank independence have played pivotal roles in this global disinflation process (Rogoff, 2003). The low inflation environment in the United States and in other developed countries has clearly helped EMEs to reduce their inflation rates. Similar to their inflation performances, the extent and the speed of this disinflation process varied considerably across EMEs. Latin American and Eastern European countries have been exposed to a more rapid disinflation process and inflation has been highly volatile. In contrast, consistent with their previous inflation processes, Asian countries have pursued a gradual decline in inflation keeping it stable.

9.3.1 The Reasons of the Decline in Inflation in 1990s

Low inflation environment in the United States and other developed countries basically helped EMEs to reduce inflation in the second half of the 1990s. This can be especially important for countries using the exchange rate as a nominal anchor during the initial stages of disinflation process. Besides the direct impact on import prices, the decline in global inflation has also increased the level of competition which tends to drive down price levels (IMF, 2001; Rogoff, 2003). Exporting an increasing volume and variety of goods at low prices, China has also been an important factor that puts competitive pressure on the manufactured goods of many countries. However, besides the contribution of benign external conditions, the disinflation process in EMEs was a consequence of their improved macroeconomic policy framework.

First of all, long years living with high inflation increased the impatience of the public towards inflation and eventually led the governments to understand the high economic costs of inflation. This basically led governments to put more emphasis on price stability. Even though external conditions are helpful, this is not sufficient to reduce inflation. Enhanced fiscal discipline together with institutional and structural reforms played a key role in their ability to achieve and sustain low inflation levels. The link between fiscal deficits and inflation is robust especially during high inflation periods (Fischer, Sahay, and Végh, 2002; Catão and Terrones, 2005; Corbo, 2000). EMEs significantly reduced their fiscal deficits in the 1990s. While fiscal deficits have remained low in Asia, Latin American countries have declined their fiscal deficits by about one-half of the levels in the 1980s (IMF, 2001).

High inflation episodes generally occurred when countries were using fixed exchange rate regimes. As evident from Fig. 9.3, since the mid-1980s, there has been a movement towards more flexible exchange rate regimes while inflation targeting has begun to be increasingly implemented. Chile, Peru, Brazil and Mexico are among the emerging countries that first adopted inflation targeting regimes since the early 1990s (Tab. 9.3). The majority of the EMEs that did not switch to inflation targeting regimes targeted the exchange rate. Countries with the highest inflation rates tended to implement exchange-rate based stabilization plans, while those with more moderate rates adopted inflation objectives. The change in the design of monetary and exchange rate regimes brought about greater central bank independence and transparency which are among the key factors for price stability. However, empirical analysis provided mixed results in the success of inflation targeting regimes in EMEs. A number of inflation targets had greater success in reducing inflation and inflation volatility relative to non-targets (Gonçalves and Salles, 2008; Lin and Ye, 2009; Batini et al., 2006) while others cannot find any evidence that inflation targeting has led to better inflation performance in emerging and developing countries relative to other countries. (Brito and Bystedt, 2010).

With the increased globalization of capital markets, capital inflows to emerging markets substantially increased in the first half of the 1990s. Higher access to global markets has played an important role in slowing down inflation reducing the need for seigniorage.

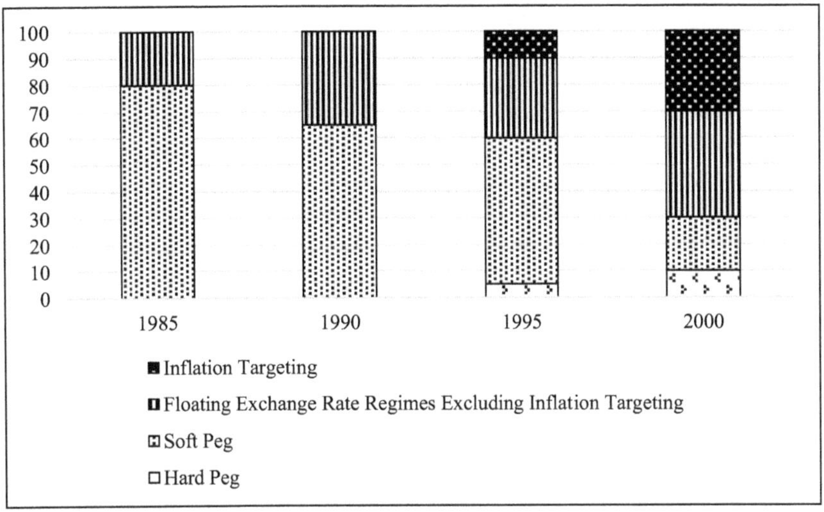

Fig. 9.3: Monetary Regimes in EMEs (Percent of all EMEs). IMF (2001), Chapter 4, Page 134

Tab. 9.3: Inflation Targeting EMEs and Adoption Years. Source: Golçalves and Salles (2008)

Inflation Targeters	**Non-Targeters**
Indonesia (2005)	*Argentina*
Philippines (2002)	*Bangladesh*
Thailand (2000)	*China*
Hungary (2001)	*India*
Poland (1999)	*Malaysia*
Romania (2005)	*Pakistan*
Turkey (2006)	*Bulgaria*
Brazil (1999)	*Russia*
Chile (1991)	*Ukraine*
Colombia (2000)	*Venezuela*
Mexico (1999)	
Peru (1994)	
South Africa (2000)	

Note: Years in parentheses are the adoption years.

The decline in the pass-through from exchanges rates to inflation can be another factor behind lower inflation since the mid-1990s. It is well documented in literature that exchange rate pass-through has been higher in EMEs than in industrial countries and it has declined over time for both groups (see among others Taylor, 2000; Campa and Goldberg, 2005; Mihaljek and Klau, 2001, 2008). One of the main explanations for reduced pass-through is the increased competition due to the globalization of economic activity which leads firms to absorb the cost increases due to exchange rate movements. A more stable macroeconomic environment and structural reforms may have also contributed to the decline in the exchange rate pass-through.

9.4 Inflation Performance in 2000s and Globalization of Inflation

As mentioned above, the decline in world inflation together with the strengthening of institutional arrangements, particularly with greater central bank autonomy, have helped EMEs to curb inflation in the second half of the 1990s. It will be correct to say that EMEs have, to a great extent, achieved removing the structural factors behind their high inflation and they have become more resilient to shocks by the enhanced policy discipline. In this way, EMEs have entered into the 2000s in a mild inflation environment. As seen from Fig. 9.4, the reduction in inflation had continued almost to the end of 2004 and the average inflation for EMEs had declined to around 6 % in the first half of the 2000s. Among different regions, East Asian countries again have had the best performance during this period reducing their average inflation rate to 3.5 %, while the average inflation rate had decreased to around 15 % and 8 % in Eastern European and Latin American countries, respectively (Tab. 9.2). Romania, Russia, Ukraine, Turkey and Venezuela are the economies in which inflation had shown persistence and was realized in two-digits in the first half of the 2000s.

As it is evident from Fig. 9.4 and Tab. 9.4, the downward trend in inflation continued during the 2005–2006 period and many EMEs faced a substantial acceleration in inflation in 2007. The surge in commodity prices is seen as an important driver of the inflationary pressures for both emerging and industrial countries in this period (Habermeier et al., 2009; IMF, 2008, IMF, 2011; Cecchetti and Moessner, 2008). There has been a downward trend in commodity prices relative to consumer prices over the past five decades which can be attributed to large productivity gains in the agriculture and the metal sectors relative to other sectors (Batini et al., 2006). However, a commodity price surge was realized in the 2002–2008 period. The rise in commodity prices was mainly due to the increased global demand, particularly

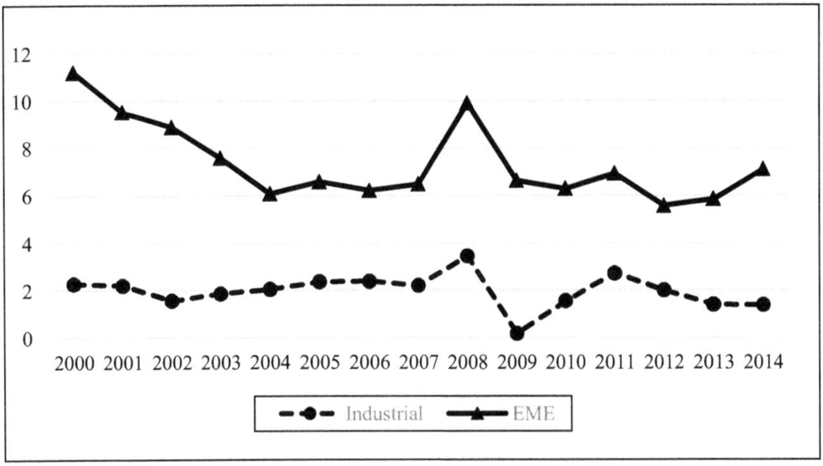

Fig. 9.4: Inflation in Industrial Countries and EMEs in 2000–2014 Period. World Economic Outlook Database, April 2016

from the strong growth of emerging economies and the slow supply growth during the late 1990s. The rapid growth of emerging economies whose growth has been more commodity-intensive based has substantially increased commodity demand over the past few decades. Following the previous low commodity prices there has been underinvestment and slow supply growth during the past two decades. Additionally, the decline in the policy interest rates of USA has raised the investment of financial investors in commodity markets (IMF, 2006b).

9.4.1 Commodity Prices as the Common Driver of Inflation in the Second Half of 2000s

As Fig. 9.5 shows, commodity prices rose dramatically during the 2002–2008 period. There was a 60 % increase in food prices in the 2002–2008 period, and fuel prices rose sharply by 226 %. While the rise in food and energy prices led to an increase in global inflation in the 2007–2008 period, the rise in inflation was gradual in advanced countries. Average inflation rose from 2 % to 4 % in industrial countries, while the average inflation increased from 6 % to 10 % on the average in EMEs during this period. The relatively higher increase in the emerging economies' inflation is mainly a consequence of the greater importance of food commodities in their consumption basket. Food commodities

Tab. 9.4: Inflation in EMEs in 2005–2014 Period. World Economic Outlook Database, April 2016

	2005	2006	2007	2008	2009	2010	2011	2012	2013	2014
Asia										
Bangladesh	7.0	6.8	9.1	8.9	4.9	9.4	11.5	6.2	7.5	7.0
China	1.8	1.5	4.8	5.9	-0.7	3.3	5.4	2.6	2.6	2.0
India	4.0	5.7	5.9	9.2	10.6	9.5	9.5	9.9	9.4	5.9
Indonesia	10.5	13.1	6.7	9.8	5.0	5.1	5.3	4.0	6.4	6.4
Malaysia	3.0	3.6	2.0	5.4	0.6	1.7	3.2	1.7	2.1	3.1
Pakistan	9.3	7.9	7.8	12.0	19.6	10.1	13.7	11.0	7.4	8.6
Philippines	6.6	5.5	2.9	8.2	4.2	3.8	4.7	3.2	2.9	4.2
Thailand	4.5	4.6	2.2	5.5	-0.9	3.3	3.8	3.0	2.2	1.9
Europe										
Bulgaria	6.0	7.4	7.6	12.0	2.5	3.0	3.4	2.4	0.4	-1.6
Hungary	3.6	3.9	7.9	6.1	4.2	4.9	4.0	5.7	1.7	-0.2
Poland	2.1	1.0	2.5	4.2	3.5	2.6	4.3	3.7	0.9	0.0
Romania	9.0	6.6	4.8	7.8	5.6	6.1	5.8	3.3	4.0	1.1
Russia	12.7	9.7	9.0	14.1	11.7	6.9	8.4	5.1	6.8	7.8
Ukraine	13.5	9.1	12.8	25.2	15.9	9.4	8.0	0.6	-0.3	12.1
Turkey	8.2	9.6	8.8	10.4	6.3	8.6	6.5	8.9	7.5	8.9
Latin America										
Argentina	9.6	10.9	8.8	8.6	6.3	10.5	9.8	10.0	10.6	-
Brazil	6.9	4.2	3.6	5.7	4.9	5.0	6.6	5.4	6.2	6.3
Chile	3.1	3.4	4.4	8.7	1.5	1.4	3.3	3.0	1.9	4.4
Colombia	5.1	4.3	5.5	7.0	4.2	2.3	3.4	3.2	2.0	2.9
Mexico	4.0	3.6	4.0	5.1	5.3	4.2	3.4	4.1	3.8	4.0
Peru	1.6	2.0	1.8	5.8	2.9	1.5	3.4	3.7	2.8	3.2
Venezuela	16.0	13.7	18.7	30.4	27.1	28.0	26.8	21.5	39.5	62.2
Africa										
South Africa	3.3	4.7	7.1	11.5	7.1	4.3	5.0	5.7	5.8	6.1

represent over one-third of household consumption in EMEs, while in advanced countries food commodities amount to only one-tenth of household consumption (IMF, 2008). Emerging economies are also more energy-intensive (which is measured as energy consumption per unit of real GDP) when compared to industrial countries. The other factor which affects the economies' vulnerability to the inflationary impact of commodity price shocks is the credibility of monetary policy. Since medium-term inflation expectations are weakly anchored in

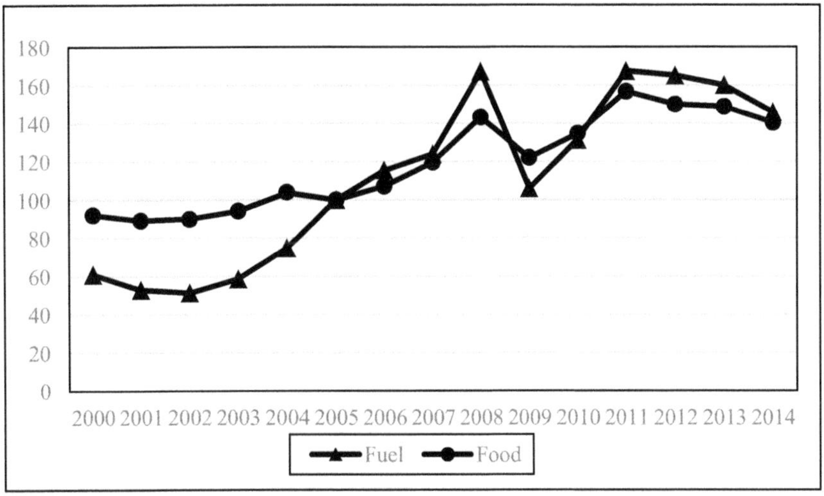

Fig. 9.5: World Commodity Prices, 2000–2014 (In real Terms, as deflated by U. S. consumer price index). World Economic Outlook Database, April 2016

many emerging and developing countries, commodity price shocks have greater effects on inflation expectations in these economies (IMF, 2011). Consequently, pass-through from commodity prices to headline inflation is much higher in emerging and developing economies relative to advanced countries.

Even though inflation pressures rose sharply in 2007 for all emerging countries, there were again significant differences in the severity of inflation pressures among regions. For instance, European countries faced stronger inflation pressures than other regions, while inflation pressures rose more modestly in Latin America. Habermeier et al. (2009) analyzed the nature and the drivers of inflation in a number of emerging and developing countries in the 2007–2008 period. Tab. 9.5 represents a summary of their findings. While surging food and energy prices were the common drivers of inflation in all regions, aggregate demand pressures also contributed to inflation pressures. This resulted in an increase in core inflation (excluding food and energy) for most economies suggesting the second-round effects. Rapid growth of EMEs over the past decade, rapid increase in the amount of credit given to private sectors and capital inflows are the main contributors of high demand in these countries. In a number of countries such as, Romania, Turkey, and South Africa, depreciation of the local currency has also increased price pressures.

Tab. 9.5: The Nature and the Drivers of Inflation in 2007–2008 Period. Habermeier et al. (2009)

	Nature of Inflation		*Drivers of Inflation*					
	Core Inflation Up	**Inflation Exp. Up**	**Second Round Effects**	*Rising Food prices*	*Rising Fuel Prices*	*Agg. Demand Pressures*	*Wages Up with Tight Markets*	*Exch. Rate Depr.*
Asia								
China	+ (limited)	+		+	+	+		
India	+	+		+	+	+		
Indonesia	+	+		+	+	+		
Malaysia	+ (limited)	+						
Philippines	+	+	+	+	+	+		
Thailand	+ (limited)	+		+	+			
Europe								
Bulgaria	+		+	+	+	+	+	
Hungary	+	+	+	+	+		+	
Poland	+	+	Likely	+	+	+	+	
Romania	+	+	+	+	+	+	+	+
Russia	+		Not clear	+	+	+	+	
Ukraine	+	+	+	+	+	+	+	
Turkey	+	+	+	+	+			+
Latin America								
Brazil	+	+	+	+	+	+	+	
Chile	+	+	+	+	+			
Colombia	+	+	+	+	+	+		
Mexico	+		Limited	+	+			
Peru	+	+	+	+	+			
Africa								
South Africa	+	+	+	+	+			+

9.4.2 Globalization and Inflation

Intensive globalization of the world economy in the past two decades has had significant impacts on all aspects of economic life. Simultaneous realization of low and stable inflation globally and the substantial increase in the internationalization of national markets (e.g. goods, services, financial and labor markets) have opened discussions on the effects of globalization on inflation. First of all, increased openness of the financial system has reduced inflationary finance of fiscal deficits. Policymakers benefit less from accommodative policies in open economies since monetary expansion has a smaller impact on output (Rogoff, 2003; Romer, 1993). Therefore, globalization has had a disciplinary effect on monetary policy. Additionally, IMF (2006a) lists a number of channels through which globalization effects national inflation such as increased incentives of policymakers to strengthen the conduct of monetary policy, the rise in price competition in national markets, and increase in aggregate supply due to the productivity gains.

According to the inflation globalization hypothesis, globalization has diminished the role of domestic factors in the inflation process and global factors have replaced domestic factors as the primary determinants of inflation. This hypothesis originated from the concerns of some monetary policy makers, in particular the Federal Reserve, during the global financial crisis. Therefore, most of the empirical studies on the relevant issue focus on industrial countries and their findings remain mixed. IMF (2006a), Borio and Filardo (2007), Pehnelt (2010) and Milani (2012) support the argument that globalization increased the sensitivity of inflation on foreign economic conditions. However, Ball (2006), Ihrig et al. (2010) and Kohn (2006) provided contrasting evidence showing that globalization has little effect on the inflation process of major industrial countries.

According to Zhang (2015), these different findings for industrial economies are in fact not surprising because of the two-way effect of globalization on their inflation processes. Higher demand from EMEs may increase commodity prices which in turn reflect in an increase in CPI for those economies. On the other side, increased integration of China and other lower-cost producers in world production networks may induce downward pressure on wages and import costs. This two-way effect can explain why the globalization-inflation relationship remains as a puzzle for industrial countries (see also Temple, 2002; Matheson and Stavrev; 2013). However, EMEs are less likely to have these offsetting effects of globalization on the inflation process, since increased trade integration has risen, and the dependence of EMEs on global supply and demand and the price levels of EMEs tend to rise when there is a rise in global prices. However, there is not a counter effect to rising prices in EMEs because there is not a flow of lower-cost labor, and products and services from industrial countries. To this end, Zhang (2015) suggests that the impact of globalization needs to be less ambiguous for EMEs relative to industrial countries. Additionally, their empirical analysis on twenty-one EMEs for the 1992–2009 period showed that domestic factors played a dominant role in driving inflation before 1999, while global economic conditions played a significant and more important role in affecting inflation after 1999. Similarly, using the data for China for the 1995–2012 period, Zhang and Wang (2015) showed that the global output gap dominantly affects domestic inflation more than the domestic output gap. Also, the results of empirical analysis on twenty-four emerging countries for the 1960–2004 period conducted by IMF (2006a) suggested that more open economies tend to experience lower inflation rates, even after controlling other inflation determinants.

9.5 Inflation in EMEs during Global Financial Crisis and Afterwards

Having peaked in mid-2008, the boom in commodity prices ended with the emergence of the global financial crisis. Coinciding with food and oil prices, the run up in inflation reversed after the second half of 2008. Since commodity prices are closely linked to economic activity, the slowdown in the global economy in the wake of the financial crisis led to a decline in food and oil prices. As falling commodity prices relieved a substantial part of the inflationary pressures in EMEs, average inflation rates decreased from around 10 % in 2008 and again to 6.5 % in 2009.

However, since the repressive impact of slowed demand during the global financial crisis was short-lived, food and oil prices surged again in 2010 and reached their 2008 peak in 2011. The rise in commodity prices propelled global inflation in 2010 and in 2011. Among EMEs, inflation rates increased 1–2 points in Asian and Latin American countries such as China, Malaysia, Pakistan, Brazil, Chile and Colombia. Given the importance of the region's high demand for commodities and its high integration in the world economy, the coincidence of the domestic price levels with the global commodity prices is the highest in Asian countries. Therefore, Asian countries faced greater increases in inflation in the periods when commodity prices were rising (see Tab. 9.3). For instance, in China, inflation jumped from -0.7 % in 2009 to 5.4 % in 2011. Similarly, Thailand's inflation rate rose from -0.9 % to 3.8 %.

In fact, inflation spillovers mainly resulted from multiple transmission channels which included the local, regional and global shocks (Osorio and Unsal, 2013). The findings of the empirical analysis by Osorio and Unsal (2013) pointed out that the main driving forces of inflation in Asia over the past two decades have been supply shocks and monetary shocks, while demand pressures have played a relatively small role. They indicated that in particular, commodity prices played an important role in driving inflation due to the high openness of these economies and their dependence on oil and food imports.

While the price of both food and fuel declined after 2011, this fall in commodity prices was more pronounced for crude oil. This trend led inflation to decline or even to remain stable in almost all EMEs in the 2012–2014 period except for oil exporters such as Venezuela, Russia, Indonesia and Malaysia. Particularly in Venezuela, the inflation rate rose from 27 % in 2011 to 62 % in 2014.[4] While rising oil prices are generally associated with inflation for oil importing countries, lower oil prices can cause inflation in oil exporting countries as in case for Venezuela, Russia, Indonesia and Malaysia.

9.6 Conclusion

Due to a number of structural and external factors ranging from monetization of high fiscal deficits to oil price shocks, high and volatile inflation was a chronic problem for EMEs until the second half of the 1990s. Among EMEs, Latin American countries had the worst performance in inflation and inflation volatility during this period, and a number of these countries experienced severe hyperinflation episodes. Since the mid-1990s, EMEs succeeded to curb inflation by their enhanced fiscal discipline together with institutional and structural reforms which included greater central bank emphasis on price stability, and greater independence and transparency. Besides these factors, a low external inflation environment was also helpful in this disinflation process. Consequently, most of the EMEs, except for a number of countries such as Turkey, Romania and Venezuela, have entered the 2000s in a mild inflation environment removing, to a large extent, the structural determinants of inflation.

However, intensified globalization of the world economy has also affected the dynamics of inflation all around the world after the 2000s. According to the inflation globalization hypothesis, globalization has diminished the role of domestic factors in the inflation process and global factors have replaced domestic ones as the primary determinants of inflation. The surge in global commodity prices has ended the downward trend in inflation in EMEs during 2005–2006 and has emerged as an important driver of inflationary pressures for both emerging

4 There are a number of factors behind Venezuela's high inflation such as lower oil prices, depreciation of national currency and shortages of goods.

countries and industrial countries since 2007. However, the change from food and energy prices to headline inflation was much higher in emerging and developing economies relative to advanced countries due to their higher share of food in household consumption, their energy-intensive production and lower credibility of their monetary policy.

Even though slowed, demand during the global financial crisis had a repressive impact on commodity prices, this impact was short-lived and food and energy prices tended to rise in 2010 and 2011. Given the importance of Asia's high demand for commodities and its high integration in the world economy, the coincidence of domestic price levels with global commodity prices is the highest in these economies. Therefore, Asian countries faced higher increases in inflation relative to emerging Latin American and European countries during this period.

While rising oil prices are generally associated with inflation for oil importing countries, lower oil prices can cause inflation in oil exporting countries. Due to the substantial fall in oil prices, inflation declined or even remained stable in almost all EMEs during the 2012–2014 period except for oil exporting countries such as Venezuela, Russia, Indonesia and Malaysia.

References

Bailliu, J. N., Garcés, D., Kruger, M., & Messmacher, M. (2003). *Explaining and Forecasting Inflation in Emerging Markets: The Case of Mexico*. Bank of Canada.

Ball, L. M. (2006). *Has globalization changed inflation?* (No. w12687). National Bureau of Economic Research.

Batini, N., Breuer, P., Kochhar, K., & Roger, S. (2006). Inflation Targeting and the IMF. *International Monetary Fund*, IMF Staff Paper, Washington DC, March, 64 pages. https://www.imf.org/external/np/pp/eng/2006/031606.pdf. Access Date: 3 May 2017.

Borio, C. E., & Filardo, A. J. (2007). Globalisation and inflation: New cross-country evidence on the global determinants of domestic inflation. BIS Working Paper, No. 227.

Brito, R. D., & Bystedt, B. (2010). Inflation targeting in emerging economies: Panel evidence. *Journal of Development Economics*, *91*(2), 198–210.

Campa, J. M., & Goldberg, L. S. (2005). Exchange rate pass-through into import prices. *Review of Economics and Statistics*, *87*(4), 679–690.

Catao, L. A., & Terrones, M. E. (2005). Fiscal deficits and inflation. *Journal of Monetary Economics*, *52*(3), 529–554.

Cecchetti, S. G., & Moessner, R. (2008). Commodity prices and inflation dynamics. *BIS Quarterly Review*, 55–66.

Corbo, V. (2000). *Monetary policy in Latin America in the 90s* (No. 78). Banco Central de Chile.

Dijkstra, A. (1997). Fighting Inflation in Latin America. *Development and Change*, *28*(3), 531–557.

Dornbusch, R. (1992). Lessons from experiences with high inflation. *The World Bank Economic Review*, *6*(1), 13–31.

Fischer, S., Sahay, R., & Végh, C. A. (2002). Modern hyper-and high inflations. *Journal of Economic Literature*, *40*(3), 837–880.

Fraga, A. (2004). Latin America since the 1990s: Rising from the Sickbed? *The Journal of Economic Perspectives*, *18*(2), 89–106.

Gonçalves, C. E. S., & Salles, J. M. (2008). Inflation targeting in emerging economies: What do the data say? *Journal of Development Economics*, *85*(1), 312–318.

Habermeier, K., Otker-Robe, I., Jácome, L. I., Giustiniani, A., Ishi, K., Vávra, D., & Vazquez, F. (2009). Inflation pressures and monetary policy options in emerging and developing countries-A cross regional perspective. *IMF Working Papers*, 1–78.

Ihrig, J., Kamin, S. B., Lindner, D., & Marquez, J. (2010). Some simple tests of the globalization and inflation hypothesis. *International Finance*, *13*(3), 343–375.

IMF (1996). *World Economic Outlook*. Chapter VI: The Rise and Fall of Inflation-Lessons from the Postwar Experience. October, Washington, D.C.

IMF (2001). *World Economic Outlook*. Chapter IV: The Decline of Inflation in Emerging Markets: Can It Be Maintained? May, Washington, D.C.

IMF (2006a). *World Economic Outlook*. Chapter III: How Has Globalization Changed Inflation? April, Washington, D.C.

IMF (2006b). *World Economic Outlook*. Chapter V: The Boom in Nonfuel Commodity Prices—Can It Last? September, Washington, D.C.

IMF (2008). *World Economic Outlook Update*. Global Slowdown and Rising Inflation. July, Washington, D.C.

IMF (2011). *World Economic Outlook*. Chapter III: Target What You Can Hit: Commodity Price Swings and Monetary Policy. September, Washington, D.C.

Kohn, D. L. (2006, June). The effects of globalization on inflation and their implications for monetary policy. In *Remarks at the Federal Reserve Bank of Boston's 51st Economic Conference, Chatham, Mass., June*, https://www.federalreserve.gov/newsevents/speech/kohn20060616a.htm, Access Date: 14 April 2016.

Lin, S., & Ye, H. (2009). Does inflation targeting make a difference in developing countries? *Journal of Development Economics*, *89*(1), 118–123.

Matheson, T., & Stavrev, E. (2013). The Great Recession and the inflation puzzle. *Economics Letters, 120*(3), 468–472.

Mihaljek, D., & Klau, M. (2001). A note on the pass-through from exchange rate and foreign price changes to inflation in selected emerging market economies. *BIS papers, 8*, 69–81.

Mihaljek, D. & Klau, M. (2008). Exchange Rate Pass-through in Emerging Market Economies: What Has Changed and Why?, BIS Papers chapters, in Bank for International Settlements (ed.), Transmission Mechanisms for Monetary Policy in Emerging Market Economies, volume 35, pages 103–130, Bank for International Settlements.

Milani, F. (2012). Has globalization transformed US macroeconomic dynamics? *Macroeconomic Dynamics, 16*(02), 204–229.

Mohanty, M. S., & Klau, M. (2001). What determines inflation in emerging market economies? *BIS Papers, 8*, 1–38.

Montiel, Peter J (1989). Empirical analysis of high-inflation episodes in Argentina, Brazil, and Israel, *Staff Papers (International Monetary Fund)*, 36(3), 527–549.

Osorio, C., & Unsal, D. F. (2013). Inflation dynamics in Asia: Causes, changes, and spillovers from China. *Journal of Asian Economics, 24*, 26–40.

Pehnelt, G. (2010). Globalisation and inflation in OECD countries. ECIPE Working Paper, no. 2007–2055. Brussels, Belgium:

Rogoff, K. (2003). Globalization and global disinflation. *Economic Review-Federal Reserve Bank of Kansas City, 88*(4), 45–78.

Romer, David. (1993). "Openness and Inflation: Theory and Evidence," *The Quarterly Journal of Economics*, Vol. 107 (November), pp. 869–903.

Singh, A., Belaish, A., Collyns, C., De Masi, P., Krieger, R., Meredith, G., & Rennhack, R. (2005). Stabilization and Reform in Latin America: *A Macroeconomic Perspective on the Experience since the Early 1990s." IMF Occasional Paper*, (238), 136 pages, Occasional Paper No. 238. Washington DC.

Taylor, J. B. (2000). Low inflation, pass-through, and the pricing power of firms. *European economic review, 44*(7), 1389–1408.

Temple, J. (2002). Openness, inflation, and the Phillips curve: a puzzle. *Journal of Money, Credit, and Banking, 34*(2), 450–468.

Zhang, C. (2015). The Effect of Globalization on Inflation in New Emerging Markets. *Emerging Markets Finance and Trade, 51*(5), 1021–1033.

Zhang, C., Song, K., & Wang, F. (2015). Economic Globalization and Inflation in China: A Multivariate Approach. *China & World Economy, 23*(3), 79–96.

Fatih Şahan

10 Global Financial Crisis and Unemployment in EMEs

Abstract: The world economy experienced a serious slowdown with the 2008 global economic crisis. Many countries recorded negative income growths and unemployment rates rose after the crisis. There is a widely discussed issue that advanced economies felt the negative outcomes of the crisis more deeply than the emerging ones on their economies in terms of macroeconomic indicators. One of the major areas where the harmful effects of the crisis were seen is on labor markets and unemployment. Within this scope, this chapter aims to scrutinize the impacts of the financial turmoil of 2008 on the labor markets of emerging market economies (EMEs). Using IMF classification, 23 EMEs were analyzed by adopting important labor market indicators for the period 2000–2014. The study was conducted by analyzing first, unemployment rates, and secondly by analyzing, labor market indicators such as employment, labor force participation rates, labor productivity, wages and prices. The conclusion of this study is that EMEs had modest negative impacts on their labor markets following the crisis. Furthermore, Asian EMEs showed lower unemployment rates and higher growth rates throughout the 2000s. They have more agriculture and industry based employment structures. Latin American EMEs, began the 2000s with high rates of unemployment and low rates of economic growth and throughout 2000s they stabilized these figures. European EMEs felt the negative impacts of the crisis more than the other countries and their recovery occurred at a slower pace. European EMEs experienced a decline in unemployment rates before the crisis, however after the crisis, the unemployment rates started to increase again, which is parallel to their economic growth trend in the post crisis period.

Keywords: Global Turmoil, Labor Markets

10.1 Introduction

In 2008, world economies experienced the biggest economic crisis since the Great Depression of 1929. The crisis began in the US mortgage sector and influenced the financial sector deeply. Large financial giants such as Lehman Brothers and Goldman Sachs collapsed, stock markets crashed and the extensive use of financial derivatives prevented the global financial system from a quick recovery. The global financial system suffered from this turmoil profoundly and the effects spread to the real sector in the form of prolonged recessions and unemployment.

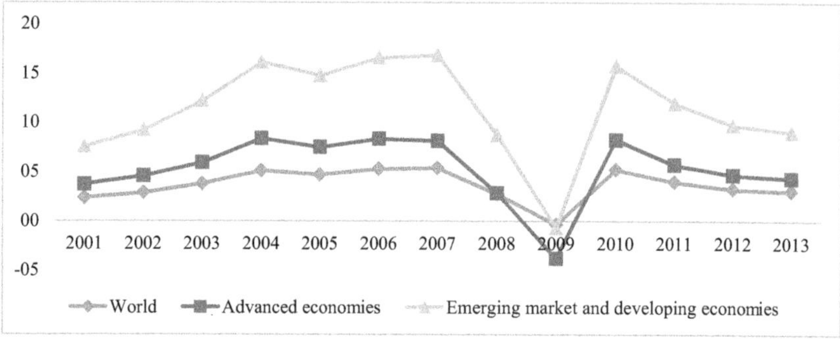

Fig. 10.1: Real GDP Growth Rates. International Monetary Fund (IMF), World Economic Outlook Database, 2014

As a result, world production decreased by 0.4 % in 2009. Advanced economies felt the slowdown more intensely with 3.4 % real decreases in production. On the other hand, EMEs recorded a 3.1 % growth in 2009 following a strong growth period in 2000s, 6 % real growth on average (Fig. 10.1).

In such an environment, many countries faced high unemployment problems after the crisis. By the year 2014, 61M more jobs were needed globally to close down the job deficit due to the crisis. About 201M people were looking for jobs by 2014 and this number is increasing (ILO, 2015:16), thus the global economy failed to recover fully from the harmful impacts of the 2008 crisis. Considering the EMEs, due to favorable macroeconomic policies and external factors, the unemployment rate is near the level of the pre-crisis period. The average unemployment rate in all EMEs was 7.10 % in 2007 and 7.21 % in 2014 which shows that they have not been affected as harshly as advanced economies (World Bank, 2015). On closer examination, it is seen that 18 of 23 EMEs have average unemployment rates in 2000–2008 period below the pre-crisis level in the period 2009–2014 on average. In this study, the unemployment rates and the labor markets of EMEs are analyzed for the 2000–2014 period by adopting different indicators.

The remainder of the chapter proceeds as follow: section two analyzes unemployment rates and their structures, section three scrutinizes employment and economic growth rate, while section four presents labor force participation rates. Section five puts forward a summary of labor productivity, wages and prices. The last section summarizes and concludes.

10.2 Unemployment Rates

The economic crisis in the 1990s affected many EMEs. As a result, the 2000s started with high unemployment rates for most EMEs. In the 2000–2008 period, most EMEs used structural reform programs which resulted in declining unemployment rates. The greatest declines occurred in Argentina (with a decrease from 15 % to 8 % between 2000 and 2008), Venezuela (with a decrease from 13 % to 7 % between 2000 and 2008) and Poland (with a decrease from 16 % to 7 % between 2000 and 2008) (Tab. 10.1). Countries such as India, Bangladesh, Malaysia, Mexico and Thailand have unemployment rates under 5 % between 2000 and 2008. Thus, in the pre-crisis period, many EMEs succeeded to decrease unemployment rates to favorable percentages.

The most severe effects of the crisis are seen in Hungary, Mexico and Turkey. Fig. 10.2 shows the average unemployment rates in these countries in pre- and post- crisis periods. Hungary had a 7 % average unemployment rate before the crisis; this rate increased to 10 % in the post crisis period. Turkey had a 9 % average unemployment rate before the crisis and this rate increased to 10 % after the crisis. Lastly, the unemployment rate in Mexico increased at an average rate of 5 % in the 2008–2014 period. The common features of these three countries are: flexible labor market institutions, lowering employment benefits and a high rate of unemployment among young people (EEAG, 2012; Kyloh, 2011).

After a general inspection, it is more helpful to examine EMEs as country groups with similar characteristics. Firstly, Latin American EMEs performed better after the crisis. Five out of 7 Latin American EMEs (Argentina, Brazil, Chile, Columbia and Venezuela) had two-digit unemployment rates in the period preceding the 2008 crisis. After the crisis, almost all these countries lowered their unemployment rates. Colombia has the highest unemployment rate in the 2010–2014 period although there is a significant decline from 20 % in 2000 to around 10 % in 2014 (Fig. 10.3).

Asian EMEs are the best performers in terms of unemployment rates in the pre-and post-crisis periods. In 5 out of 8 Asian EMEs (Bangladesh, India, China, Malaysia and Thailand) unemployment rates were around 5 % throughout the 2000s. In Indonesia, Philippines and Thailand, unemployment rates had a stable trend at around 5 % (Fig. 10.4). The major stimulus for this recovery was the amount of public spending which stimulated aggregate demand (Huynh et.al., 2010). Philippines had a volatile unemployment trend and the highest unemployment rates were observed in that country in the 2010–2014 period. Latin American countries showed a robust recovery from the crisis using macroeconomic policy responses (Marinakis, 2011). Argentina and Brazil dealt with the

Tab. 10.1: Unemployment Rates in EMEs (% of Total Labor Force). World Bank (2016)

Country	2000	2001	2002	2003	2004	2005	2006	2007	2008	2009	2010	2011	2012	2013	2014
Latin America															
Argentina	15.0	17.4	19.6	16.0	13.5	11.5	9.4	8.4	7.8	8.6	7.7	7.2	7.2	7.1	7.3
Brazil	14.0	12.5	13.0	13.7	12.9	11.4	11.5	10.9	9.6	9.7	8.5	7.8	7.4	7.1	6.8
Chile	9.2	9.1	8.9	8.5	8.8	8.0	7.7	7.1	7.8	9.7	8.1	7.1	6.4	5.9	6.4
Colombia	20.5	15.0	15.6	14.2	13.7	11.9	11.7	11.2	11.3	12.1	11.8	10.9	10.4	9.7	9.2
Mexico	2.6	2.5	2.9	3.0	3.7	3.6	3.6	3.6	3.9	5.4	5.3	5.2	4.9	4.9	4.8
Peru	7.3	7.9	7.7	8.3	9.0	8.3	7.2	6.5	6.6	4.4	4.0	3.9	3.6	4.0	4.1
Venezuela	13.2	12.8	16.2	16.8	15.0	11.4	9.3	7.5	6.8	8.1	8.4	7.8	7.4	7.8	7.0
Asia															
Bangladesh	3.3	3.3	3.4	4.3	4.5	4.3	4.5	4.0	3.0	5.0	4.5	4.5	4.5	4.3	4.2
China	4.5	4.5	4.4	4.3	4.3	4.1	4.0	3.8	4.4	4.3	4.2	4.3	4.5	4.5	4.6
India	4.3	3.8	4.3	3.9	3.9	4.4	4.3	3.7	4.2	3.9	3.5	3.5	3.6	3.6	3.5
Indonesia	6.1	8.1	9.1	9.5	9.9	11.2	10.3	9.1	8.4	7.9	7.1	7.5	6.1	6.2	5.9
Malaysia	3.0	3.5	3.5	3.6	3.5	3.5	3.3	3.2	3.3	3.7	3.4	3.1	3.0	3.1	2.9
Pakistan	7.2	7.8	7.8	8.3	7.4	7.7	6.1	5.1	5.0	5.5	5.6	5.9	6.0	6.2	5.6
Philippines	11.2	10.9	11.5	11.4	11.9	7.7	8.0	7.4	7.3	7.5	7.3	7.0	7.0	7.1	6.6
Thailand	2.4	2.6	1.8	1.5	1.5	1.4	1.2	1.2	1.2	1.5	1.0	0.7	0.6	0.8	0.8
Europe															
Bulgaria	16.2	19.9	18.1	13.7	12.0	10.1	9.0	6.9	5.6	6.8	10.3	11.3	12.3	12.9	11.4
Hungary	6.6	5.7	5.6	5.8	5.8	7.2	7.5	7.4	7.8	10.0	11.2	11.0	11.0	10.2	7.7
Poland	16.3	18.4	19.9	19.4	19.1	17.7	13.8	9.6	7.1	8.2	9.6	9.6	10.1	10.3	9.0
Romania	7.0	6.6	8.1	6.9	7.7	7.2	7.3	6.4	5.8	6.9	7.0	7.2	6.8	7.1	6.8
Russia	10.6	9.0	7.9	8.2	7.8	7.1	7.1	6.0	6.2	8.3	7.3	6.5	5.5	5.5	5.2
Turkey	6.5	8.4	10.4	10.5	10.8	10.6	8.7	8.9	9.7	12.6	10.7	8.8	8.1	8.7	9.9
Ukraine	11.6	10.9	9.6	9.1	8.6	7.2	6.8	6.4	6.4	8.8	8.1	7.9	7.5	7.2	9.3
Africa															
South Africa	26.7	26.2	26.6	27.1	24.7	23.8	22.6	22.5	22.4	23.5	24.7	24.6	24.7	24.6	24.9

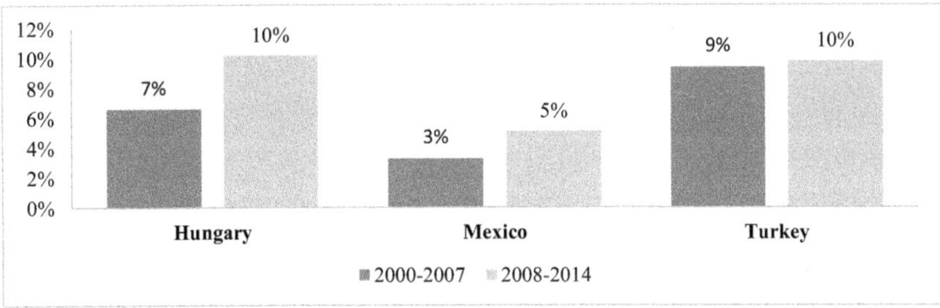

Fig. 10.2: Average Unemployment Rates for Hungary, Mexico and Turkey. Author's calculations based on World Bank (2016)

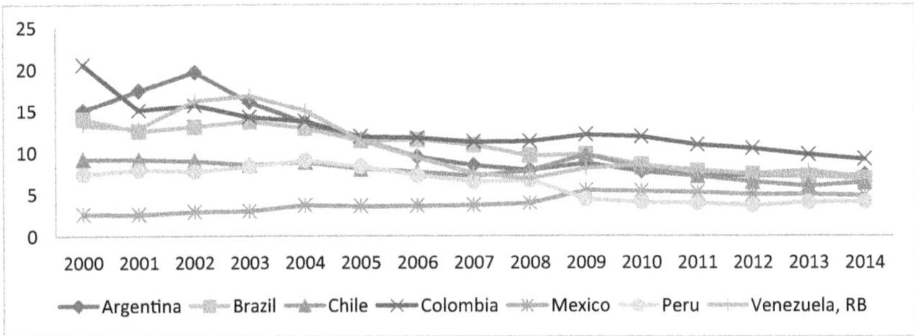

Fig. 10.3: Unemployment Rates in Latin American EMEs. Author's calculations based on World Bank (2016)

crisis by employing additional public investments to boost domestic demands and by emergency employment programs. Chile handled unemployment by allocating extra financial resources such as unemployment insurance.

European EMEs revealed a "v" shaped unemployment trend in the 2000–2014 period, i.e. the unemployment rate declined until 2008 and then began to increase after the crisis. Most European EMEs experienced low rates of fluctuations throughout the 2000–2008 period, except for Bulgaria, Hungary and Poland. Before the crisis, the Bulgarian economy was doing better by decreasing the unemployment rate from 16 % in 2001 to 6 % in 2008 but in the post crisis period, the unemployment doubled, reaching 12 % in 2012. This pattern is due to the flexibility of labor markets in Bulgaria (Maiväli and Stierle, 2013). Unemployment in Poland was around 20 % at the onset of the 2000s, after

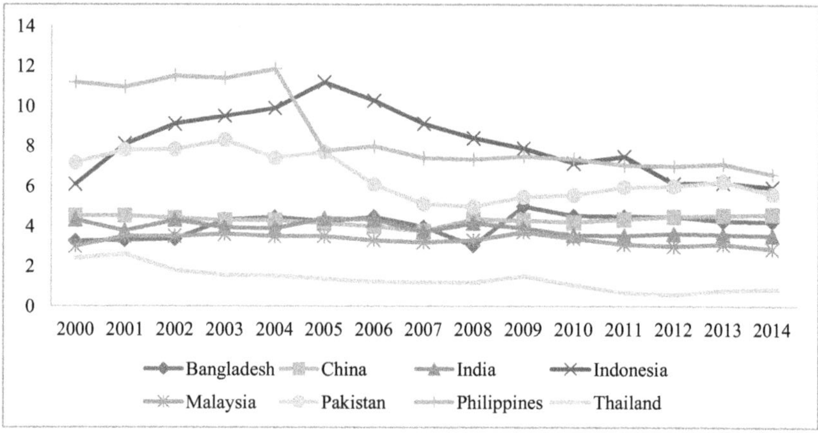

Fig. 10.4: Unemployment Rates in Asian EMEs. Author's calculations based on World Bank (2016)

EU membership in 2005, Poland's economy has gained momentum and unemployment decreased to 7 % in 2008. In 2012, the unemployment rate in Poland reached 10 % but it began to decline by the year 2014. In Hungary, the unemployment rate increased in the three-year period after the crisis until 2010, after which it began to decrease.

The highest unemployment rates are seen in South Africa with rates around 25 %. Their unemployment rates decreased to 22 % in 2008 and began to increase after the crisis, reaching 25 % in 2014. The unemployment rate among the young people is 50 % of the total unemployed population. The impact of the crisis was greatly felt after the global crisis, as it is deeply integrated into the world economy (Marumoagae, 2014) and the unemployment rate has been persistent over the 20 % level throughout 2000s.

Decomposition of unemployed people in terms of education is also worth noting. Tab. 10.2 shows the educational levels of the unemployed population. In Latin American EMEs, the share of unemployed persons with primary education decreased throughout the three periods in all countries except for Peru. In Peru, the share of unemployment among people with primary education increased in the 2010–2014 period. In Asian EMEs, in 2 out of 8 countries (India and Malaysia) the share of unemployed persons with primary education rose in the three periods. In other countries, unemployment among people with primary education declined. The highest rates of declines are in Thailand (from 50 % in

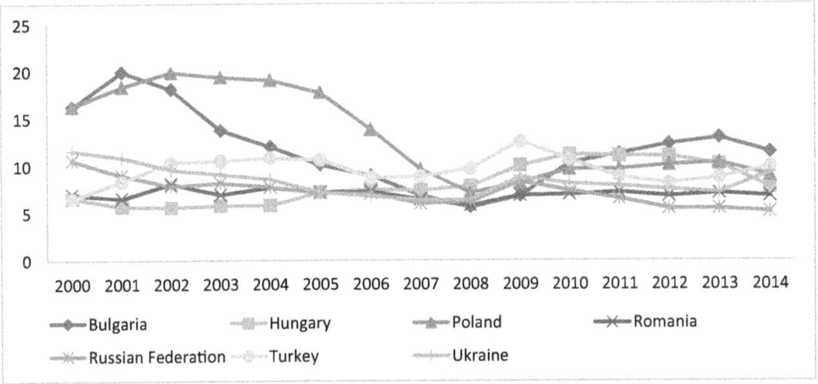

Fig. 10.5: Unemployment Rates in European EMEs. Author's calculations based on World Bank (2016)

2000–2004 period to 36 % in the 2010–2014 period) and China (from 65 % in 2000–2004 period to 50 % in the 2010–2014 period). Meanwhile, in both countries, unemployment with tertiary education increased. In Thailand, the share of unemployment among people with tertiary education increased on average from 7 % in the 2000–2004 period to 33 % in the 2010–2014 period showing a dramatic increase in unemployment in skilled labor.

As for the European EMEs, in almost all countries, except for Turkey, the highest share of unemployment was observed among people with secondary education. In Turkey, people with primary levels of education make up the largest proportion of the unemployed. In all the European EMEs, there is a significant increase in unemployment among people with tertiary education throughout the three periods. Lastly, in South Africa, the highest share of unemployment is among people with primary education.

10.3 Employment and GDP Growth

This section deals with employment rates and their relationships to GDP growths in the EMEs. Tab. 10.3 shows the employment to population ratio and GDP growth rates for EMEs. The employment to population ratio increased in all Latin American countries throughout the 2000s. Most increases were observed in Peru with an increase by seven percentage points. Moreover, GDP growth figures indicate a slowdown in these economies in the 2000–2004 period, which reverses throughout the 2005–2009 period, indicating a recovery from the early

Tab. 10.2: Unemployment by Educational Attainment (share of unemployed people). Author's calculations on ILO, Key Indicators of Labor Markets (KLIM) Data (ILO, 2016)

Countries	Primary			Secondary			Tertiary		
	2000-2004	2005-2009	2010-2014	2000-2004	2005-2009	2010-2014	2000-2004	2005-2009	2010-2014
Latin America									
Argentina	46 %	39 %	33 %	35 %	41 %	48 %	17 %	19 %	16 %
Brazil	55 %	51 %	29 %	27 %	34 %	43 %	3 %	4 %	8 %
Chile	20 %	17 %	16 %	58 %	58 %	62 %	21 %	25 %	22 %
Colombia	23 %	25 %	29 %	29 %	51 %	44 %	18 %	21 %	25 %
Mexico	54 %	51 %	20 %	22 %	25 %	52 %	21 %	22 %	25 %
Peru	26 %	10 %	44 %	43 %	53 %	27 %	30 %	19 %	25 %
Venezuela	n.a.	44 %	37 %	n.a.	28 %	28 %	n.a.	25 %	33 %
Asia									
Bangladesh	54 %	33 %	n.a.	23 %	24 %	n.a.	8 %	16 %	n.a.
China	65 %	58 %	50 %	14 %	20 %	23 %	7 %	12 %	19 %
India	28 %	28 %	30 %	40 %	22 %	24 %	31 %	19 %	23 %
Indonesia	48 %	46 %	46 %	37 %	40 %	42 %	6 %	9 %	10 %
Malaysia	14 %	11 %	15 %	65 %	61 %	54 %	18 %	25 %	27 %
Pakistan	15 %	14 %	n.a.	13 %	11 %	n.a.	24 %	28 %	n.a.
Philippines	21 %	15 %	13 %	43 %	45 %	45 %	34 %	39 %	42 %
Thailand	50 %	42 %	36 %	34 %	34 %	22 %	7 %	11 %	33 %
Europe									
Bulgaria	36 %	37 %	30 %	52 %	50 %	56 %	10 %	10 %	13 %
Hungary	34 %	32 %	30 %	61 %	60 %	61 %	5 %	8 %	10 %
Poland	19 %	16 %	14 %	76 %	73 %	70 %	5 %	10 %	15 %
Romania	23 %	26 %	22 %	71 %	66 %	64 %	5 %	7 %	13 %
Russian Federation	15 %	14 %	11 %	48 %	53 %	53 %	37 %	33 %	36 %
Turkey	56 %	53 %	52 %	27 %	27 %	24 %	11 %	13 %	19 %
Ukraine	9 %	9 %	5 %	58 %	53 %	50 %	33 %	39 %	45 %
Africa									
South Africa	52 %	40 %	51 %	39 %	51 %	33 %	5 %	4 %	6 %

2000s' sluggish economic growth. Latin American EMEs grew at a slower pace when compared to Asian EMEs.

In Asian EMEs, the employment rate in 4 out of 8 countries (Bangladesh, China, India and Malaysia) decreased. The most notable declines occurred in

Tab. 10.3: Employment to Population Ratio and GDP Growth (%). ILO, Key Indicators of Labor Markets (KLIM) Database (ILO, 2016)

Countries	Employment			GDP Growth		
	2000-2004	2005-2009	2010-2014	2000-2004	2005-2009	2010-2014
Latin America						
Argentina	49.4	56.0	56.1	0.4	4.8	3.0
Brazil	59.7	62.6	62.6	3.1	3.6	3.4
Chile	49.3	52.1	57.4	4.0	3.5	4.6
Colombia	56.4	57.8	61.0	3.6	4.7	4.8
Mexico	58.3	58.9	58.8	2.1	1.6	3.4
Peru	64.5	67.6	71.4	3.6	6.5	5.8
Venezuela	57.6	59.8	59.6	1.8	6.2	1.2
Asia						
Bangladesh	66.3	62.1	59.4	4.8	6.3	6.1
China	72.5	69.4	67.8	9.2	11.5	8.6
India	57.2	56.0	52.3	5.7	7.9	7.2
Indonesia	61.6	61.4	63.3	4.6	5.6	5.8
Malaysia	60.1	58.3	59.9	5.5	4.2	5.7
Pakistan	47.1	50.2	50.8	4.3	4.6	3.4
Philippines	59.2	59.3	60.4	4.5	4.4	6.3
Thailand	71.8	72.4	71.9	5.5	3.1	3.8
Europe						
Bulgaria	42.6	49.1	47.2	5.4	4.6	0.8
Hungary	46.3	46.1	46.6	4.3	0.6	1.4
Poland	44.9	48.3	50.9	3.3	4.8	3.0
Romania	55.1	51.5	51.3	5.4	4.1	1.5
Russian Federation	55.2	58.3	59.6	6.9	4.1	2.9
Turkey	43.3	41.7	44.9	4.4	3.2	5.5
Ukraine	51.9	54.2	54.0	8.4	1.1	0.7
Africa						
South Africa	40.9	41.5	39.1	3.6	3.6	2.5

Bangladesh, China and India. This trend seems to be related to the slowing of economic growth in these countries. The employment to population ratio in Pakistan is lower than other Asian EMEs. In China and India, the employment to population ratio declined by five percentage points.

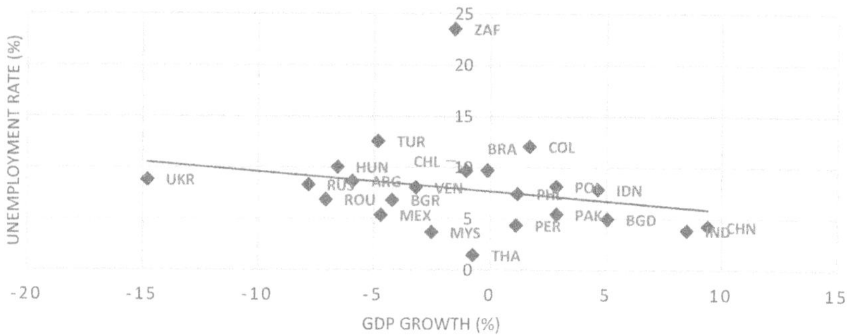

Fig. 10.6: Unemployment and Growth Rates in 2009 (%). Author's calculations based on World Bank (2016)

In European EMEs, the employment rates and GDP growth rates (especially in the 2010–2014 period) are lower when compared to other country groups. It is under 50 % in almost all these countries. Among the European EMEs, employment figures for The Russian Federation deserve special attention. A serious slowdown in economic growth was seen in The Russian Federation in the post crisis period, but it was not seen in employment figures due to the low sensitivity of Russian employment to output growth (Gimpelson and Kapeliushnikov, 2011).

The deepest effect of the 2008 crisis on economic activity was seen in 2009. Fig. 10.6 illustrates unemployment rates and economic growth rates for EMEs in 2009. Ukraine and South Africa experienced harmful effects of the crisis with high rates of contraction and high unemployment rates. Ukraine experienced a 14.8 % GDP contraction in 2009 with 8.8 % of unemployment rate. Meanwhile, The Russian Federation and Romania GDPs decreased by 7 % with 8.3 % and 7.1 % unemployment rates respectively. Also, in some countries, lower levels of declines occurred with high levels of unemployment, due to high levels of unemployment in the period preceding the crisis. For instance, in Turkey, 4.8 % of the decline in the GDP occurred with a 12.5 % unemployment rate. Asian EMEs were high performers in terms of GDP growth and unemployment. China and India had the highest rate with 9.4 % and 8.4 % GDP growth rates with 4.2 % and 3.9 % unemployment rates respectively.

The structure of employment shows different characteristics among EMEs. In Latin American EMEs, most employees work in the service sector. The share of agriculture in Argentina and Peru is below 10 % throughout all periods, while the services sector employment constitutes a level higher than 70 % in these countries throughout the 2000s. In Latin American EMEs, the structure of employment did not change to a great deal. In Asian EMEs, the share of industry sector employment is greater when compared to Latin American EMEs. In Bangladesh, India and Pakistan, agricultural employment constitutes the largest share of employment.

In Philippines and Malaysia, service sector employment has the largest percentage share in total employment. In China, the share of employment in industry increased in the 2005–2009 period and continued to increase in the 2010–2014 period. Moreover, service sector employment also rose in China significantly after 2005. This expansion in the services market absorbed the slowdown in the labor market, since the employment structure became more labor intensive (Lam et.al., 2015). European EMEs and South Africa show a similar employment structure along with the Latin American EMEs in terms of service sector employment (Tab. 10.4).

10.4 Labor Force Participation Rate

Another aspect of the labor markets of EMEs is labor force participation rates (LFPR). Tab. 10.5 presents LFPR for EMEs. In Latin American EMEs, LFPRs are above 60 % for most of the countries. Peru has the highest rates with above 70 % and the rates rose to an average of 74 % in the 2010–2014 period. Another steady increase in LFPR during the 2000s occurred in Chile, with an increase from an average of 54.1 % in the 2000–2004 period to an average of 61.6 % in the 2010–2014 period. In Asian EMEs, LFPR was also higher than 60 % in most countries, except for India and Pakistan. In addition, LFPR in 5 out of 8 Asian EMEs (Bangladesh, China, India, Malaysia, Thailand) was decreasing in the 2000–2014 period. In China, India and Bangladesh, LFPR decreased more than five percentage points. As for the European EMEs, Turkey has the lowest LFPRs, which was below 50 % in all three periods. The highest rates occurred in The Russian Federation, which was above 60 %. In other countries, LFPRs stayed under the 50 % level.

One of the main problems of EMEs is gender differences in LFPRs. In Pakistan, LFPRs are below 20 % on the average, while in Turkey and India they are 26.5 % and 31.9 % on average, respectively, through the 2000–2014 period. Remarkable increases by fifteen percentage points (from 35 % in 2000 to 50 % in 2014) in female LFPRs occurred in Chile and by ten percentage points in Columbia (from 48 % in 2000 to 58 % in 2014). Moreover, in China, Thailand and Peru female LFPRs are higher than 60 % (ILO, 2016).

Tab. 10.4: Employment by Sectors (% of Total Employment). ILO, Key Indicators of Labor Markets (KLIM) Database (ILO, 2016)

Countries	**Agriculture**			**Industry**			**Service**		
	2000-2004	**2005-2009**	**2010-2014**	**2000-2004**	**2005-2009**	**2010-2014**	**2000-2004**	**2005-2009**	**2010-2014**
Latin America									
Argentina	1 %	1 %	2 %	22 %	24 %	24 %	77 %	75 %	74 %
Brazil	20 %	18 %	15 %	21 %	22 %	23 %	58 %	59 %	68 %
Chile	14 %	14 %	10 %	27 %	42 %	24 %	59 %	45 %	66 %
Colombia	17 %	19 %	17 %	21 %	20 %	20 %	60 %	61 %	63 %
Mexico	17 %	14 %	13 %	25 %	26 %	24 %	57 %	60 %	62 %
Peru	10 %	9 %	n.a.	19 %	20 %	23 %	72 %	72 %	75 %
Venezuela	10 %	9 %	8 %	21 %	22 %	22 %	68 %	68 %	70 %
Asia									
Bangladesh	55 %	48 %	48 %	13 %	15 %	18 %	31 %	37 %	35 %
China	29 %	4 %	3 %	27 %	44 %	46 %	28 %	49 %	48 %
India	60 %	56 %	49 %	16 %	19 %	23 %	24 %	25 %	28 %
Indonesia	45 %	41 %	36 %	18 %	19 %	21 %	37 %	40 %	44 %
Malaysia	15 %	14 %	12 %	32 %	29 %	28 %	53 %	57 %	59 %
Pakistan	45 %	44 %	44 %	20 %	21 %	22 %	36 %	36 %	34 %
Philippines	37 %	35 %	32 %	16 %	15 %	15 %	47 %	49 %	53 %
Thailand	46 %	42 %	40 %	19 %	20 %	20 %	35 %	38 %	39 %
Europe									
Bulgaria	10 %	7 %	7 %	33 %	35 %	31 %	57 %	57 %	62 %
Hungary	6 %	5 %	5 %	34 %	32 %	30 %	60 %	63 %	65 %

Poland	18 %	14 %	12 %	30 %	31 %	31 %	52 %	55 %	57 %
Romania	34 %	27 %	26 %	31 %	32 %	30 %	35 %	41 %	44 %
Russian Federation	12 %	9 %	7 %	29 %	29 %	28 %	59 %	62 %	65 %
Turkey	35 %	24 %	22 %	23 %	27 %	27 %	42 %	50 %	51 %
Ukraine	21 %	18 %	19 %	24 %	24 %	26 %	46 %	58 %	56 %
Africa									
South Africa	11 %	6 %	5 %	25 %	25 %	24 %	56 %	60 %	71 %

10.5 Labor Productivity, Wages and Price Growth

This section focuses on labor productivity, measured as output per worker, and wages, which affects the standard of living of employees. This indicator points out an improvement for all EMEs through the 2000–2014 period. Tab. 10.6 presents labor productivity figures. In Latin American EMEs, there are moderate increases in labor productivity figures. Peru and Argentina experienced remarkable increases by 35 % and 29 % respectively. Meanwhile, in Columbia, there was a 20 % increase in labor productivity figures.

A significant amount of increased labor productivity occurred in China and India. In China, labor productivity steadily increased through the 2000–2014 period and soared by 152 % in the 2010–2014 period in comparison to productivity figures in the 2000–2004 period. Likewise, India experienced an 87 % increase in labor productivity in the 2010–2014 period in comparison to productivity figures in the 2000–2004 period. The least productivity improvements in Asian EMEs is observed in Pakistan by 6 %, which is the only figure that is below 25 % in Asian EMEs.

In European EMEs, the most notable increase in labor productivity was recorded in Romania with 61 %. In the Russian Federation and Bulgaria, there were also productivity increases with 41 % and 37 % respectively. The lowest productivity increases occurred in Turkey and Poland with 25 %.

If labor productivity increases are not coupled with wages, then the productivity increase will not be reflected in living standard of the employees. Tab. 10.7 represents the average wage growth for EMEs. Latin American EMEs (except for Peru) actively used a minimum wage policy to deal with the unemployment problem resulting from the global turmoil (Marinakis, 2011). Therefore, wages increased in these countries especially after the crisis. Most increases occurred in Argentina with 52 % in the 2005–2010 period and Venezuela with 33 % in the 2010–2014 period. In Brazil, Columbia and Mexico wage growth slowed down in the 2000–2014 period. In Asian EMEs, Thailand and China are the best performers in terms of wage growth, while wages in India and Indonesia grew at a slower pace through the 2000s. In European economies, wage growth was at levels in 2000–2004 period and wages grew at a lower rate in 2010–2014 period in comparison to the previous periods. The wage growth slowed most in Turkey and Romania.

Comparing nominal wages with prices will give the situation of real wages in these economies. Generally, wages rose at a higher pace in comparison to prices, meaning an improvement in terms of real wages. In all Latin American EMEs, wages rose faster than prices throughout these three periods, except for

Tab. 10.5: Labor Force Participation Rates (% of Total Labor Force). ILO Modeled Estimates (ILO,2017)

Countries	2000–2004	2005–2009	2010–2014
Latin America			
Argentina	59.0	61.6	60.5
Brazil	68.8	70.0	67.7
Chile	54.1	56.7	61.6
Colombia	67.0	65.4	68.1
Mexico	60.0	61.4	61.9
Peru	70.2	72.3	74.3
Venezuela	67.6	65.5	64.5
Asia			
Bangladesh	68.9	64.8	62.2
China	75.9	72.4	70.9
India	59.6	58.4	54.3
Indonesia	67.3	67.7	67.7
Malaysia	62.2	60.4	61.8
Pakistan	51.1	53.3	54.0
Philippines	66.8	64.2	64.9
Thailand	73.2	73.3	72.4
Europe			
Bulgaria	50.7	53.1	53.4
Hungary	49.3	50.1	51.9
Poland	55.1	54.5	56.4
Romania	59.5	55.2	55.2
Russian Federation	60.4	62.7	63.3
Turkey	47.7	46.4	49.5
Ukraine	57.7	58.3	58.7
Africa			
South Africa	55.4	53.9	51.9

Venezuela. In Venezuela, prices rose at a faster pace than wages in the 2010–2014 period. Among the Asian EMEs, in China, Indonesia and Thailand, wages grew faster than prices. In European EMEs, wage growth rose generally at a faster rate than prices. In Turkey in the 2000–2009 period and in The Russian Federation in the 2010–2014 period, prices rose faster than wages, indicating a deterioration in real wages. Moreover, in all European EMEs, real wage growth slowed down

Tab. 10.6: Labor Productivity (Output per worker) (2000=100). Author's calculations based on ILO Modeled Estimates (ILO,2017)

Countries	2000-2004	2005-2009	2010-2014
Latin America			
Argentina	92	100	118
Brazil	99	104	116
Chile	104	111	113
Colombia	92	103	111
Mexico	98	99	99
Peru	103	119	139
Venezuela	92	105	106
Asia			
Bangladesh	107	136	172
China	118	192	297
India	105	141	196
Indonesia	108	130	155
Malaysia	103	120	129
Pakistan	101	107	108
Philippines	101	113	127
Thailand	107	126	144
Europe			
Bulgaria	109	130	150
Hungary	108	125	123
Poland	107	120	134
Romania	123	177	197
Russian Federation	109	138	153
Turkey	104	129	131
Ukraine	117	152	155
Africa			
South Africa	104	114	125

in the 2010–2014 period. In South Africa, wages and prices rose almost at the same rate with prices.

10.6 Conclusion

It is widely accepted that the 2008 crisis did not affect the EMEs as much as it affected advanced economies. Emerging economy labor market indicators

Tab. 10.7: Wage Growth and Price Growth in EMEs. Author's calculations based on World Bank (2016) and ILO (2017)

Countries	Wage Growth			Price Growth		
	2000-2004	2005-2009	2010-2014	2000-2004	2005-2009	2010-2014
Latin America						
Argentina	20 %	52 %	12 %	8 %	9 %	10 %
Brazil	14 %	12 %	9 %	9 %	5 %	6 %
Chile	6 %	7 %	6 %	3 %	4 %	3 %
Colombia	9 %	7 %	4 %	7 %	5 %	3 %
Mexico	6 %	4 %	4 %	6 %	4 %	4 %
Peru	6 %	4 %	7 %	2 %	3 %	3 %
Venezuela	22 %	25 %	33 %	21 %	21 %	36 %
Asia						
Bangladesh	n.a.	n.a.	39 %	4 %	7 %	8 %
China	7 %	8 %	15 %	1 %	3 %	3 %
India	n.a.	9 %	4 %	4 %	7 %	10 %
Indonesia	21 %	13 %	13 %	8 %	9 %	6 %
Pakistan	n.a.	21 %	14 %	4 %	12 %	10 %
Philippines	6 %	5 %	5 %	4 %	5 %	4 %
Thailand	1 %	4 %	11 %	2 %	3 %	3 %
Europe						
Bulgaria	12 %	15 %	7 %	6 %	7 %	2 %
Hungary	20 %	6 %	8 %	7 %	5 %	3 %
Poland	10 %	9 %	6 %	4 %	3 %	2 %
Romania	48 %	17 %	8 %	26 %	7 %	4 %
Russian Federation	70 %	49 %	5 %	17 %	11 %	7 %
Turkey	37 %	9 %	10 %	38 %	9 %	8 %
Ukraine	28 %	26 %	13 %	11 %	15 %	6 %
Africa						
South Africa	n.a.	8 %	6 %	5 %	7 %	5 %

1 *Minimum wage is used as the minimum of monthly earnings of all employees as of December 31st of each year. Minimum wages are not reported for countries for which collective bargaining is in place for minimum wages. In cases where a national minimum wage is not mandated, the minimum wage in place in the capital or major city is used.*

2 *Malaysia is excluded since wage data is not available for this country*

3 *Growth in consumer price index is used*

support this assertion. This study examines labor market economies in five major aspects of labor markets. First, unemployment rates in EMEs present a recovery from the crisis. Especially, Asian EMEs had unemployment rates around 5 %. Latin American EMEs such as Argentina and Colombia experienced high rates of unemployment at the beginning of the 2000s, while their unemployment rate decreased considerably after the crisis. European EMEs had more volatile unemployment figures. In the pre-crisis period, their unemployment had a decreasing trend, while it had a rising trend in the post crisis period. Therefore, among these country groups, the higher volatilities in unemployment rates occurred in the European EMEs.

Second, employment to population ratios differ not only across country groups but also within them. The lowest levels of employment observed in European EMEs, whereas the highest ones are observed in Asian EMEs. Comparing it with the GDP growth reveals that the slowdown in GDP growth is reflected in employment ratios in European EMEs. Asian EMEs, continued their high rates of growth, although there exist slowdowns after 2010, and their employment rates remained higher compared to other countries. The decomposition of employment by main sector groups indicate that Latin American and European EMEs has the largest share in service employment, while Asian EMEs has the largest share in agriculture and industry.

Third, in Asian and Latin American EMEs, LFPRs are higher than European EMEs. Remarkable rates of declines in LFPRs happened in Asian EMEs, especially in China and India. Another important conclusion from LFPRs is that female LFPRs remained low compared to male LFPRs. Fourth, high raises are observed in labor productivity in most of the EMEs. This strong trend of labor productivity increases is not observed in wages in addition to the fact that wages grew at a higher rate than prices in almost all countries.

To sum up, the major challenges EMEs face can be combined in three major headings; first, there is gender inequality in labor markets where female labor force is lower than that of male labor forces in EMEs. Secondly, the youth unemployment rates are generally high in EMEs. Moreover, unemployment rate with tertiary education is increasing in most of the countries. Third challenge is flexibility of labor markets. In other words, in markets where unionization is low, wages are flexible unemployment rates have tendency to fluctuate in case of growth shocks.

Labor markets of EMEs have done well in the crisis time despite the presence of vulnerabilities. If labor market institutions can be established to secure jobs and sustainable economic growth can be attained then these vulnerabilities can be overcome. In this aspect, the results of this study shed light on important points for the policy makers.

References

EEAG. (2012). The Hungarian Crisis. In *the EEAG Report on the European Economy* (pp. 115–130). Munich: CESifo.

Gimpelson, V. Kapeliushnikov, R. (2011). Labor Market Adjustment: Is Russia Different? *The Institute for the Study of Labor (IZA) Discussion Paper No.5588*, Bonn.

Huynh, P., Kapsos, S. and Kim, K. B. (2010). Impacts of Current Global Economic Crisis on Asia's Labor Market. *ADBI Working Paper*. (No. 243).

International Monetary Fund (2014). World Economic Outlook, https://www.imf.org/external/pubs/ft/weo/2014/02/weodata/weoselagr.aspx (Last Accesion Date: 20.09.2016)

International Labour Organization (ILO). (2015). *World Employment Social Outlook (Trends 2015)*. Geneva.Retrieved from http://www.ilo.org/global/research/global-reports/weso/2015/WCMS_337069/lang--en/index.htm (Last Accession Date: 20.09.2016)

International Labour Organization (ILO). (2016). ILO Key Indicators of Labor Market Database. Retrieved from http://www.ilo.org/ilostat/faces/help_home?_adf.ctrl-state=n9g81o1zn_4&_afrLoop=24854904314945#! (Last Accession Date: 20.09.2016)

International Labour Organization (ILO). (2017). ILO Modeled Estimates. Retrieved from http://www.ilo.org/ilostat/faces/wcnav_defaultSelection;ILOSTATCOOKIE=UYv7EY43S1t6Tw_TxgSOz6rIjFWghbxsJYtnPU4G_acM1N5JAaqb!371185198?_adf.ctrl-state=1237pyk67j_4&_afrLoop=135244315086403&_afrWindowMode=0&_afrWindowId=null#!%40%40%3F_afrWindowId%3Dnull%26_afrLoop%3D135244315086403%26_afrWindowMode%3D0%26_adf.ctrl-state%3Dpf4o686og_4 (Last Accession Date: 01.05.2017)

Kyloh.R. (2011). Labor Reforms in Romania. In *the Global Crisis Causes, responses and challenges* (pp. 93–105). Geneva: International Labor Organization.

Lam, W. R., Liu X. Schipke, A. (2015). *China's Labor Market in the "New Normal"*. IMF Working Paper.(No. WP/15/151). Retrieved from ttps://www.imf.org/external/pubs/ft/wp/2015/wp15151.pdf

Maiväli, B. M., and Stierle, M. (2013). The Bulgarian labour market: Strong wage growth in spite of rising unemployment. *European Commission*, *10*(2), June 2013, 7 pages, http://ec.europa.eu/economy_finance/publications/country_focus/2013/pdf/cf_vol10_issue2_en.pdf. ISSN: 1725-8375.

Marinakis.A.E. (2011). Explaining Latin America's robust recovery from the crisis. In *the Global Crisis Causes, responses and challenges* (pp. 21–32). Geneva: International Labor Organization.

Marumoagae, M. C. (2014). The Effect of the Global Economic Recession on the South African Labour Market. Mediterranean Journal of Social Sciences, *Mediterranean Journal of Social Sciences*. *5*(23), 380.

World Bank. (2015). Recent Developments in Emerging and Developing Country Labor Markets. In *Global Economic Prospects* (pp. 49–54). Washington: The World Bank. http://doi.org/10.1596/978-1-4648-0483-0

World Bank. (2016). World Development Indicators Database. Retrieved from http://databank.worldbank.org/data/home.aspx (Last Accession Date: 20.09.2016)

Alper Sönmez

11 Foreign Direct Investment Inflows to EMEs

Abstract: The aim of this chapter is to analyze the net foreign direct investment (FDI) inflows to emerging market economies (EMEs) on a country and regional basis for the period of 2000 and 2015 by using the World Bank data. The key findings can be summarized as: (i) the FDI inflows to EMEs (current US$) have showed a steady increase; (ii) Asian region has gained increasing importance in terms of FDI inflows (current US$), while the importance of both European and Latin American regions has decreased; (iii) Europe region was more adversely affected by the 2008 global crisis when compared to Asian and Latin American regions; (iv) China in Asia, Brazil in Latin America, and Russia in Europe region have a dominate role in attracting the FDI inflows (current US$); (v) the share of EMEs in World FDI inflows has showed an increasing trend over the whole period; (vi) when economic size is taken into consideration, Chile in Latin America, Indonesia in Asia, and Turkey in Europe region have gained more importance in recent years in term of attracting the FDI inflows (as % of GDP).

Keywords: Foreign Direct Investment, Spillovers, MNCs, Emerging Economies, Globalization

11.1 Introduction

The purpose of this study is to analyze the net FDI inflows to EMEs on a country and regional basis from 2000 to 2015. The net FDI inflow is defined by the World Bank as "*the net inflows of investment to acquire a lasting management interest (10 percent or more of voting stock) in an enterprise operating in an economy other than that of the investor. It is the sum of equity capital, reinvestment of earnings, other long-term capital, and short-term capital as shown in the balance of payments. This series shows net inflows (new investment inflows less disinvestment) in the reporting economy from foreign investors*" (World Bank, 2016). For simplicity, from here on we refer to the net FDI inflows as the FDI inflows. In this study, analysis of the FDI inflows to EMEs is performed by two ways: first, the FDI inflows as current US$ and second, the FDI inflows as percentage of GDP.

This study is motivated by the large increases of FDI inflows to EMEs and importance of the FDI for the economic development of EMEs. With the globalization process, EMEs compete with each other and make numerous legal market regulations in order to attract more FDI inflows (UN, 1999; Narula and Driffield, 2012). By macroeconomic perspective, FDI was seen as a major channel for the past years by the EMEs to achieve the economic growth and development (Barro and Sala-i-Martin, 1995; Borensztein et. al., 1998; Xu, 2000). According to neo-classical theory, capital flows are very beneficial for the host countries because capital flows to poor countries increase their capital stock, increase employment, stabilize consumption volatility and raise growth (Korinek, 2017: 2). However, in the last few decades, FDI has gained more importance by the EMEs in terms of microeconomic perspective. The indirect effects of FDI (such as knowledge transfer, productivity) through externalities on the host country firms have been considered more important than the direct effects on the whole economy (such as growth, employment, foreign trade) (Kuznets, 1966; Borensztein et. al., 1998). EMEs consider that FDI inflows through MNCs can bring advanced technology into their economies (Lall, 1997; Kinoshita, 2001; Sönmez, 2013), and by this way they can increase their knowledge stock and *catch-up*[1] the developed countries (Keller, 1996). Therefore, recent literature has focused on the benefits and costs of the FDI inflows for the firms in the emerging host country. By micro-economic perspective, in the literature, there are so many empirical studies on whether the FDI inflows have any effect on emerging economies through increasing the productivity of domestic firms, leading to technology spillovers to domestic firms (Blomström and Kokko, 1998; Saggi, 2002; Görg and Greenaway, 2004; Smeets, 2008; Pamukçu and Sönmez, 2012; Sönmez and Pamukçu, 2012; Sönmez, 2013), and increasing the competition etc. (for details see Haddad and Harrison, 1993; Djankov and Hoekman; 2000; Narula and Marin, 2003). The studies reveal that only firms (or EMEs) which have qualified human capital stock, high technology capabilities, enough R&D capacity, developed infrastructure, and efficient absorptive capacity[2] can benefit from the FDI inflows (Pack, 1992; Keller, 1994; Evenson and Westphal, 1995; Pamukçu and Sönmez, 2012; Sönmez, 2013). In sum, the FDI inflows have been considered as a major channel by EMEs for economic development and growth by macroeconomic perspective, as well as for R&D and innovation activities, competition structure, technology and knowledge diffusion, improving human capital stock, and for catching-up the developed countries by microeconomic perspective[3]. Today, the FDI inflows play a major role in the evolution of economic activities in EMEs and therefore

1 For details, see Borensztein et. al., 1998.

2 See Narula and Marin, 2003.

3 For theoretical discussions on EMEs, FDI, spillovers and economic development see OECD, 2002; Aizenman, 2002; Deutsche Bundesbank, 2003; Goldberg, 2004; Meyer, 2005; Mauro et. al., 2007; Arbatli, 2011; Danescu and Nistor, 2012; Mustafa and Hasan, 2015; Korinek, 2017.

justify the aim of the study. In this chapter, we analyze the pattern of FDI inflows occurred to EMEs by using World Bank data over the 2000–2015 period.

The rest of the chapter is organized as follows. Next section analyzes the FDI inflows to EMEs (current US$) in detail on a country and regional basis and share of EMEs in World FDI inflows by using World Bank data between 2000 and 2015. Then, section three analyzes the FDI inflows to EMEs as percentage of GDP in order to take into consideration the economic sizes of the countries. The final section summarizes and concludes the study.

11.2 Analyses of FDI Inflows (current US$) to EMEs[4]

The annual average for FDI inflows (billion USD) to EMEs between 2000 and 2015 are presented in Tab. 11.1. According to the table, there is a steady increase in the FDI inflows to EMEs. For the sixteen-year period (2000–2015), the EMEs attracted a total of approximately 6.5 trillion dollars (USD) in FDI inflows; this figure corresponds to an annual average of 406 billion dollars. When examined regionally, more than half of this figure (52 %) is attracted by the Asian region, and Asia is followed by Latin America (28 %) and Europe (20 %). An interesting fact is that FDI inflows to the Asian region, when compared to the first years of 2000s, increased about six times, while they increased only four times for Europe, and three times for Latin America. The average annual FDI inflows to Asia rose from 64 billion dollars in the 2000–2003 period to 350 billion dollars in the 2012–2015 period, while they rose from 58 to 176 billion dollars for Latin America, and from 19 to 76 billion dollars for Europe in the same period.

11.2.1 FDI Inflows to EMEs by Region

In this section, the FDI inflows to EMEs on a regional basis will be analyzed in detail. Fig. 1 displays the yearly pattern of FDI inflows (billion USD) to EMEs, Fig. 11.2 shows the overall FDI inflows (billion USD) to EMEs, and Figs. 11.3 and 11.4 indicate the share (%) of the regions in overall FDI inflows to EMEs from 2000 to 2015 for three regions, i) Latin America, ii) Asia and Africa[5], and iii) Europe.

Overall FDI inflows to all three regions were approximately $150B in 2000 (see Fig. 11.2). From 2000 to 2008, the total FDI inflows to EMEs rapidly increased and reached a record level of $605B in 2008. Due to the negative impact of the

4 Foreign direct investment, net inflows (BoP, current US$).

5 South Africa (ZAF) which is actually located in the Africa region is included to the Asian region for the purposes of simplifying and interpreting the statistics better.

Tab. 11.1: FDI Inflows by Region and Country (billion USD), 2000–2015*. Author calculations based on the data obtained from World Bank World Development Indicators Database, 2016. *The values are rounded to the nearest integers.

Regions/ Countries	Annual Average					Total
	2000-2003	2004-2007	2008-2011	2012-2015	2000-2015	2000-2015
Latin America	***58***	***77***	***139***	***176***	***113***	***1,800***
ARG	4	5	9	10	7	116
BRA	21	24	68	82	49	780
CHL	4	9	18	24	14	221
COL	2	7	10	15	9	137
MEX	23	26	25	32	27	424
PER	1	3	7	9	5	85
VEN	3	2	2	3	2	39
Asia and Africa	***64***	***157***	***283***	***350***	***214***	***3,416***
BGD	0	1	1	2	1	17
CHN	50	113	207	261	158	2,522
IND	4	14	36	33	22	349
IDN	-2	6	13	22	10	154
MYS	3	6	8	10	7	111
PAK	1	3	3	1	2	32
PHL	1	2	2	5	2	37
THA	4	8	8	11	8	124
ZAF	3	4	6	5	4	70
Europe	***19***	***110***	***115***	***76***	***80***	***1,282***
BGR	1	7	5	2	4	60
HUN	4	26	15	4	12	193
POL	6	18	16	10	13	203
ROU	1	9	6	4	5	78
RUS	4	31	52	37	31	500
TUR	2	14	13	14	11	173
UKR	1	6	7	4	5	75

2008 global financial crisis, FDI inflows to EMEs fell sharply to $340B in 2009 (corresponding to a decrease of 44 % in FDI inflows). Despite this sharp decline in 2009, FDI inflows to EMEs quickly recovered in 2010 and reached their previous levels, and even broke a record at $655B in 2011, just two years after the crisis.

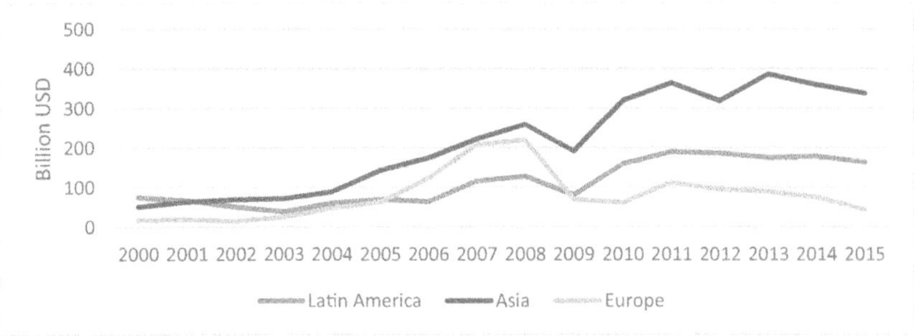

Fig. 11.1: FDI Inflows by Region (billion USD), 2000–2015. Author calculations based on the data obtained from World Bank World Development Indicators Database, 2016

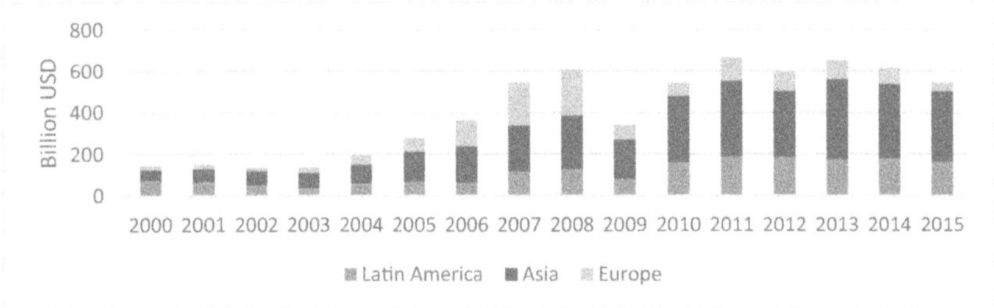

Fig. 11.2: Overall FDI Inflows (billion USD) by Region, 2000–2015. Author calculations based on the data obtained from World Bank World Development Indicators Database, 2016

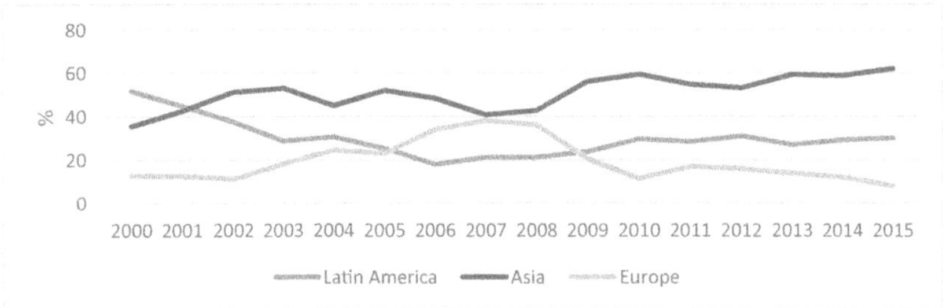

Fig. 11.3: Share of the Regions in Overall FDI Inflows in EMEs, 2000–2015. Author calculations based on the data obtained from World Bank World Development Indicators Database, 2016

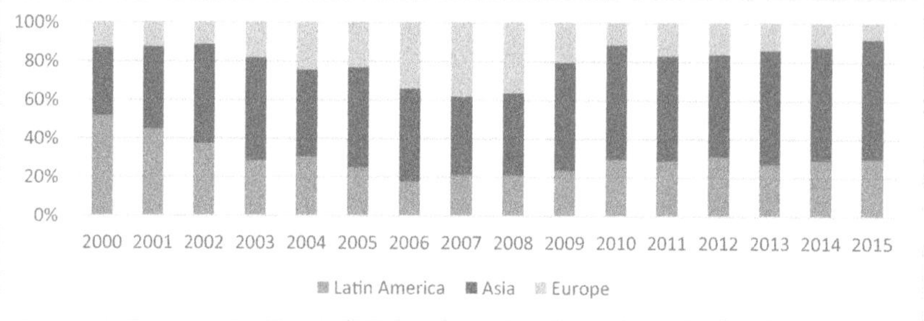

Fig. 11.4: Share of the Regions in Overall FDI Inflows in EMEs, 2000–2015. Author calculations based on the data obtained from World Bank World Development Indicators Database, 2016

In early 2000s, the majority of FDI inflows was attracted by Latin America (52 %), and was followed by Asia (35 %) and Europe (13 %) (see Figs. 11.3 and 11.4). However, as Figs. 11.3 and 11.4 show, FDI inflows to Latin America steadily decreased from 2000 to 2003 (from $75B to $39B); conversely FDI inflows to Asia increased while Europe remained stable for the same period (see Figs. 11.1 and 11.3). In 2002, the Asian region, by attracting more FDI inflows ($69B), passed Latin America ($50B) and rose to the first place with a 51 % share (see Fig. 11.3). The FDI inflows to the Asian region showed an increasing trend until 2015. In other words, FDI inflows to the Asian region increased continuously from 2000 to 2015 except for 2009 and 2012. The total FDI inflows to Asia were $3.6T from 2000 to 2015, and 75 % of this figure ($2.5T) was realized by China.

The total FDI inflows to Europe decreased in 2000. According to the data, the total FDI inflows to seven countries in Europe were only $18B in 2000, $9B of this figure (50 %) was realized by Poland, while Russia attracted only $3B (17 %). An interesting finding is that FDI inflows to EMEs in Europe experienced a rapid increase especially after the year 2003 and continued to increase until 2009 (see Figs. 11.1 and 11.3). Total FDI inflows, which were $25B in 2003, reached a record high of $219B in 2008 for Europe (corresponding to a 900 % increase in a five-year period). Moreover, for the three years between 2006 and 2008, Europe attracted nearly two times more FDI inflows ($550B) than Latin America ($308B), and Europe rose to second place following Asia (see Fig. 11.3). However, especially after 2008, due to the negative effects of the global financial crisis, FDI inflows to Europe decreased rapidly and fell to $43B in 2015.

The overall FDI inflows to Latin America were realized as $1.8T for the 2000–2015 period, corresponding to an annual average of $113B (see Tab. 11.1 and

Fig. 11.1). In early 2000s, Latin America was in first place by attracting the most FDI inflows (52 %) when compared to both Asia and Europe, but Latin America lost its place to the Asian region in 2002 (see Figs. 11.1 and 11.3). During the 2002–2005 period, FDI inflows to Latin America increased slightly, and then decreased to a record low level in 2003 ($39B). Moreover, Latin America attracted lower FDI inflows when compared to Europe and fell to third place for the period 2006 and 2008 (see Fig. 11.3). However, the FDI inflows to Latin America rapidly increased after 2009, and Latin America rose again to second place, passing Europe.

As is seen from Figs. 11.3 and 11.4, the Asian region increased its share from 35 % to 62 % in overall FDI inflows to EMEs from 2000 to 2015, while Latin America decreased its share from 52 % to 30 %, and Europe decreased its share from 13 % to 8 % for the same period. These statistics clearly show that the Asian region has gained increasing importance over the past sixteen years in terms of FDI inflows to EMEs, while the importance of both Europe and Latin America has decreased. In addition, Asian and Latin American regions started to recover rapidly despite a serious breakdown in 2009 due to the 2008 crisis, while Europe did not recover after the crisis. When compared to 2008, the FDI inflows to Asia decreased by 26 % in 2009, and they decreased by 37 % for Latin America and 68 % for Europe. These statistics show that the region most severely affected by the crisis in terms of attracting FDI inflows is Europe.

11.2.2. FDI Inflows to EMEs by Country

In this section, the FDI inflows to EMEs will be analyzed in detail on a country basis. Fig. 11.5 shows the annual FDI inflows (billion USD) by region and by country from 2000 to 2015, and Fig. 11.6 shows the share of countries (in %) in overall FDI inflows for the same period.

11.2.2.1 Latin America

When Figs. 11.5 and 11.6 are analyzed for Latin America, notably, Brazil has a very important role in attracting FDI inflows; also notable is that the FDI inflows to Brazil have continuously increased over this period. Overall, an increasing trend in FDI inflows to Brazil occurred, although there were some fluctuations especially in 2003 and 2009. According to the figures, Brazil attracts most of the FDI inflows (43 %) to Latin America, and Brazil is followed by Mexico (24 %) and Chile (12 %) (see Fig. 11.6-a). When compared to the 2000s, the annual average FDI inflows increased nearly four times for Brazil (from $21B to $81B), and six times for Chile (from $4B to $24B), while they increased one and half times for Mexico (from $23B to $32B). The share of the other four countries for total FDI

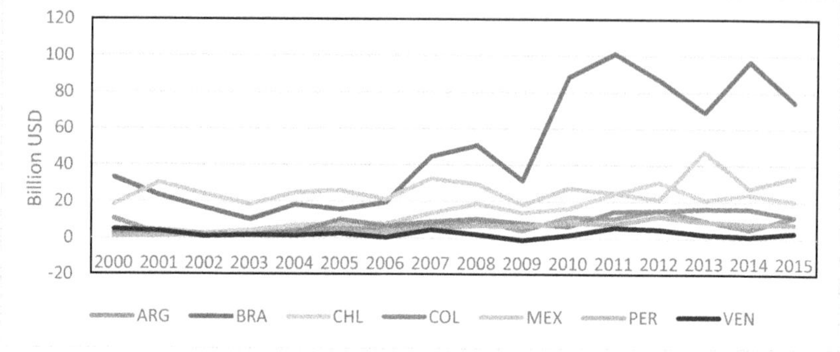

a) Latin America

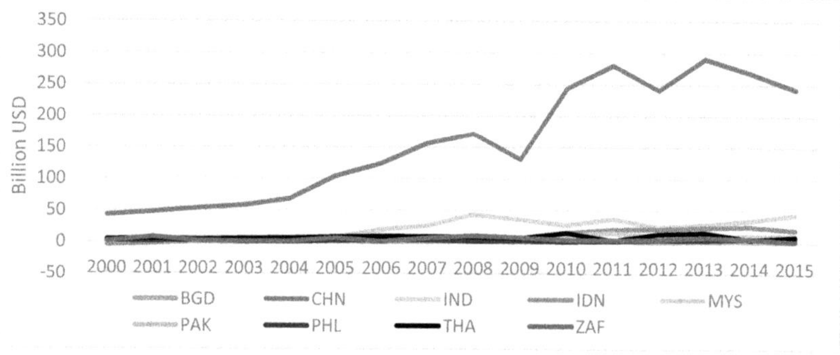

b) Asia

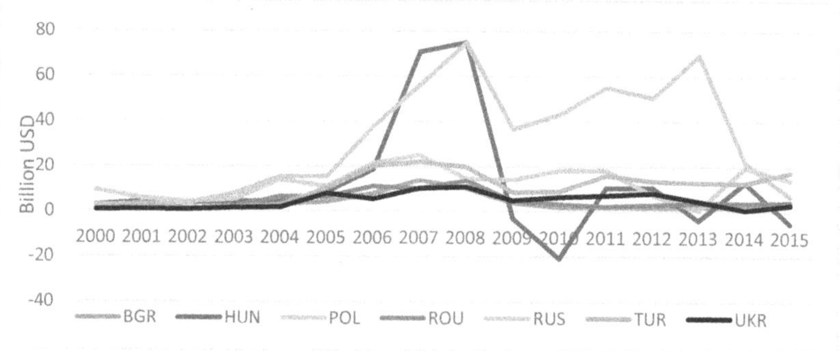

c) Europe

Fig. 11.5: Annual FDI Inflows (billion USD) by Region and Country, 2000–2015. Author calculations based on the data obtained from World Bank World Development Indicators Database, 2016

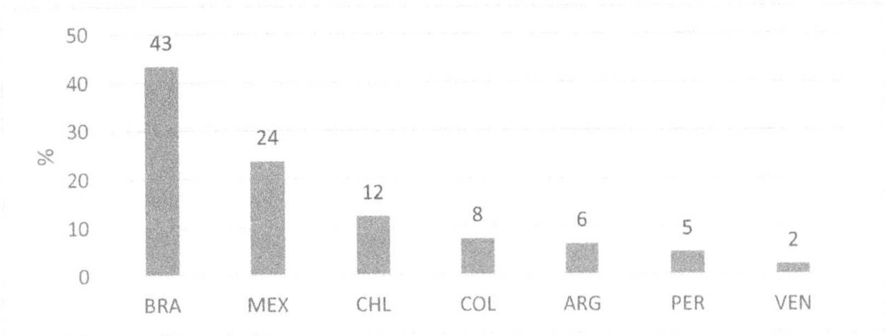

a) Latin America

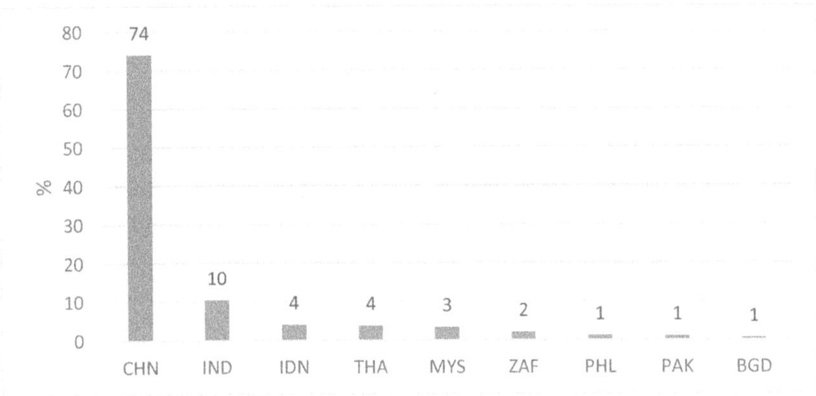

b) Asia

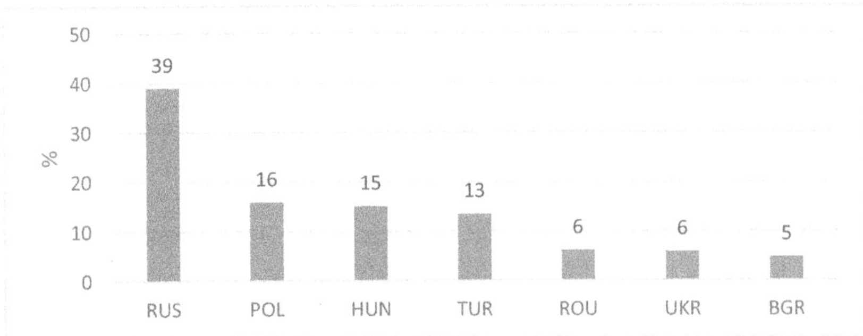

c) Europe

Fig. 11.6: Share (%) of the Countries in Overall FDI Inflows by Region, 2000–2015. Author calculations based on the data obtained from World Bank World Development Indicators Database, 2016 inflows is much lower; 8 % for Colombia ($137B), 6 % for Argentina ($116B), 5 % for Peru ($85B) and 2 % for Venezuela ($39B). An interesting finding here is that there has been a steady increase in FDI inflows to Peru and Colombia during the past years. Average FDI inflows increased nine times for Peru (from $1B to $9B), and seven and half times for Colombia (from $2B to $15B) from 2000s to 2015. Although the total amount is minimal, FDI inflows to these two countries (Peru and Colombia) have continuously increased over the period.

11.2.2.2 Asia

When the FDI inflows to the Asian region are analyzed by using the data in Figs. 11.5 and 11.6, it is clear that China dominates the FDI inflows to the Asian region. China attracted nearly 75 % of the FDI inflows for the whole period; while the remaining seven countries attracted only 25 % of the total FDI inflows (see Fig. 11.6-b). The annual FDI inflows to China increased from $50B in 2000 to $300B in 2013. China attracted a total of $2.5T in FDI inflows from 2000 to 2015, and this figure corresponds to an annual average of $158B over sixteen years. Other countries which attracted large FDI inflows in the Asian region are India (10 %), Indonesia (4 %), Thailand (4 %), Malaysia (3 %), Philippines (1 %), Pakistan (1 %) and Bangladesh (1 %). The share of India in FDI inflows to Asia has shown an increasing trend in recent years. Also, India ranks 2nd after China in terms of attracting a large share of the FDI inflows, nearly $350B in total for the whole period. Moreover, figures show that the FDI inflows to Indonesia, Thailand, and Malaysia have steadily increased in recent years, although the total amount is minimal. Another observation is that the other three countries (Bangladesh, Pakistan and Philippines) are very weak in terms of attracting FDI inflows.

11.2.2.3 Europe

It is seen from Figs. 11.5 and 11.6 that Russia is the leader country in Europe, attracting 39 % of the FDI inflows ($500B) from 2000 to 2015 ($31B annual average). Russia is followed by Poland (16 %), Hungary (15 %), Turkey (13 %), Romania (6 %), Ukraine (6 %) and Bulgaria (5 %). The annual average FDI inflows to Russia is actually much lower ($4B) for the 2000–2003 period, and the inflows started to increase significantly after 2003. When compared to the 2000–2003 period, the average annual FDI inflows to Russia increased nearly thirteen times and reached a peak at $52B during the 2008–2011 period. With the negative effects of the 2008 financial crisis, FDI inflows to Russia began to fall rapidly (see Fig. 11.5-c). Although there was an increase in FDI inflows to Russia towards 2013, Russia experienced significant declines in 2014 ($22B) and 2015

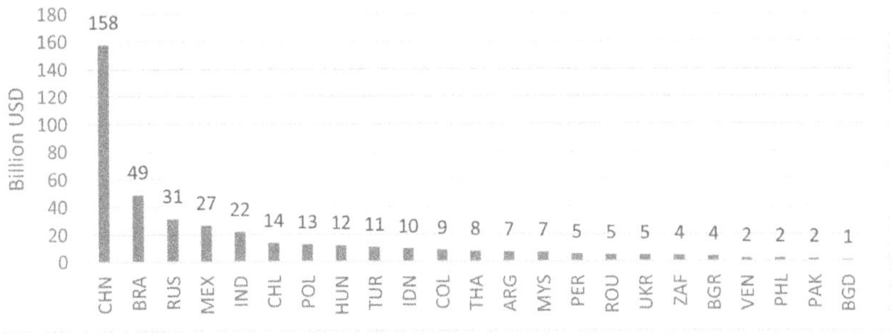

Fig. 11.7: Average FDI Inflows by Country, 2000–2015. Author calculations based on the data obtained from World Bank World Development Indicators Database, 2016

($7B). The most important reason for the declines was sanctions imposed on the country by Western countries because of the Ukraine conflict.

Another interesting finding is that the FDI inflows to Europe during the period 2003–2007 showed a rapid increase when compared to the 2000–2003 period. The average FDI inflows to Europe increased nearly six-times from $19B to $110B between these two periods. The largest share of this increase belongs to Russia ($31B), Hungary ($26B) and Poland ($18B). However, the unusually high increase in FDI inflows to Hungary and Poland for the 2004–2007 period did not continue and declined in the following years (see Fig. 11.5-c). An unusually high increase in FDI inflows to Hungary was observed for 2007 and 2008, when the FDI inflows to the country sharply rose from $19B to $71B in 2007, and to $75B in 2008. Although the FDI inflows to Turkey were low, Turkey exhibited a stable trajectory especially after 2004 with an overall of $173B (averaging $14B per year). As is seen in Tab. 11.1 and Fig. 11.6-c, the FDI inflows to Romania (6 % share with a total of $78B), Ukraine (6 % share with a total of $75B) and Bulgaria (5 % share with a total of $60B) have remained at very low levels.

Figs. 11.7 and 11.8 give the average and overall FDI inflows to all twenty-three EMEs by country, and Fig. 11.9 shows the share of countries in the overall FDI inflows to EMEs for the period 2000–2015. When the FDI inflows to all EMEs are interpreted on a country basis as opposed to a regional basis, notably, China in Asia (39 %), Brazil in Latin America (12 %) and Russia in Europe (8 %) are the top three countries which attracted the majority of the FDI inflows to EMEs (totaling 59 %) (see Fig. 11.9). Clearly, China has a dominant role in attracting FDI inflows, its share being 39 % ($2.5T) in overall FDI inflows to EMEs. Another interesting finding here is that, of all the twenty-three EMEs analyzed, fourteen

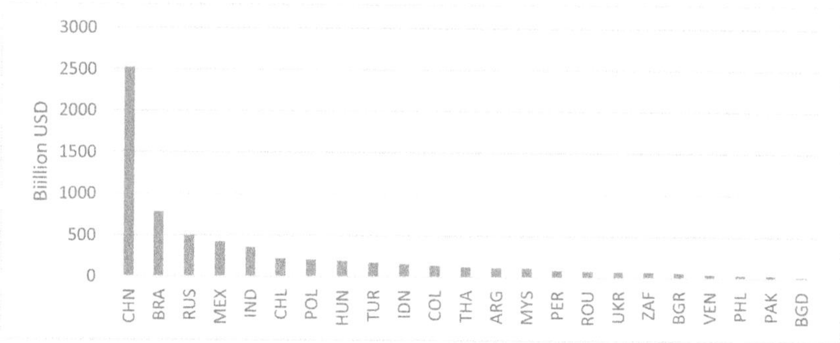

Fig. 11.8: Overall FDI Inflows by Country, 2000–2015. Author calculations based on the data obtained from World Bank World Development Indicators Database, 2016

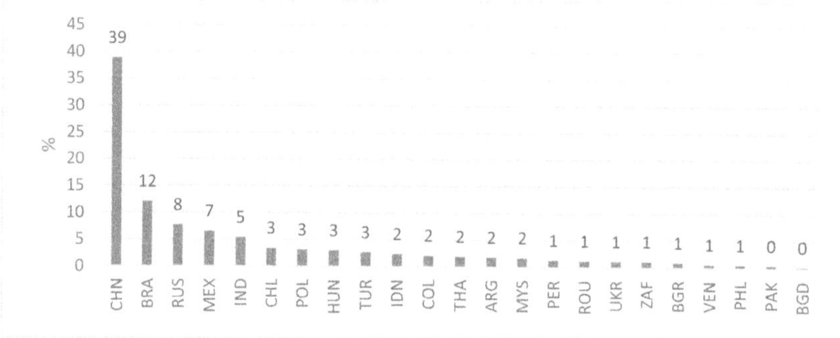

Fig. 11.9: Share (%) of the Countries in Overall FDI Inflows in EMEs, 2000–2015. Author calculations based on the data obtained from World Bank World Development Indicators Database, 2016

countries which attracted lower FDI inflows have an average of less than \$10B, and their total share is only 17 % (\$1.1T) in overall FDI inflows to EMEs (see Fig. 11.9). On the other hand, top five-countries (China, Brazil, Russia, Mexico, India) have attracted 71 % of the FDI inflows (\$4.6T) to EMEs. Also, Poland, Hungary and Turkey which are the top countries after Russia in the European region placed 7th, 8th and 9th, respectively and attracted only 9 % (\$570B) of the overall FDI inflows to EMEs.

Fig. 11.10 compares the FDI inflows (billion USD) to EMEs on a regional basis and a country basis for the years 2000 and 2015. When compared to the year 2000, the FDI inflows to Latin America doubled in 2015 (from $75B in 2000 to $163B in 2015), and this increase occurred for every country in Latin America except for Venezuela. The countries which have the largest share of this increase are Brazil, Mexico, Chile, Colombia, Peru and Argentina, respectively. The highest gain in terms of nominal value is for Brazil ($42B), but notably, the greatest gain in terms of ratio is for Peru (eight times) and Chile (four times).

When the Asian region is examined, the FDI inflows increased about seven-times in 2015 (from $51B in 2000 to $338B in 2015), and clearly China is at the forefront in Asia with $242B in 2015. The FDI inflows to China rose six-times in 2015 when compared to 2000 (from $42B to $242B). The country with the greatest increase in FDI inflows after China is India. The FDI inflows to India increased eleven-times (from $4B in 2000 to $44B in 2015).

When we analyze the European region, it is seen that FDI inflows to Europe rose from $18B in 2000 to $43B in 2015, more than doubling the amount. FDI inflows increased for every country in European region except for Hungary. The countries which have the largest share of the increase are Turkey, Poland, Russia, Romania, Ukraine and Bulgaria, respectively. The most striking finding here is that the FDI inflows to Turkey increased eighteen-times in 2015 when compared to 2000 (from $1B to $18B), and Turkey ranked in 1st place. This finding clearly reveals that in recent years, Turkey has gained more importance in Europe in terms of attracting FDI inflows.

11.2.3 The Share of EMEs in World FDI Inflows by Region

In this section, the share of EMEs in World FDI inflows by region will be examined in order to analyze the trend of the FDI inflows to EMEs. It is also important to analyze how the share of EMEs in the World FDI inflows has improved in order to understand whether or not EMEs have secured an important position in attracting more FDI inflows from the rest of the World. The shares of EMEs in World FDI inflows for the period 2000–2015 are shown on a regional basis in Fig. 11.11. According to statistics, the average share for the regions as to World FDI inflows is 12 % for Asia, 7 % for Latin America, and 4 % for the Europe for the sixteen-year period. In 2000, the share of Latin America in World FDI inflows (5 %) was greater than the share of both Asia (4 %) and Europe (4 %). An interesting finding here is that the share of Asia in World FDI inflows has significantly increased since 2001 when compared to both Latin American and European regions, and the share of Asia reached a peak at 20 % in 2014.

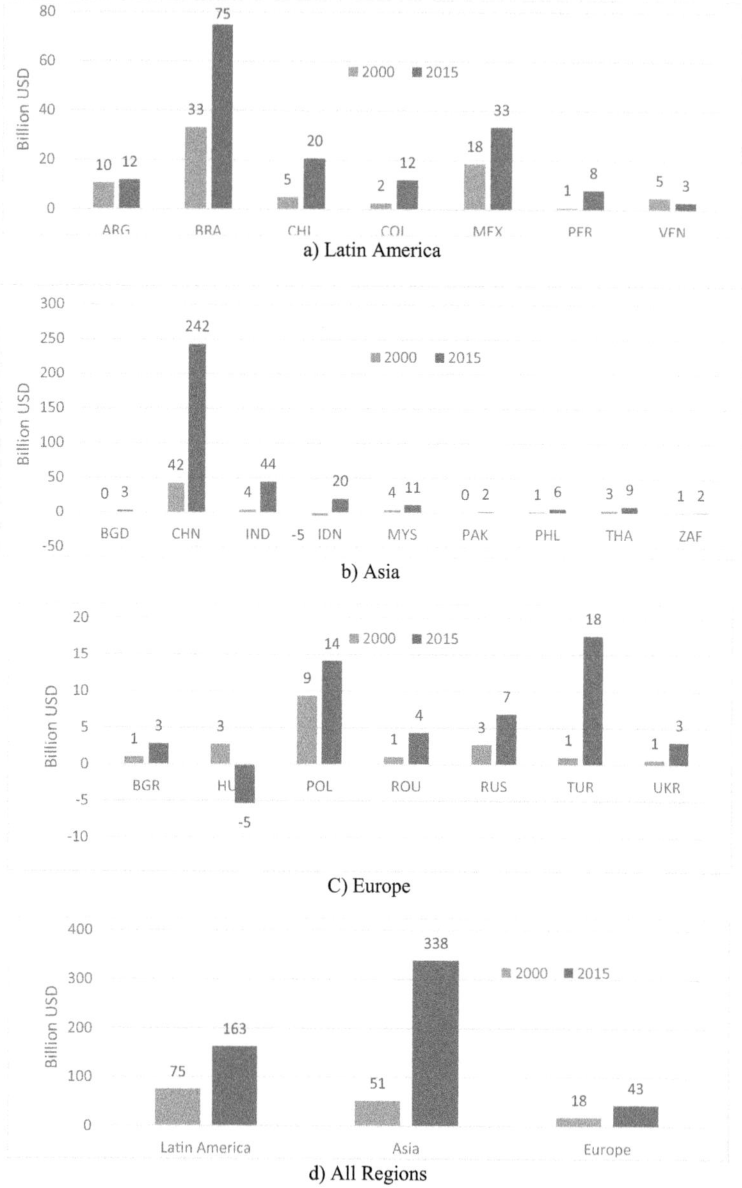

Fig. 11.10: Change in FDI Inflows by Region and Country between 2000 and 2015. Author calculations based on the data obtained from World Bank World Development Indicators Database, 2016

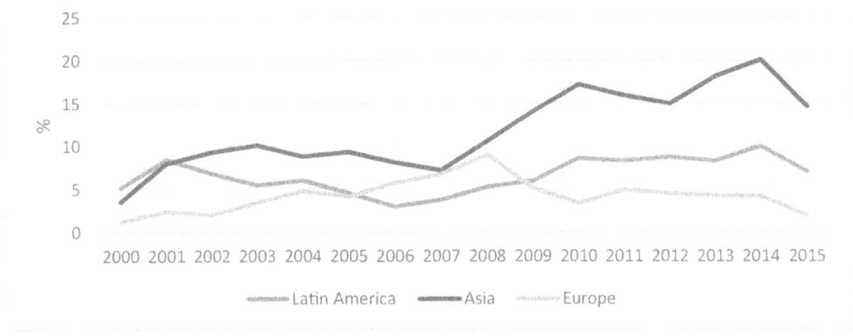

Fig. 11.11: Share (%) of EMEs in World FDI Inflows by Region, 2000–2015. Author calculations based on the data obtained from World Bank World Development Indicators Database, 2016

By the way, the share of Europe in World FDI inflows steadily increased until 2008, when the share reached a maximum level of 9 %. However, the share of Europe began to fall steadily after the crisis and reached a very low level of 2 % in 2015 (see Fig. 11.11). The share of Latin America in World FDI inflows decreased during the 2001–2006 period and fell to 6 % in 2006. However, the share of Latin America has begun to rise steadily especially after the crisis and peaked at 10 % in 2014. While the share of Latin America in World FDI inflows continuously declined until 2006, the share of Europe increased up until the crisis; however, after the crisis, the share of Europe was decreasing while the share of Latin America was steadily rising. A sharp decline was observed in FDI inflows to EMEs in European region especially after the crisis (decreasing from 9 % in 2008 to 5 % in 2009). In sum, the shares of both Asia and Latin America in World FDI inflows have continuously risen after the global crisis, while the share of Europe has decreased. Also, when we compare the year 2009 with 2008, the share of Asia in World FDI inflows increased from 11 % (in 2008) to 14 % (in 2009), and the share of Latin America increased from 5 % (in 2008) to 6 % (in 2009), but the share of Europe decreased from 9 % (in 2008) to 5 % (in 2009).

The share of twenty-three EMEs in World FDI inflows as a whole is presented in Fig. 11.12. The average share of the all EMEs analyzed in World FDI inflows was 23 % for the period of 2000 to 2015. As seen from Fig. 11.12, there is an increasing trend in the share of EMEs in World FDI inflows. The share of EMEs in World FDI inflows was 10 % in 2000 and increased more than three-times rising to maximum level at 34 % in 2014. An interesting finding here is that the average share of the EMEs in World FDI inflows was 19 % during the 2000–2009

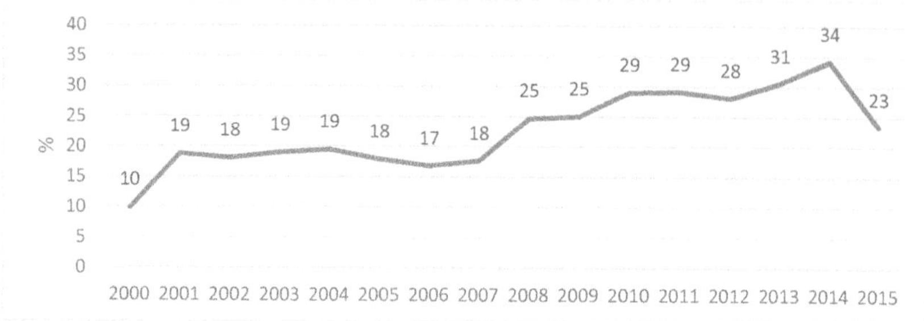

Fig. 11.12: Share (%) of EMEs in World FDI Inflows, 2000–2015. Author calculations based on the data obtained from World Bank World Development Indicators Database, 2016

period, while it was 29 % for the 2010–2015 period. This finding clearly reveals that the share of EMEs in the world FDI inflows has significantly increased after the crisis. In other words, the EMEs have started to attract more FDI inflows and have gained more importance especially after the crisis. When this fact is evaluated with previous findings, the conclusion is that EMEs in both Asia and Latin America have gained more importance when compared to EMEs in Europe, since the share of EMEs in Europe in World FDI inflows decreased after 2009. When evaluated on a country basis, China and India in the Asian region, and Brazil, Mexico and Chile in the Latin American region have gained more importance in attracting the majority of the World FDI inflows (see Fig. 11.10).

11.3 Analyses of FDI Inflows to EMEs as % of GDP[6]

In this section, the FDI inflows to EMEs will be analyzed by considering the share of GDP of EMEs. It is assumed that countries with higher GDPs attract more FDI inflows (in nominal terms) than countries with lower GDPs. It is misleading to analyze only the nominal FDI inflows without taking into consideration the economic size of the countries. Tabs. 11.2 and 11.3 summarize the FDI inflows to the EMEs as a percentage of the GDP. According to the statistics, FDI inflows to EMEs are relatively stable, in other words, there is no significant changes in the FDI inflows (as % of GDP) over the years.

6 Foreign direct investment, net inflows (%of GDP).

Tab. 11.2: FDI Inflows (as % of GDP) by Country and Region, 2000–2015. Author calculations based on the data obtained from World Bank World Development Indicators Database, 2016

Regions/ Countries	2000	2001	2002	2003	2004	2005	2006	2007	2008	2009	2010	2011	2012	2013	2014	2015
Latin America	**4**	**3**	**3**	**2**	**3**	**4**	**3**	**4**	**4**	**3**	**4**	**4**	**4**	**4**	**4**	**4**
ARG	4	1	2	1	3	3	2	2	3	1	3	2	3	2	1	2
BRA	5	4	3	2	3	2	2	3	3	2	4	4	4	3	4	4
CHL	6	6	4	5	7	6	5	8	10	8	7	10	11	8	9	8
COL	2	3	2	2	3	7	4	4	4	3	2	4	4	4	4	4
MEX	3	4	3	3	3	3	2	3	3	2	3	2	2	4	2	3
PER	2	2	4	2	2	3	4	5	6	5	6	4	6	5	4	4
VEN	4	3	1	2	1	2	0	2	1	0	0	2	1	1	..	..
Asia and Africa	**1**	**2**	**2**	**1**	**2**	**3**	**3**	**3**	**3**	**2**	**2**	**2**	**2**	**2**	**2**	**2**
BGD	1	0	0	0	1	1	1	1	1	1	1	1	1	2	1	1
CHN	3	4	4	3	3	5	5	4	4	3	4	4	3	3	3	2
IND	1	1	1	1	1	1	2	2	4	3	2	2	1	2	2	2
IDN	-3	-2	0	0	1	3	1	2	2	1	2	2	2	3	3	2
MYS	4	1	3	3	4	3	5	5	3	0	4	5	3	3	3	4
PAK	0	1	1	1	1	2	3	4	3	1	1	1	0	1	1	1
PHL	2	1	2	1	1	2	2	2	1	1	1	1	1	1	2	2
THA	3	4	2	3	3	4	4	3	3	2	4	1	3	4	1	2
ZAF	1	6	1	0	0	3	0	2	3	3	1	1	1	2	2	0
Europe	**4**	**3**	**3**	**4**	**5**	**6**	**10**	**15**	**13**	**3**	**0**	**4**	**3**	**1**	**3**	**2**
BGR	8	6	6	10	12	14	23	31	19	8	4	4	3	4	4	6
HUN	6	8	5	5	4	8	16	51	48	-2	-16	7	8	-3	9	-4
POL	5	3	2	2	5	4	6	6	3	3	4	3	1	0	4	3
ROU	3	3	2	3	8	7	9	6	7	3	2	1	2	2	2	2
RUS	1	1	1	2	3	2	4	4	5	3	3	3	2	3	1	1
TUR	0	2	0	1	1	2	4	3	3	1	1	2	2	1	1	2
UKR	2	2	2	3	3	9	5	7	6	4	5	4	5	2	1	3

11.3.1 FDI Inflows to EMEs (as % of GDP) by Region

When the FDI inflows to EMEs are analyzed in detail on a regional basis according to the % of GDP between 2000 and 2015 using Fig. 11.13, it is seen that the FDI inflows to Latin America are very stable and valued at a minimum of 2 % (2003) and a maximum of 4 % per year, and the average value for the

Tab. 11.3: Average FDI Inflows (as % of GDP) by Country and Region, 2000–2015. Author calculations based on the data obtained from World Bank World Development Indicators Database, 2016.

Regions/ Countries	2000–2003	2004–2007	2008–2011	2012–2015	2000–2015
Latin America	**3**	**3**	**4**	**4**	**4**
ARG	2	2	2	2	2
BRA	4	2	3	4	3
CHL	5	6	9	9	7
COL	2	5	4	4	4
MEX	3	3	2	3	3
PER	2	4	5	5	4
VEN	2	1	1	1	1
Asia and Africa	**2**	**2**	**2**	**2**	**2**
BGD	0	1	1	1	1
CHN	4	4	3	3	3
IND	1	1	3	2	2
IDN	-1	2	2	2	1
MYS	3	4	3	3	3
PAK	1	2	2	1	1
PHL	1	2	1	2	1
THA	3	4	3	3	3
ZAF	2	1	2	1	2
Europe	**3**	**9**	**5**	**2**	**5**
BGR	7	20	8	4	10
HUN	6	20	9	3	9
POL	3	5	3	2	3
ROU	3	7	3	2	4
RUS	1	3	3	2	2
TUR	1	2	2	2	2
UKR	2	6	5	3	4

sixteen-year period is 4 % (see Tabs. 2 and 3). When we analyze the Asian and African regions, we see that FDI inflows are also relatively stable and ranged between a minimum of 1 % (2000 and 2003) and a maximum of 3 % per year, the average being 2 % for the whole period. On the other hand, when we analyze the European region, statistics show that the FDI inflows are not stable and

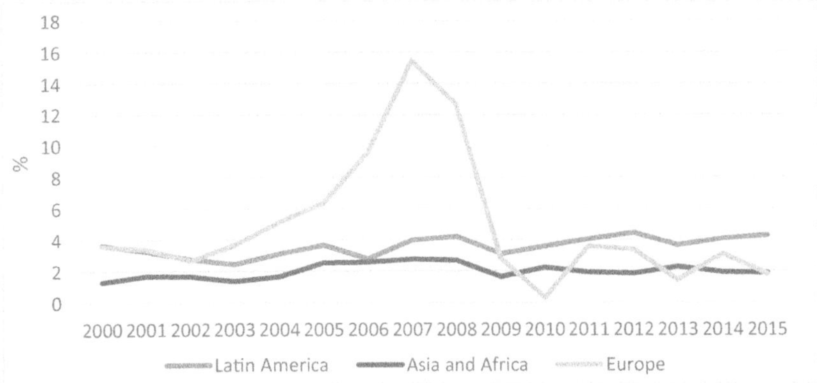

Fig. 11.13: Average FDI Inflows (as % of GDP) by Region, 2000–2015. Author calculations based on the data obtained from World Bank World Development Indicators Database, 2016

ranged between a minimum of 0 % (2010) and a maximum of 15 % (2007) per year, the average being 5 % for the period. From 2003 (4 %) to 2007 (15 %), it appears that FDI inflows to the European region rose significantly, but from 2008 (13 %) onwards the FDI inflows are declining due to the effects of the 2008 crisis and reaches 0 % in 2010. When we evaluate the average FDI inflows to EMEs on a regional basis between 2000 and 2015, Europe ranked first with 5 %, Latin America ranked second with 4 %, and Asia and Africa ranked third with 2 % (see Tab. 11.3).

11.3.2 FDI Inflows to EMEs (as % of GDP) by Country

In this section, the FDI inflows to EMEs will be analyzed in detail on a country basis between 2000 and 2015. Fig. 11.14 shows the FDI inflows to EMEs on a country basis. Fig. 11.15 shows the average value of the FDI inflows on a country basis for the sixteen-year period, and Fig. 11.16 shows the comparison of the inflows for the years 2000 and 2015 in terms of country and region.

11.3.2.1 Latin America

When the FDI inflows to EMEs are analyzed for the Latin American region, clearly, there are significant fluctuations over the years for each country (Fig. 11.14-a). Despite these fluctuations, there is an increasing trend in FDI inflows for Chile, Peru, and Colombia, while for Venezuela there is a decreasing trend. On the

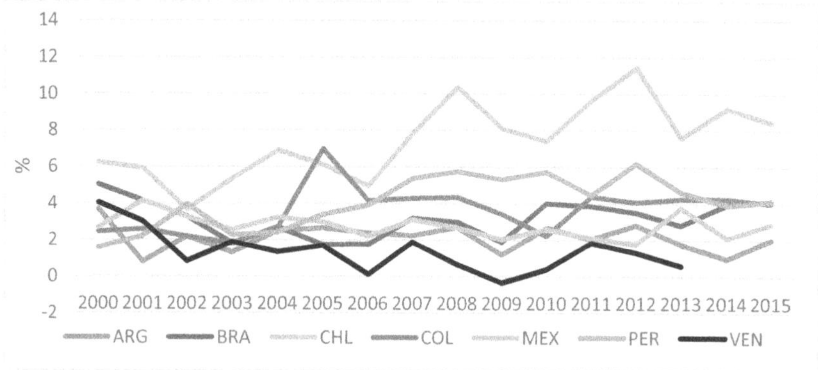

a) Latin America

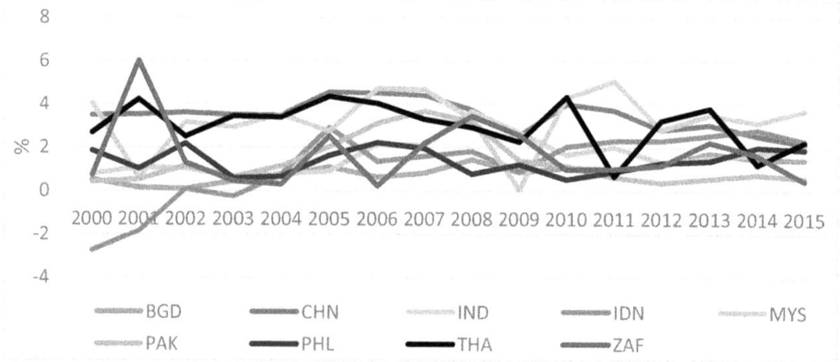

b) Asia and Africa

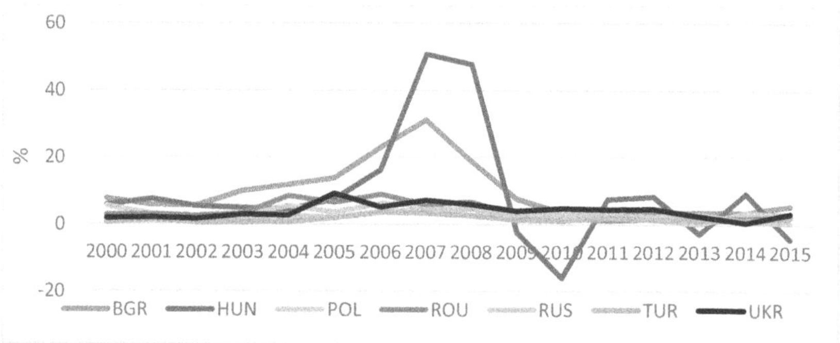

c) Europe

Fig. 11.14: FDI Inflows (as % of GDP) by Country and Region, 2000–2015. Author calculations based on the data obtained from World Bank World Development Indicators Database, 2016

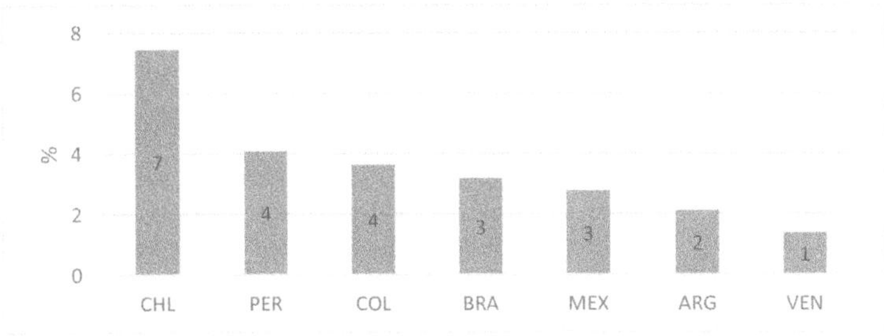

a) Latin America

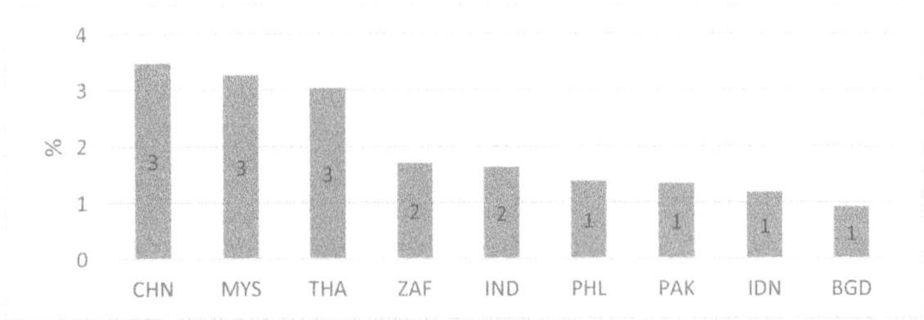

b) Asia and Africa

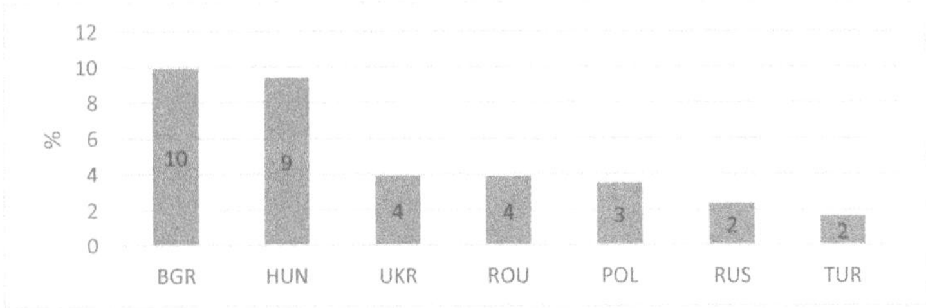

c) Europe

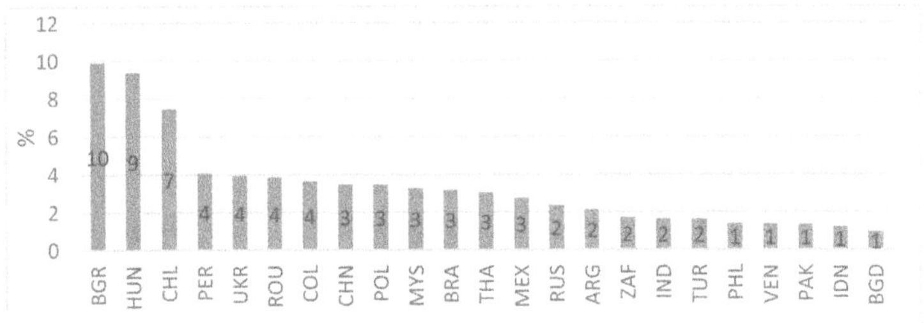

d) All EMEs

Fig. 11.15: Average FDI Inflows (as % of GDP) by Country and Region, 2000–2015. Author calculations based on the data obtained from World Bank World Development Indicators Database, 2016

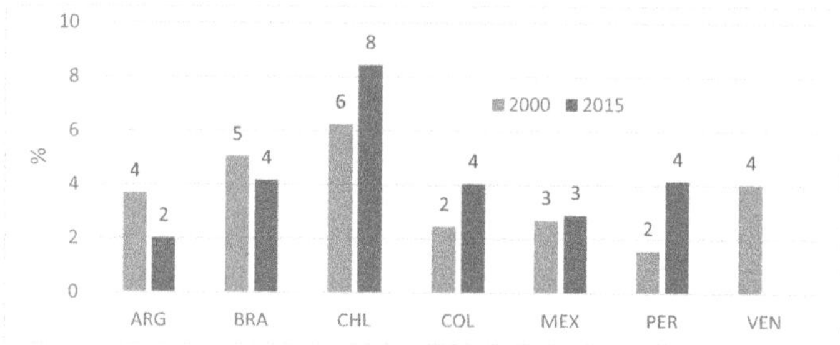

a) Latin America

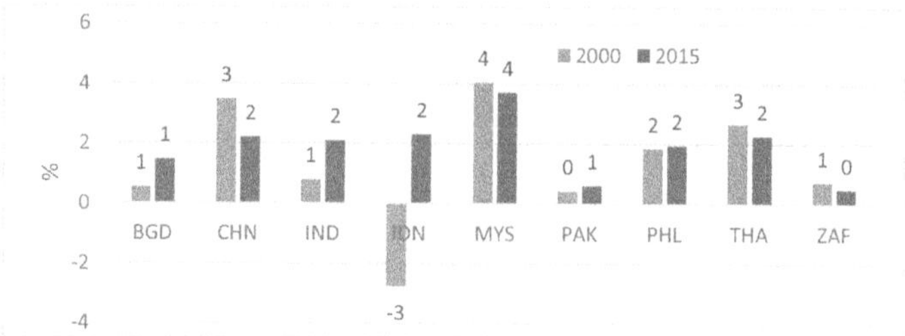

b) Asia and Africa

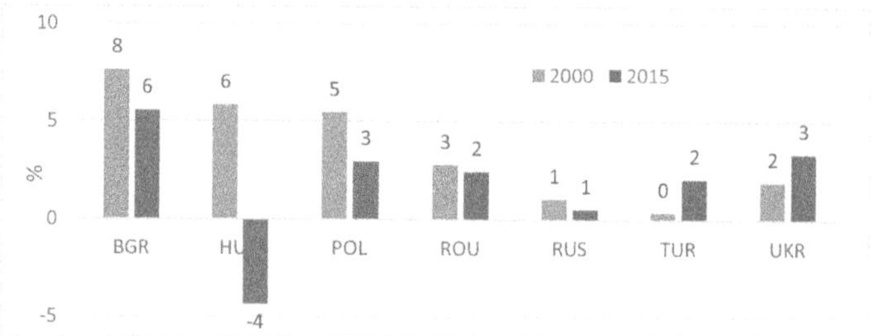

c) Europe

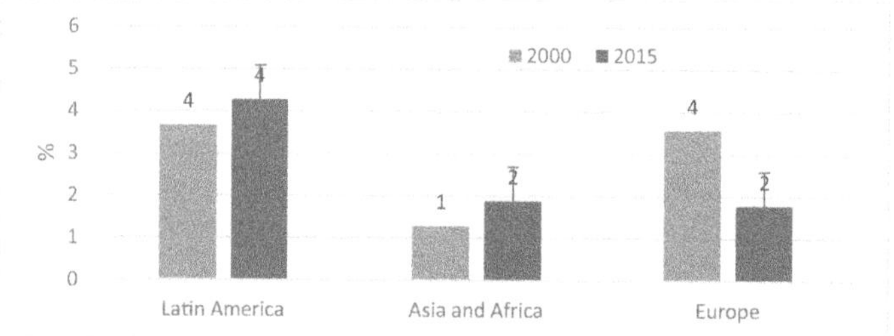

d) All Regions

Fig. 11.16: Change in FDI Inflows (as % of GDP) by Country and region between 2000 and 2015. Author calculations based on the data obtained from World Bank World Development Indicators Database, 2016 other hand, a relatively stable trend is seen for Brazil, Mexico and Argentina. When the average FDI inflows are taken into consideration for the years 2000 and 2015; Chile (7 %), Peru (4 %) and Colombia (4 %) are attracting more FDI inflows in comparison to their economic sizes (Fig. 11.15-a). Although Brazil (43 %) and Mexico (24 %) attract most of the FDI inflows (billion USD) to Latin American region (see section 2.2), these two countries fall into 4th place (Brazil with an average of 3 %) and 5th place (Mexico with an average of 3 %) in terms of average FDI inflows when their economic sizes are taken into consideration (Fig. 11.15-a). Argentina and Venezuela are in 6th and 7th place with 2 % and 1 %, respectively. In sum, Chile has gained a very important role in attracting the FDI inflows in recent years; it attracts much more FDI inflows when compared to its economic size. Chile is followed by Peru, Colombia, Brazil and Mexico.

11.3.2.2 Asia

When the FDI inflows to EMEs in the Asian region are analyzed (Fig. 11.14-b), we observe a steady trend for the EMEs (around 2 %), although cyclical fluctuations are high. The only exception is Indonesia since statistics show an increasing trend in FDI inflows for this country. The figure shows that the FDI inflows to Indonesia steadily increased from -3 % in 2000 to 2 % in 2015. The findings also point to an increasing trend for all EMEs, especially after 2005, and this increase continues until 2008, but after 2008 it falls rapidly due to the negative effects of the global financial crisis. When we look at the statistics in terms of the average FDI inflows between the years 2000 and 2015, the top three countries which attracted the majority of the FDI inflows are China (3 %), Malaysia (3 %), and Thailand (3 %) (Fig. 11.15-b). Other countries which attracted large FDI inflows are India (2 %), Philippines (1 %), Pakistan (1 %), Indonesia (1 %), and Bangladesh (1 %). Although China dominates the FDI inflows (as current US$) to the Asian region by attracting nearly 75 % of the FDI inflows (corresponds to $2.5T), she does not show a large deviation from other countries in Asian region when the economic sizes of the countries are taken into consideration.

11.3.2.3 Europe

The FDI inflows to EMEs in European region between 2000 and 2015 are analyzed in Figure 11.15-c. According to the figure, a stable trend in the FDI inflows occurs for Ukraine, Romania, Poland, Russia, and Turkey, but not for Hungary or Bulgaria. Ukraine, Romania, Poland, Russia, and Turkey tend to have low average annual FDI inflows between a minimum of 2 % and a maximum of 4 % (Tab. 11.2). The cyclical fluctuations in FDI inflows to both Bulgaria and

Hungary are quite high, although there is an increasing trend in FDI inflows. With respect to Bulgaria, the FDI inflows were much higher than the average between 2003 (10 %) and 2008 (19 %) (see Tab. 11.2). The FDI inflows to Bulgaria started to increase in 2003 (10 %) and continued to increase until 2008 (19 %), reaching a record level of 31 % in 2007. In the case of Hungary, FDI inflows started to increase in 2005 (8 %) and continued to increase until 2008 (48 %), reaching a record level of 51 % in 2007 (see Tab. 11.2). For Bulgaria and Hungary, the average FDI inflows value between 2004 and 2007 broke the record by 20 % (see Tab. 11.3). However, this unusual increase in FDI inflows to Bulgaria and Hungary did not continue and the inflows declined rapidly over the following years. Also, the FDI inflows to EMEs in Europe fell sharply in 2009, due to the negative effects of the global crisis, except in Poland (see Fig. 11.14-c and Tab. 11.2). Bulgaria and Hungary are affected more negatively from the crisis when compared to other countries. FDI inflows fall from 19 % in 2008 to 8 % in 2009 for Bulgaria, and from 48 % in 2008 to -2 % in 2009 for Hungary.

When the average FDI inflows to EMEs in European region are analyzed for the period of 2000–2015, Bulgaria (10 %) and Hungary (9 %) are the two leading countries in Europe with respect to their economic sizes (Fig. 11.15-c). These countries are followed by Ukraine (4 %), Romania (4 %), Poland (3 %), Russia (2 %), and Turkey (2 %). An interesting finding is that Russia is in the 6th place in Europe with 2 %, although she is the leading country in Europe in respect to nominal FDI inflows (current US$). Here, the following deduction can be made: the countries with smaller economic size attract more FDI inflows as a proportion.

Fig. 11.15-d shows the average FDI inflows to all twenty-three EMEs analyzed on a country basis for the 2000–2015 period. When the figure is interpreted on a country basis, Bulgaria in Europe (10 %), Hungary in Europe (9 %), and Chile in Latin America (7 %) are the three countries which attracted majority of the FDI inflows, while the remaining twenty countries account for between 4 % and 1 %. A striking finding here is that there are only two countries from Asia, i.e. China and Malaysia, among the top ten countries which attracted the largest FDI inflows, and their ranks are 8th and 10th, respectively. Although the findings in the previous section 2.2 reveal that China has a dominant role with a share of 39 % ($2.5T) in overall FDI inflows to EMEs (as current US$), it ranked 8th in the FDI inflows to EMEs with respect to the size of the economy. In a similar way, although Brazil ranked 2nd with a share of 12 % and Russia ranked 3rd with a share of 8 % in overall FDI inflows (as current US$) (see section 2.2), Brazil is 11_{th} and Russia is 14th in the FDI inflows (as % of GDP) with respect to the economic sizes. As seen in Fig. 11.15-d, the EMEs from the European region are generally in the first place and they are followed by the EMEs from the Latin American region, and the EMEs from Asia are in the last place. In other words, the countries which attracted less FDI inflows (as % of GDP) are generally in the Asian region, and the countries which attracted higher FDI inflows (as % of GDP) are generally in the European region.

Fig. 11.16 shows the FDI inflows to EMEs on a regional and country basis between the years 2000 and 2015. When the FDI inflows are compared for the years 2000 and 2015 on a regional basis (Fig. 11.16-d), the results are that the FDI inflows to the Latin American region increased slightly and stabilized at around 4 %, and the inflows rose from 1 % in 2000 to 2 % in 2015 for the Asian region; however, Europe suffered a loss with values at 4 % in 2000 falling to 2 % in 2015 (corresponding to a 50 % decrease). This finding shows that the share of Asia in FDI inflows to EMEs increased, while the share of Europe decreased.

When the Latin American region is analyzed on a country basis, the results are that the FDI inflows increased for Chile, Colombia, Peru and Mexico, while they decreased for Argentina and Brazil. The highest increase in FDI inflows is for Peru (from 1.56 % to 4 %) and for Colombia (from 2.4 % to 4 %). Although Brazil attracts the largest amounts of FDI inflows (49 %, in current US$) in Latin America, its share in terms of FDI inflows decreased when the size of the economy was taken into consideration.

When the Asian region is examined on a country basis, the FDI inflows increased slightly for Bangladesh, India, Pakistan, and Philippines, while they decreased for China, Malaysia, and Thailand (Fig. 11.16-b). Here, the most remarkable country in Asian region is Indonesia since FDI inflows greatly increased from -3 % in 2000 to 2 % in 2015. Another interesting finding is that although China is at the forefront as to FDI inflows in current US$, FDI inflows to China as % of GDP decreased from 3 % in 2000 to 2 % in 2015. In sum, there is not a significant change in FDI inflows (as % of GDP) on a country basis except for Indonesia, although there is an increasing trend in the FDI inflows to Asian region.

When we analyze the European region on a country basis, there are serious declines in the FDI inflows for the four countries. The figures showed a sharp decline in the FDI inflows to Bulgaria, Hungary, Poland, and Romania in 2015 when compared to the year 2000. The notable decline here is for Hungary, FDI inflows decreased from 6 % in 2000 to -4 % in 2015 (corresponding to a 10 % change). Although FDI inflows to Russia have decreased slightly from 2000 to 2015, they remained at around 1 % in 2015. The most striking finding here is that while FDI inflows to Europe (as % of GDP) decreased in general from 2000 to 2015 (Fig. 11.16-d), whereas they increased for Turkey and Ukraine. The FDI inflows to Turkey notably increased from 0 % in 2000 to 2 % in 2015, and inflows also increased slightly for Ukraine from 2 % in 2000 to 3 % in 2015. This finding clearly shows that Turkey has gained more importance in Europe in terms of attracting the FDI inflows.

11.4 Conclusion

This study analyzes the net FDI inflows to EMEs on a country and regional basis from 2000 to 2015. The main findings drawn from the analyses can be summarized in this way. The FDI inflows to EMEs (in current US$) demonstrated a steady increase, and the EMEs attracted a total of approximately 6.5 trillion dollars in FDI inflows for the sixteen-year period. More than half of this figure is attracted by the Asian region, and followed by Latin American and European regions. Over the whole period, the FDI inflows to the Asian region increased about six times, while they increased four times for Europe, and three times for Latin America. In the early 2000s, Latin American region was in first place by attracting the most FDI inflows, and followed by Asian and European regions. However, the FDI inflows to Latin America steadily decreased over the sixteen-year period, and FDI inflows to Asia increased continuously while Europe remained stable for the whole period. As a result, Latin American region lost its place to the Asian region. In sum, the Asian region has gained increasing importance in terms of FDI inflows, while the importance of both European and Latin American regions has decreased over the sixteen-year period.

The findings show that the global financial crisis adversely affected the EMEs and the FDI inflows to EMEs fell sharply in 2009. However, the FDI inflows to EMEs quickly recovered and reached their former levels just two years after the crisis. When examined on regional basis, both Asian and Latin American regions started to recover rapidly, while the European region did not recover fully after the crisis. In other words, European region was more adversely affected by the global crisis when compared to Asian and Latin American regions.

The share of EMEs in World FDI inflows has also showed an increasing trend over the whole period by rising more than three times. Moreover, the EMEs have started to attract more FDI inflows and have gained more importance especially after the global crisis. The findings show that EMEs in both Asian (China and India) and Latin American regions (Brazil, Mexico and Chile) have gained more importance when compared to EMEs in European region in recent years, since the share of EMEs in European region in World FDI inflows decreased after the global financial crisis.

When the findings are interpreted on a country basis, China dominates the FDI inflows (in current US$) in Asian region and attracted nearly 75 %

(US2.5T) of the FDI inflows for the sixteen-year period. India ranks second after China with 10 % (US350B) in the Asian region, and FDI inflows to India have shown an increasing trend in recent years. In Latin America, Brazil attracts most of the FDI inflows (43 %) and it is followed by Mexico and Chile. Overall, it is notable that an increasing trend in FDI inflows to Brazil in Latin American region occurred over the whole period. In European region, Russia is the leader country (39 %) in terms of FDI inflows (in current US$), and followed by Poland, Hungary, and Turkey. The findings show that the FDI inflows to Russia started to increase significantly after 2003, however, the FDI inflows began to fall rapidly in the years following the crisis. Russia also experienced significant declines in the FDI inflows after the crisis due to the sanctions imposed on the country by Western countries because of the Ukraine conflict. The other finding is that the FDI inflows to Turkey in European region have increased in recent years, and Turkey ranked in first place in 2015. Turkey has gained more importance in European region in terms of attracting the FDI inflows. In sum, China in Asia, Brazil in Latin America and Russia in Europe are the top three EMEs which attracted the majority of the FDI inflows over the sixteen-year period. China among EMEs has a dominant role in attracting the FDI inflows, and its share is 39 % in overall FDI inflows to EMEs, while the fourteen EMEs which attracted lower FDI inflows have an average of less than $10B, and their total share is only 17 % in overall FDI inflows to EMEs.

When the findings are evaluated on the FDI inflows as the percentage of GDP on a regional basis, they are relatively stable over the years, although it is more stable for both Latin America and Asia compared to Europe. By the way, the findings show that Europe region is ranked first (5 %), Latin America ranked second (4 %), and Asia ranked third (2 %) in terms of the average FDI inflows on a regional basis over the sixteen years. When economic sizes of the EMEs are taken into consideration, Chile, Peru and Colombia in Latin American region and Bulgaria and Hungary in European region attract more FDI inflows. Also, findings show that there is an increasing trend in FDI inflows for both India and Indonesia in Asian region and for Turkey in European region in recent years. It can be concluded that the EMEs with smaller economic size attract more FDI inflows. The study also reveals that Chile in Latin American region, Indonesia in Asian region, and Turkey in European region have gained more importance in recent years in term of attracting the FDI inflows when economic size is taken into consideration. Another conclusion is that the EMEs in Europe region attract more FDI inflows (as % of GDP) when economic size is taken into consideration, while the EMEs in Asian region attract more FDI inflows in current US$.

References

Aizenman, J. (2002). Volatility, Employment and the Patterns of FDI in Emerging Markets. Working Paper 9397, NBER, Cambridge, MA.

Arbatli, E. (2011). Economic Policies and FDI Inflows to Emerging Market Economies. IMF Working paper. WP/11/192

Barro, R. and Sala-i-Martin, X. (1995). *Economic Growth*, McGraw-Hill, Cambridge, MA.

Blomström, M. and Kokko, A. (1998). Multinational Corporations and Spillovers. *Journal of Economic Surveys*, 12 (2), 247–77.

Borensztein, E., Gregorio, J. and Lee, J.-W. (1998). How Does Foreign Direct Investment Affect Economic Growth? *Journal of International Economics*, 45, 115–35.

Danescu, T. and Nistor, P. (2012). Foreign Direct Investment in Emerging and Developed Economies. *Annales Universitatis Apulensis Series Oeconomica*, 14(1), 236–41.

Deutsche Bundesbank (2003). The role of FDI in emerging market economies compared to other forms of financing: Past developments and implications for financial stability. International Relations Department Frankfurt, J2 / J2-2. Frankfurt, Germany.

Djankov, S. and Hoekman, B. (2000). Foreign Investment and Productivity Growth in Czech Enterprises. *World Bank Economic Review*, 14 (1), 49–64.

Evenson, R. E. and Westphal, L. E. (1995). Technological Change and Technology Strategy. In Behrman, J. and Srinivasan, T. N. (eds.), *Handbook of Development Economics*, 3, Elsevier Science Publishers, Amsterdam.

Goldberg, L. (2004). Financial-Sector FDI and Host Countries: New and Old Lessons. Working Paper 10441, NBER, Cambridge, MA.

Görg, H. and Greenaway, D. (2004). Much Ado About Nothing? Do Domestic Firms Really Benefit from Foreign Direct Investment? *World Bank Research Observer*, 19 (2), 171–97.

Haddad, M. and Harrison, A. (1993). Are There Positive Spillovers from Direct Foreign Investment? Evidence from Panel Data for Morocco. *Journal of Development Economics*, 42 (1), 51–74.

Keller, W. (1994). Human Capital and Technology: Characteristics and Interaction. Mimeo, Yale University, NH, CT.

Keller, W. (1996). Absorptive Capacity: On the Creation and Acquisition of Technology in Development. *Journal of Development Economics*, 49, 199–227.

Kinoshita, Y. (2001). R&D and Technology Spillovers through FDI: Innovation and Absorptive Capacity. CEPR Discussion Paper DP2775, Centre for Economic Policy Research, London.

Korinek. A. (2017). Regulating Capital Flows to Emerging Markets: An Externality View. Working Paper 24152, NBER, Cambridge, MA.

Kuznets, S. (1966). *Modern Economic Growth: Rate, Structure, Spread*, New Haven, Yale University Press.

Lall, S. (1997). *East Asia*. In: Dunning, J. H. (ed.), *Governments, Globalization, and International Business*. 407–30, Oxford University Press, Oxford.

Mauro, P., Ostry, J. D., Dell'Ariccia, G., di Giovanni, J., Faria, A., Kose, A., Schindler, M., and Terrones, M. E. (2007). Reaping the Benefits of Financial Globalization. IMF Discussion Paper.

Meyer, K. E. (2005). *Foreign Direct Investment in Emerging Economies*. Policy Discussion Paper Emerging Markets Forum. Templeton College, Oxford.

Mustafa, S. and Hasan, S. S. (2015). FDI's Role in Emerging Economies. *Journal of Poverty, Investment and Development*, ISSN: 2422-846x, Vol. 16, 62–67.

Narula, R. and Marin, A. (2003). FDI Spillovers, Absorptive Capacities and Human Capital Development: Evidence from Argentina. *MERIT-Infonomics Research Memorandum Series*, 2003-016.

Narula, R. and Driffield, N. (2012). Does FDI Cause Development? The Ambiguity of the Evidence and Why it Matters. *European Journal of Development Research*, 24, 1–7.

OECD (2002). Foreign Direct Investment for Development. Maximising Benefits, Minimising Costs. OECD Report. France.

Pack, H. (1992). Technology Gaps between Industrial and Developing Countries: Are There Dividends for Latecomers? Proceedings of the World Bank Annual Conference on Development Economics, Supplement to the World Bank Economic Review and World Bank Research Observer, 283–302, World Bank, Washington, DC.

Pamukçu, M. T. and Sönmez, A. (2012). Technology Transfer in the Global Automotive Value Chain: Lessons from the Turkish Automotive Industry. In: David B. A., Erik E. L., Albert N. L. and Alexander S. (eds.), *Technology Transfer in a Global Economy*. 303–334. Springer, US.

Saggi, K. (2002). Trade, Foreign Direct Investment, and International Technology Transfer: A Survey. *The World Bank Research Observer*, 17 (2), 191–235.

Smeets, R. (2008). Collecting the Pieces of the FDI Knowledge Spillovers Puzzle. *The World Bank Research Observer*, 23, 107–138.

Sönmez, A. and Pamukçu, M. T. (2012). Foreign Direct Investment and Technology Spillovers in the Turkish Manufacturing Industry. In: Yetkiner, İ. H., Pamukçu, M. T. and Erdil, E. (eds.), *Industrial Dynamics, Innovation Policy, and Economic Growth through Technological Advancements*, DOI: 10.4018/978-1-4666-1978-4.ch003, 30–51, Hershey, PA: USA, IGI Global.

Sönmez, A. (2013). *Multinational Companies, Knowledge and Technology Transfer*. DOI: 10.1007/978-3-319-02033-4. Springer, Switzerland.

UN (1999). World Investment Report 1999. Geneva, United Nations.

World Bank (2016). World Development Indicators Database. Retrieved from http://databank.worldbank.org/data/ (Last Accession Date: 24/10/2017).

Xu, B. (2000). Multinational Enterprises, Technology Diffusion, and Host Country Productivity Growth. *Journal of Development Economics*, 62, 477–93.

Selen Işık Maden and Aykut Sezgin

12 Monetary Policies in EMEs

Abstract: The aim of this chapter is to examine the transformation of the frame of monetary policy in the emerging market economies (EMEs) in the context of economic fluctuations. EMEs have high growth potentials despite their weak institutional structures, low levels of credibility, and shallow financial systems. Some of these markets have managed to integrate into developed markets over the last decades and have had high growth performances. The economic growth performances are closely related to the monetary policies applied in these countries. In the EMEs, the Central Banks that apply monetary policies face various operational and technical constraints. In the introduction section of the study, a short history of Central Banking is presented together with the monetary policy targets. Then, the constraints which EMEs face in achieving these targets are discussed. As monetary policy applications may involve various indicators and mechanisms, we faced complex and unreliable structures when we examined country case studies. In order to discuss the applications in recent decades and their effects in these markets, the mechanism is examined in the second section under two subtitles: foreign exchange regimes and monetary transmission mechanism. During the examination, particularly two periods are utilized: the ex- and post-2008 crises period, and the effects of the crises on monetary policy is examined comparatively.

Keywords: Monetary Policy, Exchange Rate Regime, Monetary Transmission Mechanism

12.1 Introduction

In the most general sense, monetary policy can be described as an attempt by central banks to keep the amount of money on the market under control and to assure the stability of money released into the market by using certain tools. Moreover, monetary policy can be considered as a shield of the economy against internal and external shocks.

There is a consensus in literature that the ultimate aim of monetary policy is to provide price stability. Besides this initial policy aim, providing economic growth and bringing down the rate of inflation are among the main aims of monetary policy (Bernanke et al., 1999: 15).

In the historical perspective, when different policy applications have been carried out and their consequences in the countries are examined, the result is that central banks are essentially supposed to focus on price stability and it is possible to contribute more to the other aims by this way (Mishkin and Eakins, 2000: 335).

Central banks were established as a kind of private commercial bank, not as a non-profit public institute. The first banks exporting banknotes were found in the second half of the seventeenth century. The first central bank in real terms was The Bank of England founded in 1694. Especially in 1870, it was a significant development for central banking to be assigned as the ultimate loan authority (Hoggarth, 1996: 7). Germany, Norway Switzerland and Denmark began the gold standard in 1873 and central banks started to monetize only in return for gold reserve. As many countries started to apply this practice, a period in which monetary policy tools were more actively used began. The main tool used to reach the determined goals was to control the interest rates (Capie et al., 1994: 2). With the start of World War I, gold was primarily used to finance the balance of payments and gold was pulled from circulation over time. Also, loans used by governments for war expenses in that period made it impossible to provide repayment of the deposit as gold. As a result of financing the fiscal deficits by monetizing, not only inflation but also nominal interests increased (Kindleberger, 1993: 50). Within this framework all countries started to revise the monetary policies they carried out during the war. With the outbreak of the crisis in 1929, it became impossible to facilitate coordination among the countries within the scope of monetary policies especially as a result of protective policies applied by the countries. The collapse of the international monetary system eloigned central banks from their main aim to keep the external value of money stable. Central banks started to pursue a policy of decreasing the interest rates due to vulnerability and deflation in the economy. While interest rates were kept low during World War II, monetary policy was carried out by direct controls of loans (Fischer, 1994: 13). After World War II, Keynesian views dominated the economy and the Bretton Woods system was formed. One of the most outstanding characteristics of this period was that central banks were also assigned to achieve employment and growth as well as to keep the value of money stable. Upon the collapse of the Bretton Woods system at the beginning of the 1970s, the floating exchange rate regime was followed by the fixed exchange rate regime and significant changes were experienced in the tools and aims of monetary policy. In parallel to monetarism shaped from Friedman's (1968) and Phelps's (1968) ideas, it was widely believed that central banks could highly contribute to basic economic goals only by means of assuring price stability. Central banks started to focus on price stability rather than considering economic growth and full employment that were previously considered as objective functions. It was believed that the circuit velocity of money could be estimated and that objectives related to monetary growth should be implemented so as to control nominal income in the short term and inflation in the long term. These predictions directed central banks to begin monetary targeting strategy. This process went on till the mid-1980s and monetary targeting strategy collapsed as a result of the crises experienced during this period. Since the mid-1980s, central banks tended towards gradually controlling the interest rates. Monetary magnitude turned into a pioneer indicator to be pursued (Fischer, 1994: 20). As to the 1990s, main debates in central banking changed into constitutive issues such as autonomy, responsibility and reliability of the central banks from operational techniques (interest rate-monetary base control) (Capie et al., 1994: 5).

Upon a general assessment, the 1980s can be specified as a transitional period in terms of central bank autonomy and monetary policy strategies while the 1990s can be characterized as a period in which central bank autonomy was indispensable. Furthermore, it can be defined as a period of transition into inflation targeting in regard to monetary policy strategy. Moreover, in terms of monetary policy tools, the 1970s and the following years can be specified as a transition period from direct monetary policy tools to indirect monetary policy tools based on market mechanism.

The EMEs have an ever-growing importance and capacity in the global economic system with their dynamic structures. These economies had similar but more difficult times in the transformation of the aforementioned monetary mechanisms due to their fragile and complex economic and institutional structures and had to deal with various challenges simultaneously. In the following section, these challenges are examined by taking the constraints of these markets into account.

12.2 Constraints on Monetary Policy in EMEs

We would like to begin the discussion of monetary policy constraints in the EMEs with the challenges faced by central banks in these economies. Central banks came up against certain constraints in these markets. These constraints are either institutional or technical. The major constraint is that central banks do not have autonomy. In fact, central banks are contingent upon the Ministry of Finance in some emerging markets without any legal hitches. In other circumstances, apparently autonomous central banks are under political pressure especially by the Ministry of Finance. It was found that there is no relationship in developed countries between central bank autonomy and the growth rate of the countries while autonomy positively influences investments and growth in developing countries (Cukierman, 1992: 1440). Moreover, there is evidence that autonomy can increase growth in the long term by means of low inflation (Borrero, 2001: 14).

Another debate on autonomy occurs in the operational sense. If the central banks set their goals to interfere with exchange rates, then the tool autonomy on interest rates, which are fundamental domestic monetary policy tool of central banks, can become ineffective. For instance, central banks and interest rates are under the control of the government in China and Russia, which are two of the major emerging markets. Even though political authority implements related monetary policies in order to keep the exchange rate regime under control, they may not be able to maintain the desired control because of the availability to large amounts of foreign exchange reserve (Mallick and Sousa, 2012: 192).

Keeping fiscal discipline in EMEs can be considered as another constraint. Absence of long-term fiscal discipline in these countries causes pressure on central banks to revise monetary policy so that they can continuously support the fiscal policy of that country. Moreover, absence of fiscal discipline creates huge public and budget deficits in these countries. Thus, central banks are obliged to focus on governmental debt management rather than price stability, which is their main objective, while determining interest rates, which complicates the management of inflation targeting (Sims, 2005: 287).

Technical constraints experienced by central banks originated from capital movements. Vulnerable transfer mechanisms derived from the underdeveloped and shallow fiscal systems in the EMEs decreased the efficiency of monetary policy. In these markets, factors such as the inadequacy of capital in banks, uncertainty in ownership structure and low credibility which causes central banks to be slow in adapting quickly to policy changes. This circumstance decreases the efficiency of interest rates (Barışık, 2014: 8–9).

Hot money flow based on arbitrage derived from interest and exchange rate disparities and instabilities is another technical constraint which becomes effective through monetary policy depending upon openness rates of capital markets in the countries. Following liberal policies, the policy of reducing and eliminating the obstacles related to foreign trade and capital had an influence especially on emerging markets toward the increase of capital movements. As seen in the example of China, implementing a trade-open foreign trade regime, became difficult for the central bank to lead an autonomous monetary policy by managing the foreign exchange rate due to capital inflow from various channels although China endeavored to keep the inflow and the outflow of capital under control over the last decades (Yeldan, 2003: 8).

Under all these constraints, each emerging market tries to take their monetary policy decisions in their idiosyncratic structure. In the application of monetary policies, it is impossible to determine monetary mechanisms as strictly as in the theory. The countries may reveal the characteristics of more than one monetary

Tab. 12.1: Type and Categories of Exchange Rate Regimes. Table was composed by extracting information from IMF Reviews of Exchange Arrangements; 2000, 2007 and 2014

Type	Categories				
Hard pegs	Exchange arrangement with no separate legal tender		Currency board arrangement		
Soft pegs	Conventional peg	Pegged exchange rate within horizontal bands	Stabilized arrangement	Crawling peg	Crawling-like arrangement
Floating regimes	Floating	Free floating	Independently floating		
Other managed arrangements (mixed)					

regime simultaneously according to the business cycles they have. In the next section, evaluation of the policy implications in the EMEs over the last decades is explained in a systematic manner.

12.3 Monetary Policy Implications in EMEs

Reactions to global crises by monetary policy authorities in the EMEs can be examined under two subheadings. One is designing monetary transfer mechanisms against international fiscal shocks while the other is fictionalizing foreign exchange rate regimes against the concerns of these countries on international reserve loss (Allegret and Sallenave, 2015: 440).

Numerous exchange rate regime implications have been experienced from pegs to free floats in the EMEs (see Tab. 12.1). Although each economy has tried different methods in accordance with existing conditions, the general tendency has been to increase flexibility. Rapid increase in capital flow after 1980 has made it difficult for these economies to keep peg rates under control. As these economies preferred diversification in foreign trade, they had to merchandize via numerous foreign currencies and they abandoned the option to peg their national currency against one type of currency. These two factors underpinned the increase of flexibility. The crisis experienced in the 1990s supported the process as well.

When general characteristics of countries using different forms of pegged exchange rate regimes (most of these point to emerging markets) are examined, it is obvious that their degrees of involvement in international capital and commodity market is minimal. These countries follow a policy where they peg their national currency to the currency of the country they merchandize with the most. Taking this policy into consideration, as the pegged national currency is similar for many emerging countries, their response to economic shocks shows similarities. As corporate structures have not been completely formed, monetary autonomy is one of the elements ignored by these countries. Labor markets and fiscal policies are relatively more flexible and more sustainable than monetary policies. These countries are faced with capital outflow risk which puts pressure on them to keep large amounts of international reserves and high inflation figures generate pressure to carry out exchange rate base stabilization.

The global fiscal crisis starting with the mortgage crisis in the USA, spreading first to Europe and then the whole world, has created strong impacts on the monetary policies of EMEs. Different EMEs reacted to this transformation within their distinctive structures with the effect of historical process they were experiencing. In this part of the study, similarities and differences in foreign exchange rate regimes and monetary transfer mechanisms, which are official monetary policy indicators of the countries, are examined in the EMEs.

As noted on the table, 15 out of 23 countries subject to our study implemented a type of floating exchange rate regime at the beginning of the 2000s. These countries include Bangladesh, Brazil, Chile, Colombia, India, Indonesia, Mexico, Pakistan, Peru, Philippines, Poland, Russia, South Africa, Thailand and Turkey. However, their adoption of a certain type of floating exchange rate regime is based on the economic crises that some experienced in the second half of the 1990s and by the remaining countries at the beginning of the 2000s. Most of these crises can be considered as the 1997-98 Asian-Russian crises and its aftershocks. For instance, Russia was one of the countries starting to implement a closely managed float regime after the 1998 crisis. Russia made some arrangements aimed at removing some obstacles to capital movements in 2004. In this process, that can be described as a transition from an authorization-based system into a tightly controlled flow system, the Russian central bank also tried a dual currency basket system in 2005 to prevent the ruble from depreciation against other currencies. (Mohanty, 2013: 1).

Among the examined countries, Bangladesh, Brazil, Indonesia, Romania and Ukraine are ranked as countries changing from a managed exchange rate regime into a type of floating regime. The economy plan adopted in 1994 to achieve the objectives to increase the value of the Brazilian real, to correct current deficiencies and to continue foreign capital flows was interrupted as a major economic and political fluctuation subsequent to the Asian and Russian crises in 1999. In this period, The Federal Reserve Bank of the USA tried to implement a new policy which helped minimizing capital controls and restrictions and restraining hyperinflation to prevent the depreciation of the Brazilian national currency against the monetary policies implemented by FED.

As a result, Brazil transformed its exchange rate regime into a floating regime by removing the obstacles to capital flow into the country so that the exchange rate regime could be liberalized (Jawadi et al., 2014). Similarly, Indonesia experienced a major change in the conduct of monetary policy through the crises which occurred between 1997 and 2000. This change gave Bank Indonesia full autonomy in formulating and implementing policies (Geoltom, 2008).

Argentina, a striking example of a country which was affected not only by these international crises but also by internal disturbances simultaneously, could not prevent currency fluctuations although it tried alternatives in 2001–2002 such as a crawling band regime, and a dual exchange rate regime. With the advent of the crisis experienced after 2003, Argentina began to use managed floating with no predetermined path for the exchange rate system.

Before the 2008 global fiscal crisis, the majority of EMEs was began a type of floating regime. This exchange rate regime was a market-determined regime based on limited intervention. Central banks attempted a policy of minimal intervention in the markets, abandoning their former policy of tight control over the markets. Almost half of the countries that implemented independently floating were in a position to transform into conventional fixed pegs (see Tab. 12.2). These mainly include Middle Eastern and South African countries along with some Asian countries. This perspective of emerging markets presented mixed pictures as they struggled against numerous economic problems such as fiscal deficits, current deficits, capital inadequacies and high inflation.

The 2008 global fiscal crisis affected the examined markets in different degrees and in different ways during various periods. After 2010, when the impacts of the crisis relatively decreased, 15 countries out of the 23 countries which were examined in this study started to implement floating regimes based on market determined rates. Among these countries, Brazil, Chile, Colombia, India, Indonesia, Mexico, Peru, Philippines, Poland, Romania, South Africa, Thailand and Turkey changed from managed or banded floating regimes into floating regimes while Hungary and Ukraine changed into floating regimes by abandoning fixed pegs exchange rate. Most EMEs abandoned hard and soft pegs in the crises in the 2000s and chose the floating regime with the advent of the 2008 crisis. While Argentina, Bangladesh, China, Malaysia, Pakistan, Russia and Venezuela have preferred soft peg regimes during this period, only Bulgaria has used the hard peg (currency board arrangement) regime since 2000. Countries continuing to implement either soft or hard pegs used the currency of the countries that they shared intensive trade and capital partnership with as an exchange rate anchor.

Tab. 12.2: Exchange Rate Regimes of the EMEs. Table was composed by extracting information from IMF Reviews of Exchange Arrangements; 2000, 2007 and 2014

	Country	**first half of 2000's**	**before financial crisis**	**after financial crisis**
Latin America	Argentina	soft peg	soft peg	soft peg
	Brazil	floating regime	floating regime	floating regime
	Chile	floating regime	floating regime	floating regime
	Colombia	floating regime	floating regime	floating regime
	Mexico	floating regime	floating regime	floating regime
	Peru	floating regime	floating regime	floating regime
	Venezuela	soft peg	soft peg	soft peg
Asia	Bangladesh	floating regime	floating regime	soft peg
	China	hard peg	soft peg	soft peg
	Indonesia	floating regime	floating regime	floating regime
	India	floating regime	floating regime	floating regime
	Malaysia	soft peg	floating regime	mixed
	Pakistan	floating regime	Soft peg	mixed
	Philippines	floating regime	floating regime	floating regime
	Thailand	floating regime	floating regime	floating regime
Europe	Bulgaria	hard peg	hard peg	hard peg
	Hungary	soft peg	soft peg	floating regime
	Poland	floating regime	floating regime	floating regime
	Romania	soft peg	floating regime	floating regime
	Russia	floating regime	floating regime	mixed
	Turkey	floating regime	floating regime	floating regime
	Ukrania	soft peg	soft peg	floating regime
Africa	South Africa	floating regime	floating regime	floating regime

Countries such as Argentina, Bangladesh, China, Pakistan and Venezuela used the US dollar as an anchor, whereas Bulgaria used the Euro. Arrangements of the majority of the countries that did not change into floating regimes have been different from its de jure arrangements. This is mainly because central banks are not fully autonomous and there are political interventions.

The EMEs have to cope with some monetary market issues such as managing fluctuating capital movements, managing portfolio investments reaching a significant amount in reference to these countries' economies and managing the interventions in foreign exchange markets by the central banks. Basic policy instruments of the markets against these structural issues have been capital controls and regular interventions into the currency market. However, these instruments have caused difficulty in the historical use of exchange rate channels as a transfer mechanism. The EMEs struggling with double-digit inflation from time to time and trying to develop by using their high growth potentials have started to use different monetary transfer mechanisms with the advent of global fiscal crises (Mallick and Souza, 2012: 190–191).

Bulgaria, China, Malaysia, Romania, Ukraine and Venezuela can be given as examples of emerging countries using exchange rate channels at the beginning of the 2000s. As for 2004, Ukraine experienced major political change because of the Orange Revolution and in that period implemented a monetary policy supported by the IMF. Therefore, exchange rate anchor was one of the monetary policy frameworks preferred by IMF until the period when fiscal crises were experienced. Those were the years when not only emerging markets, but also many third world (underdeveloped) countries signed standby agreements with the IMF after crises and when these countries implemented IMF-supported monetary policies.

In that period Brazil, Chile, Colombia, Hungary, Mexico, Peru, Philippines, Poland, South Africa, Thailand and Turkey also passed implicitly or explicitly inflation targeting frameworks within the scope of the fight against inflation -some of them being supported by the IMF. The majority of these countries revised their legal frameworks before the global fiscal crisis to accommodate this policy. In general, these countries used their short-term interest rates as a monetary policy instrument within medium-term horizon they formed. This framework enabled the preparation of public plans based on an announced inflation target, which enabled the increase of accountability and independency of central banks.

Before changing into an inflation targeting framework, Peru's monetary policy had been based on a monetary target framework, which used the annual growth rate as a medium-term target. Peru's inflation targeting monetary policy can be described as full-fledged inflation targeting, which minimizes the risks caused by dollarization. The operational target of this monetary policy is short-term interest rates. Interventions on foreign exchange rate market by The Central Bank of Peru are considered as initiatives to minimize exchange rate volatility and to increase international reserve accumulation caused by the effect of balance of payments. This circumstance is due to the fact that a substantial part of assets and liabilities held in Peru's financial system are kept as foreign currency (Rossini et al., 2013: 246). The inflation targeting framework that Philippines set into motion in 2002, used interest rates as its main policy tool similar to Peru (Dakila, 2001: 8). In the 1990s, Poland having had a hyperinflation experience similar to the other emerging markets decided to convert its central bank monetary policy into an inflation targeting regime in 1998 after the inflation experience which came up to 1100 %. This transformation period that went on until 2010 was a gradual transition period to inflation targeting framework based on monetary independence from the openness of capital flows, which increased capital flow and exchange rate targeting (Bańbuła et al., 2011: 285). The Central Bank of South Africa, having experienced hyperinflation in 2000, used the repo rate as the policy instrument to keep the inflation level under control (Bhorat et al., 2014: 10).

The 1980s were financial liberation years for the majority of the EMEs. Monetary policy patterns which reduced capital controls, which left interest rates determination to the market and which attempted to stabilize the value of their currencies by intervening with the exchange rate became a common practice in many EMEs like Turkey. However, existing capital deficits in these countries and high capital inflows occurring from time to time caused interest rates to increase slightly when compared to developed countries. The 1990s are remembered as the years when dollarization prevailed in countries like Turkey, where national currency depreciated and high inflation figures were experienced. For instance, Turkey, which experienced a large fiscal crisis due to liquidity excess in 1994, experienced another fiscal crisis due to illiquidity in 2001 and Turkey changed into an implicit inflation targeting within a transition program framework to a strong economy in the same year. It was explicitly stated in this program that open inflation targeting would starting 2006 and monetary authorities were allowed for five-year legal and organizational preparation process. Although determination of the exchange rate was left to the free market during this process, the central bank has intervened, in case of fluctuations, on the exchange rate market through open market operations. While a strict monetary policy based only on inflation targeting was pursued until November 2008, a strategy to break the economy out of recession and to keep price stability was followed by the advent of the global crisis. The basic policy tool was short-term interest rates. The monetary base was used as the nominal anchor until open inflation targeting was implemented.

In past years, Bangladesh and Indonesia used a monetary aggregate target framework in which the monetary authority used its instruments to reach target growth rates for a monetary aggregate such as reserve money, M1 or M2. In these countries, targeted aggregate became a nominal anchor and it was used as an intermediate target for monetary policy. The Central Bank of Bangladesh, which activated new investment instruments as monetary policy tools in the 2000s, has used two main policy tools to reach its monetary aggregate target: cash reserve requirements and statutory liquidity requirements (Haque, 2013). The Central Bank of Indonesia, which also used monetary aggregate as a monetary transfer mechanism, has signaled its intent to begin a transition to an inflation targeting framework in order to reach its goals for achieving and maintaining the stability of the rupiah (currency), referring to the inflation and the exchange rate. With this intention, Bank Indonesia has announced an annual inflation target and an annual monetary policy plan (Geoltom, 2008: 309).

When we consider the period immediately before the 2008 crisis, no country among the EMEs that used the monetary aggregate target or the monetary transmission mechanism, were examined except for Argentina and Bangladesh. Bulgaria, China, Ukraine and Venezuela still used the exchange rate anchor during the subject period. Bulgaria continued using the exchange rate anchor after the fiscal crisis, whereas Bangladesh and Venezuela went on using a monetary aggregate target.

Bulgaria changing into a currency board regime in 1997 is one of the rare countries that did not change this regime despite changes in Asia, in Russia and the 2008 global fiscal crisis. Bulgaria's currency was at first pegged to the German Mark and with the transition to the Euro it was pegged to the Euro, the official currency of The Central Bank of Europe. The Central Bank of Bulgaria has used three monetary transfer mechanisms as (i) full coverage of the National Bank's monetary liabilities with liquid foreign exchange reserves, (ii) lending to the government and banks forbidden by law, and (iii) market-based interest rates (Penkova, 2011: 4).

The other countries which do not follow the general tendency are China and Ukraine. These two countries changed into monetary aggregate target implementation instead of exchange rate anchor which they implemented during the pre-crisis period. The Central Bank of the Republic of China (CBC) is significantly different from other central banks in terms of monetary policy implementations. It uses multiple tools in its monetary policy implementations. These policy tools are classified into three, which are priced based instruments, quantity-based instruments and administrative window guidance. Price based instruments are used to determine interest rates on bank deposits and lending, quantity-based instruments are adopted for reserve requirements ratio and open market operations and finally administrative window guidance is employed to influence lending of the banks. These instruments affect interbank market interest rates. The CBC attempts to achieve the monetary aggregate target by affecting interest rates (De Bandt et al., 2008: 23).

Ukraine, trying a new peg in the post revolution period between the years of 2005–2009, changed into a managed float regime in 2012. Floating currency was accepted in accordance with IMF's demand in 2014. Nevertheless, as a result of IMF policies, The Central Bank of Ukraine focused on monetary transfer mechanisms changing and adapting discount and interest rates as well as parameters adapting assets and liabilities in accordance with liquidity regulations. The Central Bank of Ukraine is attempting to reach a monetary aggregate target, like China, by affecting the interest rates (National Bank of Ukraine, 2017).

Other countries that do not fit into the three main streams mentioned are listed in Tab. 12.3 and are evaluated in the "others" category. Among these countries; Argentina, India, Malaysia, Pakistan and Russia have no explicitly stated nominal anchor. Argentina and India have been exposed to huge capital outflows since the 2008 global fiscal crisis. Due to these rapid capital outflows, central bank reserves have dramatically decreased, demand for US dollars has increased and the national currencies of these countries have had a significant decrease in value. For instance, inflation has increased even more in Argentina with depreciation of its national currency. In order to fight depreciation, capital control implementation was strictly carried out; however, the dollars started to be sold on the black market. The price of dollars increased and this increase instigated inflation even more. As Argentina was fighting against these problems, it could not change into monetary transfer mechanisms based on inflation targeting framework like the other EMEs, rather it tried to deal with inflation spiral by stabilizing the foreign exchange rate and control capital outflows with sterilized interventions for short periods. Malaysia, experiencing a similar capital outflow problem in the same period, tried to solve the dilemma by using relatively short run sterilization instruments. The Central Bank of Malaysia using overnights policy rates as a monetary policy indicator adopted an implicit targeting policy without an explicit inflation-targeting framework. In Pakistan, which has implemented overnight money market repo rates corridors since 2009, monetary policy has been considered as discretional, which means it is not transparent. It is not possible to mention any explicitly stated nominal anchors since Pakistan used rules discount rate, reserve requirements and statutory liquid ratio as its monetary policy (Hanif, 2014: 1; McCauley, 2006: 172).

The country that took the first steps to change into an explicitly inflation targeting framework is Russia. The Central Bank of Russia, focusing on depreciation of the ruble (currency), increased interest rates steadily and developed new control parameters. Russia reduced intervention in the exchange rate market and increased the flexibility of the exchange rate policy between 2009 and 2012 so that this policy could succeed. The exchange rates diminished throughout the period. Therefore, the central bank switched to a fully floating exchange rate regime which has focused on interest rates since 2013–2014 (Mohanty, 2013: 1).

Tab. 12.3: Monetary Policy Frameworks of EMEs. Compiled from IMF reports

	Country	first half of 2000's	before financial crisis	after financial crisis
Latin America	Argentina	other	exchange rate anchor + monetary aggregate target	Other*
	Brazil	inflation targeting	inflation targeting	inflation targeting
	Chile	inflation targeting	inflation targeting	inflation targeting
	Colombia	inflation targeting	inflation targeting	inflation targeting
	Mexico	inflation targeting	inflation targeting	inflation targeting
	Peru	inflation targeting	inflation targeting	inflation targeting
	Venezuela	exchange rate anchor	Monetary aggregate target	monetary aggregate target
Asia	Bangladesh	monetary aggregate target	monetary aggregate target	monetary aggregate target
	China	exchange rate anchor	exchange rate anchor	monetary aggregate target
	India	other	other	other
	Indonesia	monetary aggregate target	inflation targeting	inflation targeting
	Malaysia	exchange rate anchor	other	other
	Pakistan	other	other	other
	Philippines	inflation targeting	inflation targeting	inflation targeting
	Thailand	inflation targeting	inflation targeting	inflation targeting
Europe	Bulgaria	exchange rate anchor	exchange rate anchor	exchange rate anchor
	Hungary	inflation targeting framework	inflation targeting framework + other	inflation targeting
	Poland	inflation targeting	inflation targeting	inflation targeting
	Romania	exchange rate anchor	inflation targeting	inflation targeting
	Russia	other	other	other
	Turkey	inflation targeting	inflation targeting	inflation targeting
	Ukraine	exchange rate anchor	other	monetary aggregate target
Africa	South Africa	inflation targeting	inflation targeting	inflation targeting

* Other: no explicitly stated nominal anchor, monitors various indicators or other band arrangements

12.4 Conclusion

This chapter aims at revealing how and in which direction monetary policy implementations have changed by predicating exchange rate regimes and monetary transfer mechanisms for twenty-three EMEs included in the definition given by the IMF since the beginning of 2000s to the present. The Asian-Russian crises, global fiscal crisis and local economic fluctuations for each country by which monetary policy indicators were deeply affected are used as a research process.

Historical background of central banking indicates the stronger the autonomous decision-making abilities monetary authorities have in both technical and operational sense, the more successful and more efficient the policy is. Policy goals may not be reached due to the fact that EMEs have not settled their organizational structures yet. If there is lack of fiscal discipline, if the fiscal system is shallow; due to high political uncertainties and risks, governmental policies cannot be used efficiently even if the central banks are autonomous

Neoliberal economy policies predominantly prescribed for the EMEs after 1980 caused fluctuations in the monetary markets of most countries examined in this study. These fluctuations usually are stimulated and are influenced by each other through local, territorial or international crises. Most of the EMEs attempting to adapt to liberal policies with all their institutions seek a way to solve the problems they are confronted with through these crises by implementing deregulation and liberal policies.

One of the indicators of this situation is that they have taken a resolution toward increasing flexibility as a general tendency although EMEs have tried different methods according to the circumstances they are experiencing. These economies that have a great amount of saving gap, that keep international reserve in high quantity and that fight against high inflation figures are getting one step closer to flexibility by each new crisis they are confronted. As a reflection of this process, in brief, it is seen majority of the EMEs quitted pegs through previous crises and they changed into a complete type of floating regime by 2008 fiscal crisis.

Apart from exchange rates, another factor that EMEs operate to fight against monetary market fluctuations experienced is monetary transfer mechanisms. General tendency in this process is seen to provide price stability by keeping short-term interest rates under control and to ensure sustainable economic growth. From this point of view, a considerable part of the EMEs changed into inflation targeting framework in 2000s. When they are considered with exchange rate regimes, it can be ascertained that countries changing into inflation targeting regime are largely the ones with tendency of flexibility mentioned above.

All these findings point to the fact that monetary impossible trinity shapes market framework of the EMEs. Moreover, it can be claimed that a substantial part of these economies has a similar free capital mobility, a type of floating regime -despite a dirty exchange rate system- and limited policy autonomy with an inflation targeting focus.

References

Allegret, J. P. and Sallenave, A. (2015). Capital Flow Bonanzas and Monetary Policy in Emerging Europe: Responses to the Global Financial Crisis. *Post-Communist Economies, 27*(4), 429-447.

Bańbuła, P., Koziński, W. and Rubaszek, M. (2011). The Role of the Exchange Rate in Monetary Policy in Poland. *BIS Paper, 57*, 285–295.

Barışık, S. (2014). Merkez Bankası Bağımsızlığı, Makroekonomik Etkileri ve 2001 Tarihli TCMB Kanununun Yansımaları. *Ankara Üniversitesi SBF Dergisi, 59* (03), 1–20.

Bernanke, B. S., Laubach, T., Mishkin, F. S. and Posen, A. S. (1999). *Inflation targeting*. Princenton University Press.

Bhorat, H., Hirsch, A., Kanbur, R., Ncube, M. (Ed.) (2014). *The Oxford Companion to the Economics of South Africa*. Oxford: Oxford University Press.

Borrero, M. A. M. (2001). On the Long and Short of Central Bank Independence, Policy Coordination, and Economic Performance. *International Monetary Fund, (No. 1-19)* IMF Working Paper, WP/01/19, 24 pages.

Capie, F., Goodhart, C. and Schnadt, N. (1994). *The Development of Central Banking*. London: Bank of England.

Cukierman, A. (1992). *Central Bank Strategy, Credibility, and Independence: Theory and Evidence*. Cambridge, MA: MIT Press.

Dakila Jr, F. (2001). Alternative Monetary Policy Rules for the Philippines. *Philippine Review of Economics, 38*(2), 1–36

De Bandt, O., Frey, L., and Loisel, O. (2008). Globalization, Inflation and Monetary Policy. *Quarterly Selection of Articles-Bulletin de La Banque de France, (12)*, 23-30.

Fischer, S. (1994). *Modern Central Banking*. London: Bank of England.

Geoltom, Miranda S. (2008). The Transmission Mechanism of Monetary Policy in Indonesia. in *Transmission Mechanisms in Monetary Policy in Emerging Market Economies*. BIS Paper No. 35. 309–330. Switzerland: Monetary and Economic Department, Bank of International Settlement.

Hanif, M. N. (2014). Monetary Policy Experience of Pakistan. *MPRA Paper No. 60855*.

Haque, S. M. (2013). Monetary History of Bangladesh: 1972-2011. Paper ID: 2012-3-88-003. Date Accessed 24 January 2017. https://www.scribd.com/document/ 215039070/monetary-history-of-bangladesh-1972-2011.

Hoggarth, G. (1996). *Introduction to Monetary Policy*. London: Bank of England.

International Monetary Fund (IMF). (2000). *Exchange Rate Regimes in an Increasingly Integrated World Economy*, International Monetary Fund.

International Monetary Fund (IMF). (2007). *Review of Exchange Arrangements, Restrictions, and Controls*, International Monetary Fund.

International Monetary Fund (IMF). (2014). *Annual Report on Exchange Arrangements and Exchange Restrictions*, International Monetary Fund.

Jawadi, F., Mallick, S. K. and Sousa, R. M. (2014). Nonlinear Monetary Policy Reaction Functions in Large Emerging Economies: The Case of Brazil and China. *Applied Economics, 46*(9), 973-984.

Kindleberger, C. (1993). *A Financial History of Western Europe*. New York: Oxford University Press.

Mallick, S. K. and Sousa, R. M. (2012). Real Effects of Monetary Policy in Large Emerging Economies. *Macroeconomic Dynamics, 16*(2), 190-212.

McCauley, R. N. (2006). Understanding Monetary Policy in Malaysia and Thailand: Objectives, Instruments and Independence. *BIS papers, 31*, 172-98.

Mishkin, F. S. and Eakins S. G. (2000). *Financial Markets and Institutions*. (3. Edition). Columbia: Addison Wesley Longman, Inc, Columbia University.

Mohanty, M. S. (2013). *Market Volatility and Foreign Exchange Intervention in EMEs: What Has Changed? -An Overview*. Brasilia: Brazil Central Bank

National Bank of Ukraine (2017). National Bank of Ukraine Modifies the Monetary Policy Framework While Tightening the Monetary Policy Stance. Date Accessed 24 January 2017, https://bank.gov.ua/control/en/publish/article?art_id=14340538.

Penkova-Pearson, E. (2011). Trade, Convergence and Exchange Rate Regime: Evidence from Bulgaria and Romania. *National Bank of Bulgaria Discussion Papers, 85* , 1–46.

Rossini, R., Quispe, Z. and Serrano, E. (2013). Foreign Exchange Intervention in Peru. *BIS Paper, No:73* , 243–262.

Sims, C. (2005). Limits to Inflation Targeting. B. Bernanke and M. Woodford (Ed.), in *The Inflation Targeting Debate*. Chicago: University of Chicago Press, National Bureau of Economic Research—Studies in Business Cycles, 283–310.

Yeldan, E. (2003). Neoliberal Küreselleşme İdeolojisinin Kalkınma Söylemi Üzerine Değerlendirmeleri. *Praksis Dergisi* (7), 19–34.

Nazan Şahbaz Kılınç

13 Labor Force Participation in EMEs

Abstract: The mortgage crisis in the US caused a financial crisis which effected the entire world economy. With the emergence of the global financial crisis, the shrinking of foreign trade throughout the world and the reduction of domestic demand have also reduced production. As a result, businesses have had to lower their capacities and this has adversely affected employment. The crisis effected emerging economies in different ways and in different degrees. This crisis was reflected to unemployment variable as well. The impact of the financial crisis on labor markets changed from country to country. Almost all developed countries and emerging countries felt the negative effects of the crisis on their labor markets. Emerging economies were less affected than the developed economies. The reason for this type of asset-based loans will produce financial derivatives markets in emerging economies is not widespread. The impact of the crisis on global economic activity contradiction in demand and production decline has led to a decrease in employment and increase in unemployment. This study investigates the impact of the global financial crisis on labor force participation (LFP) in emerging market economies (EMEs). In this chapter, the concepts of global finance crisis and labor participation rate are emphasized and the effects of the crisis are evaluated in the light of various indicators. In this context, a comparative analysis of emerging economies will be made.

Keywords: Labor Force Participation, Employment, Global Financial Crisis

13.1 Introduction

The mortgage crisis which began in the US effected the entire world economy in a short period of time and became a financial crisis. Since 2008, growth in EMEs began to slow down. According to the International Money Fund (IMF) estimates; in 2014, except in India and Mexico economic growth slowed in EMEs. Unemployment rates due to the crisis increased precarious. Forms of work and increased the number of poor.

The 2008 global financial crisis also negatively affected the real sector in a short time and the production slowdown and the decline in the growth rate of the worldwide problem of unemployment has emerged. As economies slowed down, people faced unemployment, loss of livelihood and deteriorating living conditions.

This study investigates the impact of the global financial crisis on the total labor force participation and the issues of male and female employment in EMEs. This chapter examines changing employment patterns and labor market conditions before and after the 2008 crisis, particularly focusing on the differential impacts on male and female employment.

13.2 2008 Global Financial Crisis

The economic slowdown was truly global in the sense that growth declined all over the world when compared to 2007. Because of the economic downturn that began in the US housing market and the Lehman Brothers business continued, the US economy faced a deep economic crisis. This crisis, beginning with financial markets, effected the real sector within a short time and spread to other countries including European countries, due to high integration in the international markets. The crisis ultimately turned into a great recession, especially in European countries, and debt crises occurred in these countries.

Because of the crisis, the macroeconomic variables of the countries seriously deteriorated. It became clear that the output levels of emerging markets and developing economies experienced a sharp slowdown. In these countries, real GDP growth, which was 8.3 % in 2007, decreased to 6.1 % in 2008 and 2.4 % in 2009, when the real effects of the crisis were felt. The nominal GDP figure in these countries dropped $ 1.3 trillion in 2010 from the October 2007 forecast. The IMF estimated the losses at $ 2.6 trillion in the 2008–2010 period (IMF, 2010).

It was inevitable that the crisis would spread to developing countries within a short time. Because of the crisis, investors have attracted their capital even in countries where risk levels are at a minimum, which has led to the depreciation of the currencies and stock values of these countries. Decreases in exports and increases in raw material prices threw economies into a recession (Nanto, 2009: 2). This recession has had social consequences as well as economic consequences. The most important effect emerged in unemployment rates. The decrease in total demand prevented companies from receiving new orders and resulted in layoffs. (Norgren, 2010: 12). However, the increases in unemployment rates in EMEs were lower due to higher wage flexibility (Reinhart and Rogoff, 2009).

13.3 Labor Force Participation (LFP)

The labor force participation rate (LFPR) is a measure of the proportion of a country's working-age population which engages actively in the labor market, it gives a sign of the size of the supply of labor available to engage in the production of goods and services, relative to the population at working age. The LFPR is calculated by expressing the number of persons in the labor force as a percentage of the working-age population (ILO, 2015).

LFPR plays a vital role in understanding labor markets, studying factors which affect the size and the composition of a country's available human resources, formulating and implementing employment policies, planning and deciding job training needs, calculating expected life spans as well as retirement benefits, which are crucial in planning social security programs (ILO, 2014).

13.3.1 Determinants of Labor Force Participation

There are several determinants for labor force participation and earnings such as: gender, age, marital status, education, experience, possession of wealth, health conditions, quality of institutions, labor market regulations, and policy interventions (Mohamed, 2015: 2).

13.3.2 Female Labor Force Participation

There are important determinants for women's labor force participation such as: schooling, age, marital status and number of children (Dayıoğlu-Kırdar, 2010: 39). Our analysis considers a supply–demand framework for female labor force participation (FLFP) as illustrated in Fig. 13.1.

In Fig. 13.1, labor supply refers to a woman's choice of how much to work given the labor market opportunities available to her. When deciding whether to work and many hours to work, a woman must balance the returns for her labor (her wages and any nonmonetary benefits) with the opportunity costs of foregone, home production and leisure as well as other monetary and nonmonetary costs that she and her family members would incur if she works outside the home. Social stigma and norms may be important in countries like Indonesia where the roles of men and women in the home and in society are often differentiated. The household's broader financial situation will also influence labor supply: when household incomes are low, the marginal benefits of an added income are very high, thus giving women a strong incentive to work, while when household incomes are high, there is a less pressing need for the woman to supplement the household budget. These opportunities are limited by several factors, among them (i) gender-based discrimination in hiring or in wages, (ii) the quality of the work environment, (iii) the location of available jobs and commuting costs, and (iv) whether the available jobs allow a woman to balance work with obligations at home (Schaner and Das, 2016: 2).

A woman's labor market participation is decided by the intersection of labor supply with labor demand. One thing to note from the discussion above is that

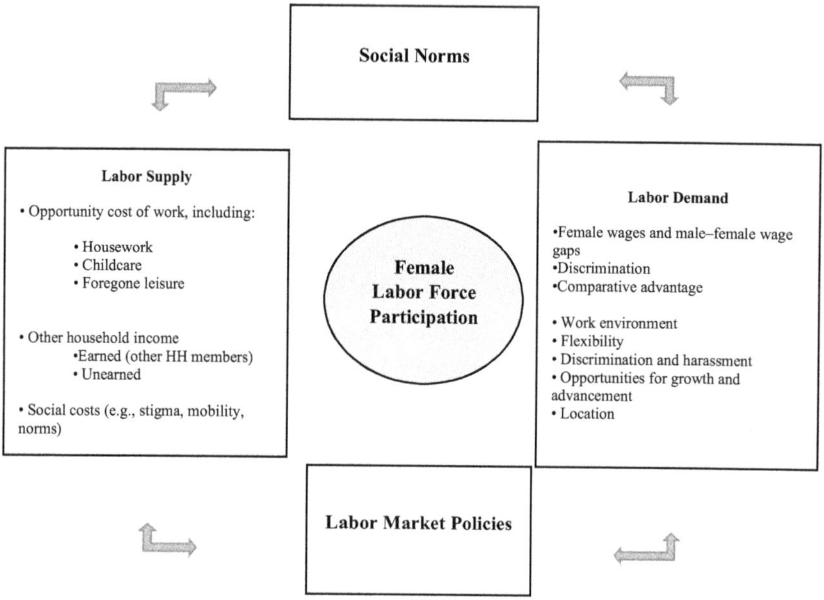

Fig. 13.1: A Conceptual Framework for Female Labor Supply. Schaner and Das 2016: 2

the impact of wages on FLFP are ambiguous. As a woman's wage rises, she may choose to work more as the marginal returns for her labor are higher (called the substitution effect in the economics literature). However, she may decide to work less as she is now effectively better off and has a less pressing need for an added income (called the income effect). Fig. 13.1 also highlights that there is a continuous feedback loop between supply-side and demand-side factors, social norms, and labor market policies. The multidirectional nature of these relationships makes it especially difficult to infer causality from observational correlations (Schaner and Das, 2016: 2)

13.3.3 Policies to Support Labor Participation

Stronger economic growth can pull more workers into the labor force if employers are paying higher wages. This situation needs more stimulus to be realized through fiscal policy such as more infrastructure investments. According to the IMF, increasing infrastructure spending can speed up economic growth by 1,5 percent in the short-term. This increased growth helps create jobs and attract

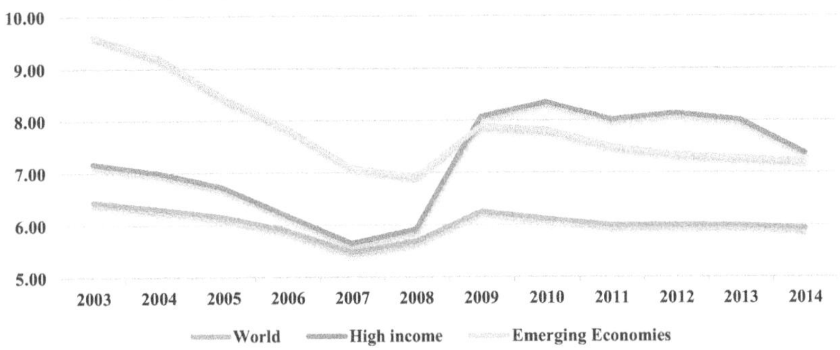

Fig. 13.2: Unemployment Rate in World, High Income and Emerging Economies (15–64 %). World Bank, 2016

discouraged workers back into the labor force, which improves the economy in the long-term (IMF, 2014).

- Some of the factors that affect women's participation in the workforce are *Elastic working-time regulations*: Policies which prevent part-time jobs will increase women's participation in the workforce.
- *Taxation*: Tax systems can also influence work-sharing decisions among couples; usually working against greater balance.
- *Support to families with young children*: Parental leave and childcare-based government support increase women's labor force participation.
- *Other policies which have a positive impact on female participation in the workforce* are: immigration policies, abandoning regulations which prevent the growth of the service industry and welfare delivered through make-work-pay system (OECD, 2016).

The trend in unemployment rates in emerging economies, world and high-income countries during the period 2003–2014 is given in Fig. 13.2. The unemployment rate in emerging economies after 2010 dropped below the unemployment rate of high-income countries. The unemployment rate in emerging market economies for 2003–2009 was above the world rate as well as the rates high-income countries. Undoubtedly, important economic changes and reforms adopted by the governments of newly industrialized countries in the 2000s gave positive results

Tab. 13.1: Unemployment Rate, Total (% of Total Labor Force). WorldBank, 2016

Countries/ Years	2003	2004	2005	2006	2007	2008	2009	2010	2011	2012	2013	2014
Argentina	16	13	11	10	9	8	9	8	7	7	7	8
Bangladesh	4	5	4	4	4	4	5	5	5	5	5	4
Brazil	10	9	9	8	8	7	8	8	7	6	7	7
Bulgaria	13	12	10	9	7	6	7	10	11	12	13	12
Chile	9	9	8	8	7	8	10	8	7	6	6	6
China	4	4	4	4	4	4	4	4	4	5	5	5
Colombia	14	14	12	12	11	11	12	12	11	11	10	10
Hungary	6	6	7	8	7	8	10	11	11	11	10	8
India	4	4	4	4	4	4	4	4	4	4	4	4
Indonesia	10	10	11	10	9	8	8	7	7	6	6	6
Malaysia	4	4	4	3	3	3	4	3	3	3	3	2
Mexico	3	4	4	3	3	4	5	5	5	5	5	5
Pakistan	8	7	7	6	5	5	5	5	5	5	5	5
Peru	6	5	5	5	5	5	4	4	4	4	4	4
Philippines	11	12	8	8	7	7	8	7	7	7	7	7
Poland	20	19	18	14	10	7	8	10	10	10	10	9
Romania	7	8	7	7	6	6	7	7	7	7	7	7
Russia	8	8	7	7	6	6	8	7	7	6	6	5
South Africa	27	25	24	23	22	23	24	25	25	25	25	25
Thailand	2	2	1	1	1	1	2	1	1	1	1	1
Turkey	11	11	11	10	10	11	14	12	10	9	9	9
Ukraine	9	9	7	7	6	6	9	8	8	8	7	8
Venezuela, RB	17	15	11	9	8	7	8	9	8	8	8	9

Note: The upper figure is rounded after the curfew.

Where the trend in unemployment rates in emerging countries for 2003–2014 shown in Tab. 13.1 can be monitered with an important decrease, it declined to 8% levels in 2014 while unemployment rate in Argentina is about 16 % in 2003.

After Argentina, the countries which succeeded in significantly reducing unemployment rates during the period 2003–2014 are Poland (from 19 % to 9 %), Venezuela (from 17 % to 9 %), Colombia (from 14 % to 10 %) and the Philippines (from 11 % to 7 %). For this period, unemployment rates showed a stable trend in countries such as Bangladesh, China, Malaysia, Mexico, Romania, Thailand and Turkey.

According to the values of 2014, the five countries with the highest unemployment rates are; South Africa (25.1 %), Bulgaria (11.6 %), Colombia (10.1 %), Poland (9.2 %) and Turkey (9.2 %). In the same year, the unemployment rate is the lowest in; Thailand (0.9 %), Malaysia (2 %), India (3.6 %), Bangladesh (4.2 %) and Peru (4.3 %). The countries which have ranked above these averages are Ukraine, Hungary, Argentina, Venezuela, Poland, Turkey, Colombia, Bulgaria and South Africa. Unemployment rates have increased, especially in times of crisis. For example, the unemployment rate in Brazil was 7.1 % in 2008, while it increased to 8.3 % in 2009, in Chile from 7.8 % to 9.7 % and in Ukranie from 6.4 % to 8.8 %. When we assess Turkey, the unemployment rate remained at the 10 % during the 2003–2014 period. Turkey experienced the full impact of the global financial crisis in 2009 when the unemployment rate increased by 3 % over the previous year. As the effects of the crisis eased, the unemployment rate in Turkey decreased to under 10 %.

The increase in female unemployment rates during the period 2003–2014 are shown in Tab. 13.2. Countries like Argentina, Poland, the Philippines and Colombia achieved notable declines in female unemployment rates. The female unemployment rates in Turkey remained at 10 % during this period. According to the data for 2014, the average female unemployment rates in EMEs were 7.92 %. However female unemployment rates for South Africa, Colombia, Bulgaria, Turkey, Poland, Argentina, Venezuela, Pakistan and Brazil were above the average. In the period analyzed, Thailand, Malaysia, China, India and Russia had the lowest unemployment rates.

13.4 Labor Force Participation in EME

According to Global-Economic-Prospects collected by The World Bank in 2015, the recent global financial crisis had a small impact on the labor markets of emerging countries. Unemployment rates have been below the pre-financial crisis levels recorded for these countries in 2010.

The LFPRs in EMEs are below the average of both developed countries and the world during 2003–2014. It has remained stable at the 65–67% level in EMEs, while the LFPRs stabilized at the 70–72% level in developed countries. During this period, the LFPR has increased continuously in the EMES and is reaching the world average (see Fig. 13.3).

The development of LFPR in the EMEs during the period 2003–2014 are given in Tab. 13.3. During this period, countries like China, Thailand, Peru, Brazil, Russia and Colombia have the highest LFPR for the population aged 15–64.

Tab. 13.2: Unemployment Rate, Female (% of Female Labor Force). WorldBank, 2016

Countries/ Years	2003	2004	2005	2006	2007	2008	2009	2010	2011	2012	2013	2014
Argentina	19	15	13	13	11	10	10	9	9	9	9	10
Bangladesh	5	5	7	5	6	6	6	5	5	5	5	5
Brazil	12	12	12	11	11	10	11	11	9	8	8	9
Bulgaria	13	12	10	9	7	6	7	10	10	11	12	11
Chile	10	11	10	9	9	10	11	10	9	8	7	7
China	4	4	3	3	3	4	4	3	4	4	4	4
Colombia	18	18	16	15	15	15	16	16	15	14	13	13
Hungary	6	6	8	8	8	8	10	11	11	11	10	8
India	4	4	5	5	4	4	4	4	4	4	4	4
Indonesia	13	13	14	13	11	10	9	9	8	7	7	7
Malaysia	4	4	4	4	3	4	4	4	3	3	4	2
Mexico	4	5	4	4	4	4	5	5	5	5	5	5
Pakistan	16	13	12	10	9	9	9	9	9	9	9	9
Peru	7	6	6	5	5	5	5	4	4	4	5	5
Philippines	11	13	8	8	7	7	8	7	7	7	7	7
Poland	20	20	19	15	10	8	9	10	10	11	11	10
Romania	6	6	6	6	5	5	6	7	7	6	7	6
Russia	8	8	7	7	6	6	8	7	6	5	5	5
South Africa	31	29	28	27	27	26	26	27	28	28	27	28
Thailand	1	1	1	1	1	1	2	1	1	1	1	1
Turkey	10	11	11	11	11	11	14	13	11	11	10	11
Ukraine	8	8	7	6	6	6	7	7	7	6	6	7
Venezuela, RB	20	18	14	11	8	7	8	9	9	9	8	9

Note: The upper figure is rounded after the curfew.

Countries with the lowest LFPR are Turkey, India, Pakistan and South Africa. In general, there was an upward trend in the LFPRs in EMEs for 2003–2014.

As of 2014, the countries with the lowest labor force participation are Turkey (54.6 %), Pakistan (55.9 %), India (56 %) and South Africa (56.4 %), while the countries with the highest rates, are Thailand (77.7 %), China (77.1 %), Peru (76.9 %), Russia (73.4 %) and Brazil (72.5 %). In the same year, the LFPR was 67.3 % for EMEs; countries below average are; Turkey, Pakistan, India, South Africa, Bangladesh, Mexico, Romania, Malaysia, Phillippines and Hungary. The LFPR is low in Turkey and Turkey is not in a good position among the countries

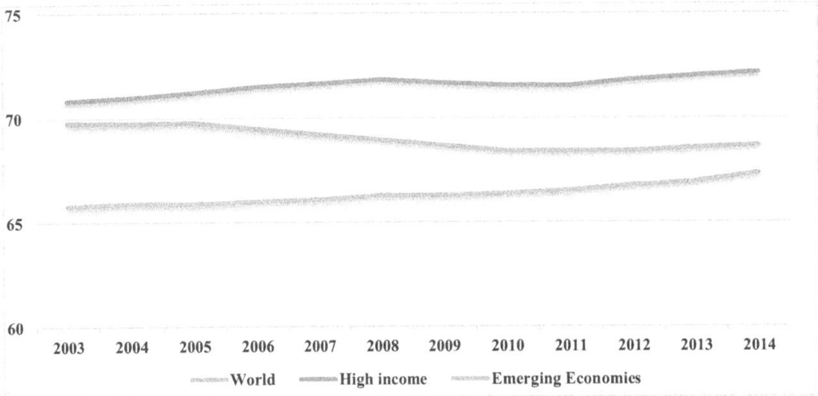

Fig. 13.3: Labor Force Partipication Rate (15–64 %). WorldBank, 2016

it is competing with. In Turkey, the LFPR showed an improvement when compared to the previous year, but it is still at a relatively low level. Therefore, to increase partipication in workforce, there is a need for innovative and stimulating economic policies in Turkey.

As shown in Tab. 13.4, female LFPRs in China and Thailand were above 70 %. Russia, Peru, Bulgaria and Brazil followed these countries. Female LFPRs have remained at a 25–35 % level in these countries. When we consider the increasing participation of females in the labor force a positive impact on sustainable development is achieved. Increasing female employment rates is a vital economic policy goal in countries such as Pakistan, India and Turkey.

13.5 Labor Force Participation Rate in Turkey

Labor participation rates are connected to the development levels of the country. The rate of participation in the workforce is low in emerging economies because the population in these countries is increasing both in the age of work force and in the labor force.

According to Turkstat, there are two reasons for the low rates of participation in the labor force. Firstly, is the low level of education in the general population. As the level of education decreases, the labor participation rate also decreases. The second reason is the low female labor participation rate (TURKSTAT, 2012: 32).

Tab. 13.5 shows the status of women in the labor market in Turkey for 2003–2014. Female LFPR has remained at the 26–34% level in Turkey. Female employment is not at the desired level, but it has increased over the years. Female

Tab. 13.3: Labor Force Participation Rate (Total, 15–64 %). WorldBank, 2016

Countries/ Years	2003	2004	2005	2006	2007	2008	2009	2010	2011	2012	2013	2014
Argentina	66	69	69	69	69	68	69	68	68	68	68	69
Bangladesh	70	69	68	68	67	66	65	64	64	64	64	64
Brazil	73	74	75	74	74	74	75	74	73	72	72	73
Bulgaria	62	63	62	65	67	68	68	67	66	67	68	69
Chile	59	60	60	61	62	64	64	66	67	68	68	69
China	80	79	79	78	78	77	77	76	77	77	77	77
Colombia	72	70	70	68	67	68	70	71	71	72	72	72
Hungary	61	60	61	62	62	61	62	62	63	64	65	67
India	62	63	63	62	61	60	59	58	57	56	56	56
Indonesia	69	70	70	70	70	70	70	70	70	70	70	70
Malaysia	64	64	64	63	63	62	62	62	64	65	66	66
Mexico	62	64	63	64	65	65	64	65	64	66	65	66
Pakistan	53	53	54	55	55	55	56	56	56	56	56	56
Peru	71	71	71	73	78	78	78	78	77	78	77	77
Phillippines	69	68	66	66	65	66	66	67	67	67	67	67
Poland	64	64	64	63	63	64	65	66	66	67	67	68
Romania	63	64	62	64	63	63	63	63	63	64	64	66
Russia	71	71	72	72	73	73	73	73	73	73	73	73
South Africa	57	56	57	58	58	58	56	55	55	55	56	56
Thailand	78	78	78	78	79	79	78	78	79	79	78	78
Turkey	50	49	49	49	49	50	51	52	53	54	54	55
Ukraine	67	67	67	67	67	67	67	67	68	67	68	68
Venezuela, RB	71	70	70	69	68	68	68	68	68	68	68	68

unemployment rate increased to 14,3 % in 2009 due to the global crisis. After the crisis the female unemployment rate decreased.

13.6 Conclusion

Many countries have long been focusing on increasing LFP and employment. Creating employment is necessary in achieving sustainable economic and social developments. Also, unemployment is a major socio-economical problem. Unemployment effects society by decreasing the amount of resources available. People who are unable to find adequate employment begin suffering since they

Tab. 13.4: Labor Force Participation Rate (Female, 15–64 %). WorldBank, 2016

Countries/ Years	2003	2004	2005	2006	2007	2008	2009	2010	2011	2012	2013	2014
Argentina	52	56	56	56	56	56	56	54	55	55	56	56
Bangladesh	53	52	50	49	48	46	45	44	44	44	45	45
Brazil	61	62	64	63	63	63	64	63	61	61	61	62
Bulgaria	57	58	57	60	62	63	63	62	62	63	65	65
Chile	40	42	43	44	45	48	48	53	55	55	56	57
China	74	73	73	72	71	71	70	69	70	70	70	70
Colombia	59	57	56	55	54	55	58	59	60	61	61	62
Hungary	54	54	55	55	55	55	55	57	57	58	59	61
India	38	38	39	37	35	33	32	30	29	28	28	28
Indonesia	52	52	52	52	53	53	53	54	54	53	53	53
Malaysia	47	47	47	46	46	46	46	46	48	49	52	52
Mexico	41	43	44	45	46	46	46	47	46	48	48	48
Pakistan	17	18	20	22	22	22	24	25	25	25	25	25
Peru	61	61	61	61	69	69	69	69	69	69	68	69
Phillippines	53	52	51	50	50	50	51	52	53	52	52	52
Poland	58	58	58	57	56	57	58	59	59	60	60	61
Romania	57	57	55	57	56	55	55	56	56	56	56	57
Russia	67	67	68	68	69	69	69	68	68	69	68	68
South Africa	50	48	50	52	51	51	49	48	48	49	50	50
Thailand	71	71	72	71	72	72	71	71	72	72	70	70
Turkey	28	25	25	26	26	27	28	30	32	32	33	34
Ukraine	63	63	62	62	63	62	62	62	62	61	62	62
Venezuela, RB	57	56	55	54	53	54	54	54	55	54	54	55

Note: The upper figure is rounded after the curfew

are unable to afford nutritious foods and basic items. Unemployed workers experience high levels of stress and depression creating social problems.

Labor markets are affected by business cycles. The recent global financial crisis affected the macroeconomic variables of many economies, especially in developing countries, such as labor participation, employment, inflation, interest rates, industrial production etc.

The aim of this chapter was to analyze changes occurring in the structure of employment and LFP in EMEs during the global financial crisis. The financial crisis had a great impact on global labor markets. Labor participation rates in

Tab. 13.5: Status of Women in the Labor Market in Turkey (Female, 15–64 %) (Thousand). Turkish Statistical Institute, 2012

Year	15+ Population	Labor	Employed	Employment rate	Labor Participation Rate	Unemployment rate
2003	24.652	6.555	5.891	23,9	26,6	10,1
2004	24.293	5.669	5.047	20,8	23,3	11,0
2005	24.686	5.750	5.108	20,7	23,3	11,2
2006	25.080	5.916	5.258	21,0	23,6	11,1
2007	25.480	6.016	5.356	21,0	23,6	11,0
2008	25.855	6.329	5.595	21,6	24,5	11,6
2009	26.317	6.851	5.871	22,3	26,0	14,3
2010	26.740	7.383	6.425	24,0	27,6	13,0
2011	27.273	7.859	6.973	25,6	28,8	11,3
2012	27.773	8.192	7.309	26,3	29,5	10,8
2013	28.197	8.674	7.641	27,1	30,8	11,9
2014	25.444	8.546	7.507	29,5	33,6	12,2

most emerging economies declined during the global crisis. This decline was due to more young people attending school or staying longer in school rather than joining the work force.

LFPRs in EMEs were below the average of both developed countries and world countries for 2003–2014. LFPRS remained at 65–67 % in EMEs, while LFPRs in developed countries remained at 70–72 %.

References

Dayıoglu, Meltem and Kırdar, Murat G. (2010). "Determinants of and Trends in Labor Force Participation of Women in Turkey", State Planning Organization of the Republic of Turkey and World Bank Welfare and Social Policy Analytical Work Program Working Paper Number 5.

IMF (International Monetary Fund). (2010). "World Economic Outlook: Rebalancing Growth", April 2010 Washington DC: International Monetary Fund, www.imf.org/external/pubs/ft/weo/2010/01/pdf/text.pdf, 04.07.2016.

IMF (International Monetary Fund). (2014). "Is It Time for An Infrastructure Push the Macroeconomic Effects of Public Investment." Washington, DC, October 2014. http://www.imf.org/external/pubs/ft/weo/2014/02/pdf/c3.pdf, 14.07.2016.

International Labour Organization (ILO). (2014). KILM 1. Labour force participation rate, http://staging.ilo.org/public/libdoc/ilo/2014/486036.pdf, 03.07.2016.

International Labour Organization (ILO). (2015). KILM 1. Labour force participation rate, http://www.ilo.org/global/statistics-and-databases/research-anddatabases/kilm/WCMS_422090/lang--en/index.htm, 03.07.2016.

Mohamed, Abdisalam A. (2015). "A Comparative Analysis of Determinants of Labor Force Participation and Economic Valuation of Social Security Programs in: China, Colombia, Egypt and Sierra Leone", Master Thesis, Norwegian University of Life Sciences Faculty of Social Sciences School of Economics and Business.

Nanto, Dick K. (2009). "The Global Financial Crisis: Analysis and Policy Implications", CRS Report for Congress, 7-5700, www.crs.gov, RL34742.

Norgren, Claes. (2010). "The Causes of the Global Financial Crisis and Their Implications for Supreme Audit Institutions", http://www.intosai.org/uploads/gaohq4709242v1final subgroup1paper.pdf, Date Accessed: 12.05.2016.

OECD (2016). Policies to Increase Labour-Force Participation of Women and Older Workers, http://www.oecd.org/eco/labour/31743892.pdf, Date Accessed: 13.06.2016.

Reinhart, C.M. and K.S. Rogoff. (2009).The Aftermath of Financial Crises, NBER Working Paper No. 14656.

Schaner, S. and S. Das. (2016). "Female Labor Force Participation in Asia: Indonesia Country Study". ADB Draft Working Paper.

TURKSTAT (Turkish Statistical Institute) (2012). Labor Statistics, https://biruni.tuik.gov.tr/isgucuapp/isgucu.zul, Date Accessed: 17.06.2016.

World Bank (2012). Global Economic Prospects, http://www19.iadb.org/intal/intalcdi/PE /2012/09744.pdf, 15.06.2016.

World Bank (2015). Global Economic Prospects, "Recent Developments in Emerging and Developing Country Labor Markets", http://www.worldbank.org/content/dam/Worldbank/GEP/GEP2015b/Global-Economic-Prospects-June-2015-Labor-trends-in-emerging-markets.pdf 15.06.2016.

World Bank, (2016). World Development Indicators, http://databank.worldbank.org/data/reports.aspx?source=world-development-indicators, Date Accessed: 07.03.2016.

List of Figures

List of Tables

About the Editors

Alper Sönmez (1980, Istanbul, Turkey) is an Assistant Professor in the Department of Economics at Selçuk University, Konya, Turkey. He received his B.Sc. in Economics in 2002 with a First-Class Honours Degree from the Faculty of Economic and Administrative Sciences at Yıldız Technical University (YTU), Turkey. After graduation, he was accepted for a *Ph.D. on B.Sc. program* in Economics at Middle East Technical University (METU), Turkey. He worked as a teaching & research assistant and continued his Ph.D. studies in the Department of Economics at METU from 2002 to 2012. He also spent one year at Cornell University, Charles H. Dyson School of Applied Economics and Management (AEM), as a Visiting Fellow in 2011. He received his Ph.D. Degree in Economics in 2012. He also received *the METU Thesis of the Year Award* granted by *METU Prof. Dr. Mustafa N. Parlar Education and Research Foundation* in 2012. In addition, he was granted a third award from *The Fourth Contest for Academic Studies* organized by *the Central Bank of the Republic of Turkey (CBRT)* in 2013. His book titled *Multinational Companies, Knowledge and Technology Transfer* was published by Springer in 2013. Since February 2013, he has been affiliated with the Department of Economics at Selçuk University, Turkey. His research interests include foreign direct investment, economies of technology and innovation, knowledge and technology spillovers, automotive industry, MNCs, global production networks, and R&D. He is married with two children.

Dilek Çetin has been an Associate Professor at Süleyman Demirel University since 2017. She received a B.Sc. from the Department of Economics at the Faculty of Political Sciences at Ankara University in 1998 and received a M.Sc. degree in Economics from Akdeniz University. In 2012, she received a Ph.D. degree in Economics from Middle East Technical University. Her dissertation was on knowledge spillovers and clusters with a spatial econometric application on Organized Industrial Districts. She was awarded the Ph.D. encouragement prize from *the Turkish Economic Association.* Her studies focus on regional economics, and research and innovation policies. In addition to these subjects she studies trade, entrepreneurship and gender issues. Econometric methods such as spatial econometrics, microeconometrics and panel data econometrics are used in her studies. She was a post-doctoral researcher for fifteen months at *the Institute for Prospective Technological Studies* (IPTS) in Seville, Spain, which is one of the seven institutes of *the Joint Research Centre of Directorate-General of the European Commission.*

About the Authors

Gülsüm Akarsu is a Research Assistant at the Faculty of Economic and Administrative Sciences in Ondokuz Mayıs University located in Samsun, Turkey. Dr. Akarsu teaches Mathematical Economics, Game Theory and Calculus for Economists. She received a B.Sc. degree in Economics from Ege University in 2003 and a Ph.D. Degree in Economics from Middle East Technical University in 2013. Her main areas of research interest include energy economics, financial economics and applied econometrics.

Emre Aksoy is an Associate Professor at the Kırıkkale University, Faculty of Economics and Administrative Sciences Department of Economics. He has been a faculty member since 2012. He graduated from Kırıkkale University and he continued his undergraduate studies in economics at Hacettepe University. He completed his Ph.D. at Gazi University in economics. His research interests lie in the area of Macroeconomics including labor economics and economic growth. He is the author and co-author of ten national and international scientific papers and two books.

Dilek Çetin has been an Associate Professor at Süleyman Demirel University since 2017. She received a B.Sc. from the Department of Economics at the Faculty of Political Sciences at Ankara University in 1998 and received a M.Sc. degree in Economics from Akdeniz University. In 2012, she received a Ph.D. degree in Economics from Middle East Technical University. Her dissertation was on knowledge spillovers and clusters with a spatial econometric application on Organized Industrial Districts. She was awarded the Ph.D. encouragement prize from *the Turkish Economic Association*. Her studies focus on regional economics, and research and innovation policies. In addition to these subjects she studies trade, entrepreneurship and gender issues. Econometric methods such as spatial econometrics, microeconometrics and panel data econometrics are used in her studies. She was a post-doctoral researcher for fifteen months at *the Institute for Prospective Technological Studies* (IPTS) in Seville, Spain, which is one of the seven institutes of *the Joint Research Centre of Directorate-General of the European Commission*.

Yasemin Asu Çırpıcı is an Associated Professor at Yıldız Technical University in Istanbul-Turkey. She received her B.Sc. from Middle East Technical University, Department of Mathematics. She has two M.Sc. degrees, one in Mathematics and the other in Economics, and a Ph.D. in Economics from the same university. She worked as a Research Assistant for seven years at Middle East Technical University and then was accepted as a Research Assistant at Yıldız Technical University in 2006. Dr. Çırpıcı became an Instructor at Yıldız Technical University in 2008 and from 2008 to 2011 she served as Assistant Department Supervisor for the Department of Economics. Currently she is working on Network Economics. Her fields of interest also include microeconomics, mathematical economics and complexity economics.

Sinem Pınar Gürel is an Assistant Professor in the Department of Economics at Pamukkale University, Denizli, Turkey where she has been teaching for 12 years. She received her Ph.D. from the Department of Economics at Ege University in 2012. Her research has primarily been in the areas of international macroeconomics, monetary theory and policy and economic growth. Her recent research focuses on monetary theory and external dynamics of economic growth. She also lectures as an instructor for undergraduate and graduate courses such as macroeconomics and monetary theory and policy.

Mine Kalay was born in 1982 in Konya. She graduated from the Department of Economics of Hacettepe University at 2006. She received her M.Sc. degree in Economics from Akdeniz University. She was a Ph.D. candidate and a research assistant in the Department of Economics, Hacettepe University. She died in October 2017 from cancer.

Duygu Yolcu Karadam is an Assistant Professor in the Department of Economics at Pamukkale University, Denizli, Turkey. She received her Ph.D. from the Department of Economics at Middle East Technical University in 2014. Her fields of research interests are international macroeconomics, growth economics, applied economics and nonlinear panel data econometrics. Her recent research focuses on nonlinear growth effects of macroeconomic variables. She also lectures as an instructor for undergraduate and graduate courses such as monetary theory and policy, international monetary theory, public sector economics, and applied panel data econometrics.

Nazan Şahbaz Kılınç was born in Afyonkarahisar. Dr. Kılınç completed her primary, secondary and high school education in Afyonkarahisar. Dr. Kılınç received a B.Sc. degree in economics from Dokuz Eylül University in 2007, and received a M.Sc. degree in economics from Afyon Kocatepe University in 2010, and a Ph.D. degree in economics from Selcuk University in 2014. She worked as a research assistant at Karamanoğlu Mehmetbey University between 2009 and 2015. Since 2015, Dr. Kılınç has been working as an assistant professor in the department of economics and politics at Kırıkkale University in Turkey.

Selen Işık Maden is an Assistant Professor and she has been working at Süleyman Demirel University, Turkey since 2006. She received her B.Sc. and M.Sc. in Labour Economics and Industrial Relations from Ankara University (Turkey) in 2000 and 2003 respectively. She received her Ph.D. in Economics from Süleyman Demirel University in 2012. Her areas of interest are urban and rural development, regionalism, regional policy, public supports and innovation management.

Ümit K. Seyfettinoğlu is an Associate Professor in the Department of Economics at Akdeniz University, Antalya, Turkey. She received her Ph.D. in Economics from Hacettepe University. She has been teaching microeconomics and urban/regional economics. Her research interests include urban economics, innovation, local and regional development, consumer and producer behavior.

Aykut Sezgin is an Assistant Professor and he has been working at Süleyman Demirel University, Turkey since 2008. He received his B.Sc. from Ankara University and his M.Sc. from Süleyman Demirel University (Turkey), Department of Economics in 2004 and 2008 respectively. He received his PhD in Economics from Süleyman Demirel University in 2014. He has also worked as a project assistant for EURODITE 6th Framework. His research interests include economic geography, innovation, local and regional development, regional policy and technology management.

Alper Sönmez (1980, Istanbul, Turkey) is an Assistant Professor in the Department of Economics at Selçuk University, Konya, Turkey. He received his B.Sc. in Economics in 2002 with a First-Class Honours Degree from the Faculty of Economic and Administrative Sciences at Yıldız Technical University (YTU), Turkey. After graduation, he was accepted for a *Ph.D. on B.Sc. program* in Economics at Middle East Technical University (METU), Turkey. He worked as a teaching & research assistant and continued his Ph.D. studies in the Department of Economics at METU from 2002 to 2012. He also spent one year at Cornell University, Charles H. Dyson School of Applied Economics and Management (AEM), as a Visiting Fellow in 2011. He received his Ph.D. Degree in Economics in 2012. He also received *the METU Thesis of the Year Award* granted by *METU Prof. Dr. Mustafa N. Parlar Education and Research Foundation* in 2012. In addition, he was granted a third award from *The Fourth Contest for Academic Studies* organized by *the Central Bank of the Republic of Turkey (CBRT)* in 2013. His book titled *Multinational Companies, Knowledge and Technology Transfer* was published by Springer in 2013. Since February 2013, he has been affiliated with the Department of Economics at Selçuk University, Turkey. His research interests include foreign direct investment, economies of technology and innovation, knowledge and technology spillovers, automotive industry, MNCs, global production networks, and R&D. He is married with two children.

Fatih Şahan is a Ph.D. candidate in the Department of Economics, Istanbul University. He has a B.Sc. from Marmara University, Department of Economics and a M.Sc. from Middle East Technical University in Economics. His research focuses on innovation economics, new economy, industrial organization and competitiveness.

Mehmet Zanbak is an Assistant Professor. He was born in Burdur. He graduated from Dokuz Eylul University, Department of Economics in 2005. He received his M.Sc. in 2008 and his Ph.D. degree in 2014 from Akdeniz University, Department of Economics. He worked as a research assistant between 2006 and 2014 and still continues his academic studies at Akdeniz University. His research areas are poverty, income distribution, consumer and producer behavior, and development.

www.ingramcontent.com/pod-product-compliance
Ingram Content Group UK Ltd.
Pitfield, Milton Keynes, MK11 3LW, UK
UKHW021848100926
8556IPUK00020B/1115

9 783631 766149